Nina Howell Starr

American Building
The Forces That Shape It

American Building

THE FORCES THAT SHAPE IT

James Marston Fitch

ILLUSTRATED

HOUGHTON MIFFLIN COMPANY BOSTON
The Riverside Press Cambridge

The Riverside Press
CAMBRIDGE · MASSACHUSETTS
PRINTED IN THE U.S.A.

To
C. R. and J. D. who
at different levels
made it possible

Preface

SINCE BUILDING is, next to agriculture, America's largest production field, it is obvious that a great many Americans are directly involved in it. To isolate this field in its exact extent, however, is not easy. It is large, complex, and loosely organized; and the interests of the millions in it are varied and contradictory. Thus, to architects and engineers a building is something you design. To a manufacturer of building material, it is a market for your product; to a carpenter, a source of employment; to a mortgage banker, a field for investment; to a landlord, a source of income. Building can be analyzed from the point of view of each of these groups — in fact, it is constantly being so studied. Each analysis always reveals the special interests of the group involved; and though it may sometimes be difficult to realize that they are all talking about the same thing, one fact at least is clear: all of these groups make their living out of the building field. In this sense they have a common identity as producers, and as such their problems differ very little from those of agriculture or transportation, or indeed of society itself.

But these groups have another and equally important identity and one which they share with all the rest of us — that of being consumers of building. And it is from this point of view, the consumer's, that building may be most fruitfully analyzed. For it is only from such a perspective that building appears as something much more than merely a thing you make drawings of, or sell your products to, or invest your money in, or get your income from. In short, it is only from the consumer's point of view that the social function of building can be fully seen and understood.

To a greater extent than perhaps any other nation, we

Americans have become an 'indoor' people. A large portion of our lives — working, sleeping, playing — is spent in buildings: buildings over whose design and construction we have little or no control; buildings whose physical and economic distribution are only remotely conditioned by our needs; buildings whose effect upon our health and happiness is only obscurely understood. Yet the impact of American buildings upon every aspect and area of American life can scarcely be overemphasized. They are absolutely indispensable tools for controlling our environment, without which modern life would be impossible. We must pay (and dearly) for the use of these buildings, in transactions much like those involving any other commodity; and, to a large extent, they condition our physical and mental well-being.

Yet in daily life this umbilical relationship between men and buildings goes largely unremarked. It takes a very large building failure, collapse, or fire to rate the same newspaper space as the smallest murder. The news-reel emphasis is always much more upon the unpredictable violence of the cyclone than upon the easily predictable failure of the building; while the woman who falls to her death down a badly designed stairway is merely reported to have died 'as the result of a bad fall.' The chronic shortage of adequate housing calls forth little more comment than bad weather, while the congestion and ugliness of our cities remain, if not largely unnoticed, then at least largely uncorrected.

Very successful buildings do not fare much better. The more suitable is a building for the use to which it is put, the more unobtrusive is it apt to become to its users, the more subtle the dividends it yields its tenants. It is difficult for the ordinary family to describe the beneficent impact upon its daily routine of a well-designed and well-equipped house — not because the improvement is not real, but because it is hard for the layman to measure or describe it. Well-being, comfort, and health seldom make good headline material.

Millions are involved in the production of buildings: all of us use them. Yet, despite this fact, few of us are able to tell a good building from a bad one or realize the importance to us of the difference between them. American building today shows immense potentials; it also has great deficiencies. To be able to discriminate between the two is thus a question of first-rate importance to everyone. For here, as elsewhere, an informed public is the prerequisite to closing the gap between what we *could* do and what we *are* doing. It is in the hope of aiding this process that I have written this book.

I have not attempted an exhaustive history: but because, in American architecture, tradition plays almost as important a rôle as the law of gravity itself, I have traced those main forces which, it seemed to me, have shaped American building. Nor have I given any more than a general analysis of its present state — in today's specialized world, anything more is quite beyond the scope of the individual. Rather I have tried to synthesize those aspects of contemporary architectural theory and practice which are of decisive importance today.

Many people have helped me in this task and I have tried to credit them wherever possible. In the case of a specific book or building, this is a simple matter: but the parentage of ideas and concepts is, of all things, hardest to establish and easiest to lose. Here many people have helped me, often without being aware of it, and I take this opportunity to acknowledge my indebtedness to them all. I am especially grateful to the Editors of *Architectural Record* for permission to reproduce the section dealing with Gustave Eiffel, and to the Editors of *Architectural Forum*, *Fortune*, and *Life* for the use of certain important photographs. Thanks are due, finally, to Mr. Paul Grotz for his design of the pictorial sections of this book; to Mr. Stirling Bowen for his index; to Mrs. Marian Schmidt for her proofreading and stenographic work; and to Miss Sighle Kennedy for her assistance in documentary research.

JAMES MARSTON FITCH

NEW YORK CITY
January 25, 1947

Contents

Illustrations

CHAPTER ONE

1620–1776: What We Had to Begin With

PERPETUATED by propaganda ranging all the way from the Rockefellers' ten-million-dollar restoration of Williamsburg down to the roofing advertisement in this week's issue of *Collier's* is the rosy legend of our colonial architecture. By some strange elision of historical and geographic fact, this legendary picture of neatly bricked physical comfort is stretched to cover the entire period from the days of the Pilgrim Fathers down to those of *Gone With the Wind* and to extend from sea to shining sea. The actual picture is more complex, for the extent of 'Colonial architecture' was much smaller in time, space, and class. The term, if it means anything, refers to that relatively standardized system of structure, plan, and ornament in use from about 1700 up to the founding of the Republic. It was largely confined to the English colonies along the eastern seaboard. It was preceded in time by the earlier Spanish building in the Southwest; by the early Dutch settlements in New Amsterdam and upper New York; and — most importantly — by almost a century of experimentation with, and adaptation of, late medieval building theories along the eastern seaboard itself. It coexisted in time with the thriving colonies of the French along the Mississippi and with the Spanish in the Southwest. It was followed by a whole series of Classic idioms. And under it everywhere and all the time, like bedrock, the common people continued the while to erect their own buildings, following the popular structural theories of their own and using materials which were nearest to hand.

1

However, if it serves no other purpose, the reconstructed Governor's Palace at Williamsburg (Fig. 16) does dramatize the extraordinary accomplishments of that first century of colonization. Together with such buildings as the State House in Philadelphia, or Saint Paul's in New York, it establishes the fact that a building technology qualitatively as high as that of Europe had been rooted in the Wilderness — that skilled artisans, processed materials, and appropriate structural theories were generally available in the urban centers. How remarkable an accomplishment this was is best demonstrated by conditions in the earliest days of the colonies.

One has only to read the fragmentary accounts of the early settlers themselves to realize that they left nothing in Europe and certainly found nothing here which resembled 'Colonial architecture.' Theirs was a wretched lot during their first days on these hostile shores. Nothing in their European experience prepared the settlers for the rigors of a New England winter or the heat of a Virginia summer. Everywhere there were extremes of heat and cold, of drought and rain, mosquitoes, flies, gnats — and hostile Indians. They had, according to one chronicler, to

> burrow themselves in the Earth for their first shelter under some hillside, casting the Earth aloft upon timber; they make a smoky fire against the Earth on the highest side; and thus these poor servants of Christ provide shelter for themselves, their wives and little ones, keeping off the short showers from their lodgings but the long rains penetrate through to their great discomfort in the night season.[1]

Again and again, the acute discomfort of these 'poor servants of Christ' is mentioned in early documents and the importance of adequate building stressed. Captain John Smith describes a Virginia church which is far different from those handsome buildings in which Richmond worshiped a century or so later:

> When I first went to Virginia, I well remember we did hang an awning to three or four trees to shadow us from the sun; our

[1] Edward Johnson, *History of New England* (1653). Cited by Briggs, *Homes of the Pilgrim Fathers*, p. 122. New York: Oxford University Press, 1933.

walls were rails of wood, our seats unhewed trees til we cut
planks, our Pulpit a bar of wood nailed to two neighboring trees.
In foul weather we shifted into an old rotten tent; for we had no
better. . . . This was our Church, til we built a homely thing
like a barn, set upon Cratchets, [and] covered with rafts, sedge
and earth; so was also the walls. The best of our houses [were]
of the like curiosity but for the most part far worse workmanship,
that could neither well defend [from] wind nor rain.[1]

In other words, in both New England and Virginia, the colonists
huddled at first in sod huts and dugouts which were technologically at a lower level than the Indian's bark and bent-wood
'long house' (Figs. 1–4).

An environment so overwhelmingly hostile to both individual
and social life left no alternative but the creation — as rapidly
as might be — of a base of operations in which the colonists
could lay their plans, husband their strength, and sharpen
their tools for the conquest of a continent. They had to build:
and build they did, 'driven by hunger and haunted by fear,'
with a savage determination which had not been seen before
and would seldom be seen again. The rich, dark continent lay
like a bride before them: lust and necessity jointly drove these
early settlers forward.

Although practically all the settlers arrived here as members
of planned, commercially inspired expeditions, it would appear
that the first ships not only forgot to bring carpenters and masons;
they also lacked adequate building tools. This omission was
partly the fault of the inaccurate and glowing accounts of the
New World which the earliest explorers had brought back.
(Captain John Smith had rushed home to publish a best-seller
in which he had described the climate, soil fertility, wild food,
and Indians in terms similar to those associated today with the
South Seas.)[2] However, the colonists soon discovered their
error, and were not long content with sod hut, lean-to, and
hillside dugout. Before the first years were out, they were

---

[1] John Smith, *Advertisements for the Unexperienced Planters of New England, or Anywhere.* London, 1631.
[2] *A Description of New England: or the Observations and Discourses of Captain John
Smith.* London, 1616.

ordering not mere man-power but specific types of skilled build-ing craftsmen — masons, carpenters, sawyers. They were send-ing detailed lists of the tools required and allowing each immi-grant family a set of carpenter's tools for their home in the New World. Of raw materials they had, of course, more than enough. Their early letters home waxed ecstatic over the vast resources in wood, stone, marble, slate, sand, and clay. However, access to these raw materials was one thing. Converting them into processed building materials was quite another.

The level of building in any given time and place stands in direct relation to the specific technological level of society — that is, to the types of skills, tools, and materials available to the building field. This was as true for the early settlers as it is for us; and the rapidity with which they established an adequate material base for their building is one of the most remarkable of their accomplishments. Unlike the Spanish in the Southwest, they found neither an established building technology ready to hand nor workers who could be readily enslaved and trained. A brick is a simple thing only to a society which has an adequate supply of skilled masons, brickmakers, and brickkilns; to the early settlers it was a precious object. A rough two-by-four timber is insignificant only to people who do not know what the world was like before the advent of the power-driven saw; and a building of these two products — brick and sawn lumber — is a social achievement whose true significance can only be grasped by people who have endured a smoke-filled dugout through a Massachusetts winter.

Structural Innovation Begins

BY AND LARGE, all of the colonists on the Atlantic seaboard were familiar with one or more of the then standard structural systems — wood framing, brick and stone masonry. The great

Many of their woodworking tools the colonists brought with them: others they quickly evolved. Under the impact of necessity, a wooden structural system of unprecedented lightness and efficiency was perfected. A skin of wood shingles (extreme left) and wood planks (left) protected dovetailed framing members (right).

Rhode Island Museum of Art

A SUMMER BEAM

ADZ
FLAT SURFACE
BROAD AX
FRAMING SAW
AUGER
TENON JOINT
HOLES
BIT & BRACE
MALLET
MORTISE JOINT
BEVEL
DRAW KNIFE
CHISEL

all-masonry construction of the Gothic periods had never been a genuinely popular building technology in the sense that peasants as well as prelates could use it in their domestic buildings. The Gothic style did not appear in America until the mid-nineteenth century — and by that time it belonged much more to literature than to building technique. Wood, however, was essential to all these systems, since no other suitable tensile material for framing floors and roof was available — then or for the next two hundred years. Although uncut stone was widely used in some parts of the colonies, it was never to become a real competitor of brick on any but a local scale. The brick's small size, standardized production, and general availability made it the pre-eminent masonry material.

But wood was to become America's principal building material, far outstripping all others in the scope and versatility of its use. Though the English unquestionably brought with them the rudiments of our modern wood-framing systems, they were crude and inexact — straight from a feudal England still largely built of wood. (The London which was leveled in the Great Fire of 1666 was a wooden city.) Moreover, English wood frames soon proved to be unsuited to our climate, whose violent and abrupt changes caused rapid expansion and contraction. This led to cracks which reduced the efficiency of the wall. Under the impact of their new surroundings, the Pilgrims modified their structural systems to meet their new thermal environment. At first they merely covered the medieval brick nogging

Without extremes of heat and cold, the English climate made it possible to leave the wooden frames exposed, the interstices filled with plastered brick or wattles. But abrupt changes in temperature made this wall system impractical in New England.

with which the English had filled in the wood skeleton with two relatively impervious skins — the clapboard exterior and the plaster interior. Ultimately, the brick disappeared altogether. Naturally, the new system was not perfected overnight: it was rather a process of small changes here and there, which resulted in new and characteristically American systems of wood construction.

Since wood was at once the most abundant and easily worked material in the new country, and since the settlers were thor-

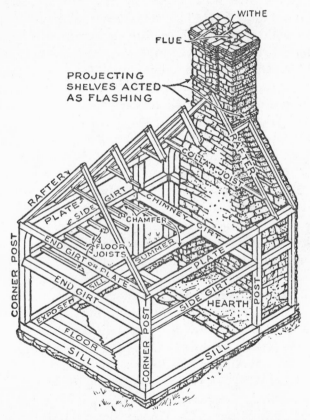

Although the wood skeleton of this early colonial house is a lineal descendant of the medieval English, important changes are apparent. The entire skeleton has been 'moved in out of the weather.' Its surfacing of shingles and clapboards shed water like the feathers on a duck.

oughly familiar with it, it is not surprising that they at once adopted it as their favorite material. What is surprising, however, is the *way* they used it. They apparently dismissed the Indian's bark-covered sapling skeleton as unsuitable from the first. They early discarded the 'stockade' — walls of sharpened logs driven into the ground and interstices daubed with mud — as impracticable. And they never employed the log cabin for the simple reason they had never heard of it. (This latter system — simplest, quickest, and relatively most comfortable of all — was the invention of the Swedes, who brought it with them to Delaware in 1638. Knowledge of it did not spread much beyond there until the eighteenth century.) Instead, the New Englanders turned directly to the wood-framed, clapboard-sheathed structure which is today called 'Cape Cod' (Fig. 10).

In many ways this was a remarkable development. It involved attacking the building problem at the point of greatest resistance. For while this system provided the most efficient structures, it also implied the most advanced equipment — specifically, power-driven saws. Both the English and the Dutch were accustomed to pit-sawing — long, straight saws operated by two men, one above, one below. But neither were familiar with sawmills, which, though known in England, were outlawed for fear of technological unemployment among the sawyers. So at first the early settlers resorted to pit-sawing. However, they soon found that hand labor was far too slow and costly for their need and — in early but typical American fashion — mechanized the process. Thus, a short thirteen years after the Pilgrims landed, they were establishing their first power-saw at the Falls of Piscataqua on the line between Maine and New Hampshire. It was a cumbersome apparatus — a huge swishing up-and-down adaptation of the pit-saw — and it must have been the source of much speculation among the villagers. There are unauthenticated reports of even earlier power mills — Maine, 1631, and New York, 1633. In any event, before there were any mills in England, the colonists had mechanized the sawing process. The basis was laid both for a huge lumber industry and for rapid advance in wood construction.

Much the same thing happened in brick manufacture. Possibly as early as 1622, and certainly no later than 1630, bricks were being commercially produced at Powder Horn Hill near Chelsea, Massachusetts. In 1628 the canny Rensselaers were producing the favorite Dutch yellow brick on their estates near Albany, New York, and selling them to all comers for fifteen florins a thousand. Even earlier, in 1611, Sir Thomas Dale had landed in Jamestown and immediately started 'many essential improvements' which included a brickyard and a smith's forge. Later the same year the colonial secretary reported that Henrico (near the present site of Richmond) boasted 'three streets of well-framed houses, a handsome church, and the foundations for a more stately one laid in bricks.' Although not founded until much later, New Orleans early provided for the establishment of brickkilns which were to be worked by convict labor from among the salt smugglers.

It is thus clear that the establishment of a material basis for the building field was the first order of business for all the colonies. Since the problem was too urgent to be left to individual initiative, early records are replete with decrees, subsidies, and interventions promoting such ventures. Even then, in a period when every man was of necessity somewhat skilled in many crafts, building labor was at a premium. Some hint of the importance of building workers in colonial economy is revealed by a choice bit of Massachusetts anti-labor legislation dated August 23, 1630:

> At the First Court of Assistants holden at Charlton [Charlestown], it was ordered that carpenters, joyners, bricklayers, sawyers, and thatchers shall not take above 2 s/ a day, nor any man shall give more, under pains of 10 s/ to taker and giver.[1]

Despite the policy of the British Crown in discouraging colonial industry, and the consequent necessity for importing glass, hardware, nails, etc., the colonists had established their own brick and lime kilns, sawmills, small foundries, and glass factories long before they gained independence.

Far to the south and west, in Louisiana and California, colonies of the French and Spanish were developing independently.

[1] *Records of the Colony of Massachusetts Bay in Massachusetts.*

When allowances are made for the different cultural backgrounds these settlers brought and for the different climatic conditions they found, their buildings will be found to differ in no important respects from those of the Atlantic seaboard. In Louisiana and the Southwest there was a much more general use of brick and stone masonry than of wood. The porch, courtyard, and balcony were becoming important features in a climate where summers were long and severe. Plastered walls and iron balustrades gave the street façades an exotic cast. But by and large their building technology was similar to, and their accomplishments about even with, those of the English seaboard colonies.

Put Another Log on the Fire

IT IS STILL not generally recognized that if the Pilgrims had landed on a near-by planet instead of the New England coast, they could scarcely have made a more abrupt switch in thermal environments. In Plymouth, England, they left a moderate climate, with a very stable temperature, without extremely cold winters or very hot summers; snows and droughts were rare; tornadoes and cyclones unknown. In Plymouth, Massachusetts, they found a thermal environment whose annual cycle was far more severe, with a temperature spread from July to December more than twice as great as in Plymouth, England. They found also heavy snowfalls, long freezes, enormous gales.

The heat of the New England summers, though doubtless uncomfortable to the settlers, was not actually dangerous to their health. They could always sit down in the shade. But the severity of the winters, with the consequent need for adequate heating sources, was a far different matter. The urgency of this problem is attested by their early buildings, the most characteristic feature of which was always the huge chimney with its fireplaces (Fig. 11). Since these served also for cooking and baking, they literally became the heart of the house. Within the limits given, these huge chimneys were cannily designed. The fireplaces themselves were none too efficient; but the mass of the chimney — located in the center of the house and occupy-

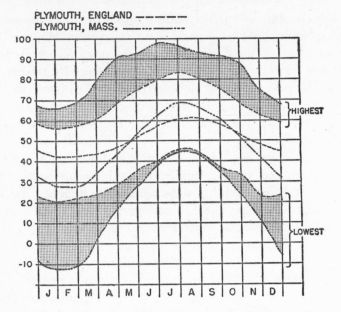

PLYMOUTH, ENGLAND _____
PLYMOUTH, MASS. ___...___...

Average annual temperature curves for the two Plym-
ouths show why the Pilgrims had to devise new heating
methods. Winters were much colder in Massachusetts
and the temperature spread was almost twice as great
as in England.

ing a disproportionate amount of floor space — absorbed the
heat of the flue gases and radiated it into the house. They were
far from ideal as heating media and — romantic legend notwithstanding — cooking on them was back-breaking drudgery.
So it is not surprising to find the fireplace beginning to be
supplanted by the stove, as soon as the rising technological level
of colonial society made that possible.

The Pilgrims had already modified their structural systems to
make their buildings weather-tight under the new conditions.
They also sought to make their heating more efficient by small
rooms with low ceilings and small windows. (This last was an
economy in another sense, for glass was dear and hard to get,
and both the British Crown and local governments had quickly
slapped a tax on it.) For such features as these, early American
building deserves no special credit. They were common prac-

tice abroad. But when Benjamin Franklin's stove appeared in Philadelphia in 1744 — a scant sixty years after William Penn had cleared away the forest — a decisive step had been taken. This stove, like an even earlier but commercially unsuccessful one by Christopher Sower of Germantown, differed in many important respects from its cumbersome European ancestors. To begin with, it was prefabricated. Using the most modern material of his time — cast iron — Mr. Franklin was able to turn out on a mass-production basis a stove which could be readily assembled from a minimum number of standardized parts. It was lightweight, self-contained, efficient, and relatively cheap. One has only to compare it with the ponderous masonry units of Europe to understand how truly revolutionary were its implications.

In its earliest form, the Franklin was half fireplace, half stove. It had no doors and its shape, grate, and raised hearth showed clearly its masonry ancestry. Its principal significance lay in the fact that it was detached from the chimney. It could be installed anywhere because it was lightweight and self-contained; and with the addition of a door, it became a stove. From this early innovation of the indefatigable Franklin, all modern stoves and most air-conditioning are lineally descended. For heating purposes, these stoves marked such an advance over the fireplace, both in terms of efficiency of conversion and efficiency of heat distribution, that they soon outstripped it. For cooking purposes, of course, their advantages were even more pronounced. In fact, it would be interesting (though not germane to this study) to trace the decisive effect of the 'range' on American cookery. The slow heat of the masonry oven naturally had led to the breads of Europe, just as the size, cost, and technique of the oven necessitated the communal baking of bread. Contrariwise, it is apparent that the stove's quick intense heat has profoundly affected our dietary habits and made possible the invention of such American breads as the biscuit, corn pone, flapjack, and waffle.

The problem of ventilation, always closely associated with that of heating, also did not escape the attention of early Americans. It was naturally more urgent in the intense heat of the South, and as the Carolinas and Virginia developed there was a steady increase in ceiling heights and window sizes. Here, too, we see the beginnings of another American invention — one might almost say institution: the porch. This grew steadily in size and importance until it became the dominant aspect of upper-class residential structures. Imagine Mount Vernon without its portico! In New Orleans, Spanish familiarity with balconies and arcades led to brilliant adaptations in masonry and iron (Fig. 35). These two streams were ultimately to meet in the reactionary ostentation of ante-bellum plantation houses, with their slave-powered, peacock-feathered punkahs, twenty-foot ceilings, and continuous many-storied galleries (Fig. 39).

The more subtle problems of fresh air in heated rooms, humidity control, and elimination of drafts had not yet risen to dog the colonists. Yet there are some prophetic signs of future advance in atmospheric and thermal control. Thus we find Benjamin Franklin taking time off from the press of diplomatic work to describe to the physician to the Emperor at Vienna a ventilation device he had noticed in France:

> Take out an upper pane of glass in one of your sashes, set it in a tin frame giving it two springing angular sides [that is, like the letter slot in a modern post box] and then replace it with hinges below. . . . By drawing this pane in more or less you may admit what air you find necessary. Its position will naturally throw that air up and along the ceiling.[1]

That so simple a device should have been the subject of correspondence between two such eminent scientists is an index of the general level which obtained in the field of heating and ventilating.

Those who incline nostalgically back to the days when gilt and crystal chandeliers shed soft light (and dripped hot tallow) on the heads of colonial dancers confuse the image with the reality. The candle which was kind to the faded beauty or the jaded swain was the same which set many a house and a hoop-

[1] Letter to Doctor Ingenhousz, written at sea, August 28, 1785.

skirt afire.   Besides being smoky and unsafe, candles were expensive; there were probably not a hundred houses in the thirteen colonies which could afford the candles necessary to illuminate properly a ballroom for an entire evening.   The vast majority of early Americans danced in the light of log fires or flaming pine knots.   For the lamp chimney had not yet been invented and the whaling fleet had not yet appeared to furnish cheap oil.   Those candlelit drawing-rooms which ornament our Christmas cards and calendars thus give little hint of the reality of colonial illumination — of dark, muddy streets and dangerous coasts without lighthouses, of workshops 'dark in the blaze of noon,' and cabins without glazed sash, so that even on the brightest winter day the wooden shutters were kept closed.

Personal hygiene was still fogged in medieval ignorance and superstition.   When teeth were brushed at all, it was with table salt and a chewed twig.   Soap was already a staple item in every household, but it was apparently more used on the family laundry than on the family itself.   Bathing the whole body was still considered dangerous, even though Benjamin Franklin had already introduced a shoe-shaped sitz bath and was cautiously advertising the benefits of bathing.

In such a context, sanitation concepts were necessarily primitive.   Table scraps were fed to the family pigs or — in the growing towns — dumped in the streets for wandering free-lance pigs to root in.   Open-pit privies were universal in both country and town.   In New Orleans slop jars were emptied into open storm sewers and drainage ditches.   In other cities, human excrement was sometimes collected by mule-drawn carts and hauled in barrels to the open country.   (Though, fortunately for colonial health, there seems to have been no use of it as fertilizer.)   Sewage-disposal systems were unknown and public water systems were still to appear.   Dug wells were the source of most urban drinking water, though farmers built their houses near good springs whenever possible.   Manually operated pumps were appearing in the towns by the time of the Revolution, though the bucket-and-windlass was the principal means of lifting water to the surface.   Since hard water was so prevalent, there was a fairly

I

A Multi-National Heritage
is Adapted to the American Scene

English settlers made scant use of aboriginal building techniques — even though the Indians' bark hut (1) and skin tipi (3) were better than the white man's first rude shelter (2).

1

2

3

Only in the Southwest, among the Cliff Dwellers, was there permanent building. The Spanish bent this native skill to their own ends.

4

5

In Massachusetts Colony, early building clearly showed
its medieval English origins. The wooden structure of Harvard College (1638) soon rotted (5).

6

Dutch and German settlers in Pennsylvania had their own way of adapting themselves to new climate and materials: the rude cloisters of the Baptists at Ephrata.

Introduced by the Swedes into Delaware, the log cabin saw its widest use when Americans moved over the Appalachians after the Revolution.

7

Spanish Renaissance blended with Indian masonry to produce the monastery later called the Alamo.

The French brought timber-and-nogging walls and tiled roofs to New Orleans in 1716.

10

By 1690, New England had a well-established woodworking industry capable of producing the clapboards, shingles, and sash which went into the Wilder house at Hingham, Mass. (10).

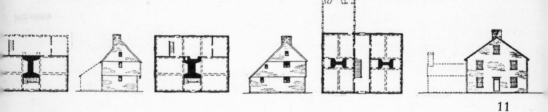

11

Growing maturity of Colonial society is reflected in morphology of its houses (11). Upper class parlors showed the sophistication of the wealthy — the Lee House in Marblehead, Mass., 1768 (12).

12

13

The granite facade of Georgian London was gracefully rendered in wood by Yankee craftsmen in this house for a wealthy trader in Portsmouth, N. H., c. 1760.

Meanwhile, the canny Dutch of Albany, N. Y., were making their favorite yellow brick for stepped gables like this one of 1657.

14

15

The Palladian formality of Philadelphia's State House (1732) gave ample evidence of the wealth and elegance already attained by the colony established only fifty years before by William Penn.

16

Further south, at Williamsburg in Virginia, an agrarian aristocracy with Royalist principles housed its governor in a Georgian Palace. . . . Charleston, southernmost outpost of the English colonies, as seen from its harbor in 1762 (17).

17

18

French adaptation to subtropic climate early produced the stilted first floor and long gallery of Madame John's Legacy (18). Subsequent Spanish influence is apparent in the old Louisiana Bank (19)

19

THE CLASSIC SPIRAL

The impact of the Renaissance upon sixteenth-century England was expressed in both the Classic imagery of Shakespeare and the imposition of Classic ornament to buildings which were still essentially Gothic in concept.

20

21

22

Inigo Jones, first modern architect of England, built this Banqueting Hall at Whitehall in 1622. The symmetry, articulation, and ornament of the Graeco-Roman world as seen through the lens of the Italian Renaissance.

The work of Christopher Wren was systematic, rational, concrete. His Chelsea Hospital (23), like his plan for rebuilding London, had unprecedented scale and orderliness.

23

With Georgian dandies, the classicism of Angelica Kaufmann was much the vogue. Her murals at Syon House (24, 26) combined poor archaeology with poor drawing . . .

. . . But a sexy romanticism made her ideal for this boudoir ceiling in a house by the Brothers Adam

25

26

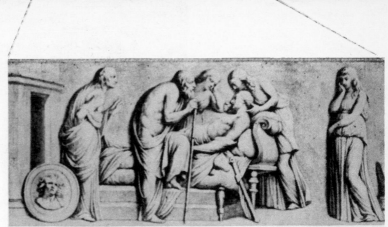

LOUIS JACQUES DAVID, ideologue of the French Revolution, was also drawn irresistibly toward the Ancients. But he saw in them the sharp, masculine lines of Republican virtue. His allegory of Socrates used singing color, luminous perspective, to teach the value of honor.

27

28

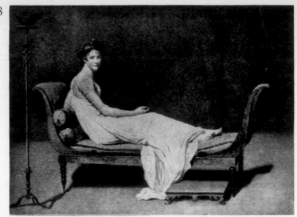

David's identification with the Romans was so complete that he clothed Mme. Récamier in Roman dress, posed her on a Roman couch. (28) Even in recording real historical events (29) he first drew . . .

29

30

his heroes nude, then clothed them decently to fit the times.

wide use of rainwater storage systems — masonry cisterns to which all the household gutters were connected. All in all, with the whole discovery of the connection between polluted water and pestilence still a century or more away, it is remarkable that colonial health was as good as it was. The principal reason was probably the preponderantly rural character of the nation and the small size of the towns.

By the time of Washington's inauguration, the building of the new Republic had consolidated itself at about the same technological level as that of Europe. It employed much the same structural theories and building materials, and was by this time largely based on its own industries. It had approximately the same percentage and types of skilled artisans and amateur gentleman architects — both of whom studied the flood of architectural and archeological handbooks which were a phenomenon of the times. If American building projects were fewer and smaller than those of Europe, this reflected more the relative immaturity of colonial society than any absolute deficiency in its means of building.

If the building of the period was abreast of Europe in most respects, it already showed certain prophetic indications of even more rapid advance in others. This was particularly the case in planning. The structure of a given society is clearly revealed in the sum total of its building plans; and the more advanced the society, the more varied and complex are its building types. Long before the Revolution, the trend toward the creation of new building types — that is, new plans — was apparent. Thus, as early as 1735, the plan of the Pennsylvania State House (Independence Hall) showed the qualitative changes taking place in government. Although clearly based on English palace types, its plan reflects the need for large democratic assembly rooms instead of small, kingly audience chambers. The new buildings for the Philadelphia City Almshouse and Hospital in 1760 likewise differed from European prototypes in their expanded facilities for separate attention to aged, poor, insane, and ill. Most unique of all new building types, of course, was our small, single-family, free-standing dwelling. Long before the Revolution this type had achieved a characteristic form and construction which was to alter very little even up to the present day.

In plan, the buildings of colonial America necessarily reflected new conditions; but they also showed the imagination and freedom with which the colonists attacked new problems. This ability to evolve new plans and new building types was the expression on an architectural plane of their fertile ability to evolve new social and economic institutions. The building type which was eventually to dominate the American scene — which was in fact to become the fountainhead of practically every subsequent advance in American building — was still missing: the factory. For this the colonists could scarcely be blamed. Such manufacturing as the British Crown permitted had not grown much beyond the scale of small localized handicraft operations. These imposed no particular strain upon conventional structural theories or plan types. Aside from water-powered flour and lumber mills, and wharfside developments in the big port cities, there was little hint of what was to come.

Yet even in this field, the colonies did not lag too far behind England and Europe. Although the development of power-driven manufacturing was well advanced abroad, it had scarcely begun to reflect itself in buildings especially designed for that purpose. It was only as the eighteenth century drew to a close that the factory began to appear as a recognizable type: and here, from the start, America was destined to excel.

The Classic Spiral

WHEN, after days of discussion made no easier by the July heat, the representatives of the thirteen colonies put their final approval on the Declaration which Jefferson had drafted for them, they adjourned to the streets of a new capital which bore a strong resemblance to the London from which they had just seceded. The very hall in which they had met might well have come from the drawing-boards of Inigo Jones. The streets and little squares through which they walked might have been laid out by Christopher Wren. The houses at which these gentlemen were guests might well have been designed by any of the famous Georgian architects. The shops they passed and all the little houses they did not notice could have been the work of any anonymous British craftsman.

The greatest difference between the two capitals was not that Philadelphia was new while London was very old. It was rather that every building in Philadelphia showed with strange consistency a common ancestry, while those of London were disparate, laid in strata, with only the most recent deposits mirroring the rising Classic tide. In Penn's city there was no such picture of long-drawn, almost imperceptible progression: no picture of a Classic idiom slowly displacing the Gothic. A century and a half of experiment in England had produced a new synthesis on this side of the Atlantic. And if the ancestors of the new capital had, in the Middle Ages, produced a highly specialized system of construction and ornament, only a scholar with prior knowledge could have deduced it here. The Gothic symbols — the twining vine, the pointed arch, the angels — had vanished from the façade as inappropriate to the new society as half-timbering or moated wall.

However many the cultures in the blood stream, they had been amalgamated, absorbed by the dominant Classic strain. Superficially, there was no cultural continuity apparent here. This Classic vernacular had its origins not in North Europe but in the Mediterranean Basin; not in the immediate past but a thousand years before; and in that interval the great Byzantine, Romanesque, and Gothic styles had risen, flowered, and died. How, then, did the Classic reappear upon the gaunt New England coast, follow the colonists as they spread south and west, ultimately blanket the nation? The key to this paradox lay in England.

Consistently, since its rediscovery by sixteenth-century England, the Classic world had dominated the English mind. With no serious interruption, it would continue to be a dominant influence for at least a century more. The basis of its appeal is apparent: conceptually, the Classic world in all its aspects was symmetrical, rational, concrete. Its large scale and fascinatingly

minute detail were equally well lighted by its spirit of free in-
quiry. For the young bourgeoisie, fighting free of the bemused
paralysis and planless growth, the bottomless pessimism into
which the Middle Ages had sunk, the Classic thus appeared as
the ideal instrument for the reconstruction of man's consciousness. They clutched it to their bosom, little knowing what they
let themselves in for. The Classic form became a unit of measurement, the standard by which they judged and the mold into
which they compressed the most varied expressions of their
culture: language, legal system, city plan; palace façade and
poem; sermon, gravestone, and essay.

But the eager Elizabethans could not approach this Classic
world directly. Separation in time and space, inadequate
scholarship, and limited means of communication prevented a
face-to-face meeting. In their lustrous naïveté, they saw it as
through a long and twisting hall of mirrors — its outlines blurred,
its features magically distorted, its imagery mixed and idealized.
Their first perspective was through the magnificent lens of the
Italian Renaissance. Shakespeare, like a social seismograph,
registered the first repercussions. Small-scale Marco Polos sailed
back to England with wondrous tales, books, drawings. The
English ruling classes, fascinated by the world they saw, were
avid for more information. Foreign sources soon proving inadequate, English scholars with their churchly Latin began their
own translations, explorations, and measurements.[1] Soon the
time would come when a knowledge of Roman architecture,
philosophy, poetry would be an essential equipment for every
cultured Englishman. A trip to the Roman capital would
replace Vignola's measured drawings of it.

The works of the German archeologist, Johann Joachim
Winckelmann, did much to systematize eighteenth-century
knowledge of Roman culture. His monumental studies of 1762
and 1764 afforded English scholars their first real information
on the current excavations at Pompeii and Herculaneum.
Winckelmann also directed their attention to a still more distant

[1] John Shute's *First and Chief Grounds of Architecture* (1563) was probably the first
handbook to bring the Roman Orders to English builders.

Classic landscape: the Greek.   Based upon inadequate Roman sources, many of the ideas advanced in his *History of Ancient Art* subsequently proved to be erroneous.   Nevertheless, his efforts brought the Grecian vista into clearer focus.   Another fascinating world was opened to the British mind, the exploration of which would in many respects duplicate that of ancient Rome.

By the close of the eighteenth century, no grand tour was complete without the Acropolis, just as fifty years earlier none had been complete without a moonlight visit to the Forum. Greek was as essential as Latin had been earlier.   Further to strengthen the sense of immediacy in this curious relationship, Lord Elgin went to Greece.   From the Acropolis, under circumstances none too savory, he brought the marble figures from the pediment of the Parthenon back to London in 1816.   And Byron, when he died there in 1824 with the Greek armies of liberation, brought the English interest in Greece to a climax. It might be said that, with Byron's death, the journey was complete for the English: the spiral had been traced out, the images disentangled, the Classic mirage explored.

This process of piecemeal rediscovery of the past was reflected with great accuracy in the architecture of England.   Indeed, architecture had been from the first one of the principal media of Classical ideology.   Already in 1550 it would have been possible to see crude Classic ornament applied to essentially medieval structures.   Here anonymous designers, moved by echoes no more precise than those which stirred Shakespeare, began to use the idiom: mask and acanthus, cornice and frieze (the style known today as Tudor).   The first great architect to show by his work a first-hand access to reasonably accurate sources was Inigo Jones.   In his buildings we find the whole Classic system — column, entablature, cornice, and pediment. Nevertheless, Jones saw Rome through the Renaissance lens, as did Sir Christopher Wren, who appeared like a phoenix from the great London fire of 1666.   In his plans for the reconstruction of the city and in his design for Saint Paul's Cathedral, Wren displayed that grandness of conception and dexterity of detail which marked the Classic at its best.   Yet he, too, was a man of the Renaissance, confusing the Rome of Michelangelo with that of the Caesars (Figs. 20–23).

Wren was followed by a number of very able men: William Kent, James Gibbs, the Brothers Adam. They were facile and well educated, completely familiar with the sources then available. However, these sources were, by modern standards, disconnected and incomplete. They made no clear distinctions between the Rome of the Empire and that of the Republic; between metropolitan and provincial Rome; or between archaic and Periclean Greece. This lack of archeological precision was characteristic and probably would not have much disturbed the Georgian architects, even had they known it. For designers such as Robert Adam and his collaborator, the decorative artist Angelica Kauffmann, were more ideologues than scholars. The whole Graeco-Roman epoch was a dazzling treasure-trove from which they could borrow at will. Under their influence, the vernacular lost in vigor what it gained in skill. This was in strict accordance with facts of their society. For the Classic concept in the hands of the Georgians had become an instrument of imperialist expansion. Even Byron's death in Greece had two aspects. It had freed the Greeks from Turkish oppression; it had also secured the Mediterranean for British trade with India and the East (Figs. 24–26).

The Georgian idiom flowered and withered, and still the Classicists had not encompassed the whole of the Classic world. Indeed the political decisions which the dissident Americans took in Independence Hall on that July day were destined to produce the most pregnant phase of the entire Classic spiral. For they led to the so-called Classic Revival, the revival within a revival, the white-hot return to simon-pure original sources. This movement was even more explicitly revolutionary than its predecessors had been, and its energy was to be expended much more in America and France than in England. Jacques David and the official artists of the French Revolution were to discover, with stunning timeliness, a very specific and politically concrete Rome, the Rome of the Republic. Jefferson would mirror this enthusiasm in this country and Latrobe would shortly thereafter discover a specifically democratic Greece. And the English intellectuals, alarmed at the literalness with which France and America were pursuing their revolutions, would begin to lose their Classic ardor. Keats would die, Wordsworth would cool, Byron would be submerged in the rising Gothic tide of Scott and Pugin and Ruskin (Figs. 27–30).

Fine as all these stylistic shadings might sometimes appear, they were nevertheless important indices to deeper changes in European and American society. Those Classic perspectives which had enthralled so many successive generations were by no means identical, similar though they may have been in general form. Politically, the movement had reconstructed man's mind beyond the wildest dreams of its founders. Always a vehicle of progress, the Classic had become an instrument of outright revolution. The Rome which inspired Christopher Wren was not the Rome which fired David; the Greece of Angelica Kauffmann was far different from that of Horatio Greenough; and interstellar space divided the Classic world of Jefferson from that of the dictator Napoleon.

Up until 1776, the Americans had found themselves one step removed from this constantly shifting image, too busy fighting the Indians to spend much time on all its nuances and subtle distinctions of emphasis. Until then architectural styles, like fashions in periwigs, were a luxury over which precious few colonists could dawdle. Like other merchandise, they were ordered from the mother country by the rich. From here they seeped slowly down into the living fabric of the nation's popular building. If they were workable they were adopted, modified, integrated into the prevailing idiom. But the Classic yeast was at work on this side of the Atlantic and the Declaration of Independence set it to work. Esthetic standards received a new, a political significance. As Jefferson was soon to demonstrate, it was time for Americans to create a concept of beauty peculiarly their own.

CHAPTER TWO

1776–1820: The New Republic Rises

Aₙy ᴇsᴛɪᴍᴀᴛᴇ of American building since the Revolutionary War must always be modified by the special conditions of American society since that time. These conditions amount to a paradox which dates roughly from the day our source of supplies in England was cut off: two separate and distinct economies — one might almost say cultures — have been simultaneously employed in creating the nation. These two moved like two successive waves across the nation from east to west and from north to south. The first was that pre-industrial economy of the seventeenth-century settlers. Gaining a beachhead on the eastern seaboard, it moved slowly but steadily westward — clearing the forests, trapping the furs, establishing a small-scale, self-sufficient, agrarian economy. This culture employed its inherited building technology, with only such modifications as I have already described.

The second wave, that of nineteenth-century industrialism, began in New England with the War of Independence. It moved slowly at first. Then, with gathering momentum, it spread out from the metropolitan centers of the Northeast like a prairie fire. In the beginning, it merely followed the first wave along the rivers and canals. With the completion of the railroads in the post-Civil War period, it overtook the first wave; and finally, with the present century, passed and completely submerged it. With the opening of the Oklahoma Territory, a geographic base for a pre-industrial economy had dwindled to the backwoods, the mountains, the submarginal lands. This new industrial economy brought, as physical evidence of its conquest, a radically improved building technology — without precedent not only in America but in the world at large.

The rapidity with which this new building was invented and developed is one of the great dramas of architectural history, and necessarily dominates the panorama of the nineteenth century. For, as the century matured, the qualitative difference between the two technologies rapidly increased, so that they soon ceased to bear more than a superficial resemblance to one another. Today, like the vermiform appendix in carnivorous animals, only the nostalgic remnants of this earlier technology remain in the form of an occasional newly built 'Colonial' city hall or 'English' suburban home.

This is the paradox which makes any cross-section of American building appear superficially as a confusing jumble of anachronism and anomaly. Because of this paradox we have 1846 slum sitting cheek-by-jowl with 1946 streamlined factory, polished city side by side with backwoods farm. The physical contrast is appalling, but intellectually the spread is even worse. Buildings, like facts, are stubborn things; many a century-old house leads a useful life today. But many a century-old building concept also lingers on, reproducing itself in new buildings which are obsolete at birth. This contradiction has been a characteristic feature of American architecture since the Revolution; and it must be constantly borne in mind if one is to understand fully the forces at play in the period which opened with Washington's inauguration.

With the close of the war, the new Republic faced, not only the task of reconstructing an exhausted and practically bankrupt nation, but of simultaneously creating an entirely new political and economic apparatus commensurate with its new status. Though Europe might not yet recognize it, the country had leaped from second-rate colony to first-rate power. For the building field, as for all other branches of the economy, this posed a new set of problems. Construction had been at a virtual standstill for the duration of the war. It was, if anything, less prepared now than before for the grandiose programs which the national, state, and local governments began to set in motion.

It was entirely logical that the first big building projects after the war were largely governmental. The sheer pressure of new governmental affairs placed intolerable strains upon available facilities. In addition, there was the natural desire to give suitable architectural expression to the intense nationalism of the period. Thus, the State of Massachusetts had the problem of housing an entire administrative apparatus, including a large new legislature. It had the equally important ideological task of housing them *appropriately*, so that the people of Boston, as of the world at large, could see the concrete affirmation of their freedom. Massachusetts moved swiftly and impressively. Already in 1795 the architect Bulfinch had laid the cornerstone of a handsome new capitol; in 1802 the state solons were settling themselves into its new-found Classic majesty (Fig. 33).

Nor were the other states very far behind, either in time or in number of columns and size of dome. The large scale, shrewd foresight and ardent optimism of these new state capitols and city halls (which were everywhere abuilding as the nineteenth century opened) were but the local reflection of an even bigger project — the construction of a new capital city at Washington. Such huge projects as this had hitherto been attempted only by the heads of old and powerful states — the French kings at Versailles, Peter the Great at St. Petersburg. This does not seem to have dismayed either Washington or Jefferson, under whose general direction the swampy site was selected. And the fact that the military engineer L'Enfant himself would die in poverty, unpaid by the Congress despite his heart-breakingly detailed memoranda of the moneys owed for the services rendered — none of this can obscure the significance of the original conception. On the very threshold of her national career, America had indicated where she was going (Figs. 31, 32).

America moved in many other ways to concretize the program of the new Republic: and each of her moves, directly or otherwise, had its impact upon the building field. Characteristic of these was the popular demand for education. As early as 1779, even before independence was assured, Jefferson had pointed out how necessary to freedom's survival was an educated public. In his magnificent proposal for Virginia, 'A Bill for the More General Diffusion of Knowledge,' he wrote:

> Whereas it appeareth that however certain forms of government are better calculated than others to protect individuals in the free exercise of their natural rights, and are at the same time better guarded against degeneracy, yet experience hath shown that even under the best forms those entrusted with power have, in time and by slow operations, perverted it into tyranny; and it is believed that the most effectual means of preventing this would be to illuminate ... the minds of the people at large ... to give them knowledge ... of the experience of other ages and countries, [that] they may be enabled to know ambition under all its shapes and prompt to exert their natural powers to defeat it.

Here Jefferson was outlining in prescient detail a system of universal, free, and compulsory education; and though his proposals were only partially adopted in Virginia, they served as prototypes to the institutions which were rising all across the land. New colleges, academies, and schools reflected the hunger for education at every level of society. Though many of them may today appear both pedagogically and architecturally unimportant, they nevertheless were the indispensable basis for modern standards in both education and school-building design.

The closing years of the century saw many other projects of an institutional nature. One of the most active building types was — ironically enough — the prison. In 1800 New York opened its new state prison, designed by the *émigré* architect, Joseph Magnin. In plan this building provided for segregation of sexes and for grouping of prisoners according to severity of crime. This represented a big advance over contemporary European practice, which threw murderer and debtor, sick and insane, all into one foul cell together. Virginia's new penitentiary went one step further (at Jefferson's suggestion) and provided for solitary confinement. And these and similar penological reforms were soon to be reflected in the design of the Eastern Penitentiary which Pennsylvania completed in 1835. This institution was so advanced for its day as to become famous —

an object of careful study by the European commissions sent
over to see it and a source of much satisfaction to American
reformers.

As economic equilibrium returned to the rich seaport cities
and the fertile river valleys, private construction revived.
Amateur designer and anonymous builder began to yield to
professional architect. Among the Portsmouth shipping gentry,
Mr. Samuel McIntire was much the vogue; in Boston Charles
Bulfinch, overestimating perhaps the strength of his popularity,
went bankrupt on an elegant group of houses modeled after
those at Bath in England; in New York and Philadelphia and
Baltimore the names of Robert Mills and Benjamin Latrobe
were becoming famous. In short, domestic architecture had
reached a level sufficiently competent to impress even the
European visitors to our shores.

Yet despite all their progressive features, these buildings —
from largest capitol to smallest jail — belonged more to the
period which was closing than to the century which lay ahead.
They were grounded upon the building technology of pre-
industrial society. They made no insuperable demands upon
the resources of conventional structural theory or traditional
technique. They were largely content with pre-Revolutionary
standards in craftsmen and building material: nor were they to
yield any important solutions to the problems of heating, ventilating, lighting, or acoustics. Their chief significance lay in their
planning — their brilliant ability to provide for the increasing
scale, complexity, and specialization taking place within the
organs of society.

These buildings were not historically retrogressive — yet.
For their time they were as well built, well lighted, and well
heated as similar buildings elsewhere. They met the special
needs of their society adequately. They were as good as they
had to be. But they were not in themselves to be the instrument
of future technological advance. For this purpose, nineteenth-
century industrialism was to employ an entirely new building
type: the factory.

Parthenogenesis in the Building Field

FROM THE MOMENT it appeared as a distinct type, with its own special characteristics, the factory was to have a twofold significance for American building of every category. Ultimately nothing would escape its impact. On the one hand, it was to supply those improved materials, equipments, and concepts without which advance in the field would have been inconceivable. (Imagine the modern skyscraper, its steel, aluminum, plywood, conditioned air, and fluorescent lighting, without the factories to turn out such products.) On the other hand, as a special type of building, the factory itself soon became the pacemaker relative to which all other types were laggard. The manufacturer demanded infinitely better performance of his building than the home-owner did of his. (It was entirely possible to produce an entire family in a wigwam; but try to turn out a single yard of cheap colored calico under the same conditions.) To make industrial processes at all possible, the factory had to perform better than building had ever done before — that is, offer a greatly expanded and far more precise control of all environmental factors. The factory was thus the parent and the first-born of modern building technology.

The beginnings were modest. Gristmills, smithies, and cobbler shops had been adequate for pre-Revolutionary handicraft production. As long as he stuck to silver (with an occasional dental plate now and then), Paul Revere could carry on in his own house, adding a room here or a shed there. It was only when he was commissioned to sheathe the new frigate *Constitution* in copper that he was forced to seek larger quarters. The level of his production had risen so sharply that the whole character of the process had been changed. As early as 1793, Samuel Slater had built a new spinning mill in Pawtucket, Rhode Island. Here water-powered machines are said to have initiated American mass production. Mr. Slater's mill was indubitably a factory: regular fenestration, angular roof, utter absence of embellishment or whimsy prevented it from being mistaken for anything else. At the same time, its clapboard walls, inadequate many-paned windows, and shingle roofs came from a long line of village gristmills. This was but one of the many structures with which New England was bidding for the industrial leadership of the nation. They spread with amazing rapidity. By 1820 they were to be found wherever water-power could be exploited.

The rapidly increasing demands of industry accelerated the development of new structural concepts and systems. Disastrous fires and structural collapses because of overloading egged on the factory designers. An entirely new scale was given to industrial operations by Francis Cabot Lowell when, in 1814, 'he revolutionized the textile industry by introducing his power loom and by organizing, for the first time, all cloth-making processes within one mill.'[1] Greater spans, greater floor strength for constantly heavier machinery demanded better building materials; increased fire resistance, better heating, artificial lighting were obviously imperative (Figs. 53–55).

The first steam-powered sawmill in the country began operations in 1803 at New Orleans, soon to become the collection point for the fabulous stands of Southern pine, cypress, and yellow poplar of the Mississippi Basin. By the eighteen-twenties, steam power and circular saw had put the production of lumber on a modern production basis. Wood had always been the country's favorite building material and the power-driven sawmill clinched its ascendancy (in 1940, 82 per cent of the nation's houses were still of wood). Though lumber in unprecedented sizes and lengths was now plentiful and cheap, it could not satisfy industry's demands for fire resistance. Iron foundries had sprung up; they were still on a handicraft scale — able to supply New Orleans and Charleston with their lovely balconies even if machine-made nails and steel structural members were still in the future.

Needless to say, the mass production of cheap lumber was no guarantee that all buildings would automatically be well built, nor that all factories would automatically become the most beautiful or efficient of our buildings. History is not so simple,

---

[1] Turpin C. Bannister, 'Architectural Development of Northeastern States,' *Architectural Record* (June, 1941), p. 68.

and quite the contrary has too often been the case. But all major advances in building technology were to be based upon the factory; and this building type, at its best, was consistently to establish new standards for the rest of the building field.

On Washington's birthday in 1817, Philadelphia's élite are reported to have danced to the light of two thousand candles — which reminds us that neither oil lamps nor glass chimneys were yet in common use. Mr. Franklin's theory on the beneficial effects of the tub bath — as well as his shoe-shaped bathtub — was still a controversial issue; and in the Capitol in Washington, the architect Latrobe was installing the first stove. The original fireplaces had proved inadequate and Latrobe was busy in 1804 installing an ingenious contraption of his own design — start of a century-and-a-half effort to keep the legislators comfortable.

Jefferson, Good Genii of American Building

TO A FAR GREATER extent than is visible on the surface of its history, Thomas Jefferson was the guiding spirit of American building during these formative years of the new Republic. He exercised his great influence through all sorts of channels, direct and indirect. By example, as in the buildings he himself designed — his home at Monticello, the University of Virginia. By virtue of official position, as in the competition for the Capitol while he was Secretary of State and in the L'Enfant plan for Washington while he was President. By persuasive argument, as when he sold the State of Virginia on the idea of duplicating a Roman temple in Nîmes for the new State House. Finally, by proxy, as in his long sponsorship of the architect Benjamin Latrobe. Through these channels he was largely responsible for short-circuiting the tortuous, elliptical course of the Classic movement and for fixing the attention of the American people directly upon the cultures and buildings of Rome and Greece.

With his enormous and well-articulated comprehension, Jefferson devoted neither more nor less of his time to building design

than to any of a dozen other pursuits. But when he turned to
it, he saw it whole, with passion, clarity, and optimism. He
saw architecture in both its theoretical and practical aspects and
he understood — as few of his contemporaries did — the inter-
penetration of the two. Equally prepared to teach a slave to
make brick, to lay out a college campus, or to design an entire
architectural curriculum, he moved with ease and sureness at
each level. He was as much interested in penological reform as
in the plans for a new prison which expressed it; and he was
more interested in an independent national esthetic standard
than in any isolated aspect of our building. As much a connoisseur in the fine arts as any London or Paris dandy, he never
for a moment let this polish blind him to buildings of the poor,
whether in Europe or at home. And history was to prove him,
on all these counts, far more perspicacious than his contemporaries.

In the design of actual buildings, Jefferson's intense practicality
matched that of Franklin. Like the Pennsylvania sage, his
diaries abound in keen observations on how to build better: an
ingenious design for a folding table, a lamp in a fan-shaped
transom which lights both sides of the door, horizontally pivoted
windows which when opened would 'admit air and not rain.'
But Jefferson's range of interests were not, like Franklin's, limited
by an almost smug immediacy. In Nîmes he could sit 'gazing
whole hours at the Maison Carrée, like a lover at his mistress.'
In Holland he was entertained at a great house whose Classic
façade he found 'capricious yet pleasing,' while in Germany 'at
Williamsbath there was a ruin which was clever.' He was more
familiar with the ruinous slums of Europe than most gentlemen,
yet he could still view as 'most noble' the old château above
Heidelberg.

The design for the University at Charlottesville is an example
of Jefferson's intelligent subordination of technique to the larger
demands of theory. Here he might teach Negro slaves to carve
a Classic column — changing the order to Ionic 'on account of
the difficulty of the Corinthian capitals.' Or, in a serpentine
wall he might, by canny use of curves, make one brick do the
work of two. But long before he had outlined the functions of a

state-wide system of education; and while he watched the masons at work, he had a very precise picture of the capstone of such a system.

> I consider the common plan followed in this country — but not in others — of making one large and expensive building as unfortunately erroneous. It is infinitely better to erect a small and separate lodge for each separate professorship, with only a hall below for his class and two chambers above for himself; joining these lodges to barracks for a certain portion of the students by a covered [passage] way to give a dry communication between all schools. The whole of these, arranged around an open square of trees and grass, would make it what it should be in fact — an academical village. . . . [Such a plan] would afford that quiet retirement so friendly to study and lessen the danger of fire, infection, and tumult.[1]

His approach here is modern, his concept functional, his program ambitious. He is not laying the cornerstone of some jerkwater college or rustic academy. He envisions a great university made up of many schools, designed to meet the expanding needs of a prosperous society. No abstractions, either pedagogical or architectural, are here to haunt him: he views the design problem from the standpoint of the ultimate consumers — teaching staff and student body. Each school must be segregated, the teacher must have privacy, the student quiet, circulation must be convenient. His argument for the plan is not its symmetry or its style but its efficiency. It will reduce the danger of fire and disease; it will make study easier for the students and discipline easier for the teachers (Fig. 37).

Like all educated men of the period, Jefferson moved in the lustrous dawn of scientific discovery, before the disciplines had congealed into specialized compartments. A smattering of natural philosophy and an inquisitive turn of mind made any man a scientist, for the line between amateur and professional was indistinct. There was nothing of the dilettante in Jefferson's excursions into science, however. His interest in the weather, for instance, did not stop with the amusing windvane and

[1] Letter to Trustees of East Tennessee College, May 6, 1810.

register which he built into Monticello, nor with the records of temperature and rainfall which he kept for many years. The relation between climate and comfort, and the rôle of building in modifying this relationship, intrigued him. He felt that the standards of construction were far short of what they should have been.

> Private buildings are very rarely constructed of stone or brick, much the greater portion being of scantling and boards, plastered with lime [that is, conventional clapboard houses plastered inside]. It is impossible to devise things more ugly, uncomfortable, and — happily — more perishable. There are two or three plans on which, according to its size, most of the houses in the state are built. The poorest build huts of logs, laid horizontally in pens, stopping the interstices with mud. These are warmer in winter and cooler in summer than the more expensive construction of scantling and plank.[1]

From a structural point of view, he was wrong about the frame house: as a piece of engineering it was remarkably efficient. Nor was it as short-lived as he assumed, thanks to the rapidly growing use of oil paints. But he was entirely correct in observing that frame construction offered a much less efficient barrier to the transmission of heat than either log or masonry. The colonists' prejudice against masonry houses was largely based upon the condensation which occurs on masonry walls under certain atmospheric conditions. This 'weeping' had given birth to wild tales of disease and death caused by malignant vapors. Calmly (in what was perhaps the first explanation of its kind in history) Jefferson undertook to show that nothing more dangerous than water vapor was involved, to explain the phenomenon clearly and precisely, and to outline measures which would prevent or minimize its occurrence.

Chronologically, Jefferson's understanding of the importance of a national architecture steadily deepened and matured. He was a critic of taste, perceptive but subjective, when in 1782 he penned his scathing indictment of Williamsburg architecture. He was, of course, born a Classicist. But there was room for sharp disagreement within the movement; and when he attacks

[1] *Notes on the State of Virginia*, 1782.

'the barbarous burthen' of Georgian ornament, he is already identifying himself with the radicals of the nascent Classic Revival. Federalist *décor* was a pallid and upper-class nationalism; its mere substitution of the American eagle for the profile of the British king was not sufficient. In all Virginia, he found only four public buildings worthy of note — the capitol, the palace, the college, and the insane asylum, all of them in Williamsburg. The capitol was, he felt, 'a light and airy structure . . . on the whole the most pleasing piece of architecture we have.' The palace was 'not handsome without, but spacious and commodious within.' As for the college and asylum — they were 'rude misshapen piles which, but for the fact that they have roofs, would be mistaken for brick-kilns.'

All in all, the picture of 'colonial architecture' which Jefferson paints is in sharp contrast with that of today's antiquarians. It seemed to him that 'the genius of architecture had shed its maledictions over this land.'

> To give these buildings symmetry and taste would not increase their cost. It would only change the form and combination of the members. This would often cost less than the burthen of barbarous ornament with which these buildings are sometimes charged. But the first principles of the art are unknown, and there exists scarcely a model among us sufficiently chaste to give an idea of them . . . perhaps a spark may fall on some young subjects of natural taste, kindle up their genius, and produce a reformation in this elegant and useful art.[1]

Here his chaste model is obviously that of Rome as against that of the Royalists. There is more than a little political animus in his position, which was natural enough, with the Revolution only now being brought to a successful conclusion. His preferences were all with 'columnar' architecture (as the Revival styles were then called), but these preferences were not yet dominantly ideological.

He proposed columns because he liked them, and brick because 'when buildings are of durable materials, every new edifice is an actual and permanent acquisition to the state, adding to its value as well as to its ornament.' Here he sounds a

[1] *Notes on the State of Virginia*, 1782.

new and significant note, the patriot's desire to see his country beautiful, wealthy, strong, and respected. As a matter of fact, this sturdy concern for the social wealth of the nation was to be a substructure for his lifelong attitude toward architecture. He wanted national greatness at every level of national life — political, social, cultural, artistic. The building field, like any other, must contribute to this greatness; and the individual building itself must satisfy, not only the needs of its owner, but also of the community as a whole.

Jefferson's advice to American tourists in Europe is a classic of shrewd selection, written by a very Baedeker of social acumen. It might pay them to have a look at the courts of European royalty, much as one might go to the circus, remembering always that 'under the most imposing exterior, [courts] are the weakest and worst parts of mankind.' But the items of real importance to American visitors were six:

1. Agriculture. Everything belonging to this art . . .
2. Mechanical arts, so far as they respect things necessary in America, and inconvenient to be transported there readymade, such as forges, stone quarries, boats, bridges (very especially) . . .
3. Lighter mechanical arts and manufactures. Some of these will be worth a superficial view; but . . . it would be a waste of attention to examine these minutely.
4. Gardens. Particularly worth the attention of an American.
5. Architecture worth great attention. As we double our numbers every twenty years, we must double our houses . . . Architecture is among the most important arts; and it is desirable to introduce taste into an art which shows so much . . .
6. Painting. Statuary. Too expensive for the state of wealth among us . . . worth seeing but not studying.[1]

This is the advice of a realist, neither snob nor hayseed. Europe had much to teach us. There were many interesting areas of activity over there and ultimately Americans must master them all. But time was short. There was a nation to build and our scale of values must be realistic. Painting and statuary might be too expensive — at least for the present. Architecture was a

[1] *Objects for Attention for an American*, June 3, 1788.

different case. Jefferson's distrust of the aristocracy extended
to the palaces which housed it. His notes on his tour of the
great English estates are almost contemptuous of the houses
themselves, critical of their gardens. Nonetheless, Europe must
be studied, the wheat separated from the chaff. Since there
was undoubtedly a lot of building to be done in the new Republic,
he was determined that it be sound, because that would increase
the social wealth. He also wanted it to be beautiful because
it shows so much — that is, the world would see our building and
judge us by it.

The Roman Idiom: Instrument of Progress

JEFFERSON's attitude toward architecture was maturing; he was
beginning to see in it an important instrument of ideological
persuasion. This concept was clearly related to his appreciation
of the situation in which the country found itself. Faced with
enormous responsibilities — mistress of a continent, her population small, her productive capacity weak — she was strong only
in potentials. No one understood this dialectic of strength and
weakness better than Jefferson. America must have time to
grow and room to expand in; and no stratagem which held at
bay the arrogant nations of the old world was too small to be
overlooked. A handsome capital city in which to receive foreign
diplomats decently — this was a real necessity in the tricky,
shark-filled shoals of international diplomacy. A 'tasteful'
dinner party in well-designed and well-furnished rooms would
serve to blur, if not to conceal, the complete absence of a naval
fleet. A lavish table with choice wines would contradict ugly
rumors of bankruptcy; and public buildings like the Classic
State House at Richmond would partially correct the rude
impact of the log cabins in the pinelands.

If years in public life had given Jefferson this attitude toward
architecture, then his long stay in France wedded him to a
specific idiom: the Graeco-Roman 'columnar' style. He had
long been partial to it. Now personal inclination deepened
into political conviction. In the French Revolution he saw the

logical extension of the American War of Independence. A close and sympathetic observer, he learned much that was to stand him in good stead when, in his battles with the Federalists a decade or so later, he was to fight for and win similar extensions of democracy for the common people of his own country. He learned, among other things, the strategic importance of the fine arts. In Tom Paine's pamphlets he had had conclusive proof of the political value of writers to the revolutionary cause. Now, in France, he saw all the arts mobilized in the democratic struggle. Painters, sculptors, writers, and architects were not only organized, their production put to explicitly ideological uses; they were themselves in the forefront of the struggle. Jacques David, official artist of the Revolution, did not content himself with heroic canvases. He participated in the drafting of the Constitution of 1791. Later, when the king tried to negate its moderate provisions, he accepted the presidency of the revolutionary Convention. The whole ponderous machinery of the Academy had begun to turn faster in the service of the revolutionary government. In return, for the first time in modern history, the government had voted the artist a living wage.

And what was the language that these radicals spoke? David, the leader, turned to the Roman Republic for his idiom. He cast his characters in the rôles of Roman allegory, clothed them in Roman togas, housed them in Roman buildings, furnished them with Roman beds and chairs (Figs. 27, 28). Others followed suit. Thus David shared with Angelica Kauffmann this historical necessity: neither could escape the reference frame of all European culture, both must return to the Classic fountainhead of Graeco-Rome for nourishment and renewal. But between Kauffmann's oversexed and misty cherubs and the lucid, sharp-edged reality of David's perspectives lay all the vast distance of their social and political divergence. She painted for the pompous, powdered British bourgeoisie, already fat with a century of power. He spoke for forces which were only now challenging the absolutism of the French kings. And, under the impact of tumultuous events, the distance between the two was constantly increasing: for, though they both revolved around the same axis, Kauffmann was repelled by the very forces which attracted David.

What was the attraction which pulled the French artists ever closer to the ancients? Tom Paine, who was always punctual in his appointments with history, showed split-second timing again:

> It is owing to the long interregnum of science, *and to no other cause*, that we have now to look through a vast chasm of many hundred years to the respectable characters we call the Ancients. Had the progression of knowledge gone on proportionably ... those ancients we now so much admire would have appeared respectably in the background of the scene. But the Christian system laid all waste; and if we take our stand about the beginning of the Sixteenth Century, we look back through a long chasm to the times of the ancients, as over a vast sandy desert, in which not a shrub appears to intercept the vision of the fertile hills beyond.[1]

It was nothing less than the historical continuity of intellectual progress which was at stake in France. The beady eyes and slavering tongues of Europe's blackest reaction ringed her round like wolves in the forest. Every weapon was needed and the artists did not fail her. On the ideological level, David's message was the same as Paine's; only their media differed.

That David, adopting the Roman idiom, was guilty of artistic anachronism is beside the point. The entire Classic movement — from Inigo Jones to McKim, Meade, and White — was by definition guilty of archeological distortion. These discrepancies are apparent only in *retrospect:* for, as Milton Brown has pointed out, the artist was not the only one who was guilty of historical bias or architectural distortion:

> His contemporaries, through a similar association, had also acquired these same delusions, with the consequence that there was no fallacy (apparent to them). It is evident, therefore, that the revolutionary approach to antiquity was no longer one of archeological or esthetic interest, but was one of social and political significance. Antiquity was valued because in it resided the virtues most desirable to the contemporary mind. Political republicanism logically gave rise to artistic republicanism.[2]

[1] *The Age of Reason*, part I, 1794.
[2] *Painting of the French Revolution*, The Critics Group. New York City, 1938.

Thomas Jefferson was by no means an unwitting victim of this ideological mechanism. On the contrary, he understood it quite clearly. Like Paine, he saw in the theocratic Middle Ages nothing but bigotry, reaction, material retrogression. The Ancients were his friends and counselors. Had he not, when they wrote him from Virginia for an original design for the new capitol, sent them instead the measured drawings of the Maison Carrée in Nîmes? For him the request had been 'a favourable opportunity of introducing into the State . . . this most perfect model' of Roman architecture (Fig. 36). He was already fully prepared emotionally to accept the new idiom: his travels along the Mediterranean littoral, his moonlight visits to the Forum, his contacts with Winckelmann's researches at the Vatican — all these served to change preference into conviction.

In March, 1789, the capital of France was full of art. But Jefferson, making the rounds of the galleries, wrote Madame de Bréhan: 'I do not feel an interest in any pencil but that of David.' His unfailing political acumen was a sure base for his esthetic standards. The art of Europe *in general* was 'too expensive' a luxury for Americans, worth 'seeing but not studying.' This dictum obviously did not include the productions of David and his colleagues, for the good and sufficient reason that they had a practical significance to American problems. Just as the French intelligentsia recognized in Jefferson the most advanced exponent of American democracy, so he recognized in them the greater political maturity of the French Revolution. One of the evidences of this maturity was the use they made of art, the effectiveness with which they had mobilized the artists in the people's behalf, and the rich and productive idiom they had chosen in the Roman Revival.

Needless to say, the Classic Revival in this country was not the subversive importation of Jefferson alone — though there were those who said it was. On the contrary, as a movement it would never have got to first base had not its symbolism corresponded to the needs of the dominant classes of the period and been consistent with their general outlook on the world. For, with the final adoption of the Bill of Rights, the state power had been wrested, by those forces which had fought the War of Independence through to a successful conclusion, from the hands of those Southern slaveholders and Northern Tories who sought to hold it. Only then was bourgeois democracy, of which Jefferson was the first great spokesman, complete and secure. The aspirations of this society were rational, expansive, optimistic, breathing confidence in Man, his native goodness and nobility, his natural rights. The desire for a truly national culture based upon such concepts was a quite explicit factor of the period. In attempting to express these concepts, to concretize them into esthetic standards, it was inevitable that the nation impress them upon its building. In the context of the period, it was inevitable that the architectural language of these standards be that of the Roman Republic.

The esthetic unity of this period, so much remarked by historians and lamented by nostalgic critics, was in fact due to the very structure of Jeffersonian society. The dominant classes — the new capitalists and manufacturers, the small-propertied people, the independent farmers — were united upon a program of national reconstruction and expansion. And, so far from being a foreign 'ism,' Jefferson's leadership suited them to the extent that, in 1804, they returned him to the White House with 162 out of 174 electoral votes. In the building field specifically, his Classicism did not yet run counter to technological development. Moreover, ownership being very widely dispersed in such a society, a far larger proportion of the population was able to participate directly in the building process. With comparatively little centralization of land-ownership and none at all of construction and design, democracy in the establishment of both esthetic and technical standards was entirely logical.

For the rest of his life after his retirement from the presidency, Thomas Jefferson was to occupy a strategic position with reference to the main lines of development in American building. And his efforts in behalf of a national architecture and a native building technology were not wasted. America built hugely and built well; and the Revival — first the Roman, then the Greek — became the absolutely universal idiom of design.

Under Jefferson's pervasive and kindly genius, a whole school of great American architects appeared: Latrobe, Magnin, Mills, Strickland. These men differed from their predecessors, and indeed from Jefferson himself, in several important respects. They were not amateurs, not dilettantes, not even necessarily gentlemen, but full-time technically trained professionals. They were largely the product of European universities (despite Jefferson's plans, it was not until 1866 that this country saw its first architectural school), with a sound footing in engineering and a diminished obsession with the more literary aspects of architecture. The environment in which they matured, and which Jefferson had done so much to guarantee, was especially favorable to the development of well-rounded designers. On the one hand, the emphasis of all higher education upon what would today be called the liberal arts was still large. On the other hand, the Industrial Revolution gave increasing importance to science and technology inside the classroom and out. Classicism could thus coexist with nascent science. One man could master both architecture and engineering. Both fields remained comparatively simple; the split between them was still a problem of the future.

For men like Benjamin Latrobe, it was thus possible to be at once an enthusiastic and meticulous Classicist and an imaginative and resourceful hydraulic engineer. He had landed in Norfolk in 1796, with no capital but an engineering degree from a German university and an apprenticeship under the English architect Samuel Pepys, one of the pioneers of the Greek Revival. A versatile young man, Latrobe had spent the first few months in this country 'idly engaged [in] designing a staircase for Mrs. A.'s house, a house and office for Captain P., tuning a pianoforte for Mrs. W., scribbling doggerel for Mrs. A., tragedy for her mother and Italian songs for Mr. T.' [1] This lapdog existence did not content him for long. His first employment was at Richmond, doing navigation work on the James River. It must have been here that he and his work first came to Jefferson's attention. In any event, two years later he was able to carry

[1] *Journal of Latrobe* (New York: D. Appleton and Company, 1905), p. XV.

with him to Philadelphia letters of recommendation from
Jefferson. Whatever the details of their meeting, the relationship between the two men was cordial, productive, and long-
lived. It is easy to understand that the young man appealed
to Jefferson. He had a first-rate technical education (hard to
find in a native-born American); he was a 'bigoted Greek' in
his esthetic standards; he had a liberal and imaginative mind.

Latrobe's career, on the other hand, owed much to Jefferson's
patronage. One of his important commissions — the Virginia
State Penitentiary — was based upon data which Jefferson had
forwarded from Europe during his ambassadorship. The Jefferson letters helped him in the Quaker City, where he was soon
designing the handsome structure for the Bank of Pennsylvania
(Fig. 40). It was here, too, that he received what was perhaps
his most notable commission — the Philadelphia Water Works.
It was certainly one of the most important building projects of
the new Republic (Fig. 41). Here Latrobe displayed exactly those
qualities which Jefferson so admired in building design: technical
progressiveness, competent craftsmanship, esthetic sophistication.
There was no prototype for a project of this complexity and
scale. It was, in itself, paradoxical: it straddled the two technologies of the period. In concept and function, it belonged
clearly to the new industrial society. In actual design and
construction, it necessarily relied upon the techniques and
materials actually available. Latrobe met and — for the moment — mastered the essential contradiction between the Classic
discipline and that of the new machines. To accomplish this
he had to resort to certain devices which would become all too
familiar as the century wore on. External symmetry did not
always represent internal balance. Chimneys did not always
leave the roof exactly over the spot where they started below.
Nevertheless, his accomplishment was great, running as it did
from the installation of the pumps and design of the conduit
system to a façade of impeccable taste. The steam pumps were
much the largest ever built in this country and the architect
risked much on them. The night of January 21, 1803, found
Latrobe himself on the scene, with only three of his closest
friends, nervously kindling the fires which would set the ponder-

ous machines in motion. They did not explode, as any boiler was apt to do in those days, and his reputation was secure.

President Jefferson recalled Latrobe to Washington in 1803 to take charge of the construction of the new Navy drydocks; and the next year appointed him to the specially created post of surveyor of building for the federal government. In this capacity he designed the south wing of the Capitol, until he quarreled with Doctor Thornton, winner of the national competition for the original design. Throughout this period Latrobe and Jefferson were closely associated. The fact that Jefferson was closely identified with the Roman, and Latrobe with the Greek, aspects of the Revival does not seem to have created any rift, despite Latrobe's somewhat didactic letter to the President declaring that his 'principles of good taste were rigid in Grecian architecture.' Actually, Jefferson was himself a Greek scholar — perhaps a better one than Latrobe — and the men were in agreement on their attitude toward architecture as a whole.

Besides, the aging Jefferson had lived to see the symbols of his beloved Roman appropriated by the Napoleonic dictatorship and indubitably turned from instruments of liberation into the heraldry of imperialism. The rise of the Directoire style was merely the esthetic expression of a much deeper political fact. The French Revolution had not only failed to hold many of the gains it had staked out for the common people; under Napoleon, it was being converted into a reactionary instrument which threatened all of Europe. Many of its intellectuals, including David himself, were now in the courts of the Bonapartes. Jefferson saw all this and his confidence, not in the Revolution but in the intellectuals, wavered.

He saw other things, too, which must have made him more sympathetic to younger men like Latrobe. In 1788 he had said that 'circumstances render[ed] it impossible that America should become a manufacturing country during the time of any man now living.' He himself had lived to see the impossible taking place. His agrarian republic was being submerged by an industrial democracy whose best exponents were men like Latrobe: Latrobe, who had designed the first drydocks in the New World, who had watched with deep interest the manufacture of his steam pumps in a Trenton factory, who was planning even then with Robert Fulton a fleet of big steamships for the upper Ohio. Jefferson was not at odds with such men; he was merely too old to keep up with them.

Practical experience in such projects as the waterworks in Philadelphia and New Orleans prevented Latrobe's getting lost in fruitless stylistic controversy. Already, before his untimely death of yellow fever in 1820, he perceived the limits of the Classic Revival — and this at the very moment it had reached its greatest peak. 'Our religion requires a church wholly different from the [Greeks'] temples, our legislative assemblies and our courts of justice buildings of entirely different principles from their basilicas; and our amusements could not possibly be performed in their theaters and amphitheaters.'[1] Such perspicacity must not be credited to native wit alone. More than any architect of his day, Latrobe had worked in manufacturing and engineering construction. Though its levels were not yet high enough to confront the designer with apparently insoluble contradictions, the crisis loomed on the horizon. And had he lived to face it, there is little doubt as to where his choice would have lain: Latrobe was not a man to be paralyzed by abstractions, no matter how symmetrical or chaste.

[1] *Journal of Latrobe*, p. 139.

CHAPTER THREE

1820–1840: Quiet Before the Storm

T HE PERIOD had opened auspiciously. The shifting relationship between agrarian and industrial economies came into a temporary national equilibrium with the election of Andrew Jackson to the presidency in 1828. For the time being, industry advanced in the North while agriculture held sway in South and West. But the nation was already half slave and half free; and ominous portents of the 'irrepressible conflict' lay in the struggle around each new state admitted to the Union. Eli Whitney had unwittingly done much to hasten and deepen the split with his invention, in 1794, of the mechanical cotton gin. Instead of five pounds, a slave could now clean five hundred pounds of cotton per day. Instead of being one of the most expensive of fibers, cotton suddenly became the cheapest. The effect on American society was cataclysmic. On the one hand, Whitney's gin laid the basis for expansion to monstrous proportions of human slavery in the South. But cheap cotton in turn made possible the rapid development of the textile industry in New England, with its liberating effects, not only upon science and technology but politics and culture as well.

The development of these two conflicting cultures — slavery in the South, industrialism in the North — had a decisive effect upon American building. As a matter of fact, the Mason-Dixon Line acted like a solid Chinese Wall around the South against which all the great progressive tides of mid-century American life beat in vain. It was the expanding industrial culture of the North which gave the nation the inventors and pragmatic scien-

46

II

The Classic Idiom
in the Service of the New Republic

American building, in the years after the Revolution, assumed a qualitatively new scale. Typical was the new Capitol at Washington (31), as planned by the unhappy l'Enfant (32). Note Latrobe's drydock (right, above), where, if he had his way, Jefferson would have permanently stored his navy.

32

33

Everywhere, as the nineteenth century opened, new public buildings were arising. In Boston, Charles Bulfinch completed his State House (33) in 1802. In New York, Joseph Mangin began the next year a City Hall (34) whose balanced elegance reflected his French origin.

34

Built under a Spanish régime, the consoled dormers and mansard roof of the Cabildo yet proved the dominance of the French in New Orleans (35). Jefferson's suggestion for the State House at Richmond (36) gave the country its first direct copy of an actual Roman temple.

Capstone of Thomas Jefferson's most cherished project — free, state-supported, universal education — was his plan for the University of Virginia (37). He envisioned no jerkwater college but a great, balanced complex of many schools. On his own home at Monticello (38) he lavished almost forty years of continual esthetic and technical experimentation.

37

The Louisiana which Jefferson cannily bought in 1805 continued meanwhile its own adaptation of the Classic: a house at Chalmette (39).

39

40

Benjamin Henry Latrobe combined those qualities which Jefferson most admired: sophistication and progressiveness. The first he demonstrated in 1799 in the Bank of Pennsylvania (40);
the latter in the Philadelphia Waterworks (41) for which he even built the boilers in 1803.

41

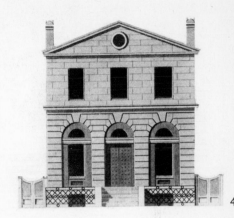

Fascination with the formal idiom of the Classic never dampened Yankee ingenuity; nor did it prevent the architect Haviland from designing this prefabricated cast-iron facade for a bank at Pottsville, Pa., in 1830.

42

By the time of Jackson, the Greek style had become the very language of Democracy, just as, two decades before, the Roman had been the symbol of Republicanism. The Greek Wars of Independence sharpened this romantic identification and led to poems, tombstones, place names and parlors (43) in the Grecian manner.

43

44

45

Boston was the center of the Grecian Renaissance and the Athenaeum was the cultural center of Boston (44, 45). Here, Washington Allston gave young Horatio Greenough drawing lessons from Greek casts. In Boston, too, Isaiah Rogers built his Greek Tremont House (1828) — that first modern hostelry with more facilities than Dickens could count or his readers believe.

46

47

Philadelphia, no less than Boston, was weaned away from the Georgian. Always famous for her institutional architecture and still the largest and most urbane of American cities, she had Strickland's magnificent Bank of America (47) . . .

. . . and Thomas U. Walter's main building for Girard Institute (48). Endowed by crusty old agnostic, Stephen Girard, the Institute's walled grounds are barred forever to clergymen.

48

49

Across the Appalachians, every capital in the Western Reserve aspired to be another Athens. Cincinnati's old Custom House (49) was in the Greek manner as was Cleveland's Public Square (50) when painted in such naïve detail by Heine in 1839.

50

51

Andrew Jackson, homely product and leader of western democracy, built a Greek plantation house near Nashville in the thirties.

52

While St. Louis's Cathedral had a granite front in the classic manner, its sides were brick.

53

Almost unnoticed, industry was revolutionizing building with its demands for greater span and strength. These 1835 views of New England textile mills show astonishing development.

54

Even earlier, in 1822, Zachariah Allen had attempted a fireproof factory in Rhode Island (55)

55

tists of the period — Fitch, Fulton, Goodyear, Otis, Morse, Bell, and a host of others. It was New England which fathered the great literary figures of the period — Emerson, Thoreau, Whitman, Whittier, Longfellow, and the pro-democratic movements for free education, woman's suffrage, trade-unionism. It is thus not accidental that the leading architects and engineers were likewise to be found in the North — Latrobe, Mills, Haviland, Isaiah Rogers, Bogardus, and Roebling.

The plantation system of production, on the other hand, had no need for advanced building types, and the slave power could not tolerate progress in building technology any more than in other areas of human affairs. It would be a mistake to think that this condition was peripheral to the slave culture. There was a certain Southern journalist who in 1857 was bitterly aware of the interconnection of events. 'We have got to hating everything with the prefix *free*,' he said, 'from free Negro to free will, free thinking, free children, and free schools — all belonging to the same brood of damnable isms.' [1] A society which did not encourage a public-school system would certainly not evolve new and better school buildings. Nor would a society based on hand labor encourage the labor-saving devices of scientists, engineers, and technicians. Instead it produced the sleazy racism of Mississippi's Doctor S. A. Cartwright, with his 'scientific proof' of the necessity of slavery. Doctor Cartwright claimed the discovery of a peculiar mental disease called *drapetomania* (sic!) which caused cats and slaves to run away at night. Also, he had found that the brain of the Negro froze in the cold climates north of the Ohio; common kindness dictated they be kept in the South!

It is to the North, then, and especially to New England, that we must turn in the period which was opening.

Like a Dream, the Grecian Vista...

THE GREEK REVIVAL was the dominant architectural style of the period. Unlike the Classic of Thomas Jefferson, however,

[1] Harriet Buckmaster, *Let My People Go* (New York: Harper and Brothers, 1941), p. 251.

the Greek Revival was not the exclusive property of one group; nor was it always the idiom of progress. To the contrary, it was used and discarded successively by the rising mercantile-manufacturing classes of the East, by the freeholders of Trans-Appalachia, finally by the Southern slave-owners. And each of these groups read into its vernacular their own particular concepts of history and used it for their own especial ends. Thus, the Greek Revival appeared first in the great humanitarian renaissance in the Boston of the eighteen-twenties, becoming for a while the very language of literature, philosophy, and art. Then it swept over the mountains into the equalitarian West of Andrew Jackson and Abraham Lincoln, where it served as the vehicle for the democratic upsurge of the rising middle class. And ultimately, turned to quite other ends than its original sponsors contemplated, it was adroitly used by Calhoun as a pedestal on which to display his monstrous 'democracy of tyrants' in the South.

By 1820 the cultural center of gravity of the nation lay in Boston, as formerly it had lain in the Virginia of Washington and Jefferson. Here was intense intellectual activity. Young George Ticknor had returned to Harvard in 1819, fresh from a triumphal tour of Europe. There he had seen Greece through the eyes of the great German humanitarians. He had met Byron, studied Greek, seen the intensive archeology of the Germans. He came back to hold his classes spellbound with tales of his discovery. And he was but the first of those who made a torrent from a tendency: Edward Everett, later the nation's first orator; Jared Sparks, the historian who met Byron and studied Greek at the German universities; Samuel Gridley Howe, who returned from Greece with Byron's helmet to write his famous *Historical Sketch of the Greek Revolution*. Like a dream, the Grecian vista lay before the whole American people. The Elgin Marbles from the Parthenon were now on display in London, and pictures, casts, and lyric descriptions of them were flooding the New World.

The children, brought up on Flaxman's outlines, knew their mythology as they knew their Bible. . . . Everyone talked mythology as everyone had begun to discuss the history of religion; and the best of the New England novels, at the turn of the Forties ... presupposed a feeling for ancient Greece as they took for granted a circle of readers steeped in the Bible and Latin authors.[1]

The architects of the period were not less enthusiastic Greeks than the teachers, artists, and writers of New England.[2] In fact, in strict chronology, the architects had anticipated the Boston intelligentsia. At the very turn of the century, Latrobe in his Philadelphia Water Works and Strickland in his Bank of the United States (Figs. 41, 47) had shown complete familiarity with the current researches into Greek architecture. There had always been a wide and eager audience for the handbooks, carpenters' guides, and architectural plates of the British publishers. As the editorial emphasis of these swung more and more toward the Greek, they carried their American audience with them. It was not long before similar works began to appear on this side of the Atlantic. Especially successful were the books of plates by the architects Minard Lafever, *The Beauties of Modern Architecture*, and Asher Benjamin, *The Practice of Architecture*. Both treatises extolled the Greek and contributed largely to the success of the Revival.

It must be remembered that these books were studied not by architects and designers alone; thousands of literate home-owners, intent on keeping up with the world, scanned them as anxiously as does a modern the pages of *House and Garden*. These books were especially influential because the prospective builder seldom engaged an architect if for no other reason than that there were as yet very few full-time professional designers in the country. Instead, he would show the local carpenter what plates in the book he wanted 'the house to look like.' This common practice led to a very wide dispersion of the Greek idiom among skilled building workers. It gave to the building of the period a remarkable homogeneity and a high degree of competence.

[1] Van Wyck Brooks, *The Flowering of New England* (New York: E. P. Dutton and Company, 1936), p. 183.

[2] The most comprehensive account of the architecture of the period is to be found in Talbot Hamlin's *Greek Revival Architecture in America* (New York and London: Oxford University Press, 1944).

Everywhere — in Philadelphia, in the Hudson River Valley, in Providence, Portsmouth, and Boston — Greek structures were abuilding. Thus, though Boston was the hub of the movement, its spokes radiated to every center in the Northeast and New England (Figs. 44–46). More important than its ubiquity was the fact that the Greek Revival was the idiom of the most progressive forces in American life. The chief proponents of the Greek were the very men and women who were most active in the great movements of the period. It was they who were bringing new libraries, art galleries, museums, and orchestras to America; they who were increasingly interested in the plight of the workingman, the poor, the sick, and the insane; it was they who acted as spearheads for the manhood suffrage, women's rights, and anti-child-labor movements of the period. When Mr. and Mrs. Charles Dickens came to America, it was Boston's institutions for wayward girls, orphans, and blind which most interested them. Finally — nodal point of the nineteenth century — it was the Boston intelligentsia who furnished the *avant-garde* in the struggle against human slavery.

That the Greek Revival had the possibilities of quite other uses — as the South was shortly to demonstrate — was scarcely their fault. The fact that historically the Greek democracy had rested on the necks of foreign slaves they overlooked, much as Jefferson and the French Revolutionists had overlooked the same phenomenon with regard to the Romans. This was perhaps partly due to faulty scholarship — archeological research was only beginning to be put upon a scientific basis. It may have been partly a deliberate (though not a conscious) oversight. But it is certainly not the first example that history affords us of the use by one society of only those aspects of another which suit its particular needs.

Nor can any honest generalizations paint the town of Boston as lily-white. For she too had her Tories and appeasers, men who had little use for the democratic propaganda and even less for the social experiments which flowed from them — the great merchants who were broken to King Cotton; the narrow Royalists who had given up George III only to accept the aristocratic pretensions of Hamilton; the rising industrialists of the mill towns who opposed chattel slavery only in so far as it threatened the eighty-four-hour week of free labor. These gentry also lived in Greek houses, worshiped in Greek churches, lay buried under Greek headstones. But this was itself an evidence of the depth and vitality of the Classic movement. It was not to the Tories that the great Boston of the period belonged.

Athens in Appalachia

MEANWHILE, west of the mountains, a new empire was abuilding. With Jackson's inauguration the middle-class frontier emerged as the driving political force of American democracy, a force which was ultimately to strike down slavery and raise New England industrialists and Western farmers to power. Jackson typified this development; himself a product of the frontier, he was the first true commoner to hold the office of President of the United States. The basis had already been laid for the continental independence of the nation: the Spanish had been driven out of Florida, the French bought out of Louisiana, and Jackson himself had smashed the meddling British at New Orleans. The way was open for the building of the West.

If the West was not largely settled by New Englanders, it was at least largely to be taught by them. Throughout the territories private schools, academies, and colleges were mushrooming. The basis was being laid for that public-school system for which the Middle West is famous; and to these seats of learning flocked the Yankee schoolmarms and the Greek professors. With them came the Boston magazines, novels, and textbooks — all the cultural forms of the New England renaissance. This coincided with the political necessities of the day. As Jefferson had seen in the architecture of republican Rome the appropriate symbols for the new Republic, so Jacksonian democrats saw in democratic Greece appropriate symbols for the America of the twenties. This philosophical identification was made much more real by the Greek Wars of Independence. How genuine was this sympathy, and how deep beyond the educated classes it extended,

Towns with Greek and Roman place names — Athens, Troy, Aurora, Venus, Olympia, Argus — show by their date and location how vivid was the identification of Jacksonian America with the Classic.   *Museum of Modern Art*

are clear both from the political rallies and money-raising campaigns to aid the living Greeks and by the adoption of the cultural forms of long-dead ones. Poems, courthouses, curricula, banks, tombstones, and dresses all bore the Grecian imprint.

An astonishing number of new American towns were given Greek place names during this period; and it is significant that most of these towns lay west of the mountains — that is, precisely in that part of the country from which sprang the main sources of Jacksonian democracy. These towns had Greek architecture as well as Greek names. Ohio knew no other idiom — she leaped from log cabins to the polished severity of the Grecian idiom (Figs. 49, 50). The Ohio River was one long line of Revival towns. In St. Louis, the spreading warehouses and the new cathedral were alike in the Greek manner, while the Springfield that nourished Lincoln was a crude but confident new Athens. The Kentucky of Audubon's time and Andrew Jackson's own house (Fig. 51) were in the Greek idiom, blurred by distance and simplified by local carpenters to meet the limited materials.

In the new Western style there was more than a trace of Jefferson's Rome; but nowhere at all was there anything left of the Royalist Georgian. We can only conclude then that this change in taste was in strict conformity to the qualitative changes in the structure of American society between 1790 and 1830.

The Deep South, the South of the slave-owners, was the last area of Greek Revival penetration. This cannot be dismissed as accidental; rather, as Parrington says: 'The pronounced drift of Southern thought, in the years immediately preceding the Civil War, toward the ideal of a Greek democracy . . . was no vagrant eddy but a broadening current of tendency.'[1] When the nineteenth century opened, slavery was merely one of the many issues which perplexed the new Republic. Jefferson and Jackson, while disapproving of the peculiar institution, could own slaves without appearing as hypocrites. Black bodies were already a valuable commodity, but they had yet to become the indispensable base for the voracious economy of cotton. It was only as the century matured that the issues began to sharpen into first-rate political controversy until, in the fifties, it became the very fulcrum on which the fate of the nation turned. In 1830, the New England liberals could extol the Greek democracy without being troubled by its more sordid aspects. Fifteen or twenty years later, this had become completely impossible. Boston humanitarianism had moved on to Transcendentalism; Goethe and Hegel and the English Romanticists were everywhere the subject of discussion; and the Greek idiom in architecture had given way to the Gothic Revival.

In the South, on the other hand, the early enthusiasm for the Greeks had gone largely unremarked. Charleston was content with pre-Revolutionary England, New Orleans with Napoleonic France, as their attitudes, literature, and architecture attest. But as slavery became more important in Southern life, its defense had to be placed on a more organized basis. From apology, the South went over to attack. Searching for the best weapon its leading ideologue, Calhoun, found the Greek Revival

---

[1] Vernon Parrington, *Main Currents of American Thought* (New York: Harcourt Brace and Company, 1930), vol. II, p. 99.

ready to hand where the Yankees had dropped it: 'They [the Southern apologists for slavery] had been moving slowly toward the conception of a Greek democracy under the leadership of Calhoun, but now under the sharp prod of Abolitionism [publication of *Uncle Tom's Cabin* in 1851] they turned militant.'[1] Calhoun spent the better part of twenty years converting the Greek Revival from an instrument of cultural liberation into a weapon of political oppression, arriving finally at his thesis of a democracy enjoyed only by tyrants. The theoreticians, professors, and architects were not far behind him. Greenough's famous article, urging Americans 'to learn from the Greeks like men and not to copy them like monkeys,' had appeared in the North in 1843. Not until ten years later, in August, 1853, did the *Southern Literary Messenger* get around to reprinting it.[2] Greenough himself was already dead — and the South chose blandly to ignore the very implications which he had drawn from his lifelong study of the Classic.

Charleston in the eighteen-twenties clung to her own version of galleried Georgian with its intricate detail — sometimes exquisite, often merely finicky. In the great houses which lined her streets, and the churches of Saint Philip and Saint Michael which towered over them, one could trace direct descent from the England of Inigo Jones, Christopher Wren, and the Brothers Adam (Fig. 17). Neither Jefferson's Virginia nor the France of David had disturbed her reading habits or architectural preferences. Pope was only now yielding to Moore and the Addisonian essay. 'We are decidedly more English than any other city in the United States,' proudly exclaimed the Tory lawyer, Hugh Legare — the same Legare who exclaimed, 'The politics of the immortal Jefferson! Pish!'; who called Jefferson 'the holy father in democracy . . . the infallible, though ever-changing, Saint Thomas of *Canting-bury*.' No, Charleston had little use for the Greek Revival until her historic rôle as intellectual center of secessionism forced her to adopt Calhoun's version

[1] *Ibid.*, p. 102.
[2] Cited by Talbot Hamlin, 'Greek Revival and Some of its Critics,' *The Art Bulletin* (September, 1942), p. 252.

of it. And by that time it was too late for it to find architectural expression in her buildings.

At the opening of the century, New Orleans — bought by the Union in 1803, fought over some twelve years later — was still only nominally a part of the United States. The sources of her culture were far different from those of the rest of America. It was from France that she got her language, her theater, her literature, and her law. Her architectural idiom was that of Mansart, architect of Versailles, cleverly adapted to the climate and merged with the Spanish (Fig. 35). But the march of cotton was lapping the shores of the Mississippi, whose rich muck was selling by the river-front foot, like lots along Times Square. Fabulous fortunes appeared in cotton overnight. Charleston might build railroads to siphon off the cotton, but New Orleans had the incomparable Mississippi; and all this swelling commerce drained into her wharves, to make her the economic capital of the slave power.

New Englanders might translate Homer, Socrates, and Aristotle, to show what heights human aspirations had reached in the past and might, with proper application, be reached again. The South would scan Plato's *Republic* for proof that slavery, and slavery alone, was the system which could make such culture possible. Thus, if by 1850, the mid-South was studded with Greek plantation houses, courthouses, banks, and capitols, it was not the same vogue which had swept through New England thirty years before. The pedimented façade had been put to other uses. In a subtle fashion the buildings themselves reveal this. For in the South the Greek Revival was a ruling-class affair. The buildings with any pretensions to elegance, or even permanence, were those of the regnant slave-owners. Not only the slave, but the poor-white also, was pushed into the squalor of the shack; independent freeholding farmers were crushed by the pressure of slavery. In the Southern countryside there was only the plantation house, the slave quarters, and the backwoods cabin. Hence there was little evidence of popular building, the anonymous structures which mark the comparatively high levels of the Ohio River Valley, the Shenandoah, New York State, or the Maine seacoast.

There was, indeed, no building technology to speak of, except in the big cities. Carved mantelpieces, marble stairs, fluted pilasters require skilled, literate craftsmen. Jefferson might train his slaves to become skilled marble-cutters and millwrights. But the slave or the poor-white who could read those carpenters' handbooks and architectural plate-books which were the stock-in-trade of every Yankee carpenter and builder might also read other literature. So the Southern gentlemen preferred to import their skilled craftsmen, their Empire furniture and damask curtains, from New Orleans, from the North, or from Europe. William Nutt, of Natchez, was one such planter. From Philadelphia he had imported not only an architect but an entire crew of Irish workmen to build his house at Longwood. The Civil War broke out when the place was but half-finished. As one man the crew laid down their tools, left the huge Moorish pile unfinished, and took the first boat up the river. The huge pile lies unfinished to this day.

A Cloud No Bigger Than Your Hand

WHAT THE ARCHITECTS of the period thought of the Greek Revival must be deduced more from their buildings than from their writings. It is true that a few of them — notably Asher Benjamin and Minard Lafever — made a comfortable living out of their vastly popular architectural books; and such books were enthusiastically Greek, as those of their predecessors had been Roman. But they involved no philosophic discussion of esthetic standards; rather, like today's women's magazines, they described how one might achieve the prevailing taste. The evidence is that the majority of architects of the period merely reflected the prevailing ideology: ready as always to trim their sails to every vagary of fashionable taste.

Like all educated men of the period, the architects were steeped in the Classic tradition, moving as freely in mythology as in the Bible. Indeed, as we have seen, the identification of past with present, of Golden Greece with Jacksonian America, was so complete, its sources so far back in our history, as seldom to call for any comment. For the building designers of that period, the Classic idiom constituted the known world. Within its limits they moved freely, with grace and knowledge. That there *were* limits, and beyond them new possibilities, seems to have occurred only to the greatest and most adventurous builders of the day.

Were these architects aware of the ideological significance of the movement of which they were a part? Nicholas Biddle, one foot in the camp of pre-Revolutionary mercantilism and one in the nascent field of modern finance, could select the Greek Revival for his own palatial residence. The financier Girard could stipulate that the Institute he was endowing be also in that style (Fig. 48). But what did Thomas U. Walter, architect for both projects, have to say on the subject? For years he had been one of the leading exponents of the Greek, evidently seeing in it the best expression of his own and his clients' aspirations. Yet by 1841 he was uncomfortably aware of the contradictions involved in the uncritical imposition of the idiom upon the reality of American life: 'If architects would oftener *think* as the Greeks thought than *do* as the Greeks did, our columnar architecture would possess a higher degree of originality, and its character and expression would gradually conform to the local circumstances of the country and the republican spirit of its institutions.' [1] And Robert Mills, designer of the Capitol and an eminently successful Greek, warned that American architects 'should never forget the original models of their country, neither its customs nor the manners of their people, . . . I say to [them]: study your country's tastes and requirements and make classic ground *here* for your art!' [2] These men were mirroring the rising nationalism which was everywhere abroad in American life and letters. Be free of Europe! We are destined to lead the world, not to follow it! Walter and Mills were here not only discussing the same problem which confronted the best minds of literature, politics and philosophy; they were also discussing it at the same level and from the same standpoint — that is, as ideologues.

[1] The Franklin Institute, *Journal*, vol. XXXII, no. 1, January, 1841.
[2] H. M. P. Gallagher, *Robert Mills*. New York, 1935.

Among the architects of the East, then, there was by the eighteen-forties a well-defined dissatisfaction with the Greek idiom. It was restrictive, with all the limitations of formality. Its rigid symmetry, stern affectations of simplicity, Spartan line, no longer comported well with the romantic naturalism, new-found wealth, and hearty appetites of the urban rich. As a system, it became inelastic and artificial before the complexities of industrial society. But what style would replace it? The more radical of the critics were actually attacking not merely the Greek but the entire Classic tradition, and proposing the Egyptian and the Gothic. Strickland was shortly to design a church in Nashville, Tennessee, in the Egyptian manner, while Upjohn's Gothic design for New York's Trinity was already a sensation.

But at first the anti-Classicists made slow headway. The Romanticist, A. J. Downing, publishing a book of plates and plans for bankers who wanted to play at country gentlemen, ruefully admitted that 'such is the rage for this [Greek] style among us just now, and so completely have our builders the idea of its unrivalled supremacy in their heads, that many submit to the most meager conveniences . . . without a murmur.'[1] Downing was able, nevertheless, to illustrate his book with examples in the Italian, Gothic, Tudor, Swiss, and 'bracketed' styles, showing how far advanced already was the collapse of the Classic vernacular.

The propaganda for the Gothic was impressive. Men like Sir Walter Scott in the field of popular fiction, and Ruskin and Pugin in the narrower realm of criticism, had huge audiences in this country. Insofar as the Romanticist movement, whether in print or in masonry, served to free building from the now-dead clutch of the Classic, it was progressive. Its liberating effect upon plan was immediate and healthy, as was its new emphasis upon the out-of-doors. As long as the basic types and character of building remained unchanged by technology, the use of historic detail and systems of ornament remained a scholarly occupation, in which gentlemen could split hairs in comfort and safety. But, unfortunately for the Romanticists,

[1] *Landscape Gardening and Rural Architecture* (New York, 1841), p. 354.

merely to switch from one set of derivative esthetic standards to another equally artificial was no longer sufficient. For history had raised a new question: not *which* of these familiar styles was most suitable, but rather were *any* of them any longer useful?

CHAPTER FOUR

1840–1860: The Schism

INDUSTRY had demanded two qualities of its building from the first — greater span and greater strength. These demands flowed from the very nature of mechanized mass production and, with the general use of steam power by the eighteen-thirties, became imperative. For the economical use of steam implied, not only that all stages of a given process be brought indoors, but more and more that they be concentrated under one roof. This meant greater spans, unobstructed floor area. Steam power also brought enormous increase in the size, power, and weight of machinery. This meant stronger floors and walls.

The traditional structural system — masonry walls and piers, wood-framed floors and roofs — soon proved inadequate. The limitations of the simple wood beam were such that experimentation with a composite element was inevitable. Hence the truss. Although implicit in the pitched roofs of the Pilgrims, the truss had only been employed in the larger public buildings, churches, and mills of the pre-Revolutionary period. The competition drawings for the United States Capitol had shown some excellent early trusses. It was now further developed as an independent structural element in the factory. But it was the bridge-builder and not the architect who really saw its potentials. The railroads had begun their march across the continent; when they came to a river, they had to cross it — rapidly, cheaply, and safely. Their problem, like that of the factory, was greater span; like the factory, they could not afford the laborious masonry arch. Instead, they turned to the truss, which, under rapidly

62

accumulating experience, ceased to be the intuitive creation of some pragmatic builder and became a formula in engineering. These early trusses were of wood.

The column was subject to no such refinement — its thickness must increase in direct ratio to its increased load. The limits of wood, stone, and brick had already been reached. What was urgently required was not a new form but a new material whose strength in compression was much greater. The answer came with iron — first *cast*, then *wrought*, and finally processed into steel. The cast-iron column was in use in England to replace wooden posts as early as 1780. Its appearance in this country seems to have been delayed by lack of adequate foundries, not ignorance. By 1840, cast-iron columns were appearing in New England factories and New Orleans business blocks. But already in 1830, Haviland had given a Pottsville, Pennsylvania, bank (Fig. 42) an entire façade of cast iron; and the next two decades saw a wide development in such uses of this material.

If advance in the building field was made possible by the factory, it was by no means confined to it. The galvanic effect of industrialism was leaving its impress on all phases of life. In the rapidly growing cities all sorts of new building types were appearing to satisfy the qualitatively new needs of the population. Typical of these was the great metropolitan hotel, a type which appeared in full flower with Boston's Tremont House (Fig. 46). Although externally this building preserved the decorous Greek proportions of its contemporaries, it was in fact the full-blown prototype of the modern Statler — complete with standardized obsequiousness, elaborate bathrooms, acres of gilded public space. Short-tempered Dickens, staying there in 1842 as befitted a famous visitor, was forced to admit that the Tremont House was 'a very excellent one. It has more galleries, colonnades, piazzas and passages than I can remember, or the reader would believe.' So immediate was the response of the traveling public (which was both rich and thick in these seaport cities) that the architect, Isaiah Rogers, found himself with a national reputation. In the eighteen-thirties, Mr. Rogers moved on to New York to build the even more lavish Astor House.

As early as 1807 the citizens of Edinburgh had been startled half out of their wits to see William Murdock, local scientist and inventor, driving around at night in a steam-powered buggy whose headlights consisted of flaming pig-bladders filled with coal gas. This was the same Murdock who had piped gas out to a lamp in front of his house, thus initiating modern street lighting. It was he, too, who spent years in perfecting a practical method for producing gas from coal and installed the first industrial lighting system (in an English foundry in 1803). His work had early repercussions. By 1812 London had its first gas-lighting company; and three years later Philadelphia — always alert to municipal improvement — was trying to launch a similar undertaking. Some trouble developed, however, and New York and Baltimore were both to get gas lighting before the City of Brotherly Love finally opened its plant in 1835.

The advantages of gas lighting — especially in industrial and commercial buildings — were so obvious that it soon became a standard. By 1860 every large city in the country depended upon gas for its principal source of artificial light. There was a steady improvement in burners, mantles, shades, etc., which constantly increased the efficiency of gas lighting. Most of these improvements originated abroad, but were almost immediately adopted in this country. The result was that, by the time of the Civil War, an entirely new concept had appeared in building design: that of a fixed, semi-automatic lighting system which *freed the building from its historic dependence upon natural daylight.* This was of enormous significance to a society whose buildings had hitherto lain idle at least half the time. It opened up the possibility of buildings which could be used on a twenty-four-hour basis, of industrial and commercial processes which could run uninterruptedly around the clock. It was, in other words, the first step toward a complete synthetic luminous environment.

Gas began to light the textile factories of New England; and factory owners were able to extend the working day to ten, twelve, fourteen hours a day. Gas began to light the theaters of New York; and the 'close-up' appeared for the first time in dramaturgy. Gas began to light the city streets; and a whole medieval world, in which all streets at night were more dangerous than a jungle path, disappeared from man's consciousness.

But the production and distribution of gas was a complex and costly operation. Its main use was in commerce, industry, and transportation. Only the rich could afford it in their houses. It did not begin to light the homes of the common people until the last part of the century, when electricity had already rendered it obsolete. Even more important, gas lighting was always purely urban. Two-thirds of the American people had no access to it at all. Instead, they used the oil lamp. By 1830 the lamp had assumed approximately its present form — cloth wick, glass chimney, and shade. The fuel was whale oil. The huge and daring whaling fleet which roamed the seven seas in American-built ships was based on this lowly lamp. The fleet rose with it and fell only after 1859, when Pennsylvania's Drake drilled the first petroleum well in history and the manufacture of kerosene began.

Like many commonplaces of modern American life, central heating is neither American nor modern in its origin. The idea of heating buildings by pipes filled with hot water or steam must have appeared shortly after James Watt perfected the steam boiler. At any rate, by 1836 London had enough experience to enable Thomas Tredgold to publish a book on the subject, which gave substantially correct methods for computing 'loss of heat radiated from buildings and corresponding methods for computing the necessary size of radiating surfaces.' Tredgold used spherical boilers of cast iron and cylindrical boilers of wrought iron. Although equipped with safety valves, these resembled nothing so much as huge and treacherous teakettles set in brick. In England, these were put to work heating the glass houses of royalty and little else.

Until well after the middle of the century, steam-heating systems were forced to remain on a custom-built basis, with the heating engineer acting as his own designer and manufacturer of pipes, couplings, radiators, and boilers. Nevertheless, Americans displayed a keen interest in the relatively great efficiency of steam and hot-water heating, and it was they who eventually put it on a mass-production basis.   Here again they could borrow from the factory, where the use of steam power forced the development of boilers, piping, etc.   New York opened a new jail in 1840 — 'a dismal-fronted pile of bastard Egyptian, like an enchanter's palace in a melodrama,' said Dickens (Fig. 56). It was immediately and appropriately called the Tombs; but it had central heating, and scarcely three months had passed before a criminal had hanged himself from the pipes in his cell. Steam-heating systems had begun to appear here and there, but by and large heating could not appear on any wide scale until industry could provide the boilers, piping, radiators, etc., and it was not until the mid-Victorian period that this would be possible.

Control of the thermal and atmospheric environment was simultaneously proceeding along another line, however.   Franklin's stove had given birth to a prodigious offspring.   The cast-iron cooking stove was rapidly becoming basic equipment for every kitchen, the cast-iron heater for every parlor.   Dickens found it 'common to all American interiors . . . the eternal, accursed, suffocating, red-hot demon of a stove whose breath would blight the purest air under heaven.'   For larger buildings, the principle of convected heat had already shifted from stove to furnace; and the concept of air-conditioning was not far away. As early as 1840, Robert Mills, architect for the Capitol and one of the great Jeffersonian school which combined architect with mechanic, had patented a system for cooling the air in summer, warming it in winter.   Such a system was actually installed in the United States Capitol a few years later but there is no record of it in operation.   In the eighteen-forties a Florida physician, Doctor John Gorrie of Apalachicola, was treating malarial patients.   In an effort to save them both from the Southern heat and their own body's fever, he conceived the idea of cooling the hospital rooms.   Using the now familiar compressor, he rigged up a working model of what was probably the first mechanical cooling unit in history.   He demonstrated this model to an unfriendly press and his experiment came to nothing.   It was to be the meat-packing industry, in the post-Civil War years, which would furnish the principal incentive to artificial ice and refrigeration.

Few buildings had central heating, and a long time would elapse before it was a standard aspect of our building. Yet two treatises had appeared in 1844 which showed that the fundamental principles of heating buildings by hot water and hot air were well understood: Charles Hood's *Warming Buildings* and D. B. Reid's *Theory and Practice of Moving Air*.[1] As in so many other instances, such works gathered dust on library shelves until the everyday world caught up with them.

By the outbreak of the Civil War, the Saturday-night tub bath was as ubiquitous as the iron stove. There might be precious few bathrooms, but at least there was no longer any fear of soap and water. On the contrary, the connection between cleanliness and health, between filth and disease, had become quite generally recognized even though — lacking a science of bacteriology — there was no real understanding of cause and effect. In the cities, disastrous fires on top of disastrous epidemics had served to raise central water and sewerage systems to the level of municipal necessities. Already in 1830, New York City had a hundred and thirty miles of sewers. Ten years later, her municipal water supply included a system of reservoirs, pumping stations, and mains. Soon it would be extended by the magnificent masonry construction of the Croton Aqueduct and reservoirs, to tap the fresh water thirty miles to the north.

With water and sewer systems, the concept of domestic plumbing could not be far behind (Fig. 61). Here and there — in the great hotels or the lordly new town houses — rudimentary facilities were appearing. Yet the bathroom did not appear as a standard feature of American houses for decades after the Civil War. The reasons for this were, again, largely practical: as in heating, the field could not advance beyond expensive handicraft until a wide range of standardized parts and fittings were generally available. In the days of the Dred Scott decision, Northern industry was not yet able to accomplish this. Its resources were taxed to the limit by historically more imperative demands. Thus it was not until 1854 that Pittsburgh could

[1] R. C. Carpenter, *Art of Heating and Ventilating Fifty Years Earlier*, American Society of Heating and Ventilating Engineers, New York, 1905.

begin to roll wrought-iron beams and — in 1855 — wrought-iron rails. Not until 1845 had John Augustus Roebling been able to assemble the necessary skills, machinery, and capital for his first suspended structure — and only then by dint of his enormous determination.

In fact, wherever one looked in the last years before the conflict, one saw the reproductive powers of industrialism straining against the limits imposed by Classical architectural concepts and handicraft building techniques. It had already been demonstrated that it — and it alone — could reconstruct the fabric of American building. But actually to accomplish this task, science and technology no less than men themselves had to be liberated. Industrial production could not advance in a nation half slave and half free.

Clearly, then, our growing technology found the restrictions of traditional architectural conventions intolerable. In many fields — manufacturing, commerce, railroads, public works — they were already being discarded. On the one hand, new demands for greater height, increased span, concentrated strength to meet concentrated load, were making obsolete the old theories of structural design. On the other, many of the new building types had little, if any, ideological function to perform. Moreover, since efficiency was the paramount consideration, esthetic standards (as factors with objective, ideological importance) fell more and more into the discard under the pressure of pragmatic mill- and shop-owners. The purpose of a New England textile mill in 1840 was to manufacture woolens, not to sell the public on the importance of democracy (Fig. 62). *That* function was delegated to the public buildings which were springing up across the land.

To cope with these problems, which covered the whole of technology and were only partially those of building, society was creating a new professional — the engineer.[1] As the name implied, he was the lineal descendant of the 'mechanick' of Jefferson's day, but with the theoretical training essential to the

---

[1] The American Society of Civil Engineers, oldest national engineering society in the United States, was founded in 1852.

mastery of much more complex processes, machines, and materials. As contrasted with the architect, the engineer's assignment from the industrialist was the simpler: to build quickly, cheaply, and efficiently, and to hell with the looks. By and large, the early engineer was not a 'cultured' man. His origins were the laboratory and the mill, the shop and the bridge gang. He was neither trained nor paid to explore the many fine shades of the esthetic problem over which the architects argued so learnedly. And as a system of formal education in engineering began to evolve out of the trades and mechanics' institutes of the early part of the century, his neglect of the 'artistic' aspects of building design began to solidify into programmatic contempt. Indeed, this tendency went so far that, by the end of the nineteenth century, many of the specialized engineering and technical curricula were to be not merely anti-art but boorishly anti-cultural as well.

There was no conscious demand for 'beauty' in the engineer's work. If, then, the American people began to see beauty in his designs (as they almost immediately did) it could only be because of his objective relationship to the productive processes themselves. They read into his work the fruitful implications of machine production. If it saved work, it could not be wholly ugly; and if it worked well, it would sooner or later be beautiful. The Americans understood (even if subconsciously) the new idiom which the engineer (also subconsciously) was beginning to develop. Form must spring not from preconceptions but from the limitations of actual material and process; form must be conditioned by the need for efficient performance in the finished product.

The appearance of the engineer as a professional with an independent status marks a decisive point in the history of American building — that point beyond which society's needs for control of its environment could no longer be filled by master builder or gentleman architect. By the same token, it marks the opening of that chasm between esthetic and technical standards which has characterized American building ever since.

John Ruskin, Romantic Tory

As THE CIVIL WAR approached, the entire structure of Classic tradition was under assault from many sides at the level of both fact and theory. By the Romanticists, under the Gothic banners of Sir Walter Scott, Pugin, Renwick, and Upjohn; by the early engineers like the elder Roebling and materialists like Bogardus (Fig. 64). But the most devastating blows were to come from two men, neither of whom was an architect and only one of whom was American: John Ruskin and Horatio Greenough.

Ruskin's impact upon American culture, especially her art and architecture, was immense. Indeed, as Henry-Russell Hitchcock has pointed out, his works received both earlier and greater recognition in this country than in England. And long after the initial impulse had ebbed, his influence was still to be traced in the Morris arts-in-industry movement, in Elbert Hubbard and his Roycrofters, in the tooled-leather-and-burnt-wood circles of the *fin de siècle*, in a hundred-odd byways and dead ends of upper-class neuroses and frustrations. The cumulative, objective effect of Ruskin's work was disastrous. This was all the more the case because he wrote for the layman. He was one of the earliest critics to direct his words, not at the closed circle of critics and intelligentsia, but at the middle-class audience which books, magazines, and rapid communication had created. There is perhaps no single individual in architectural history who has done more to retard its progress.

Yet the intellect which Ruskin brought to bear upon the subject was deeper, more perceptive and subtle, than any which immediately preceded and most of those which followed it.

Despite all his tedious deviations and asides, Ruskin explored the esthetic dimensions of building with remarkable consistency and thoroughness. For a lay audience, he defined his terms with unprecedented sharpness: he took his readers to the heart of the matter when he said: 'Thus no one would call the laws architectural which determine the height of a breastwork or the position of a bastion. But if to the stone facing of that bastion be added an unnecessary feature, as a cable moulding, *that* is

Architecture.'¹ Ruskin meant, of course, that ornament was only *structurally* unnecessary. Architecture had other and 'higher' functions to perform. The garlands and grapes, gargoyles and goddesses — why were they found only on the palaces, churches, capitols, and city halls? Why were they not equally distributed on city slum and country cottage? Why the vast and demonstrable difference between the anonymous body of popular building and the signed works of the architect? What was architecture, in short, but a specialized means of communication, 'above and beyond the common use'; a set of symbols, idioms, and concepts with which the rich and mighty spoke to themselves and the world? The architecture of the nation, Ruskin said, *'is the exponent of its social and political virtues.'*

> It is very necessary, in the outset of all inquiry, to distinguish carefully between Architecture and Building. . . . Let us, therefore, at once confine the name [architecture] to that art which . . . impresses on the building certain characters venerable or beautiful, but otherwise unnecessary. . . . It may not be always easy to draw the line sharply and simply; because there are few buildings which have not some pretense of colour or being architectural; neither can there be any Architecture which is not based on building; but it is . . . very necessary . . . to understand fully that Architecture concerns itself only with those characters of any edifice which are above and beyond its common use.²

Here Ruskin showed the uncanny precision which often characterized his criticism. He had discovered one of the basic laws of motion in the history of man's building. But he had discovered this law at a critical stage of its history. Never before had the ideology imposed upon a nation's architecture by ruling-class necessity so flatly violated the contemporary building technology. The cardinals with their cathedrals, the emperors with their circuses, the tyrants with their tombs — whatever their motives, they had not been guilty of *structural* perversion. Stone angels never weakened the Gothic vault; caryatids were satisfactory columns as well as lovely maidens;

---

¹ John Ruskin, *Seven Lamps of Architecture,* in *Collected Works* (New York: John W. Lovell, 1885), vol. III, p. 16. (Italics are Ruskin's.)
² *Ibid.,* p. 18.

since Assyrian walls were going to be surfaced in glazed tile anyway, it was a simple matter to bake in the azure lions and scarlet tigers.

The world in which Ruskin lived was quite otherwise. For two centuries or more the living fabric of western European building had been impressed into the Classic mold. For a while this had been a reasonably successful expedient; proof of that lay in the fact that the Classic idiom had penetrated down into popular building, far below the reach of scholar or architect. But by 1840 the development of building technology had made a hollow (to Ruskin, obscene) mockery of the Classic style. The architecture around him was a living falsehood, guilty of both structural and political perversion. Even the healthy body of popular building was being infected. Radical measures were called for if anything was to be saved.

Ruskin's art and architectural criticism was an organic part of the main body of his work. And however biased his view or superficial his penetration may often have been, Ruskin was a student of society itself. It was Victorian society, not just its esthetic standards, which appalled him. He represented aristocratic discontent with an industrialism which was, in England, already fairly complete. He registered the horror of cultured Englishmen at the appalling discrepancy between the promise of the machine and the actual squalor, suffering, and ugliness of nineteenth-century capitalism. It was a 'carnivorous' system, based upon an 'ossifiant theory of progress.' 'Our cities are a wilderness of spinning wheels instead of palaces; yet the people have no clothes. We have blackened every leaf of English greenwood with ashes, and the people die of cold; our harbors are a forest of merchant ships, and the people die of hunger.'[1] These 'extremities of human degradation' were not accidental; on the contrary, said Ruskin with such sharpness that his books could no longer find a publisher, they were due 'to the habitual preying upon the labour of the poor by the luxury of the rich.' But it was not only the physical and material condition of the people

[1] *Collected Works of John Ruskin* (New York: John W. Lovell, 1885), vol. XVIII, p. 502.

which alarmed him. What was happening to their artistic and
creative genius? The rationalization and specialization of industrial processes were destroying it. In the factories the craftsmen
of former times were 'divided into mere segments of men —
broken into fragments and crumbs of life.' At home they were
surrounded by a flood of machine-made articles in which Ruskin
could see no beauty — the 'paltry art' of the Crystal Palace —
while the rich monopolized 'the music, the painting, the architecture, the hand-service and horse-service, the sparkling cham-
pagne of the world.'

What was to be done? Ruskin's distrust of the machine was
equaled only by his distrust of Victorian democracy. He was
not only a Tory in British politics; he was an aristocrat in
principle. From the start he was unashamedly the spokesman
for the nobility, the landed gentry, the gentlefolk of England
whose manners, morals, and esthetic standards were now being
eclipsed by Victorian capitalism. Where the arts were concerned, he saw it as only proper that 'the decision [be] made,
the fame bestowed, the artist encouraged . . . by the chosen few,
by our nobility and men of taste and talent.' As a parallel, it is
not surprising to find that Ruskin, at first merely ignorant of
science, became in his later years profoundly anti-scientific.

Against these characteristics — anti-democratic, anti-indus-
trial, anti-scientific — was opposed Ruskin's genuine humanity,
his deep attachment to the individual man, whose talents were
being aborted, honesty deflowered, and happiness destroyed.
On this paradox turned all his arguments and rested his final
decision. Since all theories of progress were fallacious, he could
not go forward, he could only turn back. And only medieval
society, the 'magnificently human' Gothic styles of Europe,
could afford him that balance which he sought between security
and discipline.

Stripped of all rhetoric, this was a program of political, social,
and cultural reaction. To begin with, his picture of Gothic life
was historically inaccurate, as even casual reference to original
medieval sources should have told him. And to propose that
the productive forces of the British Isles be reorganized at the

level of King John and the Magna Carta was sheer escapist
nonsense. This was equally true, whether Ruskin discussed
political economy or architecture. He himself made them indi-
visible: '*The Stones of Venice* had, from the beginning to end, no
other aim than to show that the Gothic architecture of Venice
had arisen out of, and indicated in all its features, a state of pure
national faith and of domestic virtue.'[1] In building design, as
in political economy, his program was reactionary: for objective
reality made it certain that the schism between technique and
ideology would not be resolved by a mere buttering of the Gothic
or the Classic or of any other historical style.

Horatio Greenough, Yankee Democrat

OF ALL THE MEN who worked within the field of formal criticism,
none was so advanced as the Yankee stonecutter, Horatio
Greenough.

He died young, at the age of forty-seven, leaving only a small
and fragmentary collection of essays behind him. He was well
known to only a small group of his contemporaries and his
influence seems to have been totally submerged by his premature
death. But had his essays circulated as widely as those of Ruskin,
American design might well have escaped the decades of tortuous frustration which lay between Greenough and Louis
Sullivan. For Greenough, at the very dawn of industrial production, anticipated to an extraordinary degree the problems it
would raise in design.

In depth and comprehensiveness, Greenough's analysis of
technical, political, and esthetic factors in design have scarcely
been equaled by an American. This grasp of critical values is
all the stranger in a man who was a sculptor all his life — and
not a great one, at that. (He himself had feared that he would
never realize 'my idea of what sculpture should be.') But he
clearly had sharpened his wits on Italian marble. He had
begun as a student of the Classic, adoring Nature, 'but as a

---

[1] *Collected Works of John Ruskin* (New York: John W. Lovell, 1885), vol. XVIII,
p. 443.

Persian does the sun, with my face to the earth.' He ended by studying Nature, with his eyes full on her face.

Horatio Greenough was an exponent of Boston at her greatest. Graduated from Harvard in 1824, he had trained in Boston's Athenaeum in the heyday of the Greek Revival. He had taken so literally the enthusiasm for the rediscovered Classic world that he had gone abroad to be at its fountainhead. In Italy he had been a member of the large and active colony of American intellectuals during the exciting times of Mazzini. While there he had executed the famous statue of Washington — the seated General clothed only in a toga, a blasphemy which an outraged Congress would not permit in the Capitol (Fig. 69). It was in the controversy over this commission that Greenough had to take to the pen in order to explain and defend his concepts of art.

He had spent much of his adult life in Italy. But in 1851, with the Italian democrats scattered in exile, he had returned for good to his native land. It was immediately apparent that Greenough had been no lavender-tinted expatriate. He had crossed the Atlantic six times, not to escape the American, but to be closer to the Classic, mind. And when he came back for good, it was clear that he *had* penetrated to the very heart of the matter. If American architects were to profit from Greek experience, they must study it 'like men and not ape [it] like monkeys.' If they wanted to achieve truly satisfactory esthetic standards, they would have 'to learn principles — not copy shapes.' And what were these principles, where were they to be observed? Why, 'the manly use of plain good sense' would reveal them in every facet of American life: the trotting-wagon, the New England farmhouse, the clipper ships, the lighthouses and canals (Figs. 70, 71).

He strode across Manhattan — become in his absence America's greatest metropolis — and his sharp, buoyant eye was quick to see the contrary tendencies in the construction all about him. Isaiah Rogers's new Astor House, with a Classic façade for Broadway and only naked masonry for the rear. Richard Upjohn's scholarly new Trinity Church in Gothic plaster. There were not one but two Americas here, said Greenough, and 'the puny cathedral of Broadway, like an elephant dwindled to the size of a dog, measures her yearning for Gothic sublimity while the rear of the Astor House and the mammoth vase of the great Reservoir show how she works when she feels at home.' [1]

Significantly, Greenough did not ally himself with any of the quarreling schools of stylistic controversy. Like Walt Whitman, but with much more precision, he saw in the burgeoning American industry the material basis for a new esthetic standard, one which would be in conformity with advancing science and technology instead of increasingly in opposition to it. Here his confidence in the creative genius of the plain people was not vitiated, as was Ruskin's, by a Tory's fear of giving them too much freedom. It was they who would fashion the new American beauty — not the intelligentsia nor the artists nor the wealthy and well-bred connoisseurs. 'The mechanics of the United States have already outstripped the artists and have, by their bold and unflinching adaptation, entered the true track and hold up the light for all who operate for American wants.' [2]

What kind of beauty could we expect of them? Greenough answered with poetic and electrifying precision: 'By beauty I mean the promise of function. By action I mean the presence of function. By character I mean the record of function.' And where could examples of such beauty be found? Observe the Yankee clipper ships, which had already caught the imagination of the country:

> Here is the result of the study of man upon the great deep, where Nature speaks of the laws of building, not in feather and in flower, but in wind and waves, and he bent all his mind to hear and to obey. . . . If this anatomic connection and proportion has been attained in machines and — in spite of false principles — in such buildings as make a departure from it fatal, [such] as bridges and scaffolding, why should we fear its immediate use in [building] construction? [3]

---

[1] H. T. Tuckerman, *A Memorial to Horatio Greenough* (New York: G. P. Putnam's Sons, 1853), p. 118.

[2] *The Democratic Review*, vol. XIII, August, 1843.

[3] H. T. Tuckerman, *op. cit.*, p. 124.

It is apparent that Greenough had given deep and independent thought to the crisis in building design. Just as he refused to copy the Greeks, so he refused to imitate the shipbuilders. It was principle he was after, not prototypes. In a letter to Emerson, elaborating his theories, he is breath-taking in his modernity:

> Here is my theory of structure: a scientific arrangement of spaces and forms [adapted] to functions and to site; an emphasis of features proportioned to their *gradated* importance in function; colour and ornament to be decided and arranged and varied by strictly organic laws, having a distinct reason for each decision; the entire and immediate banishment of all make-believe.[1]

Greenough was no crass materialist, naïve enough to suppose that any product of man could be empty of esthetic significance; but he was searching for a new set of standards which would not be imposed from the top, and from the top of the past, at that. These standards would appear naturally, as an orderly exponent of the very process of creation. Yet, while they would be a logical — in fact, an automatic — by-product, they would not be accidental or intuitive. He stipulated that they develop within a scientific reference frame. He thereby avoided the pitfall of the Romanticists. He was under no illusion that Rousseau's 'natural' man, merely left to his own devices, will finally produce a satisfactory building. He was discussing flesh-and-blood American workmen, rapidly learning that folk-knowledge was not enough for industrial production; that the laboratory was the womb of the factory, science the seed of design.

There was, as Emerson pointed out, a similarity between Ruskin and Greenough, 'notwithstanding the antagonism in their views of the history of art.' This similarity lay in the fact that they both recognized the impossibility of discussing esthetic standards as isolates. Such standards were specialized expressions of society, complex and intricately related to every

---

[1] Ralph Waldo Emerson, *English Traits, Complete Works* (Boston: Houghton Mifflin Company, 1888), vol. V, p. 10. Greenough is here perhaps the first artist to take science as his standard of measurement.

aspect of social life; but susceptible to analysis nevertheless. And if one wished to discuss or compare or alter them, one had always to relate them to their respective social orders. On this the two men were in agreement; but never did more divergent conclusions flow from identical premises. It would be futile to analyze this antagonism without reference to the class and national platforms from which the two men spoke.

Ruskin was indisputably the spokesman for the British Tories, the mill- and mine-owners who had substantially completed the industrialization of the British Isles, the masters of an empire upon which the sun never set. He had begun as the ideologist of the old gentility. He had clashed sharply with the voracious appetites of the capitalists. He was appalled at the hypocrisy and ugliness of Victorian England. Yet Ruskin's opposition was always limited. He gave reaction its most persuasive arguments for turning the clock back. His *Seven Lamps* had given Victoria the Gothic idiom for the new Houses of Parliament (Fig. 68). He was the bosom friend and collaborator of the arch-Tory Carlyle; and his lifelong attack on the cultural potentialities of the Industrial Revolution neatly meshed with Carlyle's efforts to gut the French Revolution of its historic significance. His separation of esthetic from technique was, objectively, a reactionary maneuver. *Stones of Venice* or Houses of Parliament, book or castle, these creations were products of literature, not life; propaganda, not building. And the fact that *The Stones* would not protect an Englishman from a rainstorm quite as effectively as the House of Commons did not alter their basic similarity; they were both instruments of persuasion, designed to sell the British people the beauties of medieval serfdom. Ruskin was merely one cog in the giant obscurantist machine which was overwhelming whole sections of English culture.

Greenough, too, was the ideologue for an upper class, but with this difference: he came from the heart of Yankee industrialism at the very moment it was preparing to challenge the slave oligarchy for the mastery of the nation. Greenough had grown to manhood in the great Boston of the renaissance. He had studied Greek art at the Athenaeum and thrilled to the

III

Romanticism, Vehicle of Protest

ILLUSTRATIONS in this section are from the following sources: 56, New York Public Library; 57, Bettmann Archive; 58, 59, New York Public Library; 60, *Life*, copyright, Time, Inc.; 61, J. Clarence Davies Collection, Museum of City of New York; 62, Bettmann Archive; 64, William Gray Purcell; 63, 65, Professor Turpin C. Bannister; 69, National Collection of Fine Arts, Smithsonian Institution; 70, Bettmann Archive; 71, Peabody Museum of Salem, Massachusetts; 74, Dr. D. B. Steinman; 75, Bettmann Archive; 76, 77, 78, *Architectural Record*, Thérèse Bonney photo.

New York City's Egyptian jail was an early expression of the collapse of the Classic idiom.

Elsewhere, upper-class parlors, always a sensitive barometer of changing taste, showed a progressive corruption of classic form (57). Romantic exteriors in the 'Italian style' began to clothe plans which were discarding symmetry in favor of flexibility, informality (58, 59).

57

58

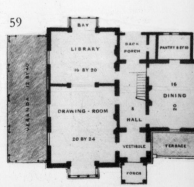

59

60

Scott's novels and Ruskin's essays, avidly read in this country, created an esthetic climate in which this Hudson River house, c. 1840, seemed quite in order. But a plumber's advertisement of the period shows quite modern concern for such creature comforts as recessed tub and toilet, spigot, hose, and fountain (61).

62

61

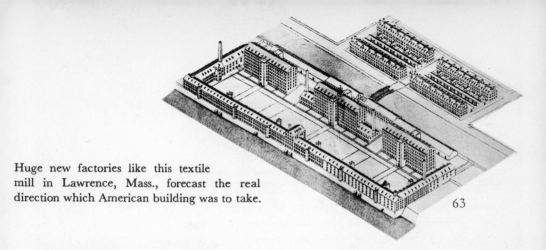

Huge new factories like this textile
mill in Lawrence, Mass., forecast the real
direction which American building was to take.

63

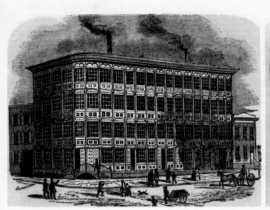

65

In the north, the remarkable builder, James Bogardus, put up a prefabricated factory in
1850 (64). Corlies used the same cast iron in 1854 in Harper's fireproof plant (65).

But athwart the path of northern industrialism lay the black power of slavery. Its might is
apparent in this bustling scene on the New Orleans levee the month that war began.

66

Bogardus's proposal for the New York Fair of 1853 recognized the potentials of industry: a spiderweb of wire cable and sheet metal covers a prefab cast-iron arena 700 ft. across.

But his design was rejected in favor of this inept mimicry of London's Crystal Palace.
67

68

By the fifties, the schism between esthetic and technique was international. Victoria had sanctioned Gothic obscurantism at Westminster (68), while in America . . .

. . . Horatio Greenough — advancing far beyond his neo-classic figure of Washington (69) — was urging our designers to 'study the past like men, not copy it like monkeys.'

69

Look, he said, at the clipper ships and . . .

71

70

. . . the trotting wagon. Here was manly use of plain good sense.

THE GOLDEN LEAP

Three great structures cast their lacy shadows
across the nineteenth-century Western world:

72

THE CRYSTAL PALACE. Joseph Paxton's
masterpiece had crystalline lightness, breath-
taking clarity, and superb scale. Only a medie-
valist like Ruskin could call it 'paltry.' The rest
of the world was enchanted.

73

74

THE BROOKLYN BRIDGE. A tension structure never surpassed and seldom equaled, it proved John Roebling a poised and finished master of theory, technique, and material.

75

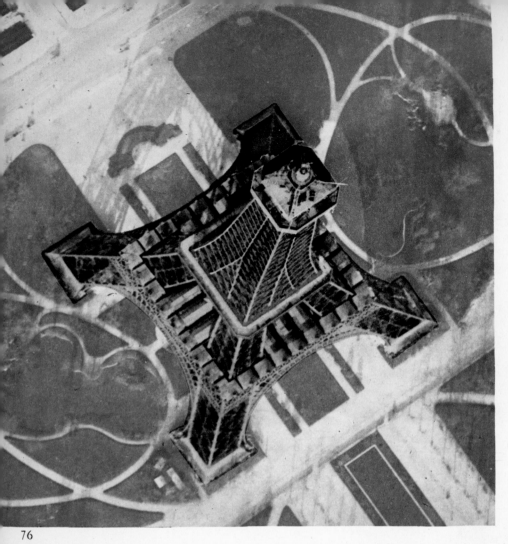

76

THE EIFFEL TOWER. A venturesome photographer in an early balloon caught the soaring thrust of Gustave Eiffel's greatest work (76). Working before modern steel or reinforced concrete, his structural detailing (77, 78) completely anticipated modern theory.

77   78

Greek Wars of Liberation. Doctor Parkman had given him lessons in anatomy, Washington Allston and Richard Henry Dana encouragement. In Paris he had done a bust of the aging Lafayette. In Italy he worked for nearly eight years on the ill-fated figure of Washington; there, too, he had seen the struggle for Italian independence under Mazzini. When Greenough spoke, therefore, he voiced the aspirations of the most progressive section of mid-century American democracy. It is this reality — democracy, science, industry — which he accepts as the essential basis for effective esthetic standards. This reality is the source of his buoyant confidence, enabling him to envisage a democracy so complete as to render esthetic falsehood impossible. His buildings would have no ulterior esthetic motive — no intangible job of intimidation, repression, or deceit — precisely because the society of which they were a part would have no such motives.

CHAPTER FIVE

The Golden Leap

THE NINETEENTH CENTURY saw three great developments in structural theory: the enclosure of great areas in the Crystal Palace; the spanning of great voids in the Brooklyn Bridge; and the reaching of great heights in the Eiffel Tower. These structures are sufficiently great in themselves, each marking the full-flowering of a new structural concept. But they are noteworthy in another respect in that they constitute historical proof of the relationship between structural theories, materials, and techniques. The interaction between these three is constant and dynamic. Together, they constitute what I have called the technological level of building. Their relation is such that an advance in one naturally and inevitably affects the other two; and this reciprocal action is the mainspring of evolutionary development.

Historically, the three factors — theory, material, technique — have seldom been in exact equilibrium at any given moment: that is, there have been few times when a lag in one did not prevent advance in the others. Occasionally, however, under the accumulating pressure of social change, a structure appears in which all three factors have combined at a high level to produce a radically new type. To borrow a term from the anthropologists, there has been a *leap* forward. Such structures were the Palace, the Bridge, and the Tower. These leaps involve not merely blind social and economic pressures. Specific human agencies are also required; live men who, by the very breadth of their understanding, are able to master all the factors involved and force the project through to completion. Such men were the designers of these three famous structures: Joseph Paxton, the English horticulturist; John Roebling, the German-American cable inventor; and Gustave Eiffel, the French engineer. The shadows of these men and their structures fell athwart the whole Western world; and nothing which came after them could remain entirely unaffected, for they had tackled and brilliantly mastered three eternal problems in structure.

Paxton, Roebling, and Eiffel were men of the new world of nineteenth-century science and thus closer to us who follow than to those who preceded them. Together they constitute an organic continuum which spans both the century and the century's chief centers of intellectual activity: London, New York, Paris. Their thinking and their works were truly supra-national in effect. Like Darwin and Marx, Morgan and Pasteur, they were citizens of world thought, at once the creators and the first great products of modern scientific theory and practice. They differed from their predecessors in this important respect: they not only worked in the field of science; they had also begun to think scientifically. Jefferson's fertile intellect might be stimulated by contemporary investigations in natural phenomena; Fulton, from God only knows what accidental contacts, might putter around with his steam boiler until the boat finally propelled itself; and Franklin might risk the thunderstorm with his kite and key. Yet they lacked in their investigations the methodology, the rigid standards, the planful accumulation of fact, which characterizes modern science. Theirs was not yet the world which, as Paxton himself put it, 'requires [of the scientist] facts instead of empiricism, and prefers scientific accuracy to blind practice.'

The Palace

OF THE THREE MEN, Paxton was the least well-educated and, as a consequence, the closest to the methodology of the preceding century. Self-made in the strictest sense of the word, Joseph Paxton began the first of a series of apprenticeships on the great country estates of England at the age of fifteen.   Under ordinary circumstances, this training would have led to the status of head gardener, but both his aspirations and abilities were much higher.   The London Horticultural Society had recently leased the gardens of the Duke of Devonshire at Chiswick and begun there a program of reconstruction and improvement; and what was to prove the turning point in Paxton's whole life came when, in 1823, he obtained employment there.

Work for a learned society offered him much greater perspectives than gardening for a country gentleman.   The whole direction and emphasis of the Society lay in extending and organizing botanical and horticultural knowledge, rather than in mere competitive display.   Young Paxton throve astonishingly in this environment.   In three years he was a foreman at Chiswick, though his salary was a mere eighteen shillings a week. He was apparently confident that he could do much better and was on the point of sailing for America when the same Duke of Devonshire, now president of the Society, offered him the post of superintendent at his country seat, Chatsworth.

Because of the wealth and prestige of the Duke, this offer could scarcely have been topped by any but the royal house itself.   Devonshire was one of the leading patrons of horticulture; in addition he seems to have been an ideal employer, for he allowed Paxton great freedom and ample funds.[1]   During his long association with Chatsworth, Paxton achieved the status of both gentleman and scholar.   In the former capacity he made the Grand Tour of Europe and Asia Minor with the Duke; in the latter, he became editor of the *Magazine of Horticulture and Directory of Flowering Plants*.   This publication appeared first in 1839, handsome in make-up and professional in content.   The very first issue reflected the curious conflict in the lowly born Paxton between snob and scholarly democrat: he dedicated it with flowery servility to the Duke,[2] but in his introduction he

[1] Paxton confirmed this years later, in 1851, at a dinner in his honor after the Crystal Palace was opened: 'By his confidence and liberality I have had placed before me ample means for various experiments without which there would never have been a Crystal Palace.'

[2] Each succeeding volume was similarly dedicated, and never to anyone less than a duchess.   Since the magazine must of necessity have been subsidized, however, we can understand these archaic attentions to the patrons.

pledged himself to keep his material 'as plain and intelligible as possible,' avoiding Latin and botanical terms except where absolutely necessary, so as to make the magazine useful to the widest possible audience.

If there is little in Paxton's work prior to 1851 to indicate a latent genius in building design, there is ample evidence of an intellect of wide range and great profundity. In his paper, 'Influence of Solar Light on Vegetation,' he anticipates the discovery of the ultra-violet band, speculating that there must be 'rays issuing from the sun [which are] distinct from the rays of heat and light — rays of chemical and magnetic influence; and who can tell to what extent glass may not intercept and transmute these rays?'[1] He was deeply interested in smoke prevention, carrying on experiments at Chatsworth in improved methods of combustion to reduce smoke and increase heat production. Here also he installed a mechanical stoker of his own design. He wrote a paper on vegetable physiology, several on the influence of climate upon plants. He took exception to the Linnaeus system of botanical classification. His interests, as reflected in his work and in his magazine, were wide and progressive.

In 1832 he designed his first orchid house and, four years later, a conservatory three hundred feet long. Neither was noteworthy; they did not differ much from those glass houses which English noblemen were building all over the countryside. In his magazine he published many designs (his own and others') of glass houses, pergolas, gate houses, and workmen's cottages which showed his familiarity with such building problems. This experience may partly explain the Crystal Palace, but only partly. Indeed, with the single brilliant exception of the Palace, Paxton's work in both garden and building design seems to have been commonplace. Before this astonishing success, his interest lay more in the great botanical discoveries and controversies of the period than in pretty landscapes. And after the Palace brought him knighthood and fame, his designs — like his dedications — showed complete subservience to the doubtful

[1] *Magazine of Horticulture*, vol. IV.

esthetic standards of the Victorian gentility to which he had just been admitted.

Whatever else he was, Paxton had become by 1849 the leading gardener of the realm. For in that year he was successful in bringing to flower, for the first time in Europe, the famous water lily *Victoria Regia*. This was a significant accomplishment in more ways than one. The lily was an exotic, an import from equatorial Africa, and though it had been grown in many tanks in Europe, it had never bloomed. To bring it to flower was a problem of the most precise environmental control and Paxton correctly saw it as such. It would have to be housed in a building which could duplicate its natural habitat; and, as Paxton pointed out, this was no easy matter; 'such plants require more light than glass will transmit and yet more heat than our open sky affords, and are consequently most difficult of culture. . . . They require a glass that transmits all possible light.'[1] It was to be many years before industry could provide a glass which was not opaque to ultra-violet light; but somehow he solved the problem, for the lily bloomed. 'Scientific accuracy and not blind practice' enabled him to study the natural circumstances of every plant, 'considering their wants, whether as regards light, heat, air, moisture, or soil.'

Two years afterward, when the Palace opened its doors to a dazzled world, it was clear that Paxton had studied another aspect of *Victoria Regia:* its structure. This remarkable plant had pads which measured eight, ten, even twelve feet in diameter: constructions strong enough to support a boy yet light enough to float. They were marvels of economy — a network of radiating and circumferential ribs which supported, and were in turn stiffened by, the thin, tough membrane of the leaf itself. The parallel between this design and the structural system of the Crystal Palace is inescapable. Cast iron and glass replace rib and membrane — though the materials necessarily differ, the principle is the same.

When the Palace was opened in 1851, it created an immediate sensation. The light and airy framing, the glittering curved

[1] *Magazine of Horticulture*, vol. VI.

vaults of glass, the full-grown trees, the fountains and tropical flowers which bloomed inside, the printing presses and harvesters and sewing machines — this juxtaposition delighted the Victorian mind. By some miracle of history, the first great exhibition glorifying modern industrialism was housed in a structure which more perfectly expressed its potential than any which ever followed it (Figs. 72, 73). The canny Queen recognized this — even if a few years before, in the much more sensitive area of government buildings, she had chosen Charles Barry's Gothic style for the Houses of Parliament (Fig. 68) — and promptly knighted the designer.

The building was, indeed, one of great beauty and many extraordinary features, not least of which was the fact that it was designed in *nine days*, after 233 other designs had been rejected. It was the first *prefabricated* as well as the first *demountable* building of modern times. Bolted together, and thus easily taken apart, Paxton himself dismantled it, moved it to a new site, and re-erected it there in 1852–54. It was far and away the largest single building the world had seen — 989,884 square feet of floor space under $17\frac{3}{4}$ acres of roof. About 900,000 square feet of glass went into it, and more mass-produced columns, girders, and beams than in any previous structure. It was erected in the unprecedentedly brief span of six months.

These statistics do not succeed in conveying the full dimensions of Paxton's accomplishments. The historic significance of the Crystal Palace lay in the fact that it was a huge shell of relatively no weight and no thickness. *It introduced the structural concept of strength through precision instead of mass.* His lily-pad system would not have made sense on a single plane, since it had no water surface on which to float. To stiffen it he had either to corrugate it — the 'ridge-and-furrow' he had long ago perfected — or bend it, as he had in the barrel vault of the great Conservatory at Chatsworth. In the Palace he did both. He used the vault only on the shorter transverse axis (it was only in the reconstructed Palace at Suydenham that both axes were vaulted), but with magnificent effect. Here was a vault which was the antithesis of its Roman predecessor — a thin curved membrane stiffened by its very shape. Elsewhere, on the long, stepped-back wings, he used the ridge-and-furrow — the same principle, in a sense, on a much smaller scale.

Nothing was more natural than for Paxton to turn to the iron ribs and glass panes of his many greenhouses. He had tried wood as a substitute for iron because, 'for our own part, the expense of metal has been one and, we may say, the chief objection' to its use. He had had to discard wood, however, because of its bulkiness. Yet the Palace is no mere blow-up of his earlier designs: it is a new and daring concept of structure. Frederick Kiesler has called Paxton's attempt to fashion a structure by such literal application of Nature's design principles essentially romantic.[1] This does injustice both to history and to Paxton. Viewed in its context of Victorian England, his design is profoundly scientific. His comprehension appears inadequate or incomplete only in relation to what we know today. It must be remembered that Paxton shared with Darwin, whom he greatly admired, the problem of perfecting single-handed a theory based exclusively upon first-hand observation. His investigations must rank among the few truly great ones of architecture.

The Palace left Sir Joseph with a world-wide reputation as a designer, a snug seat in Parliament, many important commissions. Ruskin was his only hostile critic, though the landscape architects seem to have nourished doubts as to his ability. Yet in the fourteen years between the Exposition and his death in 1865, he was never to turn out another design comparable in any way with his masterpiece. These later buildings, such as his great house for Baron Rothschild, show no kinship with the Palace, and scarcely as much competence in the accepted idiom as those of his contemporaries. To dismiss the Palace as a flash in the pan is impossible, however: rather it must be understood as the only flowering of Paxton's special genius in a peculiarly fortunate set of circumstances — the same sort of event, in fact, as the flowering of the African lily.

These circumstances were: a concrete and specific program

[1] Frederick J. Kiesler, 'On Correalism and Biotechnique,' *Architectural Record* (September, 1939), p. 68.

calling for continuous, well-lighted floor space; sharp limits to the funds and time available; the suitability of the structural system on which he had already spent so much time and energy. Even the nine days allowed for preparing the drawings were auspicious. They allowed no time to worry about appearance, so that the finished building shows his beautiful ignorance — one might almost say innocence — of current architectural controversy over idiom and cliché. As a result, the finished building was as lean and functional as a greyhound, revealing only in its smallest details (column caps, tie bars, brackets) the imprint of Victorian taste. In his later work these controlling factors were missing and without them he was lost — an ambitious, self-made man in an overawing environment. Architecturally, Paxton was destined to flower but once.

One of the enthusiastic assumptions of the Victorians concerning iron construction in general and the Palace in particular was destined to prove quite fallacious — that is, that a fireproof system had at last been perfected. Fire had always been one of society's greatest hazards and fire resistance had naturally been a most sought-after property in buildings. Unfortunately, it was seldom achieved. Until the appearance of mass-produced metals, wood had been the only building material with high tensile strength. All but a microscopic proportion of nineteenth-century buildings employed floor beams and roof trusses, and these were necessarily of wood. Thus, when mass-produced metal columns and beams appeared in mid-century, they were uncritically acclaimed. This enthusiasm was based upon the fact that neither iron nor glass will burn. It conveniently overlooked the corollary that both will melt. Under a given set of conditions, a wooden beam is more firesafe than a steel one: the steel will deform and collapse under a heat which only chars the wood. To reduce the strength of a wooden beam, you have to reduce its cross-section. Paxton's structure served as inspiration for an inexpert copy in New York City in 1853 (Fig. 67). It was completely destroyed by a twenty-minute fire, and in 1937 the same fate overtook the Crystal Palace itself.

The Bridge

EXACTLY TWENTY YEARS before the Crystal Palace, John Augustus Roebling had migrated to Pennsylvania. Neither the time nor the place was accidental. The coal fields were roaring into action, Pittsburgh was already the center of a new iron industry, and canals hardly completed were proving themselves inadequate to handle the freight. Very shortly a network of railroads would be flung across the Alleghenies. The bridging of thousands of mountain streams would become a pressing problem. There would be neither time nor money for elaborate masonry structures — even had there been a masonry tradition in this country, which there was not. In addition, the size of the rivers, with their ice floes and turbulent spring freshets, made unobstructed spans a necessity. Nor could the huge cantilevered trusses appear until after mass production of standardized steel members began in the rolling mills of the seventies and eighties. In such a context, Roebling's experiments with tension structures was inevitable.

John Roebling did not, of course, invent the suspension bridge. On the contrary, as an engineering student in Germany, young Roebling had made the chain suspension bridges of Germany and Switzerland the subject of his thesis. Neither did he actually invent steel rope. What he did was to force the parallel development of both bridge and cable. Almost alone for nearly half a century, he forced their simultaneous improvement in a series of increasingly spectacular suspension structures. Theory, material, techniques: each felt the impact of his intellect. The potentials he saw in the suspension bridge could only be exploited by a tensile material far superior to hempen rope or hand-forged chain. He achieved the first wire cables; but these in turn implied new fabrication and assembly techniques. Having perfected the latter, he could then turn his attention to still more daring designs. This ascending spiral reached its most polished statement in the Brooklyn Bridge — a design which has never been surpassed (and only recently equaled in such bridges as the Whitestone in New York and the Golden Gate in San Francisco) in its ultimate simplicity.

There is certainly nothing accidental in Roebling's accomplishment. His entire career is one of amazingly consistent preparation for his final design.[1] The initial decision to migrate to this country was a reflection of his dissatisfaction with the prospects which Europe offered a young engineer. He and his brother had made a careful study of the States before deciding upon Pennsylvania as a future home. They rejected the South because of their bitter opposition to slavery. It was, John felt, 'the greatest cancerous affliction . . . enough for us not to go into any slave-holding state, even if Nature had created a Paradise there.' Although they had initially bought a seven-thousand-acre farm at Saxonburg, John Roebling soon (1837) left it for engineering.

His first employment was on the Pennsylvania Canal, on that remarkable section where, by a system of locks and inclined railways, the barges were carried over the crest of the range. In this admirable system, the weakest links were the hawsers which pulled the barge-laden cars up the inclines; although they were woven of best Kentucky hemp, they were continually breaking. Why could these cables not be woven of wire instead of hemp? To answer the question was, with Roebling, a necessity. He set to work designing the machinery for weaving such a rope and in 1841 perfected it. This first cable was literally a steel rope composed of small spirally twisted wires. Roebling was quick to see the potentials of his new material: the availability of steel cable had the immediate effect of liberating the suspension structure from the limitations of hand-forged chains. In 1845 he completed his first suspension structure, an aqueduct for the Pennsylvania Canal. A structure quite without precedent in the New World, the aqueduct consisted of seven spans of wood flume, each one hundred and sixty-two feet long, carried by two continuous cables seven inches in diameter.

But even before he had the opportunity to erect a suspension structure with his twisted rope, Roebling had perfected a second and even more significant cable. Unlike the first, the individual

[1] The definitive biography of Roebling, as well as the most thorough analysis of his work, is to be found in D. B. Steinman's *Builders of the Bridge* (New York: Harcourt, Brace and Company, 1945).

strands were *parallel* (instead of twisted into a spiral). This meant that each individual strand would be identically stressed. Small as it seemed, this change immensely improved the efficiency and predictability of suspension structures. Roebling himself used it in all his larger bridges and it has been a standard procedure ever since.

Roebling could easily have become a manufacturer exclusively, but his interest in design was now thoroughly aroused. Building a new factory in Trenton (1848) did not prevent his building a new highway bridge across the Monongahela at Pittsburgh in 1846 (eight spans of one hundred and eighty-eight feet each) or the railroad bridge across Niagara Falls in 1854. Indeed, as the size of the structures increased, new problems arose. To reduce the danger of failure it was necessary to take over the manufacture of the wire from which the cables were woven; this involved improved metallurgy. And for such great structures the cable could no longer be woven in the Trenton plant. In the Pittsburgh Bridge, the cables were woven on the bank. Ultimately, on the Brooklyn Bridge, even this technique would not work. Again the man was equal to the job. He evolved a traveling weaving machine, which shuttled back and forth across the East River, on temporary cables, weaving the main supports as the spider does its web (Fig. 75).

All this did not exhaust Roebling's wide interests. In 1847 he advocated a system of railroads and telegraph lines to replace the canals and horse couriers. In 1850, four years before Cyrus Field became actively interested, he wrote that a trans-Atlantic cable was entirely feasible, even giving his specifications and estimate of its cost. Then, in 1857, with two bridges under construction at Cincinnati and Pittsburgh, he wrote to Abram S. Hewitt of New York City proposing a bridge from Manhattan to Brooklyn. The proposal caught the imagination of New Yorkers, but preliminaries were slow and the Civil War intervened. His son Washington went off to war with the Union army and the plant at Trenton was converted to war work. Thus it was not until 1869 that the project went through. Roebling's design was accepted and Roebling appointed chief engineer.

As much a part of American life and landscape as Niagara Falls, the structure needs no description here (Fig. 74). The scale and breath-taking clarity of its design are indelibly imprinted upon American memories. But more than this must be said if the full stature of Roebling and his bridge are to be understood. The passionate attachment to the work, which cost him his life in the first year of construction and cost his son his health in the next, was but one aspect of Roebling's mastery of the field. For, in addition to manufacturing the cable, perfecting the machine which wove it, training the workmen and supervising the over-all construction, he conceived the design itself. He thus proved himself the master of the large as well as the small. Posthumously, he displays a complete understanding of tension structures. He established criteria which are still operative; and much of what has been added subsequently reveals itself as either ostentation or ignorance.[1]

The Tower

PERHAPS the most dramatic leap of the century was that of the Eiffel Tower. Unlike Paxton and Roebling, Gustave Eiffel met the most determined — one might almost say political — opposition. He had to fight not only technological lags (inadequate supplies, untrained workmen, skeptical manufacturers); he had also to overcome hostile editors, irate property-owners, even novelists and poets! From its very inception in 1885 until long after its completion, the Tower was the center of a controversy so spirited as to appear almost incredible in retrospect. The design, appearance, cost, and safety of the structure became public issues. Prominent Frenchmen in all walks of life plunged into the discussion. Alexandre Dumas the younger and Guy de Maupassant were among the intelligentsia who signed a manifesto protesting the erection of the Tower; and the indignant

[1] Exhaustive analysis of the ill-fated Tacoma Narrows Bridge, which collapsed shortly after its completion in 1940, has recently revealed that its tendency to 'ripple' under wind pressure was the ultimate cause of collapse. Roebling had clearly anticipated this phenomenon of aerodynamic instability in both his designs and his writings.

poet Verlaine is said to have sworn never to visit that portion of Paris again. Newspapers took up editorial positions, *Le Figaro* going so far as to publish special issues on the subject. Several owners of property between the site and the Seine instituted suit against Eiffel, insisting that the courts prohibit the construction of so dangerous a structure.

Whatever Eiffel's professional colleagues thought of his project, they very wisely refrained from signing manifestoes on the subject. Only the ornate Charles Garnier, architect of the Paris Opéra, circulated a petition to have it demolished by the government. At any rate, the majority of professionals were at least respectful. Photographs taken during the construction indicate a stream of architects and engineers, top-hatted and frock-coated, being carried aloft on the dinky steam hoists and gravely clambering over the wooden scaffolding.

Gustave Eiffel fought his enemies to a standstill. When the French government, but half convinced of the soundness of his project, voted him only $292,000 of an estimated cost of well over a million dollars, Eiffel unhesitatingly supplied the balance out of his own pocket. He was confident, as he later told the Smithsonian Institution, that public opinion was on his side: 'a crowd of unknown friends were ready to honor this bold enterprise as soon as it took form. The imagination of men was struck by its colossal dimensions.' [1]

Eiffel's estimation of the temper of his age was correct. Once finished, the Tower immediately became, and has remained ever since, the most popular structure in France. In the single Exposition season of 1889 gate receipts at the Tower netted six-sevenths of the cost. It was described at great length in the world press, praised by Thomas Edison, who thanked God for 'so great a structure,' and recognized in the building field for what it was — a pacemaker for rigid structures (Fig. 76).

Dramatic as was the public controversy surrounding the project, Eiffel's mastery of the technological dilemma confronting him was even more impressive. Already the *enfant terrible* of the

[1] G. Eiffel, 'The Eiffel Tower,' *Report of the Smithsonian Institution* (Washington, D.C., 1889), pp. 729–735.

European engineering fraternity, Eiffel had won an international reputation for his designs for the famous bridge at Garabit in France, the locks for the ill-fated French canal in Panama, and the supporting skeleton for Bartholdi's Statue of Liberty. All this was valuable preparation for the Tower, although in it he confronted problems of much greater magnitude than in these former projects. Indeed, he faced an absence of all those factors which the modern designer considers essential: a wide choice of specialized building materials, factories which could guarantee their prompt and regular delivery, suitable construction methods, trained workmen.

In evolving his general design, it is apparent that Eiffel drew upon his bridge-building experience, particularly that at Garabit. By 1885 he had come to 'believe that it was possible to construct these [towers] without any great difficulty to a much greater height than hitherto.' The design was naturally based upon metal, since in such material constructions could now 'be planned with such accuracy as to sanction the boldness which results from full knowledge.' This boldness, however, did not blind him to caution: although the spread of the Bessemer process had by this time already made steel generally available, Eiffel conservatively chose wrought iron. He found its properties 'remarkable, since it may be as readily employed in tension as in compression, and can be put together perfectly by riveting.'[1]

Similarly, though the principle of reinforcing concrete with steel was already known, Eiffel stuck to stone masonry for his foundations, which rested in turn on concrete mats. And although he emphasized his faith in these foundations, he evidently realized that they were not ideal and cannily provided slots for eight-hundred-ton hydraulic jacks in each of the four piers.

Though Eiffel stuck to materials with which he was thoroughly familiar (he could not gamble on new-fangled material like reinforced concrete, about which there was as yet no basic knowledge), he used them in an astonishingly modern manner.

---

[1] This was not, of course, Eiffel's private discovery. In 1885, William LeBaron Jenney had already completed Chicago's first skyscraper, during which he would have met similar theoretical and practical problems. But the variation between American and French technology makes it unlikely that there was any direct exchange between Paris and Chicago.

Satisfied though he pretended to be with stone masonry, his foundation design nevertheless anticipates contemporary re-inforced concrete to a marked degree. Indeed, the four-inch wrought-iron bars which anchor superstructure to foundations also — 'by means of iron clamps unite almost all parts of the masonry' — act as a rudimentary reinforcing. In much the same manner his detailing of the various wrought-iron members anticipates, in both profile and general shape, contemporary design of steel members (Figs. 77, 78).

In the actual erection of the Tower, Eiffel was far ahead of the current European practice. For example, he made a clear distinction between shop and field operations, and had the entire seven thousand tons of ironwork completely fabricated at the factory, including the punching of all holes and much of the riveting. This enabled him to use a relatively small crew (two hundred and fifty) of unskilled men at the site.

He designed his own scaffolding, making elaborate (and until then unheard-of) provisions for the workmen's safety. This led one American magazine wonderingly to report to its audience: 'It was feared that, unaccustomed to a very high scaffolding, few men could be found not subject to vertigo. But in [the construction of] the Tower they did not work high in the air with an open and dangerous footing. They were on platforms 41 feet wide and as calm as on the ground.'[1] Eiffel was forced to design his own winches and rigging; and it is here that the technological lags against which he fought are most clearly apparent. By careful organization of each step in fabrication and erection processes, he was able to maintain control over the design, quality, and delivery-timing of his ironwork. But the industrial resources of his time simply did not permit a scaffold-ing and rigging system of similar efficiency. There was a time lag, between the design level of the Tower itself and that of its scaffolding and rigging, of at least half a century. This might have deterred other men: not so Gustave Eiffel. He forced the Tower through to completion without a single mishap, and

---

[1] William A. Eddy, 'The Eiffel Tower,' *Atlantic Monthly Magazine*, vol. LXIII (June, 1889), pp. 721–727.

thereby set the world new standards in the design and erection of very tall structures.

Not one of these three great designers was an architect, and only one of their three great structures can be properly classified as a building. Yet the popular acclaim which their works received shows how far removed from reality were the architects, the architecture, and the architectural critics of their day. There is little evidence that any of the three ever felt called upon to defend the appearance of their structures, much less to formulate any formal statement on personal esthetic standards. Their ignorance of contemporary architectural theory seems to have been absolute, incredibly pure. Yet it was a naïveté for which we can well be grateful. Their designs themselves carry the internal evidence of high discipline and precise selectivity — standards compared to which the turgid, flowery prose of professional critics like John Ruskin or James Jackson Jarvis appear tragically inadequate and ill-informed.

The successive impacts of these three structures upon American thought are readily traced in the periodicals of the day. Each as it appeared was added to the required itinerary of traveling Americans. The Bridge especially caught popular fancy: it was sold to yokels, woven into the music-hall routine, incorporated into our folklore. Of all sections of the population, the architects themselves seemed to have been least affected. The Crystal Palace was gracelessly mimicked in New York in 1853 and again at the Philadelphia Centennial in 1876. Roebling's bridge was quickly caricatured in the Queensborough and Manhattan spans which rose to flank it; and fragments reminiscent of Eiffel's ironwork were to be found embedded in later steel structures. Yet these were but distorted reflections of the original in which the clarity of the central concept was quite overlooked. It was as though no impulse, however strong or healthy, could remain long dominant in the ferment of post-Civil War America.

Each of the three structures was, in a way, the product of a golden moment of equilibrium, brief in time, special in character, delicate in balance. Their significance was dissipated before men of adequate stature could again appear to grasp it; and when men like H. H. Richardson and Louis Sullivan did appear, they came from a quite different background, equipped with a radically different perspective, so that they profited only indirectly from the explorations of the century's greatest structuralists.

CHAPTER SIX

1860–1893: The Great Victorians

W ITH THE CLOSE of the Civil War, the rising industrialists achieved a smashing victory over the Southern slave-owners and their allies, the great merchants of the Northeast. The way was now clear for the full industrialization of the country, and the next forty years saw the incredibly rapid development of the entire continent. The defeat of the slave-owners removed the last barriers to the full economic development of modern capitalism. Never had the shift in class forces been more abrupt or profound; never had the change in upper-class ideology been more climactic; and never had its expression in architecture been more immediate. The stylistic continuity of the previous century was shattered at a blow — it is small exaggeration to say that Greek and Roman styles 'went out like a light.' In rapid succession the architects began experimenting with the Gothic, the Egyptian, the Romanesque, the Byzantine, the contemporary French. But though archeology grew steadily more precise, use of its idioms did not regain that precision which had characterized the revivals of the past. Between and around and below them developed that characteristic set of symbols called the Victorian or (by *fin-de-siècle* snobs) the Parvenu.

The post-war period was lusty and inventive. At no time before or since has American building been so unselfconscious, so blithely forgetful, of the shadows of the past or the weight of the future. New tools, new materials, and new processes appeared with staggering rapidity to serve as new media for the builders. Mass-produced and low-cost, steel began to replace handicraft wrought iron and unsatisfactory cast iron. Portland cement manufacture, begun by David Saylor at Coplay, Pennsylvania, in 1870, gave great impetus to brick and stone masonry. There was wide development in ceramics and clay products — necessary for fireproofing the new steel skeletons. Production of glass was industrialized, and the huge plate-glass windows of the Victorians were possible. Perhaps most indicative of all was what happened to wood. This had always been (and still is) America's favorite building material. It was abundant, cheap, and easily worked. In this material, with the advent of power-driven jigsaw and lathe, the esthetic aspirations of the period found their fullest expression. In a maniacal yet curiously mechanistic enthusiasm it was cut, turned, twisted, tortured, and shaped; better than any other material it served as the medium *par excellence* for the symbols of the period.

All the buildings of the period gave characteristic expression to the narrow yet ardent interest of the American people in new machines and new processes. Even the official architecture — always a good barometer of upper-class taste — employed this lathe-and-jigsaw ideology, including even those buildings which pretended to be Gothic, Renaissance, or French. For this was the period of buoyant Victorian optimism when mill-owner and mill-worker alike saw only the promise (and not the problems) of the machine and mechanized production. It was only as the century drew to a close that 'authentic' revivals began again to be demanded.

This period saw also the further separation of the architects from the main stream of American building. Under the severe strain placed upon it by expanding industrialism, the building industry itself began to undergo a qualitative change. No longer were building operations exclusively in the hands of small independents. In the rapidly growing cities speculative housing appeared; the mobility of labor steadily increased the ratio of rented to owned dwelling units, while even those who owned houses began more and more to buy them ready-built. The mills and factories were no longer the projects of scattered entrepreneurs, but huge plants for the new trusts. By the same token the building process itself changed. The independent artisans became skilled wage-workers; specialization set in, for it was no more possible to *build* the great factories with independent artisans than it was to *operate* them with cottage craftsmen. The building process began to be industrialized, and this was the main stream from which all advance in the future was to flow.

As a result of this same process, however, the big landlords — expanding in numbers, wealth, and complex administrative tasks — began to require the full-time professional services of the architect as designer and ideologue. In this shift, control of the design process passed out of the hands of the nameless artisan into those of the professional. How closely related this shift was to the triumph of industrialism over slavery is to be seen in these facts: the American Institute of Architects was founded in 1857; the first of fifty-odd architectural schools was founded at Massachusetts Institute of Technology in 1866; and the first architectural journal appeared in Philadelphia in 1868. Nor is it surprising that the concern of all these institutions should have been, from the first, 'beauty.' They were the organs of that group of specialists in the esthetic dimension of building whose inner content was always but a reflection of the ideology of the dominant sectors of society.

This phase of American building has been the source of endless confusion to the architect himself. The contrast between the relative simplicity and homogeneity of the main esthetic currents of American building up to 1860 and the turgid flood of the three decades which followed could only be ascribed to 'an appalling decline in public taste,' which marked 'the lowest point to which American architecture had ever sunk.' Since the consistent attempt was to explain esthetic phenomena in exclusively esthetic terms, the climactic change of the mid-century has been insoluble in rational terms.

Actually, the period can only be explained in technological and social terms. Up until 1860, three salient factors determined the character of American building: (1) The esthetic standards did not seriously conflict with the technological level of building.

Neither the building materials (stone, brick, wood) nor the structural theories (post-and-lintel, load-bearing wall, arch-and-dome) differed in any important respect from those actually used by the Greeks and Romans. (2) The building types required by the economy were relatively few and simple, and could be readily fabricated with traditional materials along traditional lines. (3) The cleavage in society had not sufficiently sharpened to create wide divergencies in ideology — that is, to divide esthetic standards along class lines into 'good' (upper-class) and 'bad' (lower-class) taste. Industrialization had not yet succeeded in concentrating the production — and consequently the design control — in the hands of a small group of salaried specialists. Taste was thus still subject to some measure of democratic control.

In an indirect fashion, current concepts of the architecture of the nineteenth century are a characteristic expression of our misunderstanding of our own progressive past. For what the modern esthetician forgets, in smugly dismissing the period as 'an all-time low in taste,' is his own history. He is the product of precisely those institutions — the great architectural schools, the architectural press, the architectural profession itself — which our society perfected only in the latter part of the last century. In criticizing the 'low' esthetic standards of his immediate predecessors and praising the 'gracious, aristocratic' taste of the colonies, he is merely reflecting the contempt of many a self-made plutocrat for his own grimy origins and his yearning for the 'gracious' days of colonial slavery.

The Impact of Victorian Technology

HISTORIANS err when they overlook the work of that constellation of great scientists and inventors whose work, from the mid-century on, was to have so profound if indirect an effect upon American building. Morse with his telegraph; Bell with the telephone; Otis with his elevator; Goodyear with his gutta-percha; Edison with the incandescent bulb, the dictaphone, the central generating plant; and the host of wise men and crackpots whose ideas were flooding the United States Patent Office. For it was these men who were to release building from its centuries-old limitations of size, density, and relationship. Thanks to them, the flow of men, ideas, things, both inside and between buildings, was speeded up to an extraordinary degree. Released from the necessity of face-to-face contact by the telephone and the pneumatic tube, the scale of the department store could be almost indefinitely expanded. If freight and passengers could be moved vertically by elevators, then the sixth floor became as available as the first had formerly been. If by means of telephone, dictaphone, push-button, and loud-speaker, a manager could direct five hundred workmen instead of fifty, then the factory could be that much larger. Or if — thanks to Mr. Edison's motors, wires, and current — one operator could control machines which had required ten men before, then the building automatically increased in complexity.

Contrariwise, the same new equipments tended toward decentralization. With electric power, the shop no longer had to be at the pithead. With the trolley, the worker no longer had to live in the shadow of the shop. And with bathroom and septic tank, steam heat and acetylene, the banker could comfortably escape with his children to the country. It needs emphasizing that in building, as elsewhere, 'the machine' was not of itself responsible for the insane congestion of the century. Implicit in it was equally the tendency toward decentralization. It was the character of our society, and not merely our tools, which determined the direction of nineteenth-century urbanism.

An increase in the mobility of people, things, ideas, not only made possible much larger and more complex buildings than had hitherto been possible; it also made possible a rapid specialization of building type. Jefferson had emphasized the distinction between building types in his home at Monticello as against the Capitol at Richmond. But his concern was, after all, a formal one — more a matter of ideological effect than technical effectiveness. It was enough if the one was recognizably the seat of a gentleman and the other the seat of a state power; and the truth was that neither operation would have been too seriously impaired had the buildings been switched. Matters were different a century later: many an architect might try to make his houses look like capitols but the violation of fact was difficult. For little by little all the Victorian gadgets had become organic parts of building. Indeed, heating and sanitation systems, light and power and communication systems, had come to be quite as important (and almost as costly) as the structural shell itself. This made American building a far more precise instrument of environmental control, but, by the same token, much less susceptible to undifferentiated use.

The high rate of urban expansion of the latter half of the century, plus the accelerating rate of technological advance, raised building obsolescence to fantastic heights. In fact, an entirely new type of obsolescence appeared: *technological*. Hitherto a structure was seldom considered obsolete as long as it was physically sound. If a change in function was desired, say house into grogshop, a window was cut here, a counter built there, and a new sign hung to complete the metamorphosis. Of course, since change is uneven, many houses even today are converted into liquor stores. But the trend is entirely in the other direction.

The only important exception to this rule was in the domestic dwelling. Here technological obsolescence did not and does not operate as a law. As long as a house remained upright, it was considered by some landlord to be habitable; and, so perennial was the housing shortage, as long as a house remained upright, some tenant could be found to live in it. Except for local variations, there has been a housing shortage in America for at least a century. This is true both quantitatively and qualitatively, and all the mad and avaricious expansion of the Victorians scarcely changed the picture. Nevertheless, even in the house, the optimum standard was rising so that, by the end of the century, a house without central heating, bath, and lights was definitely sub-standard, even though the vast majority lay in precisely that category.

Today it is apparent that the origins of our most spectacular architectural accomplishments are bedded in the rich and maculate Victorian era. Those gentry clothed our cities in such confusion, waste, and appalling ugliness that it has been difficult for many critics to 'see any good' — indeed, to see anything at all — in their work.   More than refined esthetic standards are necessary to such an exploration, for their task was gargantuan and complex, and there was no time to be finicky.   Those very scientists, inventors, and builders whose grimy work seemed so remote to the stylish *fin-de-siècle* architect were in fact making great contributions to contemporary building — greater perhaps than all but a handful of the architects themselves.

It would be inaccurate to say that these peripheral developments were ignored by the building field.   Despite its general backwardness, it adopted some of them with astonishing rapidity. (For example, the elevator and the skyscraper were Siamese twins, largely perfected in a short two or three decades.)   But the resistance among the architects themselves was immense. They romantically rejected the material promise of mid-Victorian life or they accepted it piecemeal.   In neither case did they show any grasp of its potentials.   Indeed, the only coherent perspective of the period was not to be found among the professionals but in the utopian tract of Edward Bellamy, *Looking Backward*.[1]   In this remarkable book, Bellamy displayed an uncanny anticipation of the future development of technology. His utopian Boston had a twenty-four-hour broadcasting system and every room was wired for sound.   Chimneys — in fact, combustion itself with its soot and smoke — had completely disappeared: electric power was everywhere, cheap, abundant, clean.   Artificial lighting was indirect, air-conditioning was commonplace, housework was mechanized.   Yet this was the least distinctive aspect of Bellamy's perspective.   What lifted him above the ruck of mid-Victorian idealism was his naïve yet luminous vision of how technological advance was to deepen and enrich the whole course of American life.

The Boston he saw from his rooftop, that first summer morning in the year 2000, had been completely rebuilt into a modern garden city:

[1] Boston: Houghton Mifflin Company, 1887.

Broad streets, shaded by trees and lined with fine buildings, for
the most part not in continuous blocks but set in larger or smaller
enclosures . . . Every quarter contained large open squares filled
with trees, among which statues glistened and fountains flashed
. . . the public buildings [were] of a colossal size and an architectural grandeur unparalleled.[1]

The entire distributive apparatus of the city had been completely
revamped, so that each ward was serviced by a single branch
department store. Each of these was connected by pneumatic
tube to a huge central warehouse from which all deliveries were
made, also by pneumatic tube. This warehouse was the apotheosis of American rationalization — 'a giant hopper into which
goods are being constantly poured by the trainload and shipload,
to issue at the other end in packages of pounds and ounces,
yards and inches, pints and gallons.' Yet the mechanism was
only incidental to the social order it served. Satisfaction and
comfort were paramount considerations. Hence the architectural design of a typical store:

> a vast hall full of light, received not alone from the windows on
> all sides but from the dome, the point of which was a hundred
> feet above. Beneath it . . . a magnificent fountain played, cooling
> the atmosphere to a delicious freshness . . . walls and ceilings were
> frescoed in mellow tints to soften without absorbing the light. . . .
> Around the fountain was a space occupied with chairs and sofas.[2]

In Bellamy's Boston labor-saving machinery had been used
'prodigiously,' but the emphasis was upon the elimination of
drudgery rather than in the machine *per se*. Ridding the houses
of the dust-catching bric-à-brac of General Grant's epoch had
not only reduced woman's work: it had increased her social
stature. Central kitchens and dining-rooms not only took the
housewife away from the stove: they gave her the time for a
career of her own if she so desired. If there was an absence of
detail in Bellamy's architecture, it was because he was interested
in the social function of building, not its street façade. Victorian
society was drowning in detail, rich and proliferating. What it

---

[1] *Looking Backward.* Modern Library edition, p. 27.
[2] *Ibid.*, p. 80.

needed was organization. Any engineer could install his broadcasting system: the real problem was to see that the quality of
the broadcast programs themselves was good and that all had
access to them.

Bellamy managed to project a picture of urban life which
combined New England humanism with the characteristic optimism of the early Victorians. To it, however, he added a concept of organization — whether social or architectural — which
was unprecedented in breadth and completeness. He saw what
could be done with the materials at hand where his contemporaries in the building field, bemused by the sheer multiplicity of
materials, could not so much as visualize a coherent city block.

False Spring in Chicago

THE SPLIT between ideologue and technician developed most
sharply in the Northeast, as a result of the industrial expansion
immediately preceding and following the Civil War. By the
nineties this contradiction was already well developed — was,
in fact, a principal topic of discussion among the architects
themselves. Thus, in 1892, A. D. F. Hamlin ruefully observed
that:

> Engineering had monopolized whatever real progress was being
> made in building. Metal construction was coming into general
> use for bridges and for structures with large roofs, such as railroad
> stations and exhibition buildings — the most characteristic prod-
> ucts of the constructive skill of the time. These works were
> entrusted to engineers; the architects were so preoccupied with
> their mistaken efforts to resuscitate historic styles that they wholly
> failed to discover the possibilities of the new material, and scorn-
> fully abandoned it.[1]

And another prominent critic of the day, Montgomery Schuyler,
saw the situation as critical:

> The architect resents the engineer as a barbarian; the engineer
> makes light of the architect as a dilettante. It is difficult to deny

[1] *Architectural Record*, January–March, 1892.

that each is largely in the right. The artistic insensibility of the modern engineer is not more fatal to architectural progress than the artistic irrelevancy of the modern architect. In general, engineering is at least progressive, while architecture is at most stationary. And, indeed, it may be questioned whether, without a thought of art and, as it were, in spite of himself, the engineer has not produced the most impressive as certainly he has produced the most characteristic monuments of our time. . . . What may we not hope from the union of modern engineering with modern architecture, when the two callings, so harshly divorced, are again united! [1]

However clearly Schuyler saw the dichotomy in nineteenth-century building, he remained the prisoner of his time and class. He could not see that the harsh divorce between architect and engineer was the inevitable product of capitalism. On the one hand, industrial production demanded better performance of building; consequently, the industrialists were willing to subsidize progress in engineering and technology. But, on the other hand, the ideology of these same men was increasingly conservative; necessarily, they began to demand of their architects suitably imperial symbols for their new imperialism. The reintegration of esthetic with technical standards could only occur when both were developing in the same progressive direction and at approximately the same rates of speed.

In the East, then, no resolution of the harsh divorce was possible. On the contrary, the gap between technology and propaganda was steadily to deepen as the century closed. And as the gulf widened, the propaganda got steadily worse. Thorstein Veblen, observing the antics of the ruling classes in 1899 with caustic perspicacity, saw that nothing could escape the corroding effects of their new esthetic standards of 'conspicuous waste and predatory exploit.'

It would be extremely difficult to find a modern civilized residence or public building which can claim anything better than relative inoffensiveness in the eyes of anyone who will dissociate the elements of beauty from those of honorific waste.

[1] *Ibid.*, July–September, 1894.

The endless variety of fronts presented by the better class of tenements and apartment houses in our cities is an endless variety of
architectural distress and of suggestions of expensive discomfort.
Considered as objects of beauty, the dead walls of the sides and
back of these structures, left untouched by the hands of the artist,
are commonly the best feature of the building.[1]

Aside from their homes, Veblen said, the 'imperious requirements' of these bigwigs could best be observed in the architectural style they imposed on the orphanages and old ladies'
homes which they were then endowing. Here

> an appreciable share of the funds is spent in the construction of
> an edifice faced with some aesthetically objectionable but expen-
> sive stone, covered with grotesque and incongruous details, and
> designed — in its battlemented walls and turrets and its massive
> portals and strategic approaches — to suggest certain barbaric
> methods of warfare. The interior of the structure shows the same
> pervasive guidance of the canons of conspicuous waste and preda-
> tory exploit![2]

H. H. Richardson — 'Direct, Large, and Simple'

OUT IN THE MIDDLE WEST a somewhat special set of circumstances was to lead to different results. Chicago, already the
metropolis of the inland empire, had been all but destroyed in
the Great Fire of October 8, 1871. In the decades which followed it was the scene of unprecedented expansion. This
construction alone would have furnished the material basis for a
large and prosperous group of architects and engineers. But
the rise of the famous 'Chicago School' of architects — and its
unchallenged ascendancy in the nation throughout the next
several decades — cannot be wholly explained in terms of large
and numerous commissions. These men developed in the electric environment of a vigorous and progressive capital, intellectual center of the Midwest. In the older cities of the eastern

[1] Thorstein Veblen, *The Theory of the Leisure Class* (New York: B. W. Huebsch),
p. 154.
[2] *Ibid.*, p. 349.

seaboard, the Wall Street capitalists had already consolidated their power and settled down for a long period of intensifying conservatism. Chicago, on the other hand, was the pivot of industrial and agrarian forces which resisted, for the time at least, the long arm of eastern monopoly. It faced huge new problems and had no choice but to try new solutions. Internally, it was witnessing a rapid polarization of social forces marked on the one hand by the rise of the grain, packing-house, railroad, and manufacturing industries, and, on the other, by the great trade-union movements. It was thus the home both of robber barons and Haymarket martyrs, of the Pullman massacre and the eight-hour day. And beyond the city proper lay the great democratic hinterland, with its agrarian Populism.

It was this added dimension which distinguished the atmosphere of the city from that of the East, and subtly but positively affected the opinions and the work of its building designers. It must thus not be considered accidental that the great trilogy of American architects — Richardson, Sullivan, and Wright — is permanently identified with Chicago. Elsewhere they may have worked, but nowhere, during a golden era of three or four decades, did they find a more hospitable environment. They were not by any means the only fine architects in Chicago at that time — merely the greatest. With them at various times were associated Adler, Burnham, Root, and Holabird, and others — all of them loosely affiliated in the Chicago School. Whatever differences there may have been among them, there were many points in common. And these points were best exemplified in the three leaders.

Henry Hobson Richardson entered L'Ecole des Beaux Arts in Paris in 1860; and when, five years later, he disembarked in Boston, he carried with him a magnificent instrument — one that was to make him the first great architect since the days of Mills and Latrobe: the clarity and precision of French academic thought at its best. The esthetic character of his work and its impact on contemporary American building have been amply treated, notably in Professor Hitchcock's book,[1] so that it requires

[1] Henry-Russell Hitchcock, Jr., *The Architecture of H. H. Richardson*. New York: Museum of Modern Art, 1936.

IV

False Spring in Chicago

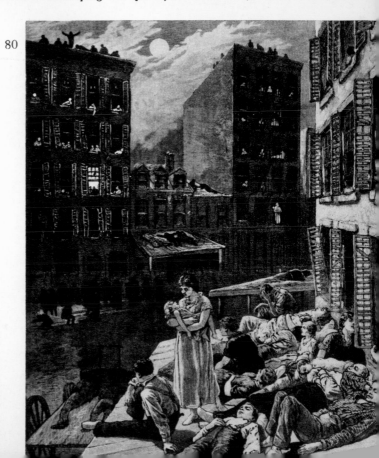

79 Frederick Law Olmsted's design for Central Park (79): the world's first great democratic recreational area, its naturalistic landscaping was quickly surrounded by airless slums (80).

80

The railroads' demands for great spans forced structural experimentation. But fires such as destroyed the fantastic wooden trestle at Portage, N. Y., forced engineers to turn to metal.

When New York's first Grand Central Station was opened in 1871, steel was still scarce. A series of open-webbed cast- and wrought-iron arches gave a fire-resistant vault 200 ft. wide.

83

84

Victorian businessmen fled the chaos of the cities they were building to suburban villas in which pretentious romanticism comported oddly with convenience. *(modern arch. is equally guilty)*

85

H. H. RICHARDSON, the New Orleans-born and Paris-trained architect from Boston, was meanwhile building a whole series of comfortable, coherent houses like this one for the Glessners in Chicago. Any one of them put the ruck of Victorian design to shame.

86

88

The strength, simplicity, and quiet good taste of Richardson's building for Marshall Field (18) marked him as a real master of his medium, the first great architect since the War.

89

LOUIS SULLIVAN

Wainwright Building in St. Louis

90 *Sullivan's "Schlesinger store"*

Richardson had an electric effect on Louis Sullivan whose Wainwright building in St. Louis (89) owed much to the Field building. But Sullivan, as he progressed through a series of big commercial structures, went far beyond his contemporaries. The last of these for the Schlesinger store (90) is probably the best architectural expression of the steel cage ever built.

COLUMBIAN EXPOSITION, 1893

Sullivan's Transportation building (91) was the only structure which disdained the dull and hackneyed idiom of the last Classic Revival . . .

The Fair's power plant (92) was hidden behind plaster columns. Yet, however accidentally, it was Sullivan's design that with uncanny fidelity anticipated the curve of vault and dynamo.

The Imperial pretensions of the Fair, as Sullivan well understood, marked the eclipse not only of the century's most progressive esthetic but of native midwestern liberalism as well.

94

95

After his defeat at the Fair, Sullivan designed this bank at Owatonna, Minn. (1907-8), one of a series for small midwestern towns. Here, among agrarian radicals, his highly personal idiom found a surprisingly warm reception.

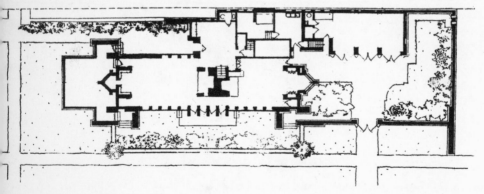

96

As early as 1907, young Frank Lloyd Wright (a sharp observer of all this esthetic fracas) demonstrated in the Robey house that training in Sullivan's office had merely given direction and form to America's most gifted and original designer.

97

little attention here except to venture an opinion that too much has perhaps been made of this aspect of his work. For Richardson's largest significance lies not so much in the architectural vernacular he perfected as in his rôle of restoring the social function of the architect to something of its former prestige.

His work in the East had already achieved the high praise of imitation when he came to Chicago in 1885 to build the famous wholesale store for Marshall Field's (Fig. 88). It created an immediate sensation. But the thing about the Field Building which Louis Sullivan was quick to appreciate was not so much the majestic scale of arched bays and rusticated stonework as the simplicity and clarity of its organization. Here he saw a 'direct, large, and simple' mind at work — the first architectural mind in half a century which showed control of the medium in which it worked. Richardson's work enjoyed then and later a great reputation for its 'composition.' But what was this composition if not an expression of the skill and understanding of the designer, a knowledge of the forces with which he was dealing, an ability to analyze their contradictions and then resolve them into a workable solution? If the churches, store buildings, and railroad stations which Richardson was then designing impressed the public with their outward appearance of order, organization, and plain good sense, it was because Richardson so largely understood the complex organisms of modern capitalism — the huge department store, the large and worldly metropolitan church, the modern library — he was called upon to house. He was like Roebling and Eiffel in this respect — capable of grasping the large outlines of the problem before him, of analyzing the forces involved, organizing them into a coherent and workable plan.

Henry Richardson died at the age of forty-eight, when his career was at its height, and one can only speculate as to what he might ultimately have achieved. The chances are that he would not have gone much farther, for his chief contribution lies in the field of plan rather than structure. He seems to have had no deep understanding of structural design or interest in constructural processes — that is, in *building*. He used current technical advances — elevators, steel frames, electricity — competently but casually. The rheostat he put into the Glessners' new mansion for dimming the dining-room lights must have caused a sensation among the guests at the housewarming; otherwise the house is technically unexceptional, differing only from other mansions in its plan — that is, its spatial organization — and hence in its form (Fig. 86). Richardson was not of a speculative turn of mind, had no philosophical pretensions, and did not commit himself to paper; so we can take Sullivan's estimation of him ('direct, large, and simple') as adequate. Yet his invasion of the Chicago scene was destined to have tremendous repercussions, leading directly to the century's most important development — the appearance of the Chicago School.

The irony was to be that Richardson had no legitimate heirs in the East. His building was widely copied, his work never really studied. His nostalgic use of the Romanesque, with its low round arches, heavy detail, and incised stonework, served merely to stimulate interest in archeology. It was always the elevation, never the plan, that stylish architects were intent on copying.

But upon one architect, at least, Richardson's work had a fertilizing effect: Louis Sullivan. If one compares the Field Building with the final design for the Auditorium Building, the direct relationship is immediately apparent. This impact of Richardson upon Sullivan is even more apparent in the earlier designs which Sullivan did for the Auditorium project. Here, although the basic plan had been developed, Sullivan had been playing around with trivial façades — cute Swiss balconies, French Renaissance towers, typical Victorian mansards. These served to obscure rather than to clarify the basic organization of the huge project. Sullivan was well aware of this dilemma but unable to escape it — until he saw the Field Building. Here were façades which precisely expressed the internal organization of the project. Fifty or sixty years later, this does not sound like an especially radical discovery, but the young Sullivan saw in it an immensely important principle, the lack of which had vitiated building for almost a century. He was quick to apply it in the Auditorium Building and to develop it theoretically into his famous axiom: 'Form follows function.'

This organizing principle was the major contribution which Richardson made to architecture. It found its most fertile ground in Chicago. Here, and almost only here, the preconditions were right for further growth.

Sullivan, Giant of the Midwest

THREE GREAT CITIES shaped Louis Sullivan's life — Boston, Paris, Chicago — and the imprint of all three is clearly evident in his buildings and in his thought. From the Boston of his birth came the warm humanism of the transcendentalists and the Whitmanesque passion for democracy; from his two years' stay in Paris came intellectual discipline, ability to study, and a profound interest in science. But from raw, expansive Chicago came the inspiration and the opportunity for the most creative years of his life. It is to Chicago that he belongs; and he sensed this fact the first time he visited Chicago as an ambitious and confident youth of seventeen. It was still largely in ashes from the Great Fire of 1871 and rocking from the current Panic of 1873; yet he found it

> magnificent and wild: a crude extravaganza, an intoxicating rawness, a sense of big things to be done. For 'big' was the word . . . and 'biggest in the world' was the braggart phrase on every tongue . . . [the men of Chicago] were the crudest, rawest, most savagely ambitious dreamers and would-be doers in the world . . . but these men had vision. What they saw was real.[1]

Sullivan went to Paris to study for two years, but there his early fascination for the precision of French scholarship had gradually given way to a healthy fear of the dry rot of French academism. Straight as a homing pigeon he returned to Chicago. In 1879 he went to work for David Adler and on the first day of May, 1881, became the partner of that brilliant man. Thus began the meteoric career of Louis Sullivan. From the first, he was destined to occupy an anomalous position in the

[1] Louis Sullivan, *Autobiography of an Idea* (American Institute of Architects, 1926), p. 200.

bustling, competitive world of Chicago architecture. Like his contemporaries — Root, Burnham, Richardson — he was a successful architect. Indeed, in the Auditorium Building he and his partner, David Adler, walked away with the largest and most costly project of the times. Unlike some of his contemporaries, he was successful in a much more profound sense, since his best buildings unquestionably rank at and near the top in American building. He was a great designer in the same fashion that Richardson was great: in his ability to analyze a complex problem, master it, solve it finally in a brilliantly articulated design. But he was more than that, as he insisted any architect worth his salt should be: he was also propagandist, ideologue, philosopher.

If Sullivan's chief impact upon American building was to be through his actual projects rather than his written word, this was due not so much to faulty thinking as to a peculiarity of the architectural profession: namely, that architectural concepts are historically visual. In the truest sense of the word, the architect has never been literate; to him a picture is worth a thousand words, and since the introduction of photography, ten thousand. Thus a hundred architects saw pictures of Sullivan's Wainright Building for one architect who read his articles or attended his lectures; and it is to these structures that we first must turn in analyzing Sullivan's effect upon American building.

Of what did this work consist? One hundred and twenty-four structures — whose dissimilarity in appearance, disparity in quality, and range of types is striking — are attributed to Sullivan.[1] In retrospect, this list seems contradictory. It is difficult at first to believe that the Auditorium and the Schlesinger Building were designed by the same man; that any design so mediocre as the Borden residence could have preceded the Babson house; or that one man could with equal ability master the plan complexities of the Auditorium and the ultimate simplicity of the Getty Tomb. Despite this, there is an inner continuity to the man's work. No architect ever had less of a

[1] According to the excellent bibliography in *Louis Sullivan*, by Hugh Morrison. (New York: W. W. Norton, 1935), pp. 294–305.

vested interest in a personal style than Louis Sullivan. He was quick to see the advantages of other men's work, and quick to adapt them to his own uses. Thus his profound respect for Richardson's Field Building was quickly reflected in his final designs for the Auditorium. Yet Sullivan was in no sense a plagiarist. He was a man in search of an architectural idiom which would be, not his own personal property, but that of the American people. It must express, not his culture, but that of his fellow countrymen. It was merely his task, as he put it, to catch and make incandescent that culture, 'as the poet, looking below the surface of life, sees the best that is in the people.' To this end, both in his buildings and his writings, he dedicated the major part of his energies. And it was only as adversity, ill-health, and isolation overtook him that his search for an appropriate idiom was reduced to the subjective metaphysics of a personal style of ornamentation.

In building design proper, his work showed a steady progression, but with equally climactic breaks. Four buildings marked this progress: the Auditorium, the Wainwright office building in St. Louis, the Schlesinger department store, and the National Farmers' Bank in Owatonna, Minnesota. In addition to his mastery of plan, Sullivan demonstrated a growing mastery of structure. The Auditorium was of traditional construction with load-bearing walls; its principal innovation was the foundations for which his partner, David Adler, was largely responsible. Yet here the multi-storied, many-windowed structure is carried as far as it could go without the steel frame. Burnham and Root's splendid Monadnock Building of four years later merely restates this fact in a style more pleasing to contemporary taste. In the almost barbaric splendor of the public rooms of the hotel and theater, Sullivan used ornament, textures, and a palette of rich color which upper-class Chicago of 1887 found well suited to its needs.

Sullivan invented neither the steel frame nor the multi-storied building; but in 1891, in the Wainwright Building in St. Louis, he produced the prototype, which in plan and façade was not to be materially improved upon for half a century (Fig. 89). Sullivan was much impressed with the esthetic potentials of tall buildings at this time and sought, by careful organization of every detail of his exteriors, to make the maximum use of verticality. Four years later, in the Guaranty Building in Buffalo, he carried this particular formula to a superb conclusion. Yet in 1893 he must already have begun to question the validity of this generalization and wonder how far it could be extended, for in that year he designed the Meyer Building. Here, for perhaps the first time in modern architecture, the deliberate emphasis was placed upon horizontality.

Now, the whole discussion of whether a skyscraper should be 'vertical' or 'horizontal' was in fact academic; structurally, the steel frame was a static cage. Floor loads are horizontally conveyed to vertical columns and thus transmitted to the ground. And when, in 1899, Louis Sullivan came to what was to prove his most pregnant design — that of the Schlesinger department store — he recognized this fact. Neither verticality nor horizontality is emphasized. Since maximum light was a prime consideration, he reduced both piers and spandrels to the absolute minimum; and then, as if to emphasize the static nature of the skeleton, he surrounded each window with a fine but very positive frame, so that the honeycomb character is inescapable (Fig. 90).

It is in the Schlesinger Building also that we find one of Sullivan's most polished statements on the subject of ornament. The first two floors are faced by a cast-iron-and-plate-glass screen, structurally and esthetically independent of the main building. The ornament is fantastically detailed and fine, so that much of it actually serves as a textural surface. All of it is typically Sullivanesque — sculpture done with a 4–H pencil, a curious *mélange* of geometry, Art Nouveau, and Classicism. But it is notable on several counts. The entire screen is designed for mass production in cast iron. As a whole, it is perhaps the first modern shop front in the country; its design is highly integrated, providing so well for hardware, awnings, ventilators, illumination, that five decades of continual use have required no alterations.

This screen has been severely criticized as being out of keeping with the rest of the building — an argument which is open to

some question, since from the sidewalk the average person sees
only the first two floors of a building. But it does clearly reveal
the two major lines of Sullivan's development and forms the
connecting link with the last phase of his career: the series of
small banks he did throughout the Midwest. In these buildings,
Sullivan was, in a certain sense, a free man. His career in
Chicago was over, cut off as sharply as with an axe. The Exposition of 1893 had been the deathblow, as he himself had been
the first to see; and in these rural clients he found a surprisingly
warm support for his esthetic theories.

The life-work of Louis Sullivan lies in two great deposits —
his buildings and his writings. The two are, so to speak, com-
plementary rather than repetitive: what he could not achieve
as a designer of actual buildings he sought to establish in the
field of polemics. They mirror the contradiction which ultimately destroyed him, although his accomplishments in both
fields make him unquestionably one of the greatest figures in
modern architecture. In the design of great and complex buildings he was without peer; his analysis of the social function of
building and the special rôle of the architect must — for its
clarity, courage, and perception — remain the classic on the
subject. There may be appalling lapses in both areas — scattered buildings of poor design or pages of florid turgidity; but
these are not central to the issue, merely the excrescences of a
fabulously fertile and diversified individual.

Although he proved himself time and again to be the most
competent architect of his period — proved it in an astonishing
variety of buildings from tombs to department stores — Sullivan
had singularly little to say about the practical aspects of building.
Perhaps it was because his executed designs so adequately expressed his opinions in steel and concrete; there was little that
needed to be added in words. In order to design a satisfactory
auditorium, one had to comprehend acoustics; to turn out a
satisfactory steel-framed skyscraper, one had to understand
structure. This was self-evident; and decades before the question was finally made obsolete by the crash of 1929, Sullivan had
furnished the prototype and the program for the tall office

building. He went much farther; though he personally was stirred by the esthetic possibilities of a tall building ('the force and power of altitude . . . a proud and soaring thing'), he was nevertheless aware of other and more important aspects. In his second tall office building (Schiller, 1891), he was already sufficiently troubled by the problem of light and air to give up a large portion of the plot to light wells. In his design for the unrealized Fraternity Temple (1891), he completely anticipated the free-standing cruciform tower, with diminishing set-backs, which the architects and promoters of the thirties were to glorify. Ultimately he came to the conclusion that the skyscraper carried the seeds of its own destruction.

> The tall steel-frame structure may have its aspects of beneficence; but so long as man may say: 'I shall do as I please with my own,' it presents opposite aspects of social menace and danger . . . the tall office building loses its validity when the surroundings are uncongenial to its nature; and when such buildings are crowded together upon narrow streets or lanes they become mutually destructive.[1]

Thus, Louis Sullivan was driven always, by the logic of his own definition of an architect, from the field of practical technique to the social, political, and philosophic speculation. Owing to his own scientific interests, his training in France, most of all to his close and fruitful association with David Adler, Sullivan could always master the most advanced technological developments of his day. With Adler there, no problem in foundations, acoustics, electric illumination, or ventilation would long go unsolved. In this respect, Sullivan's best work resembles that of Eiffel or Roebling; but unlike the great engineers, he was unable to regard his structures as isolates. It was not enough that a building perform efficiently and economically; it must in addition *express* that function. As eloquently as Jefferson and Greenough, and even more explicitly, Sullivan fought to make architecture a tool of social and political progress.

Thus he told the Chicago Architectural Club in 1899:

[1] Louis Sullivan, *Autobiography of an Idea* (American Institute of Architects, 1926), p. 313.

Accept my assurance that [the architect] is and imperatively shall
be an interpreter of the national life of his time . . . you are called
upon, not to betray, but to express the life of your own day and generation . . . a fraudulent and surreptitious use of historical documents,
however suavely presented, however cleverly plagiarized, however
neatly re-packed, however shrewdly intrigued, will constitute and
will be held to be a betrayal of trust.

The real function of the architect, he never tired of insisting,
was:

to vitalize building materials, to animate them with a subjective
significance and value, to make them visible parts of the social
fabric, to infuse into them the true life of the people, to impart
to them the best that is in the people, as the eye of the poet,
looking below the surface of life, sees the best that is in the people.[1]

If one really wanted to know the causes for the standards of
taste then prevailing in American architecture, one must look
deep. For, he said:

Architecture is not merely an art, more or less well or more or
less badly done; it is a social manifestation. If we would know
why certain things are as they are in our architecture, we must look
to the people; for our buildings as a whole are an image of our
people as a whole, although specifically they are the individual
images of those to whom, as a class, the public has delegated
and entrusted its power to build. Therefore by this light, the
critical study of architecture becomes . . . in reality, a study of the
social conditions producing it.[2]

A critical study of the conditions producing Chicago's architecture should have revealed to Sullivan precisely why so much
of it was bad. He had as clients many of those very men 'to
whom the public had delegated . . . its power to build.' And
all his abilities as a designer, all his powers of persuasion as
speaker and pamphleteer, could not bridge the sharpening gap
between the aspirations of the mighty and the needs of the
people as a whole. For a short period — roughly from the
Great Fire to the Columbian Exposition — Chicago had hung

[1] Louis Sullivan, *Kindergarten Chats* (Scarab Fraternity Press, 1934), p. 194.
[2] *Ibid.*, p. 8.

in a sort of miraculous equipoise, battleground for Midwestern equalitarianism and rapacious monopoly. And during this period Sullivan had as patrons and friends some of Chicago's richest men: they had subsidized his radical architectural theories, even attended his dinners where, after sumptuous food, he would stricture them on prevailing upper-class taste. But beneath the surface a change was taking place, illustrated in the changing character of Sullivan's commissions. In the Auditorium, he found a first great outlet for his talent precisely because of the building's social usefulness. The theater was to be a music center for a music-loving population. It became in fact the musical center of the mid-continent, a pump from which flowed a whole stream of stirring cultural impulses. But there were no such implications in the Schlesinger Building of 1899. For all its polished perfection, it remained a department store; and such a building of necessity sets sharp upper limits on social significance. In 1873, Louis Sullivan had found Chicago exhilarating; but as the century drew to a close, it was little short of explosive.

Ultimately Sullivan foundered upon this dichotomy, both as man and as architect. The Columbian Exposition of 1893 was the first evidence of his defeat. He had steadily developed his thesis of a democratic architecture, of genuinely *popular* esthetic standards which contradicted the realities of neither technical nor political progress. The architects, he had argued, must ally themselves with the people, learning from them as well as teaching them. 'Are you,' he had asked, 'using such talents as you possess for or against the people?' He was convinced (and he was largely right) that whatever success he and the Chicago School had enjoyed was due to this philosophy. And he assumed that they would fight for it as determinedly as he. Here he was wrong. The ease with which Chicago architects dropped one set of esthetic standards to embrace another and much lower one was proof of the inner political content of all concepts of 'beauty.' The first sign of betrayal came to Sullivan at the opening session of the Architectural Commission for the Exposition. Daniel Burnham was chairman of the group, which was heavily weighted with Easterners. While George B. Post (architect for the domed *New York Post*), Richard Hunt (architect for the Astors, Vanderbilts, and Goelets), and Charles McKim (architect for the Tiffanys) settled themselves around the table, Burnham began to speak. And Sullivan noticed in amazement that Burnham 'was progressively and grossly apologizing to the Eastern men for the presence of their benighted brethren of the West.'

Daniel Burnham, whose firm had done notable work in the 'form-follows-function' idiom of the Chicago School, supported the Easterners when they proposed that the Fair be designed in the Roman style. Sullivan heatedly opposed this, arguing for the application of those esthetic standards for which the Chicago School was justly famous. But when the ballots were in and counted, the Classic had carried the day. This was clearly the approved symbolism of Wall Street, as every architect on the Fair Commission could easily have testified, and its appearance in Chicago in 1893 was more than an accident of changing public taste. Louis Sullivan, with only the design of the Transportation Building to worry about (Fig. 91), was quick to see the interconnection of events:

> During this period there was well under way the [trend toward] formation of mergers, combinations, and trusts in the industrial world. The only architect in Chicago to catch the significance of the movement was Daniel Burnham, for in its tendency toward bigness, organization, delegation, and intense commercialism, he sensed the reciprocal workings of his own mind.[1]

Young Frank Lloyd Wright, asked by Daniel Burnham to join his firm just about this time, confirms Sullivan's estimate of Burnham's choice. Urging Wright to stay with the eclectics, Burnham told him:

> The Fair is going to have a great influence in our country. The American people have seen the 'Classics' on a grand scale for the first time. . . . I can see all America constructed along the lines of the Fair, in noble, dignified, Classic style. *The great men of the day all feel that way about it — all of them.*[2]

[1] *Autobiography of an Idea*, p. 314.
[2] Frank Lloyd Wright, *Autobiography* (New York: Longmans, Green and Company, 1932), p. 124.

The Chicago World's Fair was a shattering blow at the only consciously progressive effort of the century to resolve the growing contradiction between the ideology and the mechanics of American building. Historically, this was perhaps inevitable; but the loss was nonetheless disastrous. Referring to this period in post-Fair Chicago, Wright said in 1940: 'They killed Sullivan and they nearly killed me!' And the reason for the failure of this brilliant and erratic man (for though he lived until 1924, Sullivan's career was substantially ended by 1900) was, as S. Giedeon has so succinctly put it, because 'American architecture was [being] undermined by the most dangerous reaction since its origin.'

What was the *source* of this reaction? Was it merely, as Professor Giedeon would have us believe, the architect's desire to give 'an artificial backbone to people who were weak in their emotional structure'? Many things might have been said of Chicago's beef and railroad barons, but scarcely that their 'emotional structure' was 'weak.' No, the abrupt change in esthetic standards was not to be explained in terms of esthetics, but of basic changes in American society. The end of the century saw the substantial completion of the modern structure of monopoly and its absorption of the Chicago capitalists. When they exchanged local partnerships for national trusts, they did more than acquire Wall Street's stocks and bonds; they also exchanged the last remnants of their provincial democracy for Wall Street's ideology.

American building was seldom without its progressive critics at any time during the period — few of whom, significantly enough, were themselves architects. But as the century matured, most of this criticism was vitiated by the social position and affections of the critics themselves. The dishonesty of upper-class standards, the contrast between reactionary symbolism and technical advance, the widening gap between the material luxury of the rich and the suffering of the poor — these phenomena did not go entirely unremarked. But the interconnection between them and failing esthetic standards did.

The esthetic potentials of the machine came more and more

to be recognized. The more sensitive critics of the period saw with increasing clarity what industry offered building design; and they sought to extract from it a new and more vigorous esthetic, a democratic one. But what these men did not realize was that, as the century advanced, the rich and the powerful were less and less inclined to adopt social advance as their motto or the machine as their coat of arms. The lavish use of jigsaw fretwork and all manner of machine-made 'art' could be a virtue to the radical industrialists and financiers of the Reconstruction. But the cold and ruthless order of Imperial Rome was the symbol of Wall Street as the century closed.

CHAPTER SEVEN

1893–1933: Eclipse

F OR BOTH Louis Sullivan and Frank Lloyd Wright the Columbian Exposition had been climactic, a turning point. Both had refused to be party to a Classic hoax, and this courageous decision had had important effects upon their two careers. As the new century began, Sullivan was on the down grade, whereas Wright stood at the threshold to an extraordinary career. In tracing the decline of Sullivan, either as an architect or as a man, it is apparent that some personal weakness intervened to accelerate his eclipse. Objective conditions might have been hostile to his purposes. But his work had already won him many admirers and immense prestige. Why, then, his surrender? His weakness lay in the fact that he was a political Romantic. He had committed himself more completely than any other architect alive to the cause of political democracy, yet he seems to have been pathetically ignorant of the implications of this commitment and of the brutal reality of the issues involved. He shared with Edward Bellamy and Henry George the illusion that these issues existed only at the level of ideas; that eloquent after-dinner speeches or pungent essays could resolve the conflict.

Thirty years after the Chicago Fair, coming back from decades of self-imposed exile, Louis Sullivan saw all this with poignant clarity. Drafting his *Autobiography* in what was to be the last year of his life, he wrote in the third person of that earlier Sullivan:

> Of politics he knew nothing and suspected nothing, all seemed fair on the surface. . . . He had heard of the State and read some-

126

thing about the State but had not a glimmering of the meaning of the State. He had dutifully read some books on political economy . . . and had accepted their statements as fact. He had also heard vaguely something about finance and what a mystery it was. In other words, Louis was absurdly, grotesquely credulous.[1]

It may well be that no single man could have breasted that Classic tide. The architect of Louis Sullivan's day was much more the creature and prisoner of the wealthy than he is today. Even Frank Lloyd Wright, for all his splendid display of non-conformism, did not really escape. He merely found patrons who were themselves rich nonconformists. But Sullivan could scarcely have succeeded even if objective conditions had been different. His concept of democracy was a cloudy thing. It is significant that though he envisioned a generalized humanity moving in a generalized architectural felicity, improving and improved by a democratic esthetic, he failed utterly to concretize that vision.

It is not as though Sullivan lived in a world in which there were no burning social issues. Was there no recognition of the relation between decent housing and crime, prostitution and delinquency? Jane Addams saw it if Louis could not. Did the working people of America not realize the effects of badly lighted and ventilated factories upon their health? The Triangle Shirtwaist Fire stated the case in unequivocal terms, and all over the country new legislation governing sanitation, safety, and fire was being passed. Was nobody in his time aware of the relation between public education and better esthetic standards? The spread of art, music, and literary appreciation classes indicates that many people saw the relation.

For the fact was that such matters were not merely *related* to the problem of evolving a democratic esthetic: they were the bedrock upon which it must stand. Sullivan saw that architecture was, in the final analysis, propaganda itself. He knew that collectively the buildings of any society reveal the face of that society. He was aware of the monstrous evils and injustices of *fin-de-siècle* America and saw its perverted architectural taste as but a reflection of that basic social fact. He believed that 'in

[1] *Autobiography of an Idea*, p. 289.

our study of social science altogether too much importance has
been attached to heredity and too little to environment.' Yet
he never aligned himself with those people or movements which
sought to change the environment. For all his interest in the
application of science and technology to human welfare, he submerged himself in cloudy metaphysics. He was convinced that
'the so-called average mind has vastly greater powers, immeas-
urably greater possibilities of development than is generally
believed.' Yet in his personal life he showed no interest in
average people. He grew personally autocratic and egotistical,
more and more isolated from the family of men. He had no
allies when he met the aristocratic invaders from the East on
the board of the Columbian Exposition; and the defeat he met
at their hands did not drive him into closer contact with the
people. On the contrary, it had the tragic reverse of driving
him into isolation, abstraction, mysticism. Years before his
death in April, 1924, a great figure had been lost to American
building.

The Great Disciple

IF FRANK LLOYD WRIGHT succeeded where Sullivan could not,
one is almost inclined to put it down to Wright's extraordinary
tenacity — and nothing else. His accomplishment, as he himself put it in later years, was in merely staying alive. Wright's
career is unmatched in American architecture. Extending over
a period of six decades and still going at this writing, it has disturbed the profession almost as profoundly as his work has
affected our building. To do either the man or his work full
justice is far beyond the scope of this work. But some generalizations are both possible and necessary. He is the link between
the generous and humane romanticism of Richardson-Sullivan
and the harsh hopefulness of the present. He is the actual
strand of continuity between the best aspects of nineteenth-
century American building and those of the present. The three
men, adjacent in time and space, form a continuum. For all
their differences, there runs through their work an organic unity

— easy to perceive, difficult to describe; intensely personal yet symbolic of the times.

Heir though he might have been to Sullivan (whom he still calls 'The Master'), Wright did not merely sit back to enjoy his heritage. He used what they gave him, but he went far beyond that. With uncanny consistency he has hewed to his own line. He was never isolated from the world around him, yet never submerged by it. In magazines, books, luncheons, classrooms, and most of all, in his designs, he has stated and restated his convictions. Naïve, eccentric, biased they may have often been; but repeatedly they have been proved right. Was there a need for the civilized rich to break away from the formalized barbarism of Hunt's great house for the Vanderbilts? Wright's house for the Coonleys was the prototype of the break. Could no American architect conceive an urbane outdoor eating place? In the Midway Gardens on Chicago's lake front Wright showed them how to do it — a genuinely gay and lovely place, with lights, flowers, and music built in. Could mighty American business provide no more healthy or attractive an environment for its clerks than the dark warrens of its office buildings? Look to the Larkin Building in Buffalo. Could a religious congregation whose creed was rational and liturgy simple find nothing more suitable than the current ineptitudes? Wright's Unity Temple in Chicago gave them a functional assembly room, free of archaic symbolism, full of light and air.

The examples of his perception and foresight, the range of his interests, are unmatched since Jefferson. If he was far less profound as a thinker, he was a far more brilliant architect. Of *plan* he was from the start the master; in *structure* no less brilliant, though more erratic; in *mechanics* and *equipment* always forward-looking and adventurous, ready to give any new heating system or building material a whirl. But it is in the field of sheer *esthetics* that he is unique. In this specific area he has been for half a century an incendiary, putting outworn prejudice and accumulated historical bric-à-brac to the torch. Critics have for some years now been busily cataloguing his designs, indexing his 'sources,' defining his 'periods.' As for all great artists, this is essential labor — and difficult, for Wright is a man of enormous and complex culture.

But the distinct stages of his development should not obscure its continuity. For the quality which ties all the vast quantity of Wright's work together, separates it from his imitators, and raises it above his detractors, is his highly personal (one might almost say, private) esthetic standard. Although descended from Sullivan's, it is clearly not the same. Sullivan's motivation was in expressing and elevating the standards of taste of the undifferentiated masses — Wright's in deepening and enriching the perception of the individual. Sullivan wrote of the mass perversion of public taste; Wright has dwelt at length on the effect of boyhood summers on his grandfather's farm upon his concepts of beauty. One sought to be a democrat, the other was a humanist.

And this preoccupation was from the start apparent in Wright's houses (Fig. 95). Gleefully, he swept out the trash. He stripped the cornice of its brackets and the roof of its dormers; he lopped off the phony cupolas and the gingerbread; he standardized the windows and swept them almost brutally into large horizontal banks. Tortured surfacing materials gave way to sheer texture. Everywhere, a masculine and electric purpose was apparent. Indoors the same process was afoot. Dictating, and not always wisely, the design of even the fabrics, the architect swept out muddy frivolities and replaced them with body-warm colors of coral brick, sand plaster, natural oak, and raw linen. Furniture became honest, perhaps too harsh and militant, but antiseptic by contrast. Light fixtures were first rationalized into geometric patterns, then built right into the fabric of the house. Whole walls disappeared and rooms ran together, until a respectable person could scarcely say where indoors stopped and outdoors began. A fresh wind blew through American houses, and forty years later the dust has not yet died down. Wright's purpose, his whole palette and skill, is to deepen and enrich the esthetic experience of the individual. It is remarkable that so much has been said about the angularity and harshness of his houses; so little about their sensuality, their direct and immediate appeal to the senses (Figs. 145, 147).

Wright's professional career — at least until after his return from Japan — was a paradox. It was a constant struggle with the Blimps and the Plushbottoms: he never won, but he never lost. Just when the latest Wrightian eccentricity had been safely interred at some professional dinner, Wright reappeared with a new commission or another project with which to startle his colleagues and intrigue the literate public. Contrariwise, by some tragic perversity, his enemies were able repeatedly to use his personal life as a weapon against him. His separation from his first wife, in a day when divorces were *outré*; the murder of his second wife by a crazed servant; his bankruptcy — none of these strengthened his position with boards of directors, school committees, and municipal councils upon whose good will the architect must largely depend.

Frank Lloyd Wright's influence upon American building design has been immense, incalculable; for that reason it is also hard to assess. In his buildings, it has been generally progressive. The whole average level of our architecture, especially our domestic architecture, is incomparably higher than it would have been had Wright not lived. In his writing, lectures, and teaching — all of it voluminous — his influence has not always been so salutary. His not infrequent excursions into economic and social theory leave much to be desired. Throughout much of them there runs a curiously anti-scientific attitude which is in sharp contrast to his quick and intelligent appreciation of specific technical and scientific advance. His rabid individualism, fed by whole decades of criticism and now buttressed with neo-Whitmanesque generalities, leads him sometimes into absurd positions. His 'Project for Broad Acres Town' (1935) is an instance — a petit-bourgeois Utopia, Hilaire Belloc in steel-and-stucco, agrarianism with flat roofs and corner windows.

Part of Wright's immense vogue with the younger section of the profession springs from misconception of his radicalism. He was and has remained a sort of anarchist. His rampant individualism has often been mistaken for radicalism, and he himself has foxily (and quite safely) exploited this to his own advantage. But one has only to examine his clients to realize that his work has always been for the rich and mighty — a Pittsburgh merchandising magnate, a Middle-West floor-polish king, a fabulously wealthy California eccentric. He has never displayed much interest in society at large and perhaps does not intend that his social theories are to be taken too seriously. He is apt to advance fallacious arguments and then defend them — as he did upon one occasion — by holding that 'this is a case where the Truth supersedes the facts.' Yet these divagations should not be overemphasized. In a long and active life, Wright's personal courage has often carried him into dangerous waters where, like a convoy dodging torpedoes, a zigzag course was essential to survival. With a tenacity rare among mortals, Wright has clung to his own objectives and — whatever their shortcomings — they have made him our country's greatest architect.

The Wasteland

AT FIRST GLANCE, the period from 1900 to 1933 appears to be an esthetic wasteland: and a closer scrutiny of the individual buildings of the period does little to correct that first impression. Those structures which were hailed as the landmarks of the time — the Woolworth Tower, the San Francisco Exposition, the Mizner story-book houses in Florida, the *Chicago Tribune's* Gothic extravaganza, the Triangle in Washington: they all leave today's critic unimpressed. These buildings are so colorless and without significance, so magnificently sterile, as to leave one nonplussed. There may have been a certain bleak majesty in the scale of the skylines which were rising all over America. And there was a spurious romance to the suburbs of the wealthy in their shadow (Figs. 141–43). People with taste were trapped like flies in honey in the mellow compositions of Mellor, Meigs and Howe, in Philadelphia; they worshiped in such steel-and-plaster vaults as the Riverside Church afforded; they celebrated the spread of culture in the towering pile of the Chicago Civic Opera.

But the buildings which today show any recognition of reality, any creative dissatisfaction with the academic flood — these

could be counted on a single hand. Wright played Dreiser to
the architectural profession; and, like *Sister Carrie*, his houses
were long in being recognized and acclaimed. Beneath all this
froth there was, of course, an enormous quantitative expansion
in the building field. It had taken whole decades for the skyscraper to develop in the hands of Root and Sullivan. But now
it sprang up in full bloom across the land, changed hardly a jot
or a tittle from the Wainwright Building in St. Louis. Civic
centers in the cold gray stamp of dead Romans appeared at
hardly more than the press of a button. Apartments, factories,
schools, and churches — never had a people built so many in so
short a time. However badly planned and atrociously orna-
mented, they were for the most part remarkably well-built,
well-heated, and well-plumbed.

This was the great period of rationalization in American
building technology; its importance must not be underestimated.
It is one thing to build a single thirty-story skyscraper in a big
city. It is quite another to be able to reproduce them at will
across the land. This required the raising of the *entire average
level* of the building field. The real impact upon American life
of such developments as the elevator came not with Otis's
demonstration at the New York Fair in 1853, but rather with
the wide appearance of multi-storied buildings at the turn of
the century. As early as 1836, Tredgold's treatise established
the basis for steam heating: yet almost two-thirds of a century
passed before small-town heating-and-plumbing men were able
to put them into widespread use. None of the brilliant experimental work of Volta, Davy, and Franklin could mean much
to the man in the street until Edison, in the seventies, had perfected the incandescent bulb and the central generating plant.

So it was in every section of the building field. A century of
slow handicraft accretion gave way suddenly, like a log jam, to
the full flood of industrialized mass production. For three decades or more — from around 1900 to 1930 — the building field
was characterized by quantitative advance along well-established
lines of endeavor. It was perhaps a necessary gestation period,
during which the skin of hopelessly archaic esthetic formulas
were stretched to the bursting point. No building was too tall

for a Classic colonnade, no gymnasium too bulky for 'Collegiate Gothic,' no house too small for false Elizabethan timberwork.

New Avenues of Advance

HOWEVER STERILE the architecture of the period, esthetically and technically, there was a whole series of developments in allied fields of city planning, parks, and housing which were pregnant with possibilities. When Frederick Law Olmsted completed New York City's Central Park in the sixties, he ushered in a whole movement. The project created a genuine sensation. There was nothing in the country which could approach it in scale, imagination, or competence (Fig. 79). Other cities began to imitate it, even to the extent of employing Mr. Olmsted as designer. His work was the substructure to the subsequent City Beautiful movement, which had its specific architectural origins in the landscaped vistas of the Columbian Exposition. Largely an upper-class expression of civic consciousness, it gained further impetus from the rediscovery of L'Enfant's plan for Washington and the publication in 1902 of the report of the McMillan Commission for the reconstruction of the capital city. These drawings, envisioning long, empty avenues of carefully scaled elms backed by Classic façades, introduced to city councils all over the nation totally new concepts of order and civic majesty.

There was a lot of Baron Haussmann and precious little democracy in these vast geometries of befountained plazas and intersecting boulevards. Light, air, and foliage were concentrated around hypothetical water-gates and imaginary civic centers, never around housing or schools. Few of these schemes had any relation to the basic needs of the community. They all wore the obvious air of being schemes to deceive visiting notables, like the elaborate screens allegedly put up along the journeys of Catherine the Great, to hide the actual wretchedness and confusion of the land behind.

Yet they played a vastly important rôle in introducing the concept of *planned* reconstruction into the popular mind. However pompous and autocratic the solutions, they were at least admissions that real problems did exist, and that local governments did have the power to exercise some sort of control over the urban environment. Moreover, as the movement matured, it involved many well-intentioned souls who were forced by the struggle itself to realize that the problem was much more than one of simple face-lifting. The movement was also to gain important accretions from the ranks of the social and welfare workers, who were increasingly aware of the relation between the physical environment and crime, delinquency and ill-health. Their insistence upon such factors had a salutary effect upon the movement as a whole, and playgrounds, schools, and clinics began to appear alongside ornamental drinking fountains and statues of Spanish War dead.

But such movements were actually peripheral to the central fact — the crisis of the city itself. Unparalleled expansion during the last half of the nineteenth century had doubled and quadrupled the size of the older cities and produced dozens of new ones. 'Rapid transit' — trolley, subway, elevated and steam commuter trains — had made this expansion possible. Horse-drawn vehicles had merely supplemented the transportation network — filled the interstices, as it were. Essentially radial, this pattern was relatively stable because of the very nature of rail and roadbed. It was almost indefinitely expansible but in relatively fixed directions.

It remained for the automobile, in three short decades, to reduce this already inadequate pattern to a shambles of confusion. The motor car proved a disastrously flexible means for moving people, ideas, and things around the surface of the earth. It brought fantastic increases in vehicular traffic into the streets — traffic which had been hitherto tightly channelized into steel rails. In this way it profoundly altered the character and function of the street; on a city-wide scale, it made obsolete the entire street system.

A contradiction appeared. While the city as a whole continued to expand by centripetal attraction, the population within the city was flung, as though by centrifugal force, to a constantly expanding perimeter. Like cream in a separator, the wealthy and the middle class were flung to suburbs ever more distant from the center; and the rest of the population, in strict accordance with American housing tradition, moved into the backwash of their discarded homes. The automobile was a basic factor in all of this and left in its wake an urban turmoil of social, political, and economic problems. Land values, traditionally graded upward toward transportation and downward from the center out, had to be adjusted to a means of transportation which was *everywhere*. Values rose to preposterous levels at the center and along the expanding rim, while dooming the intervening 'blighted' areas to decay. Such a condition naturally played ducks and drakes with any rational pattern of land use. A given block in the path of urban expansion could easily be open farmland, stylish suburb, respectable boarding-house, and unregenerate slum — all in the span of a decade or two. It imposed increasing burdens on the whole fabric of municipal government — sanitation, police and fire protection, utilities, schools. The fabric would scarcely be complete before the tax income would begin to drop below operating costs, and the municipality would be faced with the task of supplying the same services to a whole new ring of suburbs.

Such a state of affairs penalized everyone in the community, even if in varying degrees. Naturally the waste was most readily expressed in dollars and cents; and the landowners were among the first to agitate for relief. The city councils, always responsive to the real-estate interests, began to adopt the technique of zoning as a means of controlling urban growth. There were two aspects to zoning. One was directed at maintaining some minimum standard of light and air in congested areas and among tall buildings. The other was directed at control of land use, so that an area's property values, based upon one type of use, would not be destroyed by invasion of another. Zoning had its limitations, chief of which was its essentially static intention to stabilize property values; but as it came to be integrated with the city plan it revealed other possibilities. It was directly responsible for the spectacular 'set-back' design of modern skyscrapers. More important in the long run was its tendency to establish certain minimal standards in terms of light, air, space. The effect of zoning upon housing, schools, and office buildings was in general progressive.

But external relationships *between* buildings are intimately related to spatial relationships *inside* the individual building. What was gained by pushing buildings back from street and property lines if there were to be rooms inside the building which had no access to outside light and air? What good were public sanitation systems if individual landlords were to be allowed to keep privy and pump? How could the fire departments, even with their newly motorized equipment, ever overtake the threat of spawning fire-traps?

Another whole area of social control was involved here, an area as controversial as socialized medicine today. For it clearly implied subordination of the individual's right (to do as he pleased with what he owned) to the well-being of the majority. Disastrous fires and epidemics served constantly to emphasize the necessity for such control. Gradually building laws and ordinances were passed, building inspection departments established. These were both bitterly contested and openly flouted — even though, for the most part, these controls acknowledged the *status quo* in existing structures and applied only to new construction and remodeling. Buildings erected prior to the laws would have to be obsolete, literally unfit for human habitation, before the police powers of the city government could intervene in the public's defense. There were thus great gaps in the control, whole sections of the city where physical as well as technological obsolescence ran its full course. Nevertheless, the building laws became an important and effective part of the control apparatus.

Aside from its impact upon the whole structure of the city, the automobile led to the development of a series of specialized building types, traffic forms, and recreational areas. This evolution was rapid. A short thirty years separated the county pike from the great four-lane, crossing-free, landscaped state highway; the old livery stable from the multiple-story garage;

the general store from the suburban shopping center. Since Americans have from the start regarded the automobile as a prime source of entertainment and recreation, it is not surprising to find that, as the highway approached its present form, beauty as well as speed and comfort came to be considered legitimate criteria in highway design. Many of the highways were built to provide access to recreational areas, and it was not long before the highway itself began to merge with the park to which it led. The concept of the parkway appeared. The metropolitan area of New York may be said to have pioneered this type in the nineteen-twenties in the Bronx River Parkway and the magnificent Jones Beach development on Long Island. Here a whole system of new and existing recreational areas were linked by parkways into a homogeneous unit. A motorist could theoretically drive for days amidst their landscaped splendor. In design these new traffic forms provide an interesting contrast to the earlier boulevards and plazas of the City Beautiful era. The former were static, designed so much more to be looked at than to be used that a moving pedestrian or a fallen leaf would have destroyed their composition. The new park systems, on the other hand, provided for all sorts of active and passive recreation. They were as beneficial to the communities through which they passed as to the motorist who passed through them. As the range and speed of the automobile increased, the designers showed increasing ability and confidence in a new and rapidly evolving field, until it could be safely said that some of the best architectural and landscape design in the nation lay in its park-and-highway system.

The Housing Crisis Is Discovered

WITH THE ENTRY of America into the First World War the housing problem was sharply raised on a national scale. The issue, in fact, was not new. As we have seen, the need for adequate housing for the industrial worker had been posed by the early New England textile factories. It had grown increasingly acute as the nineteenth century closed — not only for industrial workers but for all city dwellers. Thus there was already the beginnings of a housing movement. In addition to the growing awareness of the labor movement, there was an increasing body of professionals — social workers, municipal authorities, architects — who saw the urgency of the problem. With the war, the issue could no longer be dismissed as socialistic nonsense. In the Atlantic seaboard cities, housing conditions soon became an open scandal. The influx of workers into the war industries proved the inability of private enterprise to provide healthful housing at reasonable rates.

The crisis did not catch American architects wholly unprepared. English experience in housing and town planning, also accelerated by the war, had already attracted some attention on this side of the Atlantic. Sir Ebenezer Howard had launched his first Garden City at Welwyn. Although the Garden City was primarily a British solution to the problem of dormitory towns, there was much in the physical planning that was applicable to any community. The emphasis upon open spaces, individual gardens, large blocks closed to vehicular traffic, appealed especially to American designers, caught in the sterile checkerboards of real estate expansion. A small but tenacious and eloquent group of town planners and architects — among them the elder Henry Wright, Clarence Stein, Frederick Biggers — finally succeeded in getting the government to undertake housing in some of the shipbuilding cities. In this effort they were mightily aided by Charles Harris Whitaker, then editor of the *Journal* of the American Institute of Architects. To the manifest necessity of providing decent housing for the war workers, Whitaker added the weight of his own fiery pen and the writings of a whole circle of more experienced European housers.

The total number of housing units built by the two federal agencies was not impressive, and the abrupt end of the war laid both agencies open to the murderous fire of the vested interests. The agencies soon expired, the incompleted projects knocked down on the auction block, and the housers back on their own. But a beginning of inestimable importance had been made. Housing had at last been raised to the level of a permanent national issue, like the tariff or the sales tax. The architectural profession had been forced to accept housing as a legitimate part of its responsibility. The housing movement, in fact, was destined to become a veritable school for a whole generation of architects. For here, more than in any other building type, the architect was brought face to face with the basic social and economic forces at work beneath the surface of American building. It was not a pleasant picture; and the next decade was to furnish precious few examples of large-scale, low-cost housing. Wright and Stein were able to carry through their middle-class project at Sunnyside, Long Island, and their even more famous development of Radburn, New Jersey — 'Town for the Motor Age.' The Amalgamated Clothing Workers erected an apartment-house project in New York, the Rosenwalds subsidized a project for Negroes in Chicago. There was little else. But these few concrete examples were important out of all proportion to their size. They were widely published, criticized, admired. They had the salutary effect of shifting the architect's attention from esthetic abstractions to social reality. From the end of the First World War to the beginning of the Second, there was scarcely an architect who would not be to some extent involved in the housing movement — and better and wiser for it.

New Prototypes at Chicago

THESE, THEN, were the convergent movements which enclosed the architects of the first three decades of this century — beautification, zoning, planning, building laws, traffic control, housing. They were external to the individual building, and to many an architect of the period they appeared irrelevant. Actually, they constituted the reference frame for his work, without which it would be unintelligible. And the pressure of these movements upon building design was remorseless even if subterranean. Recognition of the social character of all building was slow to develop, but it had the force of fact behind it. And as this concept advanced, it had to be expressed in formal terms — that is, it had to advance its own esthetic standards.

There is irony and poetic justice in the fact that it fell to

Chicago's lot to unfurl these standards to the nation — for as far as the layman was concerned, the 1933 Century of Progress was the first statement of modern architecture in this country. The Paris Exposition of 1925 had had some small (and rather unfortunate) effects on interior *décor* and shop-front design in America. But the Paris show had really little relation to those architectural theories which were already well developed in Holland, Germany, and the Scandinavian countries; or to the work of Frank Lloyd Wright which was its American parallel. Some of this modern European work began to appear in American magazines. Some of the architects came to this country to live or to lecture. American architects, summering in Europe, began to see the work of Dudok, Gropius, Aalto. Small and tenuous as was this trans-Atlantic traffic, it served to galvanize into activity a section of younger American architects who were already reeling under the impact of the depression. For all these forces in gestation, the Century of Progress served as a catalytic agent.

One must be careful not to exaggerate the importance of those flat roofs and corner windows on the Lake Shore at Chicago. They were mostly pallid and superficial, representing a curious cross between the sophisticated International style and Yankee sanity, with its mechanical, money-saving elimination of ornament. They were not masterpieces; but neither was *Uncle Tom's Cabin*. Historical necessity is not always perfectly expressed, and the buildings at Chicago became the very war-cry of progress. Against them the Tory stylists threw the full weight of their invective. They were 'too harsh,' 'inhuman,' 'communistic,' 'barn-like,' 'angular,' 'machines for living.' In their offensive, the Classicists had the tacit support of most architectural advertising, of the real-estate and mortgage interests, of public taste itself. Their most dangerous secret weapon was the Rockefeller restoration of Colonial Williamsburg. Whatever the intentions of its founders, this project has done more to stultify and corrupt American taste than any single event in our history, the Columbian Exposition possibly excepted.

Yet life itself confined this battle to a very narrow salient — upper-class residential work, city halls, and churches. The decisive battle had been fought and won in commercial and industrial buildings. Here esthetic dogmas were quite properly subordinate to practical considerations; and here the modern architect had the full weight of fact on his side. Here and there the boards of directors who paid the bills might cling to certain esthetic prejudices. In many a plant there would be an almost comic contrast between workshop and directors' room. In the plant itself there was that sort of beauty which only a Sheeler or a Bourke-White could glorify — forms so simple and direct as to be almost abstractions, movement so immense and dramatic as to defy any medium save the camera. In the head offices one still saw Gothic paneling, William and Mary chairs, elk heads, and hunting horns. But even this was a dwindling circle, clouded by unfavorable connotations. As the nineteen-thirties closed, even the weight of propaganda shifted to the side of the modern school. The sleek, glass-and-chromium laboratory became the architectural symbol of progress.

CHAPTER EIGHT

1933–1945: American Building at the Crossroads

By THE TIME of the second Chicago Fair in 1933, the crisis in American building had become chronic. Every phase of the field was involved: concept, architect, design, and actual building. The crisis had been maturing throughout the three-quarters of a century which had elapsed since the Civil War and had been marked throughout by this curious fact: though building had been subject to many invasions by science, it had never been conquered by science. Even in the forepart of the current century, when the whole field had been rocking under the impact of technological advance and scientific discovery, building had managed somehow to preserve its profoundly anti-scientific conceptual basis. It had managed to absorb the elevator, the steel skeleton, the electric power line, without really absorbing the concepts, the philosophies, and the disciplines which made these developments possible.

Indeed, as often as not of late years, the building field has displayed an actual hostility toward science and technology, and this tendency has become very sharp among — of all people — a section of the architects themselves. In increasing numbers, these men had seen the main task of building handed over to the engineers. The struggle to meet the needs of their society had proved too great for their tender spirits, and for solace they had turned increasingly to the past. These were the men who, like the critic A. Kingsley Porter, could see only that 'good architecture came to a sudden end in America about the year

143

1850. . . . It was the machine which crushed out handiwork, it was the machine which killed beauty.'[1]

Not only architecture but human nature itself had changed for the worse. Thus the successful architect, Thomas Hastings, saw the medieval mason as a man who 'praised God with every chisel stroke . . . for him work was worship; and his life was one continuous psalm of praise. . . . Now a Gothic church is built by laborers whose one interest is to increase their wages and diminish their working hours.'[2]

There were many of scholarly temperament who accepted this analysis, but there were other conservatives who, while admitting that things were bad, still were unwilling to say that all was lost. Typical of this sort of reaction to the inexorable pressure of science and technology upon American building was the analysis of William Adams Delano. He had come to the conclusion that 'building is a business. Architecture is an art . . . to draw a distinction between building and architecture is [however] not easy, it is to be felt rather than described.'[3]

Here Mr. Delano, senior member of one of the country's most fashionable firms, was trying to draw a charmed circle of 'art' around a certain portion of building — the very top — in order to protect it from the ravages of historic fact. Unfortunately, Mr. Delano's line of exemption (which he admitted was to be felt rather than described) did not in fact exist. The contradictions raised by Mr. Porter's machine cut across the whole fabric of American building, the clubs of the rich as well as the slums of the poor.

There was, finally, that bedrock of Tory opinion which blindly and stubbornly refused to admit even the possibility that pre-industrial concepts of plan and façade were not entirely adequate to twentieth-century needs. This school was typified by John Russell Pope, whose last two commissions — the Jefferson Memorial and the National Gallery of Art in Washington — are a perfect reflection of this concept. The very existence of such structures, it might be added, are sufficient proof that Mr.

[1] Arthur Kingsley Porter, *Beyond Architecture* (Boston: Marshal Jones, 1918), p. 132.
[2] Scammon Lectures, Chicago Institute of Art, 1915.
[3] *New York Times Magazine* (April 21, 1940), p. 9.

Pope moved in no vacuum, but was rather a spokesman for a powerful laity whose concepts he accurately reflected.

Fortunately for the reputation of American building designers, there was another and less tarnished side to the coin. For architecture had scarcely achieved its modern status as an independent profession in the mid-seventies when voices within it began to be raised in defense of science and technology, and demands made that architectural concepts be forced into consonance with that fact. It was, of course, an immensely difficult problem, then as now, for the full implications of the Industrial Revolution were not apparent. Thus, in different men, according to their temperament and experience, the issue was expressed in different forms and analyzed at different levels.

Louis Sullivan, who had seemed to his contemporaries so near to formulating an effective concept, had seen it as both a political and an esthetic imperative. A democratic way of life would produce a democratic architecture; satisfactory function would produce satisfactory form. His thunderous eloquence was echoed in the architectural press by men like Hamlin and Schuyler. For Frank Lloyd Wright the issue had been at once esthetic and philosophical — he wanted organic unity restored to both architecture and life. To men like the elder Henry Wright the issue seemed largely technical and the solution physical — one had only to organize the land intelligently. Meanwhile, to his contemporary, Charles Harris Whitaker, a decent democratic architecture was an ethical if not a moral necessity.[1] Lewis Mumford had tried to express the concept in terms of man's right to mental and physical well-being. Technicians like Buckminster Fuller and prefabricators like Corwin Willson were baldly mechanistic — the problem of twentieth-century building was simply one of applying modern technique. A house was, as Le Corbusier had so famously put it, merely a machine in which one lived. Around such spokesmen as these, there had grown up the whole generation of today's social housers, planners, and economists. For them, the issue was

[1] A concept stirringly expressed in his *Rameses to Rockefeller*. New York: The Viking Press, 1934.

variously seen as one of clearing our slums, decentralizing our
cities, or lowering our building costs.

These were all attempts, by the building professionals themselves, to analyze the crisis, to formulate new concepts which
would enable them to extricate building from the slough into
which it was slipping. None of them was complete, yet none
of them was fallacious; and taken together, they did constitute
the basis for the genuine integration of building with science
and technology. Together, they were a many-faceted formula
for the resolution of the cruel dichotomy between technique
and esthetic, between bountiful promise and poverty-stricken
reality. Such concepts had been seventy years agrowing, but it
was within the twelve years between Franklin Roosevelt's inauguration and his death at the close of the Second World War
that they matured. For the building designer, the period was
indeed a stern if fruitful school. It opened with as many as
ninety per cent of all architects and engineers unemployed. It
closed with fully that percentage either in the armed services or
exclusively employed in military construction. The years between had seen our society faced with problems of unprecedented
scale and complexity — problems which involved the architect
in every level and sphere of his existence. It was in such an
atmosphere that these new concepts of the function of building
spread, deepened, intertwined, to emerge finally as the recognizable body of theory and practice known today as modern
architecture. If the period produced more ideas than buildings,
both were pregnant with change; if the buildings of the thirties
were statistically less important than those of the twenties, they
were nonetheless far more significant. For the concept which
they expressed was catalytic — namely, that the function of
American building must be the maintenance of those optimal
environmental conditions essential to the health and happiness
of the individual and to the peaceful and efficient development
of American society.

By the end of the Second World War, this ferment of architectural opinion had produced what was actually a new theoretical basis of architecture. The product of many minds, it was
necessarily more difficult to summarize; but precisely because it

represented an integration of so many points of view, it was at once more penetrating and more comprehensive than any of its predecessors. Insofar as any individual observer can synthesize a philosophy which resides in the work and minds of so many living men, the following is a synopsis of the theoretical structure of contemporary architecture.

Building Regulates the Body's Transactions

As CONTINUOUSLY as a fish in water, man moves in his own special environment, the limits of which appear to be fixed in both a temporal and a spatial sense. But unlike the fish, man acts upon his environment as well as being acted upon by it. Conscious attempts at manipulation of this environment are at least as old as man himself; and the net result of such attempts has been to give modern man a much wider knowledge of, and greater control over, it than ever before. It lies neither within the scope of this study nor the ability of its author to delineate more than a small sector of this complex relationship between man and his natural environment. However, as a result of the accumulating knowledge of the natural world, it is now both possible and necessary for us to understand certain aspects of this relationship, because building is one of the most common instruments in use to modify it.

To begin with, our environment is itself of a composite structure, formed of many distinct, coexistent, yet interacting, elements which are actually complete environments in themselves. We are here concerned with only a portion of them — those which act directly and immediately upon the human body, and which can be directly and immediately modified by building:

The atmospheric,
thermal,
luminous,
sonic,
spatial,
animate.

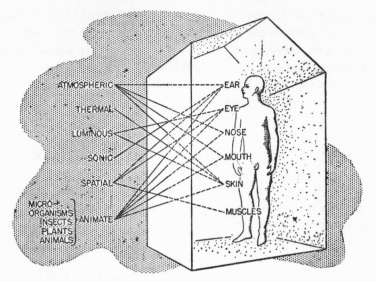

Modern building acts as a selective filter which takes the load
of the natural environments off man's body and thus frees his
energies for social productivity.

These environments are paralleled by a corresponding specialization of function in the body which, in a sense, can be compared
to a network of highways designed to handle the two-way but
highly specialized traffic between the body and the outside.
These 'highways' are likewise distinct, coexistent yet inter-
dependent. Thus, the respiratory system handles the essential
commerce between the body and its atmospheric environment
— bringing in the necessary oxygen, carrying out waste carbon
dioxide, and so forth; the skin's main task is to maintain a
'balance of trade' between the body and its thermal environment;
the ear's job is to filter the sonic environment; and so on. This
is naturally an oversimplification, for, with the marvelous complexity of the body, each of these systems has multiple functions.
Thus, the respiratory system provides our sense of smell, the
skin protects the body against attack from external forces, the
ear serves also as a balancing mechanism. But this does not
alter the basic principle involved.

The function of all these systems is to provide a *constant*

equilibrium within the body by controlling the relationship between the body's external and internal environments.   As
Pavlov, the famous Russian physiologist, expressed it: 'The
animal organism as a system exists in surrounding nature only
by means of a constant balancing [between] this system and its
environment.' By means of this balancing, the body maintains
a private internal environment whose most extraordinary feature
is its constancy.   Indeed, according to the late Doctor Walter
B. Cannon, of Harvard's Medical School:

> So characteristic is this constancy, and so peculiar are the proc-
> esses which maintain it, that it has been given a special name,
> *homeostasis* . . . [for example] there is the steadiness of our body
> temperature, a trait we share with most other mammals and with
> birds. The development of nearly thermostable state in higher
> vertebrates should be regarded as one of the most valuable
> advances in biological evolution.[1]

But as they exist in nature, the natural external environments
are not always conducive to such constancy — that is, they
fluctuate from partially friendly to being actually hostile to the
human body. Fortunately, the body is designed to accommodate
itself to fairly wide fluctuations. Its limits of accommodation
are, however, fixed; and above or below them collapse and even
death ensue. Thus, within certain limits the skin can speed up
or slow down the transfer of heat from the body to its thermal
environment — *but only within the over-all limits established by the
body as a whole;* and all the other highway systems operate under
similar limitations.

Faced with these two and often contradictory necessities, man
had to evolve external instruments for regulating the relationship
between his body's relatively constant environmental requirements and the fluctuations of an inconstant Nature. Building
and clothing are the principal instruments so evolved. Physiologically, their function is similar — they are both designed to
take the load of the natural environment off the human body.
(That they do it so imperfectly today is another question which

---

[1] *Science and Man*, edited by Ruth Nanda Aushen (New York: Harcourt, Brace
and Company, 1942), p. 290.

will be later dealt with at length.)   In some isolated examples, the difference between building and clothing practically disappears.   Thus, the electrically heated flying suit of the stratospheric aviator enables his body to maintain its thermal equilibrium quite as well as would a heated cabin, while the diving suit of the diver is actually a highly specialized sort of building. But by and large, the function of clothing is to protect the individual organism from the natural environment, while that of building is to protect an entire social operation or process. This is merely a complicated way of saying that heavy clothing might protect the individual factory worker in sub-zero weather, but so restrict his motions as to render him socially useless.   But even further, the manufacturing process itself requires a specific thermal environment without which it would operate at a much lower level of productivity.   We can, then, in all justice, paraphrase Doctor Cannon: *The development of a nearly thermo-stable state in our best buildings should be regarded as one of the most valuable advances in the evolution of building.*

The Spectrum of Health

THE LAYMAN must, therefore, judge building as he would any other tool — by its performance; and the criterion for judging building performance must necessarily be *health*.   Does the building regulate the commerce between his body and its natural environment in such a way as to provide for his optimum health? And, from the standpoint of society as a whole, do its buildings provide that precise control of environment which will guarantee maximum productivity to all its operations and processes?

As a medical term, health implies a state of normality which is extremely difficult of exact definition.   Here we are not confronted by two states of being — healthfulness and unhealthfulness — with a sharp line clearly dividing the two.   Rather we face a sort of spectrum which progresses, by slow and often imperceptible degrees, from health, through discomfort, disease, and disablement, to end in death.   For the individual, the line between any two of these stages is by no means always clear, nor is progression through them necessarily even or direct. Thus, for the blitz victims the entire progression from perfect health to extinction was telescoped into a split second; for the victim of infantile paralysis, the path may be from health to disablement in a few days, followed by a gradual return to a state of discomfort; while the normal person may enjoy six decades of perfect health with a gradual decline at the end.

Nonetheless, for our purposes, this may be described as a characteristic spectrum through which we all pass on our journey from the cradle to the grave. The object of medical and public-health endeavor is, therefore, to extend the period of health over as long a time and broad a base as possible by systematically isolating and eliminating all those factors which contribute to discomfort, disease, and disablement. Here we enter an extraordinarily complex field, of which I am prepared to discuss only one aspect: the rôle of building in relation to health.

The way in which buildings affect our health is best exemplified in that type with which all consumers are most familiar: the home. In addition to being most familiar, it so happens that the home is also most dangerous. The truism that 'home is the safest place' is nowadays cracking under an accumulating load of evidence to the contrary. Accidents in the home annually kill about 32,000 persons — a third of all accidental deaths, almost as many as are killed in automobile accidents, and more than twice as many as are killed in industry. In addition to these accidental deaths, approximately 3,000,000 persons are annually injured in home accidents — about 375,000 of them suffering some permanent disability. Expressed in economic terms — wage loss, medical expenses — it is estimated that these accidents cost the nation $6,000,000,000; property losses in home fires (second most important cause of accidents) amounted to an additional $100,000,000.

'As a cause of death and disability,' says Doctor Donald B. Armstrong of the Metropolitan Life Insurance Company, 'the home accident problem may significantly be compared with some of the hitherto major diseases of mankind, many of which have yielded to scientific control.' Some idea of the epidemic proportions of the problem may be gathered from the fact that *home accidents are the eighth most important cause of death* — exceeded only by heart disease, cancer, cerebral hemorrhage, nephritis, pneumonia, tuberculosis, and motor accidents!

What is the cause of these appalling statistics? How can they be reduced? Their cause is overwhelmingly due to deficiencies in the building itself, not in the building consumers; their cure, therefore, is primarily one of redesign of the dwelling. Naturally, no home can be one hundred per cent accident-proof. The factor of human fallibility enters into the use of the house just as it does in that of a motor car, so that a certain degree of education must parallel an increased safety factor in the design. But, in a statistical sense, *the main burden of blame rests on the house, not the user*. This is clearly established by recent surveys which show that home accidents of a given type happen to people of a given age and sex, while occupied with given tasks, at given places in the house!

Falls, for example, are the source of over two-thirds of all serious injuries sustained by consumers of housing. At first glance, this might appear to be the most difficult thing of all to pin on the building itself; actually, it is the easiest. All buildings should be organized for optimum speed, ease, and safety of movement. This movement usually resolves itself into two characteristic patterns — people moving toward things or things moving toward people. In the case of the house, movement is almost exclusively of the former type, while in the factory, the opposite is largely true. The housewife who prepares, assembles, and serves a meal usually has to move around the kitchen, up to the pantry shelf, into the dining-room, down to the basement. Unlike the industrial worker, few time-and-motion studies have been made of her at work. Most of her equipment consists of instruments — beds, chairs, dishes — whose essential design has remained unchanged for centuries; all of it is poorly organized with reference to her physical and psychical needs; and usually it is worn out. No wonder, then, that she falls from a bad ladder, trying to get an archaic plate from a shelf which should never have been there in the first place. No wonder children slip on stairs whose pitch is too steep, surfaces too slippery, rails too high — with none of it adequately lighted. No wonder, either, that old people fall in climbing out of a bathtub, after having tried to get cleaner in water which got progressively dirtier.

Much the same thing holds for the burns, cuts, poisonings, and other accidental injuries that occur in the home. Sufficient investigation of the causal relations will reveal that the vast majority of burns could be prevented by fireproof construction and by heating and cooking units designed to minimize the possibility of burning the user; by knives stored out of the children's reach; by poisons in special locked and lighted compartments, and so on. As we shall later see, and in more detail, the causes of such accidents can be isolated, and in most cases removed, by redesign of the building.

Many danger points in our houses are unconsciously avoided without our being aware of the issue of safety *per se*; but many others remain for the same reasons. Accidents in the home are the result of characteristic movements and processes which require the closest scrutiny if they are to be reduced or eliminated. This does not always imply that the house is structurally bad. An interior stairway may be inherently dangerous because it is steep, slippery, badly lighted, and/or winding; but it may be none of these, and still be a source of accidents because the only telephone is at its bottom and the housewife is always in a hurry when running down to answer it. The first instance would imply redesign of the stair; the latter would indicate need for two telephones — one at the top and one at the bottom.

This problem arises in many forms throughout the building. Thus, there is the problem of collision with objects in a dark room — stumbling over furniture in the bedroom or over toys on the living-room floor. Both of these are statistically important sources of accidental injury. In the first case, the plan of the bedroom either does not make adequate provisions for the necessary furniture or the furniture is not suitably arranged in the room. In the second case, the children of the household should have either a room of their own or (at the minimum) storage space for their toys. A child cannot be taught to put away his toys unless he has some place in which to put them.

Not all areas of the house are equally dangerous, nor are different types of accidents evenly distributed through the house. Outside stairs and porches are over seven times as dangerous as the bathroom. This of itself constitutes impressive proof that accidents in the home are not due merely to 'human nature,' but to very specific factors which can be isolated and eliminated by scientific design. Where there's an accident there's a reason; and this reason may be partly due to what safety experts call 'unsafe conditions' and partly to 'unsafe practices.'

Reference to industrial experience sheds new light on this situation. Here scientific research has yielded many control and preventive measures which resulted in a sixty-nine-per-cent reduction in accident frequency and a fifty-per-cent reduction in accident severity in the period from 1926 to 1939 inclusive. In such industrial safety work, three factors are investigated: the condition of the building itself; the processes carried on in the building; and the practice of the workers. The same analysis must be applied to the home if we are to understand why it is so dangerous and how it may be made safer. Take the kitchen, for instance — the most dangerous single area in the house. What characteristic processes are carried on here? To what extent can redesign of the room itself increase its safety (omission of live storage space above eye-level, inclusion of electric dishwasher, and the like)? To what extent can the processes themselves be made safer (elimination of deep-fat frying or the washing of cutlery by hand)? And to what extent must the housewife herself learn safer practices (to cut bread away from the body, to keep explosive or poisonous chemicals locked out of children's reach, and so on)?

The only large-scale opportunity to apply this analysis to house design has fallen to the Federal Public Housing Authority. But the results indicate that an effective set of safety standards can achieve marked reductions in accident frequencies. The general home accident rate of 4.65 per thousand has been lowered in USHA projects to 1.85 per thousand — that is, by sixty-one per cent. Subsequent investigations have shown that further changes in design would result in a further reduction in accidents of thirty-one per cent, and in fires of fifty-nine per cent.

Whether accidents result from poor building design or human frailty, it is thus amply clear that they are entirely susceptible to scientific analysis and prevention. But for American buildings to be really safe, more than accident-proof design is necessary. 'Ordinary care in eliminating physical hazards in buildings is not adequate,' the New York Safety Council has said. 'Extraordinary care, constant inspection, prompt maintenance and repair are required to assure the minimum . . . of personal injuries.'

Building: Source of Illness and Disease

THE FOREGOING applies only to one type of damage to the health of the building consumer — the accident. There is yet another (and perhaps even more important) one to consider: the contribution of buildings to illness and disease. Current practice makes a sharper distinction between accident and disease in relation to building use than the facts seem to warrant. Both constitute an impairment of health, and both may be wholly or partially traced to deficiencies in the building. Obviously, the sequence of cause and effect is more apparent in the case of a sudden fall down a stair (an accident) than an obscure and imperceptibly worsening case of allergy from the dust-laden air of a felt factory (disease). But the precise difference between the two is likely to be more important to the medical statistician than to the building consumer, who is merely interested in preserving his health against both forms of attack.

However, it is a difficult and risky business to try to plot the causal relations between deficient buildings and disease. As a study by the United States Public Health Service puts it:

> The existence of excessive rates of sickness and mortality in the slums or overcrowded districts of cities is an accepted fact, but the extent to which poor housing *per se* is responsible for these differences is very difficult to ascertain because of the interaction of many economic and sociological factors.[1]

[1] Britten, Brown and Altman, *Certain Characteristics of Urban Housing and Their Relation to Illness and Accident.* New York: American Public Health Association, 1941.

In other words, one must be careful not to attribute to deficient buildings those maladjustments, illnesses, and diseases which in fact are caused by deficiencies in the social order. Thus, the coincidence between tuberculosis and bad housing at one time led many housing specialists to conclude that slums were the *cause* of this social evil. Subsequent investigation has shown this to be incorrect: the fact is that both slums and tuberculosis are the *result* of poverty. No amount of clean, sunny interiors can cure starvation; nor can ample space in which to relax prevent the destructive tensions of unemployment, insecurity, and want. These are the products of our social environment, against which no building yet devised can offer any protection.

Nevertheless, there are many aspects of illness and disease which are demonstrably dependent upon bad building, and which can be demonstrably reduced by good building. In subsequent chapters, we shall see in more detail what these aspects are and how building can reduce or eliminate them. Here it will suffice to cite one example — the significant relationship between a group of digestive diseases (diarrhea, enteritis, colitis, typhoid and paratyphoid fevers) and the presence or absence of private indoor flush toilets. The Public Health Service found that the frequency of such digestive diseases in households without sanitary facilities was seventy per cent greater than in those with them! Any interpretation of such findings, the survey adds, must bear in mind that

> in households not meeting this standard (of indoor toilets) there will probably be concommitant deficiencies (especially, lack of screening and poor facilities for refrigeration of food) which may have an effect on the illness rate from this group of digestive diseases. . . . We are confronted with an expression (or standard) which tends to measure poor housing as a whole.[1]

In other words, buildings which do not provide adequate control of the animate environment (that is, prevent invasion by germs and insects) are not likely to provide the special thermal environments necessary for food preservation. Deficiencies in one direction usually imply deficiencies in others; the task of

[1] *Ibid.*, p. 178.

exactly tracing the relation of each to the maintenance of health only emphasizes the over-all importance of good building.

The Social Function of Building

ALTHOUGH POPULAR ATTENTION has usually been focused upon the columns, walls, and roofs of our buildings — in other words, upon their visible aspects — of much greater significance has been the space which they enclosed. For this relatively microscopic enclosed space has served as the base of man's operations, from which he has conquered the physical world. Within this minute space he laid his plans and sharpened his tools. With building he was able to exercise control over his natural environments. He could not stop the winter's gale; he could not heat the whole outdoors; nor could he kill all the tigers in Africa or the enemies around his door. All these interrupted — where they did not actually threaten — his work. He could only control them within limited areas by barriers which they could not penetrate.

Building is usually described as having the function of 'sheltering' or 'protecting' man against the elements. This is a negative statement of the case. Actually, building does much more. For it is not enough that man keep the natural environments out of his enclosed spaces; he must also replace them with synthetic ones better suited to his needs. Though his original motives might have been purely defensive, man's building long ago ceased to be a purely defensive weapon. Thus, when he heats the rudest hut against the cold, he does more than ward off the natural thermal environment. He simultaneously replaces it with a synthetic one, and the more advanced his equipment, the more complete the substitution. The crudest oil or latest mercury vapor lamp creates, not mere imitations of daylight, but synthetic luminous environments. And a soundproof broadcast studio today does much more than merely exclude the external sonic environment: it creates an entirely new one, designed to man's own specifications and having no precedent in nature.

As has been seen in previous chapters, the range and depth of this manipulation has steadily increased in American building. In World War II, it reached a climactic stage: how complete a control of all environmental factors was necessary to an industry which ultimately split the atom is graphically demonstrated by the late W. F. Austin's description of an airplane plant designed by his firm.

> Each precision part made in this plant . . . must conform to tolerances as exacting as any ever specified for the mass-production metal working industries. If the sun were to strike castings ready for machining, the expansion caused by the resulting heat would frequently be sufficient to render castings machined in this expanded state entirely useless. Then, too, the parts have to be protected against the danger of rusting which is sometimes caused by perspiration from a mere finger mark. In the face of these facts, and the need for highly efficient continuous operation . . . complete control of light, temperature and humidity seemed to offer the only solution.[1]

Historically, advance along these lines nearly always originated in the factory and had to fight its way into the building field proper. Moreover, in the context of nineteenth- and twentieth-century life, these advances were forced by fundamental economic pressures. It was the drive for increased productivity, not for employee health, which impelled the factory owner to install the first electric lights. Artificial refrigeration was developed to preserve Chicago beef, not to cool the brow of the fevered. And it was to facilitate the conquest of Charleston by the Union army, not to make night baseball possible, that the floodlight was perfected. The mill, the factory, the battleground — these were the crucibles of technological advance.

In general, advanced standards of environmental control are introduced into industry for one of two reasons — either because the process itself demands it or because it will raise the productivity of the workmen. Under these twin impulses, the industrial development of controls has been little short of extraordinary. The environments — thermal, atmospheric, luminous,

---

[1] 'Advanced Lighting Technique for Windowless Factories,' *Proceedings* of Illuminating Engineering Society Convention, Spring Lake, New Jersey, 1940.

sonic, and spatial — have been manipulated to almost any desired degree and in practically every direction. Testing chambers for motors can easily duplicate the coldest weather on
earth. The atmospheres of bakeries can be cleansed of microscopic wild-yeast spores so that the cultivated varieties can work
without competition, while enough silver dust can be reclaimed
from the air of a film factory to quickly pay for the necessary
equipment. The sonic environments obtaining in the laboratories of the electronics industry are quite without parallel in
either history or nature. In the great mass-production industries
of the country, mechanization has to all intents conquered space
— moving, lifting, carrying is done by the building itself instead
of the workman.

These techniques have begun to infiltrate architecture, usually
through the so-called service industries. Here, under intensely
competitive situations, the comfort of the customer is almost as
important as the goods he buys. Indeed, on a hot summer's
night, the neighborhood movie's real feature is often its refrigeration plant. Restaurants find that acoustical control is an important item on the bill of fare, transport advertises its soft lighting.
Thus, although its motives may not differ from those of straight
industrial applications, this section of building has served to
expose and dramatize another aspect of these environmental
controls: their deliberate application to problems of human
comfort.

The causal relation between building and accident, discomfort and disease, is today a generally accepted concept, however
complex the line of cause and effect may be and however much
of it remains to be explored in detail; and this in itself marks a
great advance over the architectural theory of even a few years
ago. Yet it remains merely the negative side of a much greater
discovery; for these techniques of environmental control promise
not merely the eradication of age-old deficiencies in building;
they also yield totally new concepts of human comfort, health,
and safety.

So it appeared to an increasing number of modern architects
during the stormy nineteen-thirties. They could not escape the

liberating effect of industrial practice upon building design. Yet as the decade closed they could not avoid the conclusion that these techniques did not yield the increased physical and mental well-being they seemed to promise. The contradiction was thorny and complex; and the remainder of this book is largely devoted to it. Let it here suffice to say that air-conditioning was found to be no substitute for democracy, sound control no panacea for economic insecurity.

The physics of light and air and sound we are well on the way toward mastering; but when it comes to control of the animate environment, matters are complicated by the fact that we ourselves are animals, exploiting not only all the rest of the kingdom but also other men. This fact introduces a dichotomy into our building, whereby standards of performance have usually been most advanced in factories (where control techniques effect economies in the production of goods or services) and most backward in houses (where such techniques could raise the health of the American people). Stated another way, the best building is generally found in those areas of most intensive competition — large-scale industry, big business, chain-store commerce. Where advanced design does not promise increased efficiency or economy, the general level of building is much lower, and improvement comes only to the degree that competition demands or that national or local legislation is enacted and enforced. And even in those areas where high standards do obtain, their very unevenness and exploitative application too often nullify the physiological benefit.

This is not to say, of course, that the application of these control techniques has always been mechanistically determined by the profit motive. Whatever its low points of urban and rural slum, the *average* technological level of American building is probably the highest in the world. And this is largely due to the participation of the public — the building consumers themselves — in the demand for better buildings. Significantly enough, this demand has nearly always been expressed in terms of 'health and safety.' Popular pressure for ever better schools has been a constant factor in our national history. Great plagues like those of New York in the eighteen-thirties made

political issues of inadequate sanitary facilities. Especially horrifying building failures like the Triangle Shirtwaist Fire served
to galvanize the public into action against the criminal negligence
of the owners. In such cases the issues were building deficiencies
which involved the welfare of the entire community, not merely
the owners or tenants of a particular building: the community
acted accordingly. But it must be admitted that, valid and
necessary as they are, such pressures have served merely to put
a floor under building performance. They established minima:
it was up to the building designer himself to establish optimal
standards of environmental control.

The Way to Measure Building Performance

AMONG OTHER THINGS, the discovery of the relationship between
building and health served to expose the complete inadequacy of
existing criteria for analyzing building performance. Most discussion of building has been always in primarily visual terms.
Consciously or unconsciously, explicitly or implicitly, judgments
based on vision have dominated architectural opinion: Have
you *seen* the new Jones house? What does it *look* like? It *seems*
somehow out of scale; it doesn't quite *express* its function.
Actually, of course, there was quite as much justification for
measuring buildings on any other sensory bases: Have you *heard*
the new Jones house? What does the kitchen *smell* like? How
do the stairs *feel*? Do the windows *get on your nerves*? Won't the
sink be *tiring* for the cook? The truth is that, though we are
trained to think otherwise, we experience building through all
our senses equally; our entire nervous and muscular system is
involved.

But the matter goes much deeper, for none of the senses are
very reliable in estimating a building's performance. How woe-
fully inadequate they are is amply testified to by the number of
persons who — despite the use of their senses — are annually
killed or injured in buildings (35,000 fatalities, 3,000,000 dis-
abilities — 375,000 of them in dwellings *alone* in 1945). The
nose is sharp enough to smell only the smoke from the actual

fire, not to detect the hidden defective wire which caused it. The eye can tell you if the column is perfectly proportioned, but it can't read the internal stress organization or estimate how near it is to collapse. The ear will accurately register more noise than the nerves can stand, while the sense of touch comes into play too late to save you from breaking your neck on a slippery floor.

There are, in addition, a host of situations which arise in the day-to-day use of all sorts of buildings which cannot be sensed at all: they have to be *understood*. Under such a head fall the accidents involving electric shock, spontaneous combustion, and explosions; hookworm, typhoid, and dysentery spread by bad or nonexistent sanitary systems; silicosis, asphyxiation, and allergy due to atmospheric pollution; fatigue due to bad lighting, ventilation, or acoustics. To measure accurately such factors, more than the rule-of-thumb techniques of the past are required. In the light of modern knowledge and in the face of modern building, it is no more possible to measure the performance of a building by the senses alone than it is to operate a bomber without instruments.

The corollary is obvious: it is no more possible for an architect to design a satisfactory building by traditional methods — a knowledge of Vignola and Williamsburg, a 'feeling for materials,' and a couple of handbooks on plumbing and heating — than it would be possible for the local tinsmith to design a modern plane. Thus, from both the standpoint of the user and that of the designer, health-protecting and health-extending building implies the fullest application of the scientific method, the widest use of technical resources. Recognition of this fact is the historical contribution of the moderns to architectural theory. It is to show what this concept in all its richness promises — and what in all its complexity it entails — that the remaining portions of this book are devoted.

CHAPTER NINE

Skeleton and Skin

ALTHOUGH ISOLATED BUILDINGS have, for many thousands of years and in all parts of the world, shown a superb and daring grasp of one or another aspect of structure, a scientific *theory* of structure has only been established in the last one hundred years. The gabled Parthenon, the soaring vaults of the Baths of Caracalla, the magnificence of Chartres and Rheims — all of these are the products of entire schools of design: each represents the most brilliant statement of a specific phase of structural theory based upon one specific set of objective conditions. They lack, however, the internal continuity and common denominator of scientific method. They represent accumulated knowledge and experience only within themselves. The Greeks were isolated from Egyptian technology. The Romans acquired only a portion of what the Greeks knew. The Gothic builders were largely ignorant of the magnificent engineering of the Romans. Renaissance men discarded all Gothic knowledge in favor of the resurrected Classic. And the Victorians borrowed from everybody without understanding any of it. The planful accumulation of structural knowledge, the systematic exploration and development of applied mechanics, the standardized testing of natural materials and the deliberate search for new synthetic ones — all of these essentials to a scientific theory of structure had to await the Industrial Revolution.

This historical process has been telescoped into three centuries of American building. Moreover, this process has been superimposed upon a rapidly growing and polyglot people, inheritors of many specialized building techniques; upon a country which was constantly meeting new climactic and geographic conditions; upon a nation which was for three hundred years always partly settled and partly wilderness, partly agrarian and partly industrial. Under such conditions, it is not surprising to find that neither our theories of structure nor our methods of building have remained static for long. Rapid and violent change, uneven and undisciplined, replaces that slow, almost imperceptible accumulation of experience which characterized the sudden flowering of the great building schools of the past. Consequently, any discussion of contemporary theories of structure must be simplified, diagrammatic, and misleadingly symmetrical.

The Function of Structure

BUILDING is the sum total of those structures which we erect to keep the natural environment out of a given space and that equipment necessary to replace the natural environment with a synthetic one. Building is thus a specialized instrument for modifying our environment in any desired direction or degree. This may range from the comparatively simple case of a bandstand (where the curved shell merely concentrates the sound in a desired direction and the sloping floor merely organizes the spatial relationships so that the entire audience may see) to the enormously complex problem of the broadcasting studio (where the building is called upon to furnish a complete and flexible control of every environmental factor).

Capacity for visible — or at least measurable — transfer or conversion of energy is the line which usually divides structure from equipment. This is a necessary oversimplification. Actually the electric cable which carries current from switch to vacuum cleaner is clearly engaged in a transfer of energy: it is considered equipment. The steel truss which takes up and distributes the earthquake shock in such a way as successfully to resist it is also engaged in a transfer of energy: yet it is called structure. In the last analysis, all of the building is dynamic. The air-conditioning apparatus which forces cold air into the room is no busier controlling the environment than the insulation in the wall which, inch by inch and molecule by molecule, opposes the transfer of heat from the blistering outside to the cool interior. Thus, the distinction between structure and equipment is largely one of active versus passive function.

The nature and function of contemporary building equipment is discussed in succeeding chapters, in relation to the respective environments which they modify. We are here concerned with structure, the envelope whose function it is to enclose, support, and protect the synthetic environments thus created. Modern structure is itself usually composed of two visibly distinct elements — skeleton and skin, framing and surfacing — for the simple reason that Nature subjects man's building to correspondingly distinct forms of attack. When humidity rusts unpainted steel, her attack is *chemical;* when winter cold penetrates the too-thin wall, it is *physical;* when earthquake shatters the wall or snow load caves in the roof, her attack is *mechanical.* Commonplace as it sounds, such an analysis was only possible with the advent of modern science; and structural designs which reflected it were only possible with the rise of modern technology. Prior to that, in the load-bearing wall, in the masonry dome and vault, structure had been largely undifferentiated. A single element was depended upon to resist Nature's attacks in all its forms.

Contemporary structure, then, is specialized. To the surfacing is assigned the primary task of resisting chemical or physical attack, while to the frame falls the lot of resisting gravity, windstorms, snow, and earthquakes. The frame or skeleton is subjected to two sets of forces:

vertical
- the weight of the structure itself
- the weight of the equipment, people and goods inside it

horizontal
- windpressure (hurricanes, tornadoes)
- earthquake

In its simplest terms, the function of the frame is to absorb these forces and convey them to the ground. There are literally hundreds of different ways of doing this, employing different materials and concepts. When a house shakes before the blast of a winter gale, it is busy resolving such loads, breaking them up into their component parts and sending them along to the structural members best qualified to handle them. The building frame thus converts 'raw' forces into characteristic stress patterns called, in engineering parlance, *normal* (compression, tension, and bending) and *tangent* (shear and torsion).

There is another type of load in which the critical element is time and not force: vibration. All building materials have some elasticity, depending upon their internal structure. Up to a given limit each will deflect under a load and snap back into shape when the load is removed. Beyond this elastic limit is a second stage of resistance to load wherein the material deforms — that is, supports the load but is permanently misshapen as a result. Beyond this point of deformation lies that of ultimate failure — the material ruptures under the load. But the cumulative effect of a series of even small loads rapidly applied can telescope this process. Certain types of vibration will alter the crystalline structure of metal and radically modify its properties. Sound waves at a sufficiently high pitch will set up vibrations in a water glass which can shatter it. Soldiers marching in lock step across a bridge will set up an oscillation which can literally destroy it, although the same men, marching out of step or standing still, would not use more than a fraction of its total strength.

If the job of the skeleton in resisting mechanical attack is complex, that of the skin is even more so. Until recent years it was possible to consider it merely as a barrier, a surface which kept the cold out and the heat in and offered the maximum resistance to corrosion, rot, and insects. Today, this concept has been modified in two important respects. In the first place, it is now clear that there is no single material which is literally and permanently resistant to all forms of chemical, physical, or mechanical attack. By the same token there is no possibility

of a wall which is literally impervious to the penetration of heat
or sound. But, even more important, it is now clear that a
building skin should not be conceived in such terms anyway.
An efficient wall is actually not a barrier but a filter. It is
composite, each of its membranes with a specialized task. It is
selective, admitting those phases of the natural environment
which are desired and excluding those which are not.

In the succeeding chapters, we shall see how intricate the
functions of a building skin may become. The wall which
admits sunshine in the daytime will, unless equipped with addi-
tional membranes, also lose artificial light at night. The wall
which admits fresh air may also admit pollen, while that which
excludes the glare of the summer sun may also exclude the cooling breeze. A soundproof wall is apt to be lightproof as well;
while one which is opaque to the infra-red rays of the sun may
also be opaque to its ultra-violet band. To unlock these contradictions, it is clear that no single sheet of any known material
will suffice. Instead, by the sheer logic of the problem, the
contemporary designer is forced to evolve increasingly complex
skins composed of many membranes. Moreover, to maintain
an internal constancy against external fluctuations, many of
these membranes must be adjustable. They must be able both
to reflect and absorb, to act alternately as exit or as access.
Some contemporary wall designs indicate this tendency quite
brilliantly (Figs. 98–100).

Naturally, the complexity of the building skin will vary with
the precision of environmental control required: the ordinary
five-room bungalow will not have requirements as stringent as
those of the acoustical laboratory. Yet the difference between
the two is more one of degree than of kind, for the same principle
must be applied to the house if it is ever to approach the efficiency
of the laboratory.

Man's structures are peculiarly susceptible to another form
of attack — that of fire. In a certain sense, fire merely tele-
scopes the ordinarily slow and imperceptible processes of chemical, physical, and mechanical attack into a single cataclysm —
a process of decay which makes up in intensity for what it lacks

in time. With its threat to life and property, fire has always exercised an important influence upon building design. But with the growth of modern urban society, the demand for fire-resistance has become a controlling element in all structure. Nevertheless, despite many advances toward the goal, the genuinely unburnable building has yet to appear.

The first iron-frame buildings were widely hailed as fireproof. A few disastrous fires sufficed to prove the fallacy of this. Steel frames were then encased in concrete and ceramic sheaths: still fires raged. The LaSalle Hotel in Chicago was a 'fireproof' building: and the day after sixty-one persons lost their lives in the fire which swept through it on the night of June 5, 1946, the LaSalle was probably *structurally* as sound as the day it was put up. Actually, the fire had fed, not on the structure proper, but on its furnishings and equipment — on curtains, carpets, paneling, even the grease in the elevator shafts and the paint on the walls. As a result, many of the people who died in this fire were not burned to death at all: they were asphyxiated.[1]

It is, of course, obvious that, had the LaSalle been built of wood rather than of steel and concrete, the loss of life would have been much greater; property destruction probably would have been complete. Hundreds of thousands of fires rage in this country every year, usually in buildings which are structurally as inflammable as their contents. In 1945 some eleven thousand persons lost their lives in these fires, many others were injured: property losses ran to $500,000,000 for the year. It is probable that no more than ten per cent of all American buildings reach even minimum levels of fire-safeness. As for the remainder, there is no doubt that more fire-resistant structure would greatly increase the margin of safety of the people who live in them. Yet the fires which occur in the upper ten per cent — the 'fireproof' portion — indicate that the problem is only partially one of incombustible structure. As long as the contents are combustible, the buildings cannot be literally fire-proof, no matter what they are built of. Realization of this fact has, in late years, served to widen enormously our concepts

---

[1] This was also true in the famous Cocoanut Grove fire in Boston in 1942, where 487 persons died by asphyxia, flame, and trampling.

of fire prevention and control. The field now includes measures covering city and building planning, structure, fire-fighting equipment (both inside the building and out), and the training of tenants and personnel in fire-safe practices. Only by the most careful control of all these factors can the incidence of fires be measurably reduced.

Many purely architectural problems remain to be solved, however. For example: the natural tendency of stair towers, elevator shafts, and halls to act as flues which can rapidly fan a small fire to disastrous proportions; of air-conditioning systems to pick up and spread smokes and gases to remote parts of the building; or the toxic by-products of combustion from synthetic plastic materials. All of these hazards, and many more like them, are implicit in contemporary buildings. It is difficult to see how they can be eliminated (though they can often be minimized by skillful design). Hence even the most advanced buildings have had to assume that some hazards will always exist and to establish secondary lines of defense. Of such a nature are the familiar fire extinguishers and sprinkler systems. They are effective but far from perfect. One of the most promising developments along this line has been the carbon-dioxide sprinkler systems. Widely used in aircraft during the war, these systems carry liquid CO_2 capable of extinguishing all types of fires, including those which water does not affect. In aircraft, these systems penetrate every portion of the plane, including even the interior of the motors themselves. Thus CO_2 acted almost like the white corpuscle in the bloodstream — omnipresent throughout the mechanism, it was ready to counterattack at the first alarm. It is in such terms that fire-fighting equipment in buildings should be conceived, especially in large buildings or in congested areas.

Modern building abounds in examples of fantastically intricate structures, but they are logically concentrated in industry and many of them can scarcely be called architecture. Their significance for the building field proper lies largely in their pioneering theory. Thus, the formulation of an over-all theory of structure has been immensely facilitated by a whole spectrum of laboratory techniques: photo-elasticity, micro-photography, crystallography, X-ray, polarized light. These new techniques enable us not merely to calculate, but actually to see what goes on inside a loaded structure. They reveal the movement and behavior of forces at every scale and level of structure — molecule, crystal, I-beam, or skyscraper. And they lend added significance to Frederick Kiesler's comment: 'Since the building designer deals with forces, not objects, design is in my definition not the mere circumscription of a solid but a deliberate polarization of natural forces towards a specific human purpose.[1] They make one wonder at the name and definition of that basic course in engineering — statics, 'the science of bodies at rest.'

Steel, the Mathematician's Material

FROM A PURELY STRUCTURAL STANDPOINT, the least efficient structures in the world are the Pyramids, which occupy all but the merest kernel of the space they displace. From the same narrow viewpoint, the molded plywood PT boats and plane fuselages of World War II are among the world's most advanced structures. 'Advanced' and 'efficient' are, however, relative terms: that structure is most advanced and efficient which most closely conforms to the configuration of its own stress patterns. To put it another way, that structure is best which does the most work with the least material or — as the engineers say — whose strength-weight ratio is highest. Crystal Palace, Brooklyn Bridge, Eiffel Tower — all three were remarkably efficient structures. However, two of them were not buildings at all, and the Palace itself was a very special sort of showcase, with few of the complexities in plan or function which characterize even the simplest five-room cottage.

Of great significance is the fact, however, that all three were of iron. The historic accomplishment of men like Roebling and Paxton was the concept of structural strength achieved through precision instead of mass. To realize such a task it was necessary

---

[1] Frederick Kiesler, 'Design Co-Relation,' *Architectural Record* (September, 1939). p. 67.

to analyze the problem of structural efficiency theoretically — that is, mathematically. Only thus could one determine precisely under what set of circumstances a given amount of material would support the greatest load. Such theoretical investigations were scarcely possible until the development of modern steels. For steel is a mathematician's material because it is almost perfectly isotropic — that is, its physical characteristics are such as to make it react identically in all directions from a given point when stressed. Natural materials, such as timber or granite, because of their internal construction, do not react identically in all directions from the point of load: nor do they, because of their natural flaws and impurities, react predictably.

Structural theory fed chiefly on steel during the latter half of the nineteenth century. The properties of all types of steel structures were common property before the other materials got started. The commercial production of steel was assured when Sir Henry Bessemer read his famous paper on his process before the British Association at Cheltenham in 1856, although William Kelley in this country had come to the same conclusion even earlier. In essence, the Bessemer system was simply a practical technique for converting cast iron into steel by blowing air through the iron in a molten state. By 1860 Bessemer was manufacturing steel in sizable quantities, and within a decade or so its manufacture was widespread in this country.

Although the immense importance of steel to building was immediately apparent to architect and engineer alike, its liberating effect was channelized principally into cage-type skeletal structures. The steel cage moved in rapid progression from early mill construction, through the completely articulated steel skeleton of Sullivan's Schlesinger Building, to its final apotheosis in Rockefeller Center. Meanwhile, steel tension structures came to early and perfect flowering in Roebling's bridges only to languish in neglect for the next fifty years. While the steel truss and cantilever grew mightily in size and variety, the arch, reduced to cast-iron prettiness by the Victorians, reappeared as an important structural element only in the nineteen-thirties as the hinged arch. The old post-and-lintel, long ago absorbed into the cage, reappeared as the rigid frame only in very recent building; and the brilliant potentials of steel in shell and stressed-skin structures were explored, not by the building field, but by the aeronautical engineer.

This one-sided development of steel structures was not accidental. The wooden truss and the framed house, with its light skeletal cage and thin stiffening membranes of clapboard and plaster — these had been the basic structural forms in this country when the metals first appeared in the building field. They had channelized American technique; and it was entirely logical that cast-iron or steel columns or beams be first considered as merely improved substitutes for the wooden ones. It was only gradually that the concept of a complete steel skeleton, designed for steel, was evolved and the skyscraper appeared as the first American building type specifically based on steel. Even here a great debt was owed the earlier wooden structures, for it was they that had made the first clear differentiation between skeleton and skin. Such a specialization was necessary if the efficiency of either was to be increased. Such a specialization was impossible, either conceptually or actually, in solid masonry construction.

Once this distinction was made, the wall ceased to have much structural significance despite its visual importance. The sleek walls of Chicago's Monadnock Building gave it the appearance of a true skyscraper. By dint of solid masonry walls seven feet thick, it reached sixteen stories and thus visually challenged LeBaron Jenney's genuine steel cage near-by. In reality, there was a great conceptual gap between the two. The Monadnock was the old load-bearing wall pushed to its utter limit. LeBaron Jenney's block was the new light steel cage with a masonry skin hung on the outside. The function of this skin was confined to (1) creating an envelope within which a synthetic environment could be created and (2) protecting the skeleton against external attack from fire and corrosion. By the same token this division of labor enabled the skeleton to concentrate on the single task of load-carrying. This process was in fact a specialization in tissue which closely corresponded to that which took place in the animate world: as in the higher vertebrates, it was the precondition to further evolutionary advance.

The steel cage was an important development, as the appearance of the huge skyscrapers of the nineteen-thirties bears ample evidence. Yet its importance is apt to be exaggerated by the sheer mass of an Empire State or Radio City Building. Actually, the latest and largest skyscraper marks only a quantitative advance over Sullivan's Wainwright Building. Architecturally, the skyscraper was an outstanding invention, but from a purely structural standpoint, the first one was practically as efficient as the last; and the steel cage was by no means the ultimate application of steel to building design.

Until recent years the fabrication process itself served to restrict the use of steel to rectilinear structures, since the only practicable method of *jointing* steel members was riveting. With the perfection of electric arc welding, this limitation was removed. Not only are welded steel skeletons much more efficient than riveted ones; welding also permits steel to enter the more advanced fields of shell and stressed-skin structures. So far, the building field has been slow to recognize the significance of this development, and the most interesting examples are to be found in such specialized structures as spherical oil-storage tanks, airplanes, and tanks (Fig. 123). Welding has already contributed one distinctly new structural system to the building field — the so-called 'diagrid' or 'Lamella' shell. Although the engineering is complex, this system is in reality nothing more than a diagonal metal grid or lattice, whose members increase in number as they decrease in depth. In a single plane such a lattice is effective; but when it is curved it becomes, in effect, a remarkably efficient vault.

Electric welding will unquestionably have a profound effect upon future building theory and design, as it already has had upon naval and aeronautical engineering. In addition, the development of new steels — alloys of incredible strength, hardness, resistance to impact and corrosion — serves further to increase the versatility of the metal. The future will show that steel is by no means limited to the structure which first won for it the nation's breathless admiration — the skyscraper.

Concrete, the Original Plastic

ALTHOUGH METALS dominated the building field from the eighteen-fifties on — capturing the imagination of designers and public alike with their remarkable potentialities — they only eclipsed the other two basic building materials, concrete and wood. Both reappeared; and both followed a line of theoretical evolution closely parallel to that of steel.

Of the two, concrete rose most quickly to prominence. The manufacture of true Portland cement preceded that of steel, since it was being turned out in both France and England, in fairly large quantities, before 1850. But the concept of re-inforcing concrete with steel, whereby the compressive strength of the former is allied with the tensile strength of the latter, was later in appearance and slower in its spread. The actual inven-tion is attributed to a French gardener, Jacques Monier, who in 1868 hit upon the idea of using small steel rods in concrete pools.

Prior to Monier's discovery and for some time thereafter, concrete's chief use was as a binder in masonry construction. Perhaps because of this its real identity as a distinctly new material was overlooked. And even after ferro-concrete emerged as a new structural medium, it was for a long time still regarded as a 'mass-material' — ugly, gross, and inaccurate. Under the variable conditions of on-the-job mixing and empirical reinforc-ing, it was in fact often both ugly and inaccurate. But once begun, the technique of ferro-concrete progressed rapidly. Great advances were made in the chemistry of concrete — its formulae, mixing, pouring, and curing. Thanks to the rapidly expanding knowledge of reinforcing, ferro-concrete was soon converted into a precision material. Thus, in the present century it has be-come unchallenged in such constructions as highways, dams, and canals. Indeed, such masterpieces as the Grand Coulee and Boulder Dams are inconceivable in any other material.

Concrete is by definition a plastic material. Poured into any form, it assumes and permanently holds that shape. It is all the stranger, therefore, to see how seldom this property of plas-ticity has been exploited by American designers (the hydraulic

V

Modern Structure: Its Morphology

DESIGNERS of the structures in this section: 98, Fellheimer and Wagner, architects; Clarence R. Jacobs, acoustical engineer; 99, Wurster and Bernardi; 100, Costa, Niemeyer, Reidy, Leao, Moreira, Vasconcelos; 104, Konrad Wachsmann and Paul Weidlinger; 105, Austin Company; 107, New York Department of Parks; 109, United States Engineers; 112, William Lescaze; 116, Robert Maillart; 117, United States Bureau of Reclamation; 118, James Workman; 119, Frank Lloyd Wright; 120, 121, Wallace Neff; 125, E. H. Bennett, H. Burnham and J. A. Holabird; 126, Simon Breines; 127, Buckminster Fuller; 128, Bertrand Goldberg; 129, 130, Paul Nelson; 131, 132, Herbert Stevens.

ILLUSTRATIONS in this section are from the following sources: 98, Ezra Stoller photo; 99, Roger Sturtevant photo; 100, George Kidder Smith photo; 101, *Life*, copyright, Time, Inc.; 102, New York City Housing Authority; 103, American Institute of Steel Construction; 104, Anna Wachsmann photo; 105, Austin Company; 106, Timber Structures, Inc.; 107, A.I.S.C., Rodney Morgan photo; 108–110, 114, Timber Structures, Inc.; 115, Roof Structures; 116, *Architectural Review*; 117, *Life*, copyright, Time, Inc.; 118, *Architectural Record*; 119, Torkel Korling photo; 120, 121, 123, *Life*, copyright, Time, Inc.; 124, United States Plywood Corporation; 125, Hedrich-Blessing photo; 127, *Architectural Forum*; 128, Hedrich-Blessing photo; 129, Museum of Modern Art; 130, *Architectural Record*; 131, 132, Stoller photos.

98

Only with structural specialization could the building skin become a flexible means of filtering the environment. By revolving its louvers, this broadcast studio can modify its acoustical response (98) while the fixed sunshades in a California building (99) and the movable louvers in a Brazilian office building (100)
give control of sunlight.

100

99

CAGE CONSTRUCTION, the serial use of the old post-and-lintel, is our simplest skeletal system. Whether in wood (101), concrete (102), or steel (103), it is static, discontinuous.

A brilliant adaptation of the rectilinear truss, Wachsmann and Weidlinger's 'mobilar' system is entirely of steel tubing. All connections are hinged, like piston rod and crankshaft.

105

SKELETAL CONTINUITY is already well advanced in 'tree form' framing (105) or in laminated wood arches (106). Here post flows into lintel. . .

106

. . Continuity of true arch is dramatized in this New York footbridge.

107

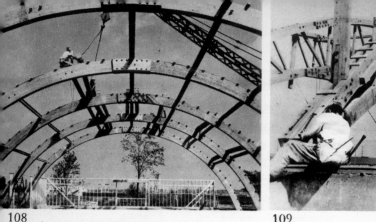

108   109

VAULTS quite unlike their masonry predecessors result from the repetitive use of many of the new structural elements — rigid frames, arches, crescent trusses — in wood or steel.

110   111

DOMES are achieved when these same elements are revolved around a vertical axis (112). In a midwestern bandshell, a semi-conical shell was achieved by the use of wooden trussed arches of steadily diminishing radius (113).

112

113

114   115

The diagrid system can be used in either flat or curved plane and in wood (114), steel (115), or concrete.

116

PLASTIC properties of concrete have been best exploited in curvilinear structures of highway and hydraulic engineers.

117

118

In concrete, the morning-glory shape is a structural element of great efficiency and beauty; Workman's concentrically rippled plate is 40 ft. across, 2 in. thick at edge (118). Wright's similar columns at Racine have hollow shafts (119).

119

SHELLS are a structural form in which shape more than material is a source of strength: concrete 'igloos' molded on inflated rubber forms (120); stressed-skin plywood railroad car (122).

120   121   122

123

124

One of the highest expressions of purely structural efficiency is found in the spheroid metal shells of the chemical industries (123) and the light molded-plywood boat hulls (124) whose strength-weight ratio is greater than steel.

125

SUSPENSION structures, by a system of cables and masts, yield great, unobstructed spans with minimum material in these two halls — one in Chicago (125), one proposed for Moscow (126).

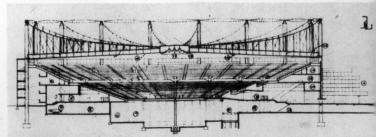

126

127

128

Structures hung from a central mast have long fascinated designers: Fuller's first Dymaxion House (127), Goldberg's demountable ice-cream stand (128), and the two schemes by Paul Nelson — a house hung from two tree-form steel frames (129), a huge Museum hung from a mast (130).

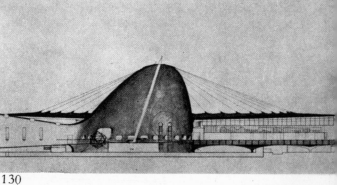

129

130

A slightly higher internal atmospheric pressure supports the roof of Stevens' proposed arena for Baltimore. Roof membrane could be of light aluminum and clear plastic — water- and fireproof.

131

132

engineers always excepted). In building design, its principal use has been in rectilinear skeletal structures — that is, as a competitor of steel and wood. Except in very tall buildings, concrete could and did compete with steel. Here it even had certain advantages: it carried its own fireproofing, it required somewhat less skilled labor, it could be used for floors and walls which would have been impractical in wood or metal. And a ferro-concrete skyscraper was, to a much greater extent than a steel-framed one, a homogeneous unit.

Yet all such structures ignored concrete's most important properties, or rather failed to exploit them properly. For the mere fact that it could be poured into any shape did not mean that concrete was equally efficient in all of them. European designers were much quicker to grasp this fact than Americans. In his famous bridges in Switzerland, the engineer Robert Maillart shows a totally different concept of the material from that of his American contemporaries. By an exquisitely detailed knowledge of ferro-concrete he was able to achieve forms which no longer bore any resemblance to their steel or masonry ancestors. Basically, Maillart used the simplest concrete elements — the reinforced mat or slab and the beam; but he used them in a revolutionary manner. He saw that by bending the slab or beam he could reduce its thickness without diminishing its resistance to a specific load. In fact, to all intents and purposes, he reduced both slab and beam to a two-dimensional plane which he stiffened by bending — sometimes in the vertical plane, sometimes in both vertical and horizontal. Thus, in a series of structures each more brilliant than the last, he moved ferro-concrete from the field of conventional cage structures into that of the shell and the stressed skin. He achieved this by utilizing the special plasticity of concrete, isolating and exploiting this property in such a way as to establish new levels of structural efficiency (Fig. 116).

Prior to World War II, there was little that paralleled Maillart in this country. The 'monolithic' buildings, so widely publicized by the trade associations, were not very significant structurally. Essentially, they were derivative forms, reflecting earlier experience with solid masonry and wood and metal skeletons. Even

Wright's famous earthquake-proof hotel in Tokyo falls into this category, though it had special features which could only have been achieved in concrete. However, there is ample evidence of a rapidly changing attitude among building designers: John Early's research in diaphragms, James Workman's concentrically corrugated slabs, Frank Lloyd Wright's 'morning-glory' hollow columns. The thin spherical shell, with and without ribs, is appearing with increasing frequency in single-story buildings where unobstructed span is essential. The construction of small, thin shells has been greatly facilitated by the use of inflated

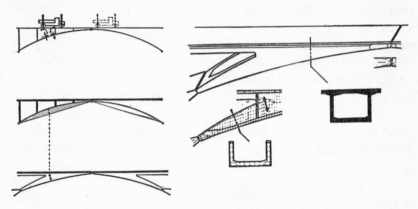

rubberized forms. Here a fabric sack of appropriate size and shape is inflated; concrete is sprayed on with an airgun, the reinforcing web is placed, more concrete is sprayed on together with a final coat of waterproofing. When the concrete has set, the form is deflated and removed through a door or window. Although this technique has obvious limitations, it has significance for small single-story structures, where it yields genuine shell structures of great efficiency: rigid, lightweight, permanent, and easily adaptable to a wide range of acoustic and thermal surfacing (Fig. 120).

Wood, the Universal Material

WOOD has always been America's favorite building material. It still is. In 1940, eighty-seven per cent of all dwelling units in the nation were built of wood. But this quantitative ascendancy can be deceptive: almost from their first appearance, steel and ferro-concrete displaced wood as a qualitatively important structural material. This eclipse was largely due to the inherent limitations of wood as a natural material (although such misconceptions as the 'fireproofness' of steel played their part). Wood was not isotropic, hence it could not be calculated accurately. It was not uniform in texture or strength, thus requiring large factors of safety. Finally, it was a very lively material, responding quickly to changes in the moisture content

His astonishing knowledge of the stress patterns in loaded structures enabled Maillart to pare his designs to the bone. Note (left) how he resolves an arch into a system of thin, folded planes or (right) employs a horizontal curve to stiffen a vertical one.

Museum of Modern Art

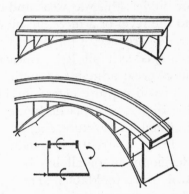

and temperature of the air. In its natural form, wood was not suitable for large or complex structures.

Certain properties of great significance to structure lay dormant in wood, for nineteenth-century technology had neither the theoretical nor the technical means of isolating them. In the form of lumber, it lent itself naturally to skeletal use, either in trusses or in cages. Thus, for popular building it was ideal — plentiful, easily worked, yielding a fairly efficient structure with a minimum output of material or labor. But its peculiar characteristics — high tensile and compressive strength, flexibility, immunity to fatigue and vibration — were not adequately exploited until modern plywoods appeared. These have so little in common with the lumber of the past as to constitute a totally new structural material.

The use of thin sheets of wood as a decorative veneer was apparently known to the Egyptians. It was widely used in nineteenth-century furniture. But the production of laminated plywoods on a mechanized basis did not begin until the eighteen-eighties in Russia, and around the turn of the century in this country. In multi-ply laminations, the properties as well as the form of wood were radically altered. It became relatively iso-tropic, for placing the grains at right angles in successive layers served to equalize the tensile strength in both directions. By the same token, plywood became more stable and uniform — movement or flaws in one layer being largely corrected by the others. The weakest aspect of the early plywoods was the glue or binder: this was weak and unreliable and held plywood down to the level of a mere finishing material. It has only been with the emergence of the synthetic plastic binders that plywood has emerged as a full-fledged structural material. These new binders have great adhesive strength: under test loading, the individual plys will rupture before the joints between them give way. In addition, these plastic binders render the plywood resistant or immune to moisture, fire, fungus, and insect attack.

From a structural standpoint, perhaps the most significant development of all has been the perfection of plastic binders which are moldable. These introduce into plywood structures the same possibilities which Maillart exploited in ferro-concrete. Plywood landing craft, torpedo boats, and airplanes were widely used in the war (Fig. 124); and the performance of such struc-tures gives great promise for the peace. In its resistance to mechanical, physical, and chemical attack, molded plywood is in most respects equal, and in some superior, to steel. In the critical strength-weight ratio it probably surpasses any known material.

Today plywood may be molded into any shape, no matter how complex the form or compound the curve. The process is at once cheaper and more flexible than the die-stamping of metals, since comparatively low temperatures and pressures re-place the costly and inflexible die. The resulting form is per-manent and, of course, both continuous and homogeneous. The technique can be applied either to skeletal structures (trusses, arches, frames), or to stressed-skin and shell structures (vaults, domes, spheres), or to combinations of the two. For small or medium buildings, molded plywood offers the contemporary designer a new medium of first-rate importance.

There have been limited advances in the use of conventional lumber — such as the substitution of connectors for nails in heavy engineering structures — but they fall outside the main line of wood's development. Indeed, there are many scientists today who hold that the use of wood as a building material in any fashion at all is a barbaric practice. This is based upon the fact that, under the impact of modern chemistry, wood has become a fabulous source of raw materials of all sorts: newsprint, rayon, film, resins, lignin, etc. Even before the war, the Nazi scientific hierarchy had dubbed wood a 'universal material.' Wood was to furnish their autarchy sugar, cattle (possibly even human) food, alcohol, rubber. However extreme this view, or inapplicable to American conditions, it is apparent that our estimate of wood must be sharply revised. In the light of modern chemical and engineering knowledge, it has become a precise, high-performance material, fertile basis for structural advance.

The tendency toward a functional distinction between skeleton and skin has had a pronounced effect on the development of all building materials. While steel, concrete, and wood have seen immense development in the skeleton, a large and complex family of surfacing materials has appeared to challenge the conventional wood and plaster: glass, cotton, ceramics, paper, rubber, cork, synthetic plastics. The first result of this trend has been to reduce brick and stone to the category of a surfacing material. The fact is that, in all but residential building, solid load-bearing masonry has practically disappeared. We have never had a genuine masonry tradition in this country: even in its heyday, the masonry building relied upon steel or wood for framing its roof and floor. Our genuine vaults and domes could be counted almost upon the hands. And for all the pretensions of its recent appearances (in the Triangle in Washington or Saint John the Divine in New York) masonry has dwindled to a surfacing material — a skin or a membrane in the skin. As a surfacing material, masonry has both potentials and limitations. A sheet of polished granite or glazed tile will resist the attack of the elements long after a sheet of linoleum or cork has disappeared. But the cork has acoustic properties beyond the challenge of the granite, the clay tile can never offer the resiliency of a linoleum floor. This is merely another way of saying that stone, brick, and tile must now compete with a growing host of newer, more specialized surfacings. Glass, plastics, metals, rubber, cork, fiber- and asbestos-board, plywood, and synthetic fabrics: the list is long and constantly growing. As a whole, they offer the building designer a fabulous array of special properties: by combining them properly the building skin can become a truly selective filter.

The Line of Increasing Efficiency

STRUCTURAL THEORY could not develop and cannot exist·in the abstract. Today's impressive knowledge of the subject represents the accumulated experience of a century or more: and historically most of this experience has been pragmatic, planless and asymmetrical. This is by no means a purely technical phenomenon: on the contrary, the controlling factors are often economic, geographic, even political. The theoretical aspects of ferro-concrete structures were largely the by-product of factory, dam, and highway construction. Similarly, the intensive development of the steel truss and steel cage were the by-products of great railroad and skyscraper expansion. Each material had its characteristic potentialities, each had its limitations; as a consequence, each became associated with certain types of structures. This parallelism between material and structure has served to accelerate the development of certain specialized aspects of structural theory: but it has also often served to distort or stultify the development of others equally efficient. Here three factors are in constant interaction: structural system, material, and production method. A change in one inevitably affects the other two and, consequently, the entire complex. Sometimes this change is startling. By means of a new method (thermo-pressure molding) an existing material (plywood) can appear in a radically new structural system (stressed skin).

It is true that literally all structural forms are related, despite their differences; that some lines are more advanced than others, either relatively (because of more intensive cultivation) or absolutely (because of the laws of mechanics); and that there has been in all lines a progression towards these higher forms. The quality which these higher structural forms have in common is encompassed in one word: *continuity*. Continuity of material or continuity of direction or both. Now it may not come as a surprise to the layman — though it certainly has to many an architect and engineer — to learn that loads, rather like fluids, are conveyed more efficiently around a smooth bend than around a sharp angle; or that loads are carried more effectively by one homogeneous member than by several, no matter how well the several are bolted together. The point is clearly made in the eggshell of a hummingbird or the mammoth arc of Boulder Dam. Both are remarkably efficient structures with reference to the load each is designed to resist. And in both structures, continuity in direction and material is the dominant feature of the design.

The seams are the weakest points in all of man's constructions. From whatever angle the problem is surveyed, this is profoundly true. The chemical and physical attacks of the environment always find their first toe-hold here. Joints and seams are the weakest point in any skeleton when it comes to the transfer or conversion of any type of load. For just as a chain is no stronger than its weakest link, so is a skyscraper no stronger than its weakest rivet. The danger of failure can, of course, be decreased by dividing the load amongst an increased number of rivets. But the stresses remain concentrated there around the rivet holes, since it is only there that the forces can bridge the gap from one beam to the next. As if to make matters worse, the joints in most man-made structures occur always at angles or intersections. Thus, the stress pattern in any loaded structure is further complicated by discontinuity in direction as well as in material.

There is little reason to hope that man's constructions will ever be literally seamless, as Nature's are. The building designer would have to cross from dead to living tissue to make that possible. But there is no doubt that the principle of continuity, applied to building design, will result in much higher levels of structural efficiency. Nor does this imply that all buildings need become egg-shaped domes; on the contrary, continuity has three aspects which cut across all types of structure:

(1) continuity in the skeleton
(2) continuity in the skin
(3) continuity between the skeleton and the skin

In the ordinary frame bungalow there is a relatively low level of continuity in all three. Yet if the nails were everywhere replaced by one of the incredibly strong modern adhesives, this one change alone would greatly increase the total load resistance of the structure. To carry the process to its logical conclusion, of course, the entire bungalow should be redesigned for continuity. This would imply change in its method of assembly as well as in its final appearance. Instead of roofs made up of small shingles and walls of narrow clapboards, we would find surfaces composed of large sheets of composition materials — metal, plywood, plastic, glass. Instead of joists and rafters meeting studs at sharp angles, we should find all the members flowing into each other in smooth short-radius curves. Instead of the skin and skeleton being merely nailed together, we should find them solidly and continuously joined into a homogeneous unit. Thus, the skin would be carrying a more just portion of the load, instead of just hanging on as is now the case. In short, we should find the basic structure only modified, with discontinuity in both material and direction reduced to the minimum. It must be added, however, that we should almost certainly find these houses being largely completed in a factory, since their production in the field would be impossible.

There are, of course, many factors in addition to professional conservatism which militate against continuity in architectural structure. In building proper, there can be no such 'pure' structure as is natural to the Brooklyn Bridge or the B-29. The social operation to be housed is too imperative in its demands in plan. And traditional planning concepts in this country are all right-angular: the corners square, the line plumb, the floor and ceiling level. To a large extent, these conventions grew in turn out of the limitations of earlier structural systems like the Classic post-and-lintel. They reflect, too, the impress of early American surveying and land-plotting techniques, where all boundaries of necessity conformed to the cardinal points of the compass. Actually there is no fixed and absolute reason why rooms should have corners, why walls need be an exact ninety degrees to the floor and to each other, why the ceiling need be flat. On the contrary, as will be seen in the discussion of the various environments, there are many sound reasons for none of these conventions to exist. A room which provides optimum control of heat, atmosphere, light, sound, and human movement will normally tend to become curvilinear in plan and section. It will remain rectilinear only with difficulty.

Post-war structure will be more nearly freed from its Procrustean bed of right-angle planning than at any time in modern history. It must not be forgotten, however, that if there is no intrinsic merit to the straight line and right angle, there is also room for error in the curve. The one is as subject to abuse as the other, at least in architecture. Recent history abounds in horrific curvilinear examples — the Art Nouveau movement, Rudolph Steiner's nightmarish buildings for the Anthroposophical Society in Switzerland, *moderne* filling stations and bars in this country. In such buildings a romantic and essentially antistructural concept demolishes both structural efficiency and esthetic integrity. The curves of continuity structures must be determined by stress patterns, not literary intuition.

Straws in the Wind

CONTEMPORARY AMERICAN BUILDINGS fall, structurally, into four broad groups. The first and by far the largest are rectilinear skeletons — the cage, the truss, the rigid frame. Next are the arches — the vault, the dome, the hinged arch. Closely allied to these are the shells — the stressed-skin or semi-monocoques. Then there are suspension or tension structures, such as the tent. There is even speculation on the possibility of inflated structures

— tension in reverse, so to speak — where a small differential between outside and inside atmospheric pressure would be utilized to support a flexible shell.

Unfortunately, American building boasts very few examples which more than approximate the theoretical possibilities of the structural groups listed above. This is due to a number of factors. There is, first, the time lag between discovery and application. The professional schism between architecture and engineering, so clearly stated by Hamlin and Schuyler at the close of the last century, is not yet entirely healed. Because of its peculiar character, the building industry is not yet truly industrialized; as a consequence, its products still show handicraft's inability to assimilate scientific and technical advance. On the other hand, American building consumers do not, except in isolated examples in industry and commerce, demand the same high performance from their buildings that they expect from their battleships or their autos. Such factors as these all contribute to the structural backwardness of our buildings. Yet another fact remains: *the design of a building is by no means a purely structural problem.* The needs of a social unit like a congregation or a family are seldom as symmetrical, as sharply defined, as a structural formula. Thus, an efficient plan may easily dictate inefficient structure. The more complex the social unit or the more complete the environmental control desired, the less likelihood there is of a perfect structural system. Each building raises its own special set of requirements and the final design can only resolve them at the highest possible level.

In frame and cage structures, the principle of continuity is breaking down the formal distinction between horizontal beam and vertical column. Naturally, in the multi-story building, this tendency is restricted by the repetitive character of the cage. Continuity of form and material is confined to the actual point of intersection — the joint itself. But even here the use of continuous material and short-radius curves eases the flow of stresses from horizontal to vertical member and yields quite surprising increases in the over-all efficiency of the loaded structure. Welding makes this development possible in steel construction, eliminating open joint and right angle (Fig. 105). In concrete the same tendency is to be observed: thus Wright, in his famous 'morning-glory' column, has used a wide-throated column cap which literally flows into the slab which it supports (Fig. 119).

However, it is in single-story buildings that the principle of continuity has all but revolutionized structural design. Here, with no necessity for a rectilinear profile, a wide range of handsome and efficient structural elements has been developed: tree-form columns, rigid frames and bents, hinged arches. In varying degrees, all of these new forms mark an advance over traditional post-and-lintel methods of conveying loads into the ground. From these it is, of course, but a step to the barrel vaults and the domes. A series of hinged arches in a row produces a vault incomparably more efficient than its masonry predecessors (Fig. 108); while half of a rigid frame or a hinged arch, when revolved about a vertical axis, produces a ribbed dome both handsome and efficient (Fig. 112). All of these new structural forms are equally suitable to fabrication in steel, reinforced concrete or laminated wood.

There are many situations in which, for various reasons, lightness is a more critical value in structure than continuity. This has led to interesting variations in the internal design of elements which retain their over-all rectilinearity. In general, the tendency here is to increase the number of elements while at the same time reducing their individual size. This produces a three-dimensional honeycomb structure, of which the lattice-like Lamella system is an example (Figs. 114–115). A sensational application of this principle is to be found in the 'mobilar' system designed by Konrad Wachsmann and Paul Weidlinger (Fig. 104). Instead of the conventional trusses, purlins, and columns, they have evolved an articulated skeleton of steel tubing. Using this system in one design for a hangar, they are able to achieve a huge cantilevered roof, 192 by 192 feet, which is carried by two pairs of piers near the center — a feat which it is difficult to imagine in any other medium.

However, some of the most advanced examples of structural efficiency lie outside the building field proper — in storage tanks, airplane and boat bodies. Shell forms such as these afford astonishing examples of structural efficiency (and, incidentally, of beauty). Here objective conditions have reduced the margin for error to the vanishing point. The designers have been compelled to examine their calculations, their stress patterns, the very cellular structure of their raw materials. Though their work cannot be copied by the building designer, it must be studied by him if he is to meet American society's need for better buildings. Fortunately, there is evidence that he has begun to do this.

Suspended structures have offered the building designer an especially fertile field for speculation, though few have so far been actually built. Here the structure is turned inside out, as in the cylindrical gas-storage tanks used by the public utilities. The skeleton is moved to the outside and the skin or envelope which holds the gas is merely hung from it. An application of this principle is to be seen in the Railroad Building at the 1933 Chicago exposition (Fig. 125). To free the interior of the huge octangular shed from the interruption of columns and girders, the designers have hung the entire structure from a circle of steel masts outside the building proper. The system has obvious advantages over conventional cage structures. Properly designed, a suspended structure will automatically accommodate the expansion and contraction of large wall and roof surfaces, as well as great variations in load due to rain or snow.

Paul Nelson's proposed 'suspended house' is an interesting demonstration of the same sort of principles applied to residential design (Fig. 129). Here again the main objective is flexibility of plan — interior space which can be organized, subdivided, and rearranged without reference to the structure proper. A series of free-standing hinged arches carries the entire weight of the envelope: instead of being transmitted directly to the ground, the weight of walls, floors, and roofs is hung from the sky. Since steel in tension carries a far greater load than the same size column in compression, Nelson's interior space is free of interruption. The shape, size and relationship of his rooms are no longer aborted by the Prussian discipline of the post and lintel.

SKELETON AND SKIN 189

In his famous 'Dymaxion House' of the early nineteen-thirties, Buckminster Fuller employed the same concepts (Fig. 127). In his design, the envelope was hung from and around a central mast, like the tent of the American Army. Because of this, his house was hexagonal in plan — a limitation which is perhaps offset by structural economy. In 1938, using the identical concept on a far larger scale, Nelson produced his spectacular design for the proposed Palace of Scientific Discovery in Paris (Fig. 130). The purpose of this museum was to have been the presentation, in a coherent and balanced exhibit, of the story of the historical development of the sciences. In view of their rapid and uneven development in the modern world, it was obvious that flexibility of interior space was of paramount importance in a museum of the sciences. Moreover, concentric circulation around a central control point provided a very efficient plan for a museum. Hence Nelson adopted a central mast supporting several circular floors, one above the other. Besides being the principal structural element of the design, this huge hollow mast carried stairs and elevators as well as all utilities for the building and exhibits. Traffic and utilities radiated from this point in all directions at each floor. Fantastic as it might have seemed to pre-war eyes, it was not impractical from a technical point of view. On the contrary, it was a brilliant demonstration of the application of modern scientific knowledge to the problems of building design, wherein the contradictions between structure and plan were resolved at the highest possible level.

In his prize-winning design in the first competition for the Palace of the Soviets in Moscow, Simon Breines utilized an ingenious tension system in his structural design (Fig. 126). A ring of steel masts, outside the structure proper, was joined at each floor level by a system of steel cables radiating from the building's center. By tightening these rings, the entire skeleton was kept in tension. The radial nets support floors and roof, while the walls are carried by the circle of masts outside them. Both skeleton and skin being in tension, Breines achieved great rigidity and load capacity with far less material than would be required by conventional structural systems.

The intention of all these structures is, of course, twofold. On the one hand they seek to vastly increase the structural efficiency of building, to carry great loads with less material, by substituting precision for mass. On the other hand, they seek to liberate the space thus enclosed from structural interruption. Perhaps the most audacious of all proposals along these lines is that of a young New York engineer, Herbert Stevens, for inflated structures (Fig. 131). According to this designer, buildings of almost unlimited size could be raised and held in place by nothing but compressed air, like an automobile tire. The structure would consist of a single membrane which would be weatherproof, fireproof, resistant to sound and heat, flexible and lightweight. Semi-spheroid in shape, it would be inflated to an atmospheric pressure somewhat higher than that out of doors; and this differential between the two would be maintained by air locks at the doors. The differential, according to the designer, would be too small to cause any physiological hardship on the people using the building. In this proposal, structure is reduced to its absolute minimum. Skin and skeleton become one: and the air, instead of the earth, supports the load. Yet it, too, is entirely feasible technically: a wide range of fabrics — metal, rubber, plastic, glass and asbestos — is already available. A combination of them could readily yield a 'structure' such as Roebling would have delighted in and a skin such as Paxton never dreamed of.

Even this project does not, however, exhaust the possibilities of inflated structures. In 1946 the architect William H. Tuntke proposed a blimp-supported roof for St. Louis' famous open-air opera. Used only on summer nights, this open-air auditorium has little need of a roof and none at all for a permanent building; yet the hazard of rainstorms during the season is a serious one. In light of this requirement, the Tuntke design is not as far-fetched as might appear at first glance. A transparent, helium-filled balloon, anchored over the auditorium, will drop a glass-fiber tent down along nylon ropes to protect the audience from sudden showers. Operated by motors in the gondola, this tent can be pulled back up to the blimp when the shower stops. The gondola — which will also house spotlights for the stage — will be independently powered. Thus, when not needed, the entire structure can be parked elsewhere in the grounds. This is probably the ultimate in structure, for here the problem is one of holding the roof to the earth instead of holding it up.

Designs such as these can be all too easily dismissed as nonsense. So, too, were Paxton's Palace and Eiffel's Tower. But the fact remains that they are completely logical projections of certain current trends in American structural theory. Where strength-weight ratios are used as criteria, they are probably among the most efficient structures ever conceived. Opposition to them is much more apt to be based upon tenacious concepts of what a building should look like than upon a rational analysis of what a building should do. Deeply ingrained prejudices in favor of maximum *permanence* in structure tend to obscure the fact that maximum *performance* is what we should demand of our buildings today.

The great majority of American building is, unhappily, not structurally very advanced: much of it is not even structurally very sound. This reality serves to establish an immense spread between what is theoretically possible and what is actually accomplished. In this context, even modest advances in structural theory achieve great significance — especially in housing. According to the 1940 Census, almost one out of every five dwelling units in the United States is in need of major structural repairs. In some categories, the figures are much higher. As might be expected, farmhouses are more decrepit than urban ones: for the nation as a whole, 33.9 per cent of all rural dwelling units are structurally defective. Tenant-occupied farmhouses are in even worse condition — 38.8 per cent, or some one-and-a-quarter million units were in need of major repairs: in the South, this percentage ran to 42.9.

With all of our building booms, it is surprising to see how old most of our country's housing is: in 1940, only 16 per cent was less than ten years old. Forty-three per cent was from ten to thirty years old, and the remaining 41 per cent was over thirty years old. The suspension of civilian construction during the war years has certainly sharpened the colors of this depressing picture. Allowing for both physical deterioration and technical obsolescence, it is thus apparent that much — perhaps the majority — of American housing fails to meet even minimum standards of structural efficiency.

Comparable figures for the structural condition of the nation's non-residential building are not available, but it is likely that their average quality is higher, and their average age lower, than that of dwelling units. The vast expansion of industry during the war and since — much of which has employed quite advanced structural design — has considerably raised this hypothetical level. Even so, our industrial plant does not approach that level of structural efficiency which modern knowledge makes possible.

Structurally, a large portion of American building needs replacement. In terms of the welfare of the country as a whole, it will not matter greatly which of the many structural systems and materials are employed. Each has its merits, each its deficiencies. The problem facing the building designer is to raise both the average level of actual structure *and* the level of structural theory. In the last analysis, it is more important that the gap be narrowed between the average and the maximum than that we have a few very advanced structures in a sea of obsolete and decrepit ones.

CHAPTER TEN

Fair and Warmer

W E ARE INCLINED to refer to our climate here in America as 'temperate'; and, compared to the heat of the Sahara or the cold of Alaska, this is indeed the case. Yet if we had no buildings at all, there is scarcely a spot in the continental United States where life above the level of the Neanderthals would be at all possible. Except for the southernmost parts of Florida, Texas, and California, Nature moves in a definite climatic cycle. Within this cycle there are violent fluctuations — temperatures which range from 30 degrees below zero in January to 110 above in the July shade, or fluctuate thirty or forty degrees within a single day.

Except for man, all forms of life adapt themselves to this thermal cycle by alternating intense activity with dormancy, migration, or hibernation. After an active summer, the oak drops its leaves, the bird flies south, the bear just goes to sleep. During a very hot day all animal life will lie in a state of suspended animation, quietly awaiting the return of night. But for human society seasonal dormancy and hibernation are out of the question, while seasonal migration is possible only for the idle rich and the migrant poor. And for American society in particular, with its extreme dependence upon industrial processes, these thermal extremes are intolerable: too hot in August, too cold in January; too much change between night and day; too much variation between one city and the next. The principal deficiency in our natural thermal environment is thus its *discontinuity* relative to human activity. For each of our million-

fold processes has its own thermal requirements; and these requirements must be met wherever or whenever the process takes
place. In many phases of American life, this need for thermal
constancy reaches almost fantastic proportions. To meet such
needs as these we have steadily extended and deepened our
control of the thermal environment, until today our buildings
lead the world in this respect.

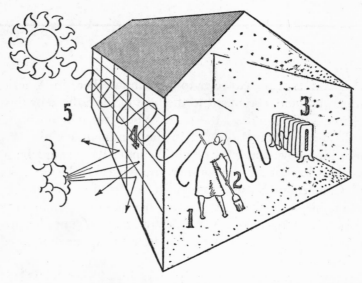

In order for the muscular system (1) to accomplish its task (2)
with maximum efficiency and minimum effort, the building —
by its equipment (3) and structure (4) — must create and
maintain a constant set of thermal conditions seldom found
in the natural environment (5).

Here we meet a strange paradox; for despite our accomplishments, *most* of our buildings continue to offer very inadequate
control of the thermal environment. Only fifty-eight per cent
of American homes boast a central heating system, while some
fifty thousand out of millions of work places are air-conditioned.
If thermal constancy be our criterion, it is clear that these
scattered and disparate units do not meet it, for the rest of the
nation's buildings — homes, schools, workshops — have very
primitive heating or cooling systems; many have none at all.

Compared to these, the buildings with heating and cooling equipment of advanced design offer thermal asylum to only a portion of the population, and that for only a portion of the time.

Heat—Better to Lose than to Gain It

AT FIRST GLANCE, the question as to why we heat buildings in winter or cool them in summer seems too obvious to require an answer. Yet the obvious response is actually so crude as to be meaningless. Our sensations of coolness and warmth are not only relative, but highly subjective. Scientifically, they are inaccurate, since in thermodynamics there is no such thing as cold. Above absolute zero ($-460°$ F.), the point at which molecular activity theoretically ceases, science recognizes only varying degrees of heat. Moreover, buildings neither warm nor cool us. Under all circumstances, the human body produces more heat than it needs; consequently, it is always losing heat to its environment. The function of building is to control the *rate* at which this heat is lost.

The amount of heat produced by the body varies very widely with activity and age: a man engaged in violent exercise may produce ten times as much heat as he will when in bed and asleep; a ten-year-old boy will produce more heat than an elderly man. But the body is only about twenty per cent efficient in the performance of work, which means that approximately eighty per cent is waste in the form of heat. This constant surplus of heat must be dissipated, since the body is very sensitive to its accumulation. Indeed, a fundamental requirement for health is that the total net heat loss from the body shall balance the heat produced under given conditions of muscular activity. In order to be comfortable at any task — cooking a meal, operating a lathe, or typing a letter — a person must lose eighty per cent of the total energy required in the form of heat. If more than this is lost, he will begin to feel 'cold'; if less, he will complain of feeling 'hot'; and if either sensation were indefinitely extended, he would ultimately become 'sick.'

Within fairly narrow limits the body has an extraordinarily efficient system of balancing heat production against heat loss to maintain a constant temperature of 98.6° F.   Only when this temperature rises above 105° F. or falls below 80° F. is the human body in danger of collapse and death.   To maintain this internal thermal constancy, the body has a complex system of controls.[1]

In either case, the actual point of heat transfer is the skin, which relies upon three principal methods of getting rid of its heat — convection, evaporation, and radiation.   A fourth method — conduction — occurs only when swimming or bathing.   It is the most rapid of all, and often has disastrous results, as when persons are rescued from drowning only to die from exposure.

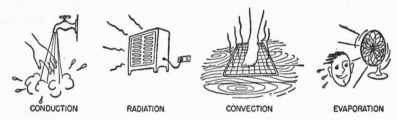

CONDUCTION   RADIATION   CONVECTION   EVAPORATION

The four methods by which heat transfer is effected between the body and its environment.

Convection, evaporation, and radiation are all physiologically effective within given limits.   Actually, all three methods are used by the body all the time, since nowhere in nature do conditions permit the transfer of heat by one means exclusively. But the degree to which they are used varies with external conditions.   Here four distinct factors govern heat loss from the body: the movement, temperature, and humidity of the air, and the radiant temperature of surrounding surfaces.   In nature, these four factors are in constant flux and infrequently achieve

[1] As the outside temperature drops, the pores of the skin close up, the surface veins contract, the heart — pumping slowly — husbands the heat of the bloodstream deep in the body.   Hence the phrase 'blue with cold.'   On the other hand, if the outside temperature rises, the heart accelerates, the arteries and veins expand, and the overheated blood is rushed from the vital organs to the surface for cooling. When this proves insufficient, the pores open and the sweat glands begin to work. Hence the phrase, 'damp and flushed with fever.'

that exact balance required for human comfort. When the air temperature is below that of the skin, its movement along the skin's surface will remove heat by *convection*. Even when the air is warmer than the skin, air movement will still remove body heat by *evaporation* of the sweat which the body automatically produces when the first method fails. However, evaporation has sharp upper limits, beyond which sweat runs off without evaporating. This limit is established by the relative humidity of the air. Thus, as the temperature of the air rises, the humidity must fall, or discomfort, collapse, and death will ensue. It was thus as much high temperature and high humidity as shortage of oxygen which caused the deaths in the Black Hole of Calcutta; the victims were as much burned as suffocated to death.

Finally, and irrespective of atmospheric conditions, the body is constantly losing heat by *direct radiation* to surfaces cooler than itself. As light flows from an electric bulb, so invisibly radiant heat flows from every point and pore of the body. Like light, this heat moves in straight lines, at high speed, and unaffected by intervening air; like light also, it may be reflected. Naturally, this process also works in reverse — that is, the body receives radiant heat from all surfaces warmer than itself. Thus, the nude skier will sweat freely on a sunny snowbank — even with the temperature around zero — because snow is an ideal reflector of solar heat.

Thermal Continuity Is Important to Health

IT IS EASY to dramatize thermal extremes — heat so intense or cold so severe as to result in disablement or death. Actually, such cases are statistically unimportant in modern America. For one farmer who dies of heat prostration, or one seaman who dies of exposure, there are a thousand clerks or factory workers who suffer from much less apparent (but quite as important) deficiencies in their thermal environment. These may be small — a few degrees too hot here or too cold there — but their cumulative effect can often be quite disastrous. No illness or disease can be blamed exclusively on one single environmental deficiency. Life is never that simple. There are usually a complex of factors involved in any illness, each of which 'contributes' something to the final *débâcle*. Unfortunately, this too often serves to confuse all diagnosis: a sort of shell game is operated wherein *cause* (bad building, bad clothing, bad diet) can never be directly related to *effect* (discomfort, bad health, disease, and death).

Despite this confusion, it is now generally recognized that deficiencies in our thermal environment are factors of prime importance in a number of respiratory ailments: pneumonia, tuberculosis, influenza, grippe, common cold, and rheumatism. The United States Public Health Service observes that 'debilitation and breakdown of human resistance to cold in ill-heated, ill-ventilated habitations are . . . regarded as conducive factors to pneumonia'; that 'dampness and cold are considered to be important predisposing factors' to rheumatism; while 'there was a marked association between degrees of crowding and the frequency of influenza.'

But deficiencies in the thermal environment are not always or immediately expressed in terms of bad health or illness. Mostly they are expressed in terms of discomfort too vague for the individual to be directly aware of them — jittery nerves, short tempers, lassitude when it is hot; shivering, sneezing, gooseflesh when it is too cold. Such discomfort, if continued indefinitely, may well lead to illness and disease; at any rate, it certainly leads to incalculable losses in working efficiency from day to day. It has been estimated that two-thirds of our adult population suffer from colds each year between October and March. This means that more than fifty million adults suffered loss of vitality, efficiency, or working time because of colds.

The steel worker who 'don't mind sweating' may not realize that he is dead tired at the day's end, not so much because of energy expended in work as because of excessive sweating. He doesn't know that it is the perspiration he never sees, not the sweat which he 'don't mind,' that cools him. He is unaware that profuse sweating leads to a heavy loss of vital body fluids and salt reserves, to physio-chemical disturbances of the internal environment which may lower blood pressure enough to lead to a circulatory breakdown. The man who opens the window wide on the coldest night because it is healthy may not realize that, unless he has enough blankets, his body will lose heat equivalent to walking two miles an hour all night long. The fact that he eats a huge breakfast next morning is not necessarily a sign of health; more than likely, it means he is merely replacing the calories lost in a night of very inefficient sleeping.

It is apparent that the body is well equipped to maintain the thermal equilibrium so necessary to its survival under varying circumstances. Indeed, Cannon regarded this 'as one of the most valuable advances in biological evolution.' The external thermal environment is by no means always friendly to such constancy, however; and though the body is designed to accommodate itself to fairly wide fluctuations, its limits of accommodation are fixed. It is to take up the discrepancy between what we need and what we get, that we heat and cool our buildings. We thus create a synthetic thermal environment which takes the load off our own shoulders, in much the same way as the shell protects the unhatched chick.

The task of building, then, is not merely to keep us from freezing or burning to death; not only to maintain conditions which reduce or eliminate the causes of respiratory disease; not even to stop with maintaining comfort conditions for steel worker and stenographer: but to provide the exact thermal environment required by the whole spectrum of modern life.

How Buildings Are Heated and Cooled

WHATEVER THEIR SPECIAL FEATURES, all heating and cooling systems have a common cycle. They must have a *primary source of energy* — coal, wood, oil, gas, or electricity. They must *convert this energy* into heat or cold by combustion, compression, or electrical resistance. After producing heat or cold, they must have a *medium for distributing* it throughout the building — this may be air, steam, water, or some chemical of special properties. Finally, these systems have available two *methods for transferring* heat to and from the building's tenants — convection and radiation. It is within these limits that heating and ventilating engineers have worked for over a century. To improve the mechanical efficiency of the system — that is, the ratio of useful heat delivered relative to the energy units put in — has been the constant goal. The direction of these efforts, however, has been largely conditioned by historical accident. Because wood, coal, oil, and gas became available in approximately that order, most nineteenth-century heating was premised upon simple combustion. Electricity was not generally available until after the turn of the century and the internal combustion and Diesel motors came even later: hence compression and resistance appeared very late as conversion methods.

With our earliest heating apparatus — the fireplace and the stove — the air was heated at the point of combustion. This had the obvious disadvantage of requiring a stove or fireplace in each room. This led to the idea of heating the air in one central chamber and carrying it by ducts to the various rooms. Such hot-air furnaces relied solely upon the tendency of heated air to rise. This, too, had its limitations and fans were soon introduced to push the heated air through the ducts. From this it was but a step to the 'air-conditioning' system of today, where the air can be heated or cooled, dried or moistened, as conditions require, and then forced through the ducts in any rate and volume desired.

Industrial experience with the steam boiler made it an early contender with the stove and furnace in the heating field. Unlike them, the boiler did not have to await the appearance of the motor-driven fan to circulate its heating media. In a closed circuit, steam or hot water moved of its own accord from a central boiler to the various rooms and was there, by means of radiators, transferred to the air. (Radiators, incidentally, were misnamed: less than a quarter of their heat is radiant, the rest being discharged by convection.) To increase the efficiency of the radiator — that is, to enable it to heat more air faster — fans were later placed behind it to force the air across its heated fins in a steady stream. In such cases, the radiant action disappears almost completely and the unit becomes a convector.

Endless variations and permutations to meet special conditions are by now in common use; but these are the basic features of ninety-eight per cent of our central heating and cooling systems. Together with parallel advances in combustion and refrigeration — oil burners, mechanical stokers, and gas burners for burning fuel more efficiently — and automatic-control instruments — thermostats, thermometers, pressure gauges, etc. — these constitute the basis of America's undisputed leadership in the field. The advantages of these systems over all previous methods of controlling the thermal environment are apparent. Their mechanical efficiency is so much greater that they have, for all practical purposes, removed all limits of size and location from our buildings. A small house, a large factory, an entire city may be heated by a single plant. An air temperature of 72° F. may be maintained anywhere from the Equator to the North Pole with equal precision. This is indeed an historic accomplishment in the evolution of building, the importance of which cannot be overestimated. For the first time society has at least the prospect of being able to produce and maintain the special thermal environments required for each of its processes and operations, wherever and whenever it desires them.

Convection systems, however, have several disadvantages. The first is economic — the entire air mass inside the building must be heated or cooled before the tenants can be comfortable. Hence, more fuel is required than when the tenants are heated or cooled directly, as in the radiant method. If our buildings were as efficient in holding air-borne heat as our systems are in producing it, this would not be as serious a matter; unfortunately, most of our buildings are anything but airtight.

Another set of disadvantages to convection systems are physiological and thus, from the standpoint of health, more serious. Warm air always rises, cold air always falls. This leads to a phenomenon familiar to everybody — temperature stratification, where the air temperature at the ceiling may be from ten to twenty degrees higher than that at the floor. This is physiologically undesirable; for health, the air temperature at the level of the feet should be *equal to or greater than* that at the level of the head. While it is true that modern air-conditioning systems can overcome this stratification, they do so only by greatly increasing the complexity and cost of the system. In the last analysis, it is always inefficient to go against a natural law when the same result may be achieved by other means.

To maintain comfort conditions, convection systems manipulate the temperature of the air; and for most of the nation most of the time, this manipulation results in sharp differences between inside and outside temperatures. This is also physiologically undesirable, involving the danger of thermal shock for those people who pass in and out of the building. The shock is somewhat offset by wearing extra garments in winter and, logically, we should undress when leaving air-cooled buildings in the summer. The real problem is much more complex, however. It is undoubtedly true that people who work in shops or offices which are air-warmed in winter and air-cooled in summer are able to work efficiently. But — since they spend the remaining sixteen hours of each day in buildings which are inadequately heated and almost never cooled — their over-all health may not be improved. It may be actually impaired. This sort of thermal discontinuity is perhaps the paradox which explains why air-conditioning has not achieved the spectacular reductions in respiratory ailments which was first anticipated.

Radiant Heating

WELL KNOWN to the Romans and widely used in their public buildings, radiant heating was, until a few years ago, relatively unknown in America. Recently, however, there has been great advance in both theoretical and practical experience with this type of heat transfer. Mechanically, the radiant system differs from the convectional in only one important respect: the actual method of heat transfer. It depends upon the same fuels — coal, oil, gas, electricity; it is assembled from the same equipment — boilers, piping, controls; it employs the same media — steam, water, air, electricity. Radiant systems consist of a central unit where the medium is heated or cooled; a system of pipes (for water or steam), ducts (for air) or resistance coils (for electricity) which carry the medium to the various rooms. But instead of radiators or registers, the radiant outlets are coils embedded in floors, walls, and/or ceilings. These surfaces become in effect heating and cooling plates.

The advantages of radiant over convection systems are several. Mechanically they are more efficient, since radiant heat warms only the people in the room (and only indirectly and secondarily the air mass itself). They are more economical, since the heating medium can be used at lower temperatures, thus reducing fuel consumption. Unless the system is electrical, it can be reversed — that is, used to circulate a heating medium in winter and a cooling medium in summer. They are invisible in the finished building, their temperatures being low enough to permit any type of surfacing — paper, paint, linoleum, plywood, etc.

There seems to be no reason why the steel reinforcing of concrete floor and ceiling slabs cannot be made to do double service as heating coils. Wall-boards of all sorts could have built-in resistance coils, so that they need only to be plugged into the house current to become sources of radiant heat. Doors, shutters, and screens made of these boards could thus become sources of heat gain, instead of loss, as at present. We shall probably even see electrically heated curtains (with the resistance coil woven right into the fabric) which can be pulled across the window at night to reproduce the heat from the sun in the daytime.

The most severe mechanical limitation to radiant cooling systems is the problem of condensation in the summer when humidities are high. Under such conditions, radiant surfaces would sweat like a glass of iced tea. This limits the use of radiant cooling to those parts of the country where summer humidities are low, or to those buildings where the air is artificially dehumidified.[1]

Even more important than mechanical efficiency, however, are the physiological advantages of radiant systems. It makes little difference to the body whether it loses its excess heat by convection, evaporation, or radiation; the important thing is

[1] Such equipment is seldom used except in conjunction with refrigeration. But wartime developments in hygroscopic absorbents (such as silica gel or lithium chloride) indicate that relatively simple and efficient means for drying air may soon be available. This would sharply raise summer comfort conditions inside buildings even without cooling of any sort.

that the loss equal the surplus. Thus, a fully clothed man at rest will be comfortable in a steam-heated room whose air is 71° F. The air temperature could drop to 59° F. and he would still be comfortable, provided the walls were heated to 85° F. Contrariwise, the air temperature could rise to 90° F. and the man be comfortable provided the walls were radiantly cooled to around 60° F. Naturally, this ratio can be extended further both ways, the only limitation being that the radiant sources would have to be confined to the ceiling, since it is both uncomfortable and unhealthy to walk on floors which are much hotter or colder than the skin. Theoretically, it would thus be possible to keep our buildings comfortably warm in winter and cool in summer with the doors and windows wide open. Actually with radiant systems, optimum comfort conditions can be maintained with smaller temperature differentials between indoors and out than with convection systems.

The second physiological advantage of radiant systems is that temperature stratification is largely eliminated, as radiantly heated rooms maintain approximately the same air temperature from floor to ceiling. They thus come much closer to meeting the standard previously mentioned — air temperature at the feet equal to or higher than that at the level of the head.

Radiant systems promise solutions to all sorts of complicated building problems which until now seemed insoluble: the hospital operating theater, for example. Here two contradictory criteria are apparent — one for the patient, another for the surgeon and his staff. The patient needs warmth at exactly the time when the staff, under severe nervous tension, needs to be cool. Since it might easily mean death for the patient if he gets too cold and only discomfort for the surgeon if he gets too hot, most operating rooms are kept at the temperature required by the patient. With radiant sources, it is now possible to meet both criteria simultaneously: the patient can be warmed by hot air while radiant-cooling plates around the walls can be 'focused' on the staff.

These, then, are the two methods of heating and cooling buildings: both have advantages; both have drawbacks. In complex buildings, a combination of the two is often desirable. A recent office building for the Bankers Life Insurance Company in Des Moines, Iowa,[1] employs both methods of thermal control and may be taken as an illustration of the current level in the field. This building has both a complete air-conditioning system and radiantly heated and cooled walls. These two systems are independent but co-operate in an almost human and entirely fascinating way. Both are subdivided into zones, any one of which can run full tilt while the other is running on low or not at all. This flexibility is important. Summer or winter, most American buildings are engaged in a terrific battle with their natural thermal environment, but any building in Iowa is subject to particularly severe temperatures, which may easily run from 20° F. below to 110° F. above — that is, a span of 130° F.

On a day in August, this building will be assaulted on all sides and from above by a very high air temperature. In addition, its southeast, south, and southwest walls will, at some time during the day, be assaulted by high radiant temperatures from the sun. This total thermal load is both enormous and uneven. Now unless this unevenness were provided for, the thermal environment inside the building would be dangerously uneven. The cooling system could work itself to death and still lose the battle. Thus, like a modern army, this new building is flexibly designed for concentrated defense against concentrated attack. On this August day, the ventilating system will automatically rush more cooled, dried air to the rooms along the south than to those along the north, which are of course in shade. Similarly the radiant coils in the south wall will work overtime, combating heat penetration into the building by circulating more cold water here than in the north wall.

On a bitter day in January, conditions will be largely reversed and the two systems will reverse their tactics accordingly. Now the ventilating system rushes more warmed air to the north wall where — because of shade and prevailing winds — the heat loss is greater than in the south; and the coils in the north wall step up the circulation of hot water, to slow down heat loss through the walls.

[1] Designed by the late Leland McBroom of the firm of Tinsley, McBroom & Higgins, architects. Charles Leopold was the heating engineer.

Day and night, winter and summer, the building responds automatically to these outside stimuli, compensating one against the other to maintain a stable thermal environment for its tenants. Indeed, the building is now acting in a fashion closely parallel to that of the human body itself; and this is not accidental, for it becomes more and more apparent that nature itself offers the best criteria for building design. The more we understand the body's relationship with its external environments, the better will we be able to design efficient building.

New Sources of Heat and Cold

WE HAVE THE TECHNICAL MEANS for maintaining thermal continuity in our buildings to a degree hitherto undreamed of. But no heating or cooling plant is better than the building which contains it. Heat passes in and out of our buildings — even the best of them — like water through a sieve. Ironically, this situation has been aggravated by the disappearance of the old load-bearing masonry wall which — for all of its structural shortcomings — was a tolerably good thermal insulator. While a functional differentiation between skeleton and skin — such as we see in the modern skyscraper — was a necessary and desirable one, it has raised a host of new problems, particularly where the skin is concerned. In recent years there has been considerable research in thermal insulation, with the result that our newer buildings are more heatworthy than ever before. These insulation materials usually rely upon a porous spongelike structure to slow down the transmission of air-borne heat; and a building whose walls and roof are so insulated loses less heat in winter, gains less in summer. For radiant heat an entirely different sort of barrier is required — a reflective surface like polished copper or aluminum foil.

With such insulators, it is entirely possible to increase greatly the heat-holding capacity of the building. It is theoretically possible to achieve such perfect insulation that buildings could be heated just from waste body heat, as many theaters already are during peak loads. But here we come to another irony.

From a strictly physical point of view, the building's thermal task is the same the year around — to act as a barrier to the passage of heat through its outer skin. Actually, from the standpoint of the designer, trying to balance the constancy of human needs against seasonal variation, the problem is somewhat different. In cold weather there is an absolute shortage of heat in nature. Except for what can be gained from winter sunshine, this heat has therefore to be produced by the building and conserved by it to the maximum. This impels the designer toward the concept of a hermetically sealed, heatproof envelope. But in warm weather, although there is a surplus of heat, there are many ways in which the building can borrow coolness from its environment with little or no mechanical energy. In most cases, the designer's principal task will be to prevent solar radiation from penetrating into the building. The simplest method is to prevent the sun's rays from even impinging upon it. The natural shade of trees and vines presents an ideal barrier but where this is not available a whole series of architectural devices have been developed. Roof pools and roof sprays are proving very effective, reducing summer roof temperatures by fifty degrees and more; and interior air temperatures by ten and fifteen degrees. There is an increasing use of ventilated roof and wall construction. Here the skin is composed of several separate membranes with moving columns of air between. The South Americans, plagued with a tropical sun, have developed the *brise-soleil* or exterior sunshade to a remarkable degree (Fig. 99).

From developments such as this, it is clear that the ideal building skin would not be an impenetrable barrier but rather a complex and flexible filter. Ideally, this filter would operate automatically and on a highly selective basis, to exclude or admit the natural thermal environment. Such building skins are by no means improbable.

Current practice in thermal control might thus seem to have reached a high level. From one point of view, this is true: our best examples are much more efficient, convenient, and healthy than those of the past. But if one measures even the best of current installations against theoretical possibilities, the picture is altered radically. Already at or past the laboratory stage are a number of developments which promise to make obsolete much of our present equipment, if not indeed our very concepts of how buildings may be efficiently heated and cooled.

One such development is that of liquid heat. It has long been apparent that we needed a medium with a much greater heat-holding capacity than water — a fluid which could be heated to 500° or 600° F. without evaporating. Packed with such heat at a central boiler, the medium could then be piped all over a building or group of buildings not only to heat and cool them but to power domestic cooking and refrigeration units. The John B. Pierce Foundation had worked on this problem since 1935, but it was not until ten years later that it finally succeeded in perfecting such a liquid. Called tetrasylsilicate, the new compound has remarkable properties. Although it does not boil until it reaches a temperature of 817–825° F., it does not freeze at −65°; it is non-inflammable, non-explosive, non-poisonous, and non-corrosive; it is chemically stable; and it is relatively inexpensive.

With the liquid heat perfected, the Foundation set up a demonstration unit to check its practical application.[1] Using a conventional coal-fired boiler, they heated a little over five gallons of the medium to 550°. When continuously circulated through the unit, this proved adequate to run a house heating plant, hot-water heater, refrigerator, cook stove with griddle and toaster and two separate ovens. The efficiency of the system was rated at eighty per cent and the operating cost was found to be half that of conventional domestic utilities. Since different fixtures would require different temperatures, the Foundation also perfected a fully automatic temperature control. Under test, this control was successful in maintaining any setting within the range of the system itself.

Liquid heat should prove particularly useful in housing. A single insulated system could largely replace the maze of water, steam, air, gas, and electrical conduits which are now required by conventional utilities.

[1] See 'Liquid Heat Powers Domestic Utilities,' *Architectural Forum* (April, 1946), pp. 211–213.

In the field of conversion, the heat pump is a development of great potential significance. Although all mechanical refrigerators are heat pumps, removing thermal units from one area and discharging them somewhere else, they have not until quite recently been considered as possible sources of heat. The fact that they were efficient producers of cold served for a long time to obscure the fact that they had, by the same token, an important by-product of heat. One had only to run them backwards, so to speak, to make heating machines of them. Practical application of this principle has produced the so-called reverse-cycle installation, a number of which are in successful operation today. Mechanically, they are quite efficient, yielding from three to five units of heat for each unit of electrical energy put in. There is no fuel in the ordinary sense of the word. In cold weather the heat pump takes outside air or well water (depending upon which is warmest) and pumps the thermal units out of it into the heating system proper. The waste product in this case is ice. In hot weather, the system is reversed: excess heat from inside the building is discharged either into the outside air or into the well water.[1]

Aside from its efficiency, the reverse-cycle system has much to recommend it. Since combustion is completely eliminated, there is no problem of fuel-handling and storage. There are no objectionable by-products in the form of smoke, ash, soot, or fumes. The system is completely automatic, requires no seasonal change-over. It is surprisingly compact — a two-story building of 170,000 cubic feet requires only two 20-horsepower compressors for complete heating and cooling. Because there is no combustion, the installation is completely independent of chimneys and may be placed anywhere in the building. The main obstacle to its wide use is the high cost of electric current which, in the nation as a whole, is around $3\frac{1}{2}$ cents per kilowatt hour. Most of the existing installations have been made by utility companies in their own buildings, where access to electrical power at cost made them economically feasible. However, the

[1] For detailed descriptions see 'The Heat Pump' by Philip Sporn and E. R. Ambrose, *Heating and Ventilating Magazine* (January, 1944, pp. 68–78); and 'Two Heat Pump Air-Conditioning Systems,' by Sporn and Ambrose, *Heating, Piping and Ventilating* (June, 1944), pp. 377–385.

reverse-cycle system can already compete with ordinary fuels in those areas where power rates do not exceed .01½ cents per kilowatt hour.   In any event, the mechanical efficiency and social desirability of the heat pump is sufficiently great to guarantee a much wider use in the future.

The heat pump thus raises the practical possibility of communities from which the whole wasteful and dirty process of combustion will have been banished.   Such a change in heating methods would, of itself, bring about radical changes not only in building design but in urban life in general.   But even a prospect such as this palls into insignificance beside that of atomic fission.

The energy extracted from a pound of coal by combustion is roughly 12,000 B.T.U.; the energy released from the same pound of coal by atomic fission is at least 12,000,000,000 B.T.U. This fact establishes the scale against which the efficiency of all conventional thermal systems must henceforth be measured.   Irrespective of all the technical, political, and economic obstacles which today obscure the peaceful applications of atomic energy, it is apparent that fantastic changes in our concepts of the thermal environment are inevitable.   The centralized heating and cooling of entire cities will become a necessity.   Here we will heat and cool not merely their buildings, but their streets, parks, playgrounds, and airfields as well.   Indeed, the manipulation of the climates of whole regions will become a commonplace.   Then the control of the thermal environment will have been raised to the level of climatological manipulation.   Torrid climates will be cooled, cold ones warmed, damp ones dried, and dry ones moistened.   Thermal continuity — one of the most basic requirements of modern industrial society — will have been accomplished.   Far from increasing the complexity of buildings, this will tend to simplify their design since one of their principal environmental loads will have been permanently removed.

CHAPTER ELEVEN

Pure as the Air You Breathe

THERE PERSISTS IN THIS COUNTRY a fixed opinion that somewhere — in the Yellowstone, in the Smokies, in Atlantic City —
there is such a thing as 'pure air,' that such atmospheres are
'good for you,' and that they constitute the 'natural' standard
relative to which all other atmospheres should be judged. The
fact is, of course, that the air of the Yellowstone is certainly no
more sterile, and probably no freer of inorganic impurities, than
that of Chicago or Los Angeles. The nearest approach to a
'pure' atmosphere in Nature is probably that of the Poles — no
dust, few pollens and bacteria, etc. Yet it is obvious that polar
atmospheres are hostile to man because of one great deficiency
— low temperatures. Again, the stratosphere may be free of
Kansas dust and goldenrod pollen, but is deficient in two other
respects — pressure (too low) and composition (too little oxygen).

Nowhere in Nature is there such a thing as pure air; natural
atmospheres are by definition impure, freighted with a vast
cargo of bacteria, molds, pollens, spores, seeds, insects, and
dusts. The atmosphere is Nature's most important transportation system and she employs it to the maximum. What we
usually mean when we talk about the advantages of the countryside's clean, fresh air is that it is free from *man-made* pollution.
And this is obviously true. The full effects of the synthetic
atmospheric environment in which the urban half of the American people live have yet to be fully investigated. It is safe to
hazard that the cost in terms of health is enormous.

This does not mean that all our ills are due to bad air, or that

211

they will automatically disappear if we go back to the farm, as many agrarians and decentralists would like us to believe. The natural atmospheric environment is good for some of the people some of the time, but it is already pretty generally recognized that natural atmospheres no longer offer a valid citerion for all human activity. The real problem involved is not one of *abstract purity* but *specific control*; the real criteria cannot be literary abstractions from Longfellow's whispering pines and hemlocks, but scientific determination of the comfort requirements of a specific workman at a given job. Furthermore, there is an increasing range of human activities for which no historical or anthropological precedent exists — flying, tunneling, operating a comptometer, a tractor, or a high-speed rotary press. These are new occupations. They require new atmospheres.

In this field, the American people have at least two achievements to their credit: they have, at the same time, destroyed more natural atmospheres and created more synthetic ones than any other nation in history. It is of course technically much easier to destroy a natural atmosphere than to create a synthetic one. For every air-conditioned theater or office building whose atmospheres are designed for human comfort, there are whole regions where not only production but life itself is menaced by atmospheres which have been destroyed: the Dust Bowl, where a gas mask was almost as great a necessity as clothing; Copper Hill, Tennessee, where chimneys belching acid scarified hundreds of thousands of acres of verdant plant life (oddly enough, no records exist of what such atmospheres did to the workers); even the average city, where the addition of smokes, dusts, gases, and vapors has had a markedly deleterious effect on plant life and presumably on humans.

Today it is safe to say that we have already mastered the technical means for controlling the atmospheric factors listed above over a very wide range. We are remodeling natural atmospheres. We are reconstructing ruined atmospheres. We are creating completely new atmospheres, atmospheres for which there is no precedent in human experience. We are reproducing authentically all sorts of natural atmospheres and are even importing foreign varieties.

The atmosphere is a very complex affair. Webster tells us hopefully that air is the 'invisible, odorless, and tasteless' mixture of gases which surrounds the earth. In its natural state, air is principally composed of nitrogen and oxygen (in proportions of about four parts to one). In addition, air has argon, carbon dioxide, water vapor (the humidity discussed in the last chapter); minute quantities of helium, krypton, neon, and xenon; and varying small parts of ammonia, nitrous and nitric acid, and sulphurous and sulphuric acid. Together with its suspended burden of bacteria, spores, dusts, etc., and its varying pressure, this mixture constitutes man's atmospheric environment. Three vital factors — chemical composition, pressure, and impurities in suspension — are thus involved in the control of the atmosphere.[1]

Some Atmospheric Arithmetic

MR. SIGMUND SPIELBERGER arose one March morning at eight-fifteen to notice that his pet terrier, Buddy, 'was rolling on the floor and acting queerly.' He took Buddy out to the street for air, and the dog promptly lost his alarming symptoms. Relieved, Mr. Spielberger re-entered his apartment only to find his eldest son lying unconscious on the floor. Another son was sent out for help, an alarm was sounded, and only then was it discovered that Mrs. Molly Geller, her son Bernard, and daughter Jean were all dead in their beds in an adjoining apartment. 'Coal gas' — probably carbon monoxide — escaping from a defective furnace in the basement had killed them.

The workers at the Arlette Dress Company's shop in midtown New York have reason to remember a certain winter morning in 1941. It was a Monday and cold, and consequently the windows were not opened. No one thought much about that until at nine-thirty, in rapid succession and with only the

[1] From the standpoint of the human body, the motion and temperature of the air are largely functions of its thermal environment and have been discussed in the preceding chapter. This classification is borne out in everyday life by the fact that, in both theory and practice, handling of air masses inside buildings is regarded as an integral part of thermal engineering.

slightest preliminary blanching, thirty-eight men and women quietly passed out. The foreman, Mr. Harry Goodman, got as far as the next shop with the alarm before he, too, keeled over. An emergency squad rushed to the scene in time to rescue all thirty-eight workers. Investigation showed that pilot lights on three pressing machines had been accidentally left burning over the week-end. The pilots had consumed the oxygen and the closed windows had prevented its replacement.

The Gellers all died because something had been *added* to their environment. The garment workers got the fright of their lives because something had been *subtracted* from theirs.

These true stories illustrate the only two important ways in which changes in the chemical composition of the air affect our health; addition of some noxious gas like carbon monoxide or subtraction of the absolutely indispensable oxygen. On the average, a person will take in about five pounds of air for every pound of food and water consumed; but he can go for days without water, weeks without food, and a lifetime without light or sound, whereas a matter of five or ten minutes stands between him and death if his access to air is cut off. The atmospheric environment is so indispensable a requisite that life is literally inconceivable without it. Here the body operates within extremely close tolerances, without the reserves to which it has recourse in other environmental difficulties. Fortunately, the composition of the atmosphere varies very little in nature, and insufficient oxygen is seldom a threat.

Fatal instances of chemical pollution are not very common in everyday life, and the building consumer is seldom particularly aware of them.[1] However, the atmosphere is far more often and more extensively damaged than is commonly realized — especially by addition. In certain industries, this pollution is very common, assuming the status of an 'occupational hazard.' As a rule, the concentrations are not high enough to cause

---

[1] There are, of course, all sorts of specialized situations in which the alteration of the air's chemical composition is desirable. Thus it has been reported that the substitution of helium for nitrogen prevents the dread caisson disease of divers, while the addition of oxygen to the atmosphere of a pneumonia patient or high-altitude flyer is by now routine. The future will probably see more applications of this sort.

immediate illness or death; if they were, the cause would be more promptly discovered and eliminated. Rather, the gases are present in small proportions. The body absorbs them gradually until, by a process of accumulation, they result in weakened resistance and ill-health. Since such poisonings could only take place inside buildings, our buildings must take the blame for them. Simple ventilation is ordinarily all that is required, although where toxic concentrations are unavoidable, safety measures should include both gas masks and automatic gas alarms.

The pressure of the atmosphere varies with the altitude; but on all except the highest mountains the body easily compensates for this by increasing the rate of breathing, and any temporary discomfort usually disappears with acclimatization. Theoretically, if a person went far enough up he would explode, like a deep-sea fish yanked suddenly to the surface; or, if he went far enough down, he would be crushed like a sunken ship. Unnatural atmospheric pressures are no longer the exotic experiences of lone divers hunting for sunken treasures, however; for thousands of American 'sandhogs' they are part of the normal working environment. Bridges, tunnels, dams, subways — all require subterranean work; and it was the Roeblings who first demonstrated that the most efficient method of preventing a cave-in was not steel or wood shoring but air. Under the East River in New York, beneath the towering skyline of downtown Chicago, all over the country, thousands of sandhogs work in air pressures held at around twelve pounds above normal. The hundreds of thousands of Air Force men in World War II, on the other hand, fought in abnormally low atmospheric pressures. In other words, it is no longer possible to think of man as working in a fixed pressure zone. His business increasingly takes him into many others, and it is the task of building to protect him there. Although resistance to extremes of atmospheric pressures is not a function of ordinary building, there are many specialized instances in which structure is called upon to resist great differentials. In very tall buildings, wind loading can reach very large dimensions. And if the buildings in the tornado and hurricane belts of the southern United States are ever to approach storm-proofness, they too will have to be designed to handle great pressure differences.   There is even the possibility, as seen in Chapter Nine, that we will use air pressure to support certain structures where uninterrupted spans are essential. Meanwhile, in aviation and in industry, the maintenance of low vacuums and high pressures has become a commonplace. The building field can easily draw upon such experience if it needs to.

Impurities in Suspension

ALL ATMOSPHERES carry a suspended burden of 'foreign' matter — dust, bacteria, spores, pollens, and other microscopic particles. It has been pointed out that this is as true of natural as of synthetic atmospheres.   In nature, the foliage of trees acts as a viscous impingement filter, removing dust and air-borne organisms from the atmosphere.   This natural air-conditioning will produce an atmosphere at the center of a forest which may easily be twenty-five per cent cleaner than at its fringes.   It is only within the last few decades that we have been able to define — much less produce — perfectly pure and sterile atmospheres.   Yet men have for centuries sensed that the air could carry a lethal burden.   In medieval plagues, the people wore masks whose inefficiency seems at once tragic and comic today. Colonial ladies were afraid of 'night air' and fearfully retreated indoors to atmospheres which were even more murderous, had they but known it.   In ante-bellum New Orleans, there was great dread of the 'miasma' which was alleged to rise at night from the swamps and lowlands and give fever to all who inhaled it.   Buildings were supposed to offer some protection against this menace, though flight to the hills was considered advisable in hot weather, when all the windows were open.   It remained for Walter Reed, the great American doctor, to find that it was the swamp mosquito, and not the swamp air, which caused malaria and yellow fever.   Even so great and so recent a scientist as Darwin, lacking bacteriology, was forced to fall back upon the miasma in explaining the propagation of certain tropical diseases.

The natural atmospheric environment has always been immensely important to Nature as an avenue of propagation; she has freighted it down with spores, pollens, and seed pods. Not all of these are 'good' for the human respiratory system, and it is incorrect to suppose that the contemporaries of John and Priscilla Alden were any more comfortable in this ocean of pollens than are we today. There is no reason to believe that hay fever, asthma, and allergy are modern inventions. Like most of the diseases and ailments which afflict mankind, we are constantly learning more about them. Our diagnosis grows more accurate and for this very reason last year's statistics are not comparable with those of fifty or even ten years ago. Even today, there is no way of knowing how many millions of persons are suffering from one form or another of atmospheric pollution by spores and pollens. But for the first time in history, we know something about the subject and we now have the equipment which can rid our buildings of ninety-eight per cent of these hostile invaders.

Like the ocean, the air also supports a complicated hierarchy of microscopic organisms — bacteria, parasites, and viruses. Many of these are friendly or beneficial to man: some of them (like the bacteria which causes milk to sour or those which 'fix' nitrogen in the earth) are indispensable. But between them, they also cause most of the common diseases afflicting mankind. Some of them are free agents, riding around on drops of moisture from human throats and nostrils; some of them hitch rides on insect hosts. For many others the exact method of transmission is not understood. The viruses — those strange substances that bridge the gap between the living and the non-living, and thus obscure what was once considered to be a sharply defined line between living cell and chemical molecule — these viruses may move through the air on mosquitoes and cause malaria and yellow fever; on flies to cause infantile paralysis; on tsetse-flies to cause sleeping sickness; or on droplets exhaled from the nostrils to cause influenza.

There is now no doubt that air-borne pollens can cause hay fever and allergy, and that air-borne dusts cause silicosis; but do air-borne microbes similarly cause infection and disease? Oddly enough, the whole theory of infection by air-borne organisms is still the subject of cautious opinion, though there is a growing body of evidence to support it. The layman who thinks he 'catches' cold or influenza in crowded places has common sense on his side but not yet completely proven fact. For scientific investigators the problem is complicated by the fact that many common diseases including colds and flu appear to be caused by viruses. The behavior of the virus is not completely understood. Not until the perfection of the electronic microscope in 1941 were we able even to see it; and we still do not know definitely whether it can move directly and independently through the air from the respiratory system of one person to that of another.

If we must, with the experts, withhold final judgment on the air-borne transmission of disease, we can at least observe that the atmosphere supports millions of bacteria of all sorts; that inside buildings the number of such organisms per square foot of air rises in proportion to the human population; and that many of these organisms closely resemble those known to cause respiratory diseases. To this we can add the notorious coincidence between overcrowding and contagious diseases of all sorts; and from it we can conclude that the freer our buildings are of air-borne bacteria, the better will be our health.

Then there are the insects which use the air as a highway — the mosquitoes, flies, gnats, bees, moths, and hosts of others. A few of these are friendly to man in general. Aside from making honey, for instance, the bees carry on the immensely important task of pollenization. But relative to most of man's activities — especially those which take place inside buildings — insects are, without exception, *persona non grata*. Even where they are not carriers of some dread disease, they are the cause of damage (termites, clothes-moths) or pain (wasps).

It is clear that a building 'fit to live in' should provide an atmospheric environment free from all such dangerous or noxious invaders. The fly-screen and mosquito netting have done pretty well in keeping out the insects.   Modern insecticides like DDT have immensely improved our chances of controlling them.   In recent years we have perfected the means for filtering the smaller and more dangerous invaders out of enclosed spaces.   We shall presently see how these filters work and what they promise to do for our building.   There remains, however, one last class of atmospheric pollution — the most extensive and perhaps the most dangerous of all — that produced by man's own activities.

In November, 1939, the city of St. Louis was blanketed by the worst smoke pall in its history.   For nine days on end, the sun did not shine — indeed, there was scarcely any daylight at all.   Visibilities at noon were reduced to a matter of a few feet. Lights burned everywhere — in schools, shops, homes, factories — as though it were night.   If anything, it was worse than night, for no artificial light could penetrate an atmosphere so polluted that it cut out the sun itself.   Factories slowed down, schools were dismissed, transportation crawled to a standstill: the city was all but paralyzed in an atmosphere of its own making.

What had happened?   Merely that the wind and the weather had conspired to hold down over the city the immense amounts of soft-coal smoke which it produced on a normally busy day. It was a condition of which many St. Louisans had been long aware — prophecies of just such a situation had been issued as early as 1927.   A whole series of smoke-abatement ordinances had already been passed by the city.   But it took the nine black days to galvanize the town into taking the steps necessary to prevent their repetition.   By April of 1940 a complete program had been put into effect which controlled every phase of the combustion cycle for every power and heating plant in the city. The famous 'St. Louis Plan' had begun.[1]

Smoke from a fire, like a squeal from a brake, is a sign of inefficient energy conversion: the perfect fire yields no smoke at all.   The St. Louis pall, like those in many other American

[1] For a detailed description, see 'A Smoke Elimination Program that Works,' by Raymond R. Tucker, *Heating, Piping and Airconditioning*, September, 1945, through February, 1946.

cities, was thus a sign of monstrous waste. But this primary waste served merely to obscure a much more extensive damage to the health, property and livelihood of every citizen of the city. Hence the marked success of St. Louis's smoke-elimination program has yielded the conservation of much more than mechanical energy.

In the five years of its operation, the program has achieved an average over-all reduction in smoke of 73.1 per cent: in areas where smoke had previously been densest, this reduction has run to 80.8 per cent! Figures comparing the last year before the program began with the five subsequent years with it are startling:

TOTAL SMOKE

Season	In Days	In Hours	Reduction (per cent)
1939–40	82	716:30	——
1940–41	46	197:15	72.5
1941–42	47	184:05	74.3
1942–43	39	142:00	80.2
1943–44	69	251:10	65.0
1944–45	46	189:58	73.5

Measured in concrete terms, the results of this sharp drop in atmospheric pollution are impressive — even if they are not as yet definitive. Owners and operators of buildings of all sorts are without exception enthusiastic.[1] Smoke, soot, and their accompanying acids not only soil and stain buildings inside and out: they attack and eventually destroy paints and sheet metal. It is estimated that smoke reduction had extended the life of painted surfaces by at least twenty-five per cent, while that of sheet metal is expected to treble. Cleaning specialists say that the rate of exterior soiling has been reduced from three to four times. Decorators have noticed a sharp drop in damage to interior finishes of all sorts — one large apartment-house owner estimating the increase as being as much as fifty per cent. The hotels estimated their savings in cleaning, decorating, and maintenance at about thirty thousand dollars annually, while office

[1] The following data are taken from a paper by J. H. Carter, 'Does Smoke Abatement Pay?' *Heating, Piping and Airconditioning* (April, 1946), pp. 80–84.

buildings reported similar benefits. The department stores reported that stock spoilage was at an all-time low. The local utility company says that St. Louisans save seventy-five thousand dollars annually on their light bills. Dry cleaners and laundries seem to be the only enterprises adversely affected by the cleaner atmosphere.

But evidence of far more significant savings comes from the horticulturists and physicians of the city. The Missouri Botanical Garden was quick to note the dramatic results of cleaner atmospheres upon its plant life. Smoke damage had previously been of two sorts — instantaneous and cumulative. Such plants as begonias, cinerarias, and tropical water lilies might be entirely defoliated by a single smoke pall of less than twenty-four hours duration. Hardier plants would be slower but no less certain to show the effects of smoke in abnormal browning or dropping of leaves, drooping or discoloration of flowers. The beneficial effects of the program were so marked that after only a few months the Garden *Bulletin* declared: 'certainly there has been such a marked improvement that one is inclined to become optimistic about the possibilities for successful gardening in the city.' Five years later the city forester said: 'Now we feel safe in planting evergreens and even juniper in our downtown areas. Previous to the adoption of the city smoke ordinance, this was unthinkable.'

To see if parallel improvements in human health had been observed, a survey was made of the ear, eye, nose, and throat specialists of the city. Of the thirty-three doctors who replied, only four could report no improvement: the other twenty-nine almost unanimously agreed that 'there has been a very definite reduction in infections of the upper respiratory passages and of the tracheo-bronchial tree.' Prolonged exposure to the old smoke-laden air had caused serious and permanent damage to the membranes of nose, sinus and lungs and rendered them more susceptible to infection, the doctors reported; they agreed that smoke abatement had reduced such infections and had made those which did develop easier to treat. One eye specialist said that 'there has been a very noticeable improvement in the incidence of eye infections since the smoke program has been adopted'; while the reduction of conjunctivitis, and of inflammation and irritation caused by chemical and mechanical irritants was particularly noticeable.

Obvious though the damage to health and property may be, every American city is busy polluting its atmospheric environment, soiling its own nest, with a wide variety of smokes, dusts, and gases. (New York City, for example, has an atmosphere which deposits as much as nine hundred tons of soot per square mile per year!) Unfortunately, not many cities have taken the thoroughgoing corrective measures adopted by St. Louis. None of them, needless to say, have had the opportunity to adopt the new energy sources described in the last chapter. These would largely eliminate atmospheric pollution. Nor is it only in the cities that we pollute the atmosphere with noxious smokes and gases. The air of a mine, a cement mill, or a tunneling operation can be equally lethal in the heart of the wilderness. In the great dust storms of the nineteen-thirties, suspended soil particles rendered large, purely agricultural regions literally unfit for human habitation.

It should go without saying that it is as dangerous to breathe polluted air as to drink polluted water. While typhoid epidemics are more tragically spectacular, air-borne dust and smoke are probably as great a threat to health as nature's microbes and pollens combined. Certainly, air-borne dusts always and everywhere play into the hands of the microbes. To the evidence of St. Louis's doctors can be added such facts as the one that, in the lead and zinc mining areas of Missouri, the death rate from tuberculosis was nearly two and a half times that of the nation as a whole. To a greater or lesser extent, all urban and industrial atmospheres are polluted. This condition not only leads directly to such diseases as silicosis but also prepares the ground for the active intervention of bronchitis, pneumonia, tuberculosis, etc.

Discomfort, disease, and death from atmospheric pollution is a prosaic and slowly developing process. Hence the conditions in our cities and buildings have to be pretty terrible before we are moved to do anything about them. Here again we see the pattern: a long-range accumulation of small discomforts which, if indefinitely extended, lead slowly but surely to disease and premature death.

All the foregoing is very recent history. It is only within the last thirty or forty years that we have begun to realize the exact degree to which all atmospheres are polluted by germs, dust, spores, and pollen. It is even more recently that we have begun to realize how adversely this pollution affects our social and individual health, and begun to evolve means to correct it. Characteristically, the first steps were taken to promote industrial efficiency rather than public health, *per se*. It was in those industries where dust interfered with the process itself that the most effective measures were taken and the most efficient filters evolved. Industrial dusts in the painting shops of Detroit's automobile plants and the film laboratories of Hollywood picture companies made first-rate paint jobs or movies impossible, even though the workers suffered no serious effect. In mining or quarrying, industrial dusts did not affect the process itself, but they annually damaged the lungs of thousands of workers. In the first case, we find industry eagerly fostering the development of all sorts of equipment to filter the air to fantastic degrees of purity; in the latter case, we find Congress itself unwilling to pass legislation requiring elementary health measures to protect the worker's lungs against the dreaded silica dust. Be that as it may, the first effective air-cleaners originated in industry and are just now trickling down to the consumer.

There are several ways to rid the air of its unwelcome burden of suspended matter: washing, mechanical filtering, and electric precipitation. A stream of air can be passed through a fine spray of water which will wash out most of the larger particles of smoke, dust, pollen. However the air comes out loaded with moisture, which is often undesirable. A stream of air can be forced through a many-layered screen of fine metal filings or glass threads. This method also gets only the larger particles, allowing all the smaller to slip through; in addition, the filter offers high resistance to the air flow. Finally, by electric precipitation, the air can be passed through a metal grid or ionizer which bombards the particles with ions and thus gives them an electrical charge. The air then passes through another grid whose plates are alternately positive and negative. The charged particles are attracted to this second grid and held there, whence they can be periodically removed by washing.

Of the three methods, precipitation appears to be the most efficient, since it removes dusts, pollens, and bacteria whose diameters are small enough to pass through all other filters. The principle of precipitation is not a new one and was known for some years in industry, but it was not until recent years that its excessive use of current and its odd habit of occasionally producing ozone and nitrous oxide were overcome. The applications of the electric precipitator in commerce and industry are endless and fascinating. A large film-manufacturing company is using it for the reclamation of silver nitrate which was formerly lost in the air. It is at work in laboratories and telephone exchanges, where extremely delicate equipment demands dust-free atmosphere; in libraries and archives, where books and manuscripts must be kept dirt-free. Installed in stores, the precipitator greatly reduces atmospheric damage to merchandise and building. But it is in the field of health that the air-cleaners offer their greatest promise.

Despite their relatively high efficiency, most air-cleaners cannot be relied upon to remove all air-borne germs. The precipitator removes upwards of eighty-five per cent of all foreign particles from the air; but the microscopic bacteria largely slip through in the remaining fifteen per cent. Besides, the only safe germ is a dead germ; it is not enough to catch it — you also have to kill it. Now the germicidal properties of sunlight are well known; the germ-killing rays lie in the invisible portion of the spectrum, near (but are not identical with) the ultraviolet rays which tan our skins. Research into this phenomenon has resulted in a new lamp being placed on the market which reproduces these bactericidal rays. Its application promises spectacular results. Together with the air-cleaner, the bactericidal lamp promises completely clean and sterile atmospheres for the first time in the history of mankind.

The new lamp can be used in any of several ways. Placed alongside the air-cleaner, it can irradiate all incoming air after it has been filtered. It can be used to irradiate the air in any given room or any specified portion of the room, including its surfaces.[1] Finally, it can be used to form a barrier between different parts of the building, an invisible door through which no germ can pass save at peril of his life. The implications of this are obvious, especially in such buildings as hospitals. The atmosphere of the entire hospital can be kept completely sterile; certain areas like operating rooms and baby wards can be sterilized, or such areas as isolation wards can effectively prevent cross-infection.

Obviously, this technique could be applied to all buildings — homes, schools, theaters, even railway trains and buses. In a controlled experiment in three Pennsylvania schools, ultra-violet irradiation in the classrooms of the primary grades reversed the trend of a measles epidemic. Only a third as many cases were reported in the primary grades as in the upper ones, where irradiation was omitted. (There are usually three times as many measle cases in the lower grades as in the upper.) In similar experiments in 1943–44 the Navy, at its Training Center at Sampson, New York, found ultra-violet radiation in selected barracks reduced colds, German measles, and scarlet fever by twenty-five per cent. Samples of the air in these barracks showed only half as many germs of all sorts as in non-irradiated buildings. The artificial lighting of tomorrow's buildings may well combine visible and ultra-violet rays, so that all artificial light would be automatically hostile to microbes.

There are many specialized processes in which certain micro-organisms are not only welcome but essential guests, and the job of many factory buildings is to provide that none but these special organisms are present in the atmosphere. Thus, in brewing or baking, a particular strain of 'cultivated' yeast may be introduced; thereafter contamination by air-borne wild yeasts and other microscopic fermentative agents must be avoided.

---

[1] The rays have been proved to be effective not only on air-borne micro-organisms but also against bacterial colonies on any surface on which the rays may fall — clothes, skin, furniture, floors, etc.

Sterilization of all incoming air is easily accomplished by ultra-violet irradiation. Cheese-making requires both bacteria and molds, but certain cheeses require special cultures as well as other special atmospheric and thermal conditions. Until recently, such cheeses could only be produced in some odd cavern in Italy or Greece. Now it is possible to recreate these exact atmospheres — complete with wandering microbic population — in any factory and, by irradiating all incoming air with ultra-violet, to avoid the presence of any other organisms. Other fields in which control of air-borne micro-organisms is important are the manufacture of surgical and pharmaceutical products, cosmetics, and food processing, where putrefaction, food poisoning and decay are a constant hazard.

Most of this magnificent equipment should be used to modify or supplement the natural atmospheric environment to meet our special needs, yet it is, in fact, busily duplicating it. If, during St. Louis's 'nine black days,' there was a single building equipped for removing all air-borne dust particles from the air, and if it had an equally efficient lighting system to replace the lost daylight — then its occupants were lucky. They were breathing clean air and had enough light to see by, while the rest of the town stumbled around in a suffocating pall of its own making. Here was irony compounded: this building was at great expense merely producing environmental conditions which under 'ordinary' circumstances would be free for the asking. Moreover, it is almost certain that the building's power and heating plants were going full tilt; that like all the other buildings it used soft coal for fuel; that therefore its chimney was also belching sooty smoke — so that the building was simultaneously destroying without what it strove so hard to produce within!

The insanity of this proposition does not make it the less probable. As a matter of fact, it is a characteristic contradiction of all urban building. We have met it before and we shall meet it again. A single building, no matter how advanced its design or excellent its performance, cannot stand alone. It affects, and is affected by, all its neighbors in its struggle with the natural environment; unless they work together in a mutually satisfactory plan, they will not work at all.

CHAPTER TWELVE

'Oh, Say, Can You See . . . '

A SUNSET is a pretty thing to look at and a leaping deer a lovely thing to see. But it is scarcely in such terms that the evolution and function of human vision can be discussed. For, as Hans Blumenfeld has so succinctly put it:

> We did not develop the ability to see just for the fun of it, but in order to grab and avoid being grabbed. The good, the true and the beautiful light is the light which enables us to perceive real bodies. We want to perceive their exact size, shape and distance; and to perceive them safely, easily and quickly.[1]

And lest this strike one as too blunt or too simple a definition for the function of sight, one needs only to remember the darkened European cities with their searchlights fingering the sky 'in order to grab but avoid being grabbed' by hostile planes; or to turn the tables of industrial accidents and occupational diseases to see the number of workers who — annually losing their ability to 'perceive the exact size, shape and distance' of real bodies — lose their jobs.

The human eye has been conditioned by the natural luminous environment for millions of years before it became human, and for scores of millions before it became an eye. The environment in which it increasingly moves is the product of the last century. And it has been roughly parallel to this increasing control of both natural and artificial light that we have come

[1] 'Integration of Natural and Artificial Lighting,' *Architectural Record* (December, 1940), p. 49.

to understand the mechanism of vision and the physiology of the human eye.

The natural luminous environment shares with the thermal and the atmospheric the quality of discontinuity. There is not only the periodic fluctuation between night and day, but also the constant fluctuation in both intensity and color composition of daylight itself. Unlike the other environments, however, these luminous fluctuations have not been the source of much inconvenience until modern times. Nightfall, naturally, had always brought discomfort as well as terror to primitive people, but it did not seriously interfere with their activities. There was ample daylight for hunting, agriculture and shepherding; and the long night provided the necessary recovery of energy from the day's strenuous activities. This remained true for even so relatively advanced a society as that of pre-Revolutionary America. There might have been a cobbler here or a student there who felt that 'God had made the night too long.' But by and large there was no overwhelming compulsion to extend the light and all society remained geared to the dawn-to-dusk rhythm.

It remained for the industrial revolution first to raise the question of, and then produce the means for, continuous light around the clock. In pointing to the primitive state of artificial illumination in George Washington's America, we must not make the mistake of simply comparing it with our own standards of today. We have to ask, rather, how that society differed from ours. What sort of synthetic luminous environment did it require? Little research is required to show that it actually had little need of artificial light. When this country was founded *nineteen people out of every twenty* had to spend their time producing food for themselves and the twentieth person. A hundred years ago *eight people out of every ten* had to work with the soil, producing food for the whole ten. Today about *two people out of every ten* produce the food for the whole ten. It is thus apparent that ninety-five per cent of early Americans had relatively little need of more or better light, since even today agriculture is almost exclusively carried on in the natural luminous environment. Our forefathers rose with the dawn, worked by the light of the sun, and stopped at dark. They went to bed early both from choice (because they were sleepy) and necessity (because they had no light to read by and few books to read; in addition, few people in those days knew how to read).

Today, this situation is almost precisely reversed. Eighty per cent of the American people today live in an almost exclusively synthetic luminous environment, where neither the amount nor the quality of daylight is adequate. Upwards of ninety per cent are literate: newspapers, magazines, and books are published by the hundreds of millions: artificial light sources are cheap and plentiful.

Another change must be observed: ninety-five per cent of pre-Revolutionary Americans used their eyes naturally. Their seeing tasks nearly all involved far- or middle-vision — stalking game or shooting Indians, plowing a field or sailing a ship. Only the craftsmen — bookkeepers, printers, watchmakers — and the housewives (with their sewing, knitting, and weaving) had tasks which lay primarily in the field of near-vision. Many colonists could not read at all, while the per capita use of papers, books, and magazines was microscopic. More important still, few children went to school and so used their eyes naturally during that most formative period.

Today, this situation is likewise reversed. The vast majority of us move in a world of near-vision, of prolonged and critical seeing tasks, of concentration on a field of vision rarely farther from the eye than arm's length. All of us read. With universal education, American children are nowadays plunged into this world of near-vision at six years or earlier, there to remain for from eight to sixteen years.

The nineteenth century's fascination with artificial illumination was expressed in its enthusiasm for such spectacles as gas street lighting. Here natural laws had been repealed. Night had been outlawed from streets which had previously become useless at dark to all but the hardy or the suspect. With the appearance of lighted streets, the temporal limits of social intercourse had been measurably extended. The sheer novelty of artificial lighting continued to hold a fascination for the entire century. The early torchlight parades, the 'illuminations' with which mid-century political rallies were decorated, the electric illumination of the Columbian Exposition, whose fairy-like appearance left all America breathless: these were the spiritual as well as physical proofs of the Victorian conquest of darkness.

However, it was scarcely to make streets safe or fairs beautiful that American society spent so much on artificial illumination. It was rather that industrial production could not develop to the maximum in the natural luminous environment. The need of industrialism for a constant luminous environment sprang from two distinct but closely related facts. The first was the discovery that a machine (unlike a slave or a horse) is most economically operated when it runs all the time. The second was that, even in its primitive stages, a machine is a precision instrument — that is, works to close tolerances and hence demands good vision from its operators. Both of these facts imply artificial light: the first, *more* light and the second, *better* light, than nature gives us.

The economy and culture of industrialism not only changed the lighting of our factories but literally of our entire lives. It has even changed the way in which we use our eyes. From simple and imprecise operations like chopping down a tree or plowing a field, it put us to work indoors under artificial suns, running the lathe and the loom — operations involving close and accurate vision. It could not even stop there. An industrial nation is by definition a literate and educated nation. The Three R's are essential to all but the simplest mechanical tasks. So, a century and more ago, American children started streaming to public schools to take up seeing tasks which were both historically and anthropologically revolutionary.

Without realizing it or being able even to hazard its full implications, a profound shift in our living habits has taken place in American life. This involves two immensely important factors, the full implications of which we are only now becoming aware: on the one hand, we have moved from a *largely natural* to an *almost completely synthetic* luminous environment; on the other, we have shifted from the world of *far-vision* to that of *near-vision*. It is during the last century that the American people have superimposed upon the natural luminous environment a synthetic one, more extensive and complex than any the world has seen. In general, we have developed artificial light sources to the point where, in many building types, they have actually replaced natural light. There is little question but that most of the technical and industrial achievements of which we are so proud would have been inconceivable without this mastery of light.

Yet it is a debatable point as to whether the *average* American eye is any better off in this synthetic environment than was its colonial ancestor in a largely natural one. Certain it is that for every American building whose lighting standards are optimum, there are many whose standards are little short of criminal. For every window glazed with heat-resisting (infra-red filtering) glass, there are millions glazed with ordinary glass that excludes most of the beneficent ultra-violet rays. For every adequately lighted home, there is at least one which is inadequately lighted by oil lamps or completely dark from unpaid electric bills.

Historically, this new environment was developed primarily to expedite mechanical processes (such as photo-engraving or textiles) and not to increase health, and today it bears the characteristic imprint of this history. Its development has been uneven, with enormous technical lags between its highest and lowest examples, with instances of grossest deficiency side by side with extravagant waste. Manhattan is a dramatic example of this contradiction. Visible at night from thirty miles away because of its lavish use of light, it has the million bulbs of Times Square and thousands of ill-lighted streets and houses — many even with no electricity at all. Here we meet again the familiar contradiction of an entire synthetic environment which is much less efficient than its component parts, whose productive aspects seem hopelessly mixed up with its waste.

What We See and How

THE EYE is the original camera and, to date, the best. Although designed to cover, with marvelous precision and flexibility, a wide range of distances under the most varied of luminous conditions, the eye is primarily an instrument of far- and middle-vision. The so-called normal eye focuses at approximately fifteen feet away from the head, and is effective from there on out to infinity. If the focus is closer the vision is called near-sighted; if further than fifteen feet it is called farsighted. All eyes have this in common — that as they grow older they tend to become more farsighted.

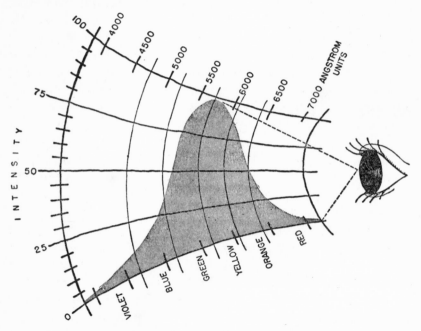

The eye perceives only a small portion of that form of energy called light.

The eye is like the ear in that it perceives only a portion of its special environment — the visible spectrum which is only a portion of the total. Thus below the violet of the visible spectrum (3800 angstrom units) lie the ultra-violet rays, while above the red at the other end of the visible spectrum (7200 angstrom units) lie the infra-red rays. Although invisible, both these rays constitute an important part of natural light.

Thus, the limits of vision of the eye are, in effect, three-dimensional — the horizontal unit of measurement being spectral, the vertical one of intensity, and the axial one of distance. But within this range, the eye works with extraordinary precision. Moreover, it is well equipped to adapt itself to extreme fluctuations in the luminous environment. It has a control mechanism — the iris, which permits wide accommodation. When that is not adequate to cut out extreme intensities, it has the eyelid. In addition it is protected from sky brightness by eyelash and eyebrow.

Actually we know very little about the connection between deficiencies in the luminous environment and defective eyesight.

How many Americans have defective eyesight, what are the major types of eye defects and disease, and with what occupations are they associated? To begin with, about 131,700 persons in this country have no eyesight at all — they are totally blind. Among adults, about ten per cent are congenitally blind, twenty-nine per cent have lost their eyesight from disease, and thirteen per cent as a result of accident or injury, with the balance of undetermined origin.[1]

The Selective Service System, in rejecting 400,000 out of 1,000,000 draftees because of medical and health defects, found that 45,000 (or more than one out of ten) men had defective eyesight. This is a much lower percentage than that given by Doctor Matthew Luckiesh, who estimates that three per cent of all persons have defective vision at birth; that twenty-five per cent of persons at high-school age, thirty-three at college age, and fifty per cent at middle age need glasses. The discrepancy between the Army and Doctor Luckiesh is not as great as first appears, however, when it is remembered that the Army's minimum vision standards were relatively low with and without glasses.

The number of people who 'have trouble with their eyes' is sufficiently impressive to indicate the presence of basic maladjustments between the organ and its environment. Since most of the manipulation with the luminous environment takes place inside buildings, it is obvious that building design plays an

[1] According to estimates of the National Society for the Prevention of Blindness, New York.

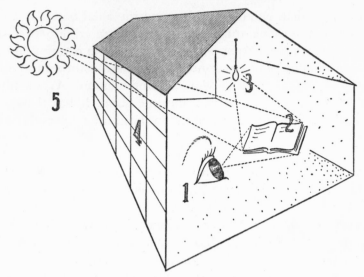

In order for the eye (1) to accomplish its task (2) with maximum precision and minimum strain, the building — by its equipment (3) and structure (4) — must create and maintain a set of luminous conditions seldom found in the natural environment (5).

important, though as yet vaguely understood, rôle in this maladjustment. It is necessary to isolate these factors and in so doing indicate wherein better building design can contribute to better eye-health.

Common sense indicates that three factors are involved: the eye, the seeing task, and the luminous environment. If the three are in perfect adjustment — and barring all other considerations — vision should be maintained at optimum efficiency. It goes without saying that they seldom are, and that adjustments are therefore necessary. Such adjustments can be made at three points. With glasses, the eye can be changed as a seeing apparatus. Here prismatic, tinted and/or polarized lenses serve as an auxiliary to the eye. Or the seeing task can be shifted from a person with one type of vision to another whose vision is better suited to it. Or the luminous environment can be corrected to make seeing easier. For example, the pay envelope of a normally farsighted 'looper' in a hosiery mill depends upon her ability to do piecework some eight inches from her eyes. A pair of glasses could correct her vision to take part of the load of continuous adjustment off her eyes; artificial lighting especially designed for that seeing task would further relieve her optical difficulties. A better solution would obviously be to shift her to a job whose visual field coincided with her own point of adjustment; and assign a naturally short-sighted person to the looping job. Finally, there is the possibility of mechanizing the seeing task so that the machine does its own looping.

In any case, a luminous environment specially designed for the seeing task must be considered irreducible minimum — both for the health of the individual and society as a whole. And it must be remembered that glasses are no economic substitute for light. In a series of tests carried out by Luckiesh, glasses raised the visual acuity of a selected group by twenty-three per cent; increased light (from one to one hundred foot-candles) increased it thirty-three per cent without glasses!

The specific requirements for good vision vary with the seeing task involved but, generally speaking, we need enough light, of the right sort, properly distributed. For most tasks involving close seeing, two qualities are generally desirable: the average level of illumination should be high and the contrast in brightness values within the room should be small. The amount of light is called brightness. (Light falling *on* a surface is measured in foot-candles; light flowing *from* a bright surface is measured in foot-lamberts.) Minimum brightness levels for various tasks are being constantly revised upwards. Levels which a few years ago were considered to have been adequate are today known to be totally insufficient. Today's practice calls for fifty foot-candles for moderately critical or prolonged seeing such as ordinary reading, clerical work, sewing on light goods. For a host of precision tasks such as one finds increasingly in industry, the minimum is around one hundred foot-candles. For such specialized tasks as surgery or fine inspection the minimum may range from one thousand to two thousand foot-candles. Anyone with a light meter can easily prove to himself that he spends most of his time in buildings whose brightness levels seldom approach these minima. In view of the fact that the eye developed in the natural luminous environment whose brightness levels can easily reach up to nine thousand foot-candles, it is entirely probable that society will demand much higher levels than these in the future.

Intimately connected (and often confused) with the factor of brightness is that of glare. Glare occurs when light strikes a highly polished, light-colored or crystalline surface and is thrown back into the eyes of the observer. Because there are few such surfaces in nature, glare usually occurs only on snow, sand or — under certain circumstances — on water. This accounts for the fact that we find the brightness levels in nature restful while the same values would be intolerable in or around the city.[1] In order to avoid glare inside our buildings — especially in our homes — we often resort to reducing the brightness level instead of altering either the light source or the color and texture of the room surfaces.

Except for certain industrial processes like color-matching, the color quality of the light is not of such great importance. For all ordinary eye tasks the spectral quality of daylight remains ideal — that is, the special balanced white light of the north sky. Most artificial light sources only approximate this. For purely decorative effects, of course, the use of colored light has great possibilities which have scarcely been explored, much less adequately exploited.

It is obvious that in all these terms — brightness, glare, distribution, and color — the urban areas differ radically from the primeval landscape or the countryside today. It is a truism also that they suffer in comparison with nature. In the city street the daytime glare is far greater than anywhere in nature, while inside the city's buildings the gloom is worse. Outdoors we are surrounded by light-colored, reflective surfaces, inside by dark, absorptive ones. Outside there will be brightness levels up to five thousand foot-candles, inside we are lucky if we get twelve.

Instead of the 'deep' view of Nature, we move in the 'shallow'

---

[1] A lawn under the nine thousand foot-candles of the midday midsummer sun is no brighter than this page under five hundred foot-candles.

frame of man-made perspectives. Aside from the fact that most of our work involves near-vision, there is the added problem of spending most of our leisure time in the same fashion. Our horizon is usually limited by the walls of a room (bedroom, office, workshop, or classroom) or a very limited perisphere (out the window, down the block, out the subway window). Many of us probably go for weeks on end without focusing our eyes on anything further away than the movie screen from the front row in the balcony.

This raises a problem which may have important implications for building design — the physiological importance of the far-view. Ever since air-conditioning and artificial lighting made windowless buildings practical, designers have been obscurely conscious of there being something awry. In many windowless factory and office buildings there have been definite indications of discomfort on the part of employees — discomfort so definite that some designers have reverted to the use of windows for what has been called the 'psychological effect.' They put in a few windows so the workers won't feel 'cooped up.' The designers of a small windowless factory in Cleveland were aware of this when they installed photomurals on the end walls to give the optical illusion of space. But clerical people, bench workers, and school children probably gaze out the window to rest their eyes by focusing them in the field of far-vision. In this case, then, the window fills both a psychological and a profound physiological need: and no mural is an adequate substitute.

There is even some reason for believing that continual use of the eyes in an urban environment actually tends to make them more nearsighted than they would ordinarily be, while continual life in the country would tend to make them more farsighted. This seems to be one conclusion to be drawn from Army Air Forces statistics on visual acuity of recruits. Here boys from rural regions were found to have better eyesight and better far-vision than boys from urban homes. In other words, the luminous environment of the city can both change and damage vision. Obviously, no inherited tendency is involved here, since men have lived in cities for only the merest fraction of time required for evolutionary changes. Rather it appears to be a question of the impact of a special luminous environment on the individual organ which is itself highly flexible and adaptable. The prevalence of corns and bunions as a result of improperly designed shoes has by no means become an hereditary trait of mankind, even though many generations have worn them for thousands of years. But they do set up special environments which cause marked and characteristic deformations of each generation of feet. Might not the synthetic luminous environment of our cities cause similar deformations of our vision?

Actually, the effects of the luminous environment upon the human body are to be measured not in terms of vision alone but of the health of the entire organism as well. An incorrect or inadequate environment may thus produce not only impaired vision but a whole train of functional disorders. This fact has been impressively demonstrated by the recent work of Doctor Darrell B. Harmon of the Texas State Department of Health. On the basis of experimental work in the Texas public school system, involving over 160,000 school children in 4,000 classrooms, Doctor Harmon has shown that improved classroom illumination will quickly and radically improve the health and intelligence of the students.[1] By a series of comparatively simple changes in the daylighting, decoration, and seating pattern of existing classrooms, Doctor Harmon was able to reduce eye troubles in certain schools by almost two thirds, nutritional difficulties by forty-four per cent, ear, nose and throat infections by thirty per cent! In one school, fifty-three per cent of the children had retractive eye problems: after six months in the new environment, these had been reduced by fifty-seven per cent. In the same period, non-retractive eye problems were reduced by ninety per cent. Improved health was paralleled by improved mental growth. Children in the experimental classrooms grew an average of 10.2 months in educational age while those in uncorrected classrooms registered a mental development of only 6.8 months.

[1] Darrell B. Harmon, 'Lighting and Child Development,' *Illuminating Engineering* (April, 1945); and Biesele, Folsom, and Graham, 'Control of Natural Light in Classrooms' (October, 1945).

The exact area of building's responsibility in this complex relationship of eye, seeing task and environment is by no means clear. Here we are confronted with much the same confusion of cause and effect as was observed in our discussion of the thermal and atmospheric environments. By a process of elimination, however, some important facts can be isolated. To begin with, certain types of eye defects can be definitely related to certain occupations; and these occupations can, in turn, be related to certain building types and hence to certain characteristic luminous environments. For example, the incidence of certain types of eye trouble among clerical and white-collar workers is known to be appreciably higher than among common laborers, farmers, and other occupations which do not involve long hours of near-vision. It is likewise obvious that clerks work in a far different luminous environment from that of the farmer or common laborer. It must be inferred, therefore, that an inadequate luminous environment is as hard on the eye as an unnatural seeing task. The office which provides inadequate lighting for clerical work is as much to blame for eye trouble as the clerical work itself.

In this connection, Luckiesh cites a significant instance from the records of the United States Naval Academy. The class of 1934 began with 647 men. By graduation in 1934, this number had been reduced to 464; of the graduates 12.7 per cent (one out of eight) were subsequently rejected by the Navy for defective vision! These figures are all the more remarkable in that they show a high rate of deterioration of vision among a selected group of men who, four years earlier, had passed rigid physical examinations (including vision); and whose general health and welfare had been maintained at much higher than average levels throughout the entire period. With all the accidents of civilian life removed from the equation, one can only conclude that their vision was damaged by (1) a special visual routine in (2) a deficient luminous environment. Whatever the routine, it is clear that the Academy's buildings did not provide an optimal environment for it.

One thing is clear — today's world of industry is a world of near-vision. There is no gainsaying that, nor any point to romanticizing about the beauties of the natural world of far-vision. Society cannot eat its cake and have it too. Rousseau and Henry Ford cannot coexist. The contradiction must be resolved at a higher level. Obviously, if we can't eliminate near-seeing, we can mechanize it. Indeed, in the more advanced areas of American industry, this is already happening on quite a large scale. Thanks to the photo-electric cell, many processes involving critical seeing, such as fine inspection and color-matching, are being automatized. This is a clear gain on two counts: it saves human eyesight and is more accurate than human vision. But such advances — even if general — do not absolve building of the responsibility of providing the optimal luminous environment of all seeing tasks, near and far alike.

Modern Light Sources

SINCE THE DEVELOPMENT of the dynamo in 1877 made possible the production of electrical energy on a large scale, all artificial light sources but those dependent upon electrical energy have become obsolete. The most spectacular aspect of this develop-ment has been the increase in efficiency of these light sources — the best being some five hundred and fifty times as efficient as the candle. These light sources fall into four general cate-gories: arcs, filaments, luminous vapors, and fluorescents. Since each has widely varying characteristics, it is necessary to describe them briefly:

Arcs: Displayed as a scientific curiosity by Davy in 1809, the arc merely awaited the appearance of the dynamo to become the earliest of all practical electric lights. It consists of the luminous bridge which is formed when an electric current jumps across the gap between two electrodes. Although tremendously improved since that day in 1878 when it first flooded Cleveland's Public Square with a sputtering blue-white glare, the arc is no longer important in building illumination. A brilliant but very hot and inflexible light source, it is principally used in search-lights, where millions of candle-power have been achieved, and in television and movies.

Filaments: These are the basis of the ordinary 'Mazda bulb.' Here a current is passed through a coiled tungsten filament inside a sealed, gas-filled glass bulb. The filament's resistance to the current raises it to a white heat: hence the light. This is of course the standard light source of the world, whose efficiency has been increased from three lumens to thirty or thirty-five lumens per watt in the past forty years. Its advantages scarcely need listing: its principal shortcomings are the high percentage of energy lost in form of heat and its spectral deficiencies. In order to get colored light (other than its characteristic yellowish-white), a tinted bulb must be used which wastes ninety-eight per cent of the light for blue, sixty per cent for yellow.

Luminous vapors: This is a complex and growing family, of which the best known (but by no means most important) is the neon. They are all based on the fact that passing an electrical arc through certain vapors and gases makes them luminous. Electrons strike the gas-atoms and jar them; as a result of such displacement, the atom emits radiant energy in the form of light. The color and wave length will be determined by the particular atom or element. In other words, each gas has its characteristic spectrum.

Sodium vapor lamps are very efficient, producing from forty-five to fifty-five lumens per watt; but they operate at high temperatures (400° F. and more), and the sodium is dangerous under certain conditions. Most serious deficiency, however, is that the light lies in the deep-yellow portion of the spectrum, so that all objects appear either yellow or black. Its use is therefore limited to such lighting jobs as highways, bridges, and crossings.

Neon vapor lamps operate on the same principle, producing the now ubiquitous orange-red light; use of similar gases and colored-glass tubes produces a wide range of other colors. They are unsuited for general illumination, however, because of relative inefficiency, low intensities, and dangerously high voltages. Their use is largely confined to outdoor signs and decorative lighting.

Mercury vapor lamps emit a light which is heavy with blue and violet but totally deficient in red; hence they are not suitable for general illumination of buildings. But because of their efficiency — certain types can get up to fifty-five lumens per watt — they are in wide use in industry where this spectral deficiency either does not matter or actually helps, as in photography. But because mercury vapor lamps are rich in non-visible ultra-violet rays, they constitute the base for two of the most important recent developments in the field — germicidal and fluorescent lamps.

By certain modifications in the design, and the use of a special glass which is transparent to short-wave ultra-violet, the mercury-vapor lamp may be converted into the so-called 'black light' lamp; here the output of visible light is quite low. These lamps have great significance as germicidal agents, as we have seen in the field of atmospheric control. Also, they will probably be widely used in hospitals, nurseries, and schools to supplement the ultra-violet in daylight, most of which is excluded by window glass.

Fluorescents: The most spectacular applications of this low-pressure mercury-vapor lamp, however, is in the field of fluorescent illumination. Here the tube is of ordinary glass, the inside of which is coated with a fluorescent material. The ultra-violet rays excite the material, causing it to glow with visible light; in other words, the fluorescent agent converts the energy from invisible to visible form. Since the mercury-vapor spectrum is itself deficient in red or heat rays, and the light of fluorescing materials the coolest known, the result is a lamp with a very low heat output. The ordinary filament lamp is from four to five times hotter than the fluorescent tube. Other advantages of the lamp include its wide color range including a close approximation of daylight, and its efficiency — from twenty-five to seventy-five lumens per watt depending upon the color. Because it represents an even source of diffused light (as contrasted with the incandescent lamp with its high concentrations) it is an important addition to indirect lighting.

Although still in the experimental stage, there is a further possibility in fluorescent lighting. The use of fluorescent paints and dyes on walls, ceilings, and rugs which could be illuminated by black light. So far this principle has been employed mostly for novelty effects on the stage. But the chances are that it may see a fairly wide application in those areas where an even, soft luminosity is required.

The application of these new light sources is a complex and fascinating subject, and constitutes an independent field in itself, that of illuminating engineering. Singly or in combination, using a wide variety of shades, reflectors, and lenses, the new lamps provide the means for effectively meeting almost any illumination problem for any type of building. The germ on the microscope slide may be pinpointed with the same ease and precision that the huge interior spaces of Willow Run are bathed in glareless, high-level light. Here, as elsewhere, industrial and commercial applications have set the pace. But flowing from developments in these areas has been the steady (if still far from adequate) improvement of artificial lighting in schools, offices, hospitals, etc. Last to respond has been the house itself. This has been partly due to the tenacity of anachronistic concepts of what a light source should *look like*. But the larger deterrent has undoubtedly been the comparatively high cost of installing and operating efficient artificial lighting. In any event, the average house or apartment today offers a much less satisfactory luminous environment than it should.

Closely linked to advances in lighting has been an unprecedented interest in color. This was, of course, inevitable, since it is only by the surfaces on which light falls that we perceive the light itself. This perception is measured in terms of how much light the surface reflects and what color the reflected light has. The esthetic aspects of color in building were dramatized for millions of us who saw the New York and San Francisco Fairs in 1939. These were the country's first large-scale demonstrations of brilliantly colored exteriors. Not only were they illuminated with colored light at night; they were also brightly painted for daytime color. And, at the San Francisco Fair at least, the colors were not necessarily the same — that is, a coral-painted building might at night be given a golden flood or a green building washed in electric blue. The results were spectacular, serving to demonstrate the timidity and pallidness of the conventional architectural palette.

The use of color in interior design has made great progress during the past decade. However, this has been more a question of pigment than of light, and employed more for esthetic effect than for any demonstrably practical reason. There seems to be little doubt that the color of a room has a perceptible influence upon the mood of the people in it. But there is little agreement among colorists as to how important this influence is or how it operates. Blues and greens are generally assumed to have a tranquillizing effect while reds and yellows are considered exciting. There is evidence aplenty that complaints about cold rooms may be remedied by merely changing the wall color from blue to yellow. But the subject is complex, involving as it does both objective and subjective factors. Social convention and individual taste both play an important part in our attitudes toward color. Until more precise and comparable data are available, the only safe position to assume is that interior color is psychologically of undetermined importance.

More significant from the standpoint of health has been the control of color in industrial operations. Here the color of the light, of the walls, and of the tool itself may be of critical importance to the safe and efficient performance of a given task. Enough evidence is available to show that, when considered scientifically in relation to all the other factors involved in quick, easy seeing, the choice of colors may be of considerable importance.[1] Such colors may be proved to be safe and healthy but it does not necessarily follow that they will be esthetically pleasing.

The Window Reconsidered

THERE IS NOWADAYS much talk of windowless buildings. Under existing conditions, many factories, stores, and offices are finding

[1] Safety records, covering the wartime operation of 26 United States Army depots, show that use of a standard safety color code for marking physical hazards reduced some types of accidents from a frequency of 46.14 to 5.58. One depot estimated that use of the code reduced disabling accidents from 13.25 to 6.99 per 1,000,000 man-hours. Another reported a yearly reduction of $5,000 in property damage by use of a special marking at a single hazard on a loading platform.

it easier to maintain precise control of the environments by entirely eliminating the windows and depending upon artificial illumination. This effects important economies in heating and cooling during the daytime (since conventional windows are an important source of heat loss and gain) and in lighting at night (since as much light goes out of a window at night as comes in in daytime). In addition, of course, the workers are often given an unfluctuating luminous environment much better adapted to their specific seeing task. This trend was given added emphasis in the early days of the war, when many vital new plants were 'blacked-out' at night by simply having no windows to cover up.

But it would be foolish to mistake this very limited and special solution for the *ideal* for all types of buildings, now and hereafter. Talk of generally excluding all natural light from our buildings is a vulgar oversimplification of an enormously complex problem. It is characteristic of American illuminating engineering that, historically, it solved the technical and optical aspects of its problem before it solved the physiological; or that, once a new source of light were perfected, its use would, for a time at least, obscure its basic subordination to natural light. Both tendencies have been noticeably true of all our work in environmental control. Only in recent years has the interest of the lighting specialist broadened from an obsession with the efficiency of his light source to include a consideration of its effect upon human vision. Similarly, artificial light is only now being understood as a supplement to, rather than a substitute for, natural light. Increased awareness of this fact has led to the new field of 'daylighting.'

The manipulation of daylight in buildings is more the architect's responsibility than the engineer's, since it involves the shape, size, and articulation of the various elements of the structure. And architects are still not sufficiently aware of how profoundly the luminous environment of a building may be altered by a few changes in the size, shape, and location of its windows. In the experimental Texas classrooms already mentioned, Doctor Harmon was able to achieve astonishing improvements by merely installing translucent diffusing screens across the windows and raising the reflectivity of the room surfaces by light paint. By such means, huge contrasts in brightness (one of the greatest hazards to vision) were reduced from a ratio of 217:1 before renovation down to 8:1 afterward. Prior to his work, Harmon found that although some desks near the window got as high as 100 foot-candles on their working surface, others along the inside of the room got as little as 5.4 foot-candles. After renovation, the darkest desk had been raised to 21.5 foot-candles without any artificial lighting at all.[1]

In another experimental classroom at a Salem, Massachusetts, school, similar results were achieved by similarly simple means. Brightness contrasts between unshaded windows and surrounding wall surfaces had been of the order of 150:1. By use of vertical-louvered venetian blinds, this ratio was reduced to 7:1. Inside desks which previously had gotten only 2 to 3 foot-candles of natural light, even on bright days, received 17 foot-candles after renovation. And with the lights turned on, this level could be raised to a minimum of 40 foot-candles.

These cases serve to illustrate two things about the average American building: its shocking deficiencies as regards the exploitation of the natural luminous environment; and the immense improvements which can be made without any artificial light sources at all. The full potentials of scientific daylighting were just beginning to be appreciated before the outbreak of World War II: hence there is scant evidence of its application in contemporary buildings. There is, however, every reason to suppose that it will play an important rôle in the building design of the next few years. (See also Chapter 15.)

We have already seen the optical importance of windows as a source of relaxation from near-vision tasks; and have seen their parallel (but perhaps less important) psychological value. There remains, however, still another important aspect of natural light: the physio-chemical. This cannot be ignored in any discussion of windows, even though the ultra-violet rays do not directly affect vision. Indeed, the more we learn of the physio-chemical relationship between light and all forms of life,

---

[1] *Architectural Record* (February, 1946), pp. 86–89.

the less likely it seems that the buildings of the future will simply exclude natural light. Rather we will want to admit more of it than ever — but on our own terms: that is, we will *filter* it.

The idea of filtering water or even air is no longer a novelty to the layman. But the concept of filtering light — and for the same reason, health — is not so familiar. Yet the principal function of windows has always been to filter the natural luminous environment. With its accumulated paraphernalia of centuries — shades, blinds, awnings and curtains — it has served as a crude and inefficient filter, keeping out many elements which it should have let in (diffused light, ultra-violet rays) and admitting much that it should have excluded (glare and infra-red rays in summer). But the window has always had the dual purpose of admitting air as well as light. This is its basic limitation: in trying to do both, it does neither well. (Any bedroom on a hot summer night shows this paradox — lights on, no breeze; open windows, no lights.) Yet to discard natural light because of inefficient windows is to throw the baby out with the bathwater.

Tomorrow's sunlight will not enter tomorrow's buildings through holes punched in solid walls; rather it will be absorbed by the entire building, there to be filtered and mixed in the right proportions with artificial light to form a synthetic environment designed to our specifications. Tomorrow's buildings may open and close automatically with the sun, like morning-glories; or, like sunflowers, revolve slowly to keep their 'faces' toward the sun. This comparison to growing plants is not mere romancing, for it is already clear that building design must finally adopt nature as its criterion — not by copying its forms but by learning from its processes.

Nor is the comparison in any sense far-fetched or Utopian. Many of the necessary materials and equipments are already available. First of all, there is that miraculous control instrument, the photo-electric cell. Responsive to the most minute variations in light, it is already at work turning off and on classroom lights, closing and opening doors, counting people entering rooms, trapping burglars, etc. This is the logical control for almost any type of automatic light problem. Motor-driven movable walls are a commonplace in American industry, while there are many installations of movable roofs which slide to one side at the press of a button. In Buenos Aires, where the brilliance of the sunlight poses a terrific problem in light control, there are several new buildings whose entire exteriors are covered by a sort of giant venetian blind of reinforced concrete (Fig. 100). From this it is but a step to huge blinds of metal or plastic, motor driven and automatically adjusted to the sun.

Tomorrow's buildings will use glasses which are transparent to ultra-violet (growth) rays, which common glass largely excludes, and opaque to infra-red (heat) rays, which common glass largely admits. Instead of cumbersome combinations of shades, blinds, and curtains for privacy, there will be sheets of 'one-way' glass (you can see out but they can't see in) or of water-clear polarized-glass windows which become opaque as a granite wall at the flip of a hand. Such materials can naturally be combined into dozens of varying combinations, depending upon the specific problem involved. The thing to bear in mind is that the problem is not one of window versus no windows, but of the optimum luminous environment for the specific activities involved.

This does not mean that all buildings need constantly to be opening and closing and turning (so that, in inviting people over for dinner, you'd have to say 'remember, our house faces due west at exactly six-thirty-five summer time this coming Friday'). As a matter of fact, there is no excuse for the miserable use our buildings make of sunlight, even with present limitations accepted. Most of our cities have streets running east-west and north-south, as though our ancestors were determined that as little sunlight as possible would find its way into our buildings. Most houses have windows whose number, size, and location are determined by some arbitrary standard of 'taste' or 'balance' with little or no reference to their main function. Yet the simplest use of the principles of orientation would make our buildings better lighted and infinitely more comfortable.

It is perhaps not the most important thing in the life of the average city dweller that, by the techniques and equipment just described, he has been slowly but surely transplanted from his natural luminous environment into another and artificial one. For many specific seeing tasks, this new environment is much more suitable. Yet, as our cities are built and lives are ordered today, this shift involves immense and needless sacrifice. The city dweller has lost the bright yet glareless illumination, the rich varied colors, and deep perspectives of the natural landscape. He spends a large part of his life moving in and between buildings which exclude sunlight and, at night, prevent his enjoying either moonlight or plain ordinary darkness. In exchange for detailed advances in illumination, beneficial to only part of his day at best, he has accepted a luminous environment which, in its total aspect, is sadly distorted and inadequate.

Thus the city dweller's theoretical advantage over the farmer is actually quite narrow. For many it is nonexistent. Yet the farmer's situation is not idyllic either, immersed though he may be at the center of a natural luminous environment. It is true that much of his work is carried on out-of-doors, with little or no need for artificial light. But much farm work — especially that of the wife — is carried on indoors. Here the illumination requirements are little if any different from those of any family, anywhere. Well over a third of all American farm homes are without electricity today — being lit, presumably, by oil lamps, candles, or open fires. Such homes can scarcely provide a suitable environment for any task involving close or precise seeing. And since the general illumination of the other two-thirds is not likely to be very advanced, it is apparent that the countryside also lacks a balanced environment.

The solution of this paradox is not the responsibility of the lighting specialist alone: on the contrary, it can only be solved by the building field as a whole. Only when buildings are designed not as isolates but as units of integrated groups, communities and towns — only then will a satsifactory balance be struck between the régime of the sun and that of the lamp.

CHAPTER THIRTEEN

Silence: Men at Work

Unlike the environments we have discussed, there is nothing 'wrong' with the sonic. The other natural environments may fluctuate wildly, resulting in acute discomfort if not death for man. Not so the sonic: there is no such thing in Nature as too much or too little sound. Most of the time in Nature, sound drops below our powers of perception; at its highest pitch (thunder or Niagara Falls) it cannot hurt us. Until comparatively recent years, a simple sonic environment was the natural state of man. Our colonial ancestors heard few sounds and most of them were pleasant: the song of a bird or the wind in the pines, the cry of a baby or the blacksmith at his anvil. Although some of these sounds might have been dangerous by implication — rattlesnake whirring, panther crying, despot ranting — they were not of themselves dangerous to health.

All the more ironic, then, that today the man-made sonic environment constitutes a real threat to the well-being of urban America. For it was left to modern industrial society to create new sound to the point where sound levels in many plants and offices are at the threshold of pain; where most urban areas have an average loudness level that makes protection against it necessary; where noise has become a recognized factor in pathology. How has this come about?

Society creates a synthetic sonic environment deliberately (as when it broadcasts a symphony) and incidentally (as when it stamps out a mudguard or rivets a ship). In the first case, the sound is the end-product of the process, with tangible social

250

value. This might be called productive sound. In the second instance, the sound is a by-product of the process and represents social waste. This, which might be called destructive sound, is usually known as noise.

However, even productive sound remains socially useful only so long as it is socially controlled; otherwise, it too often becomes mere noise. This is easily demonstrated by reference to our symphonic broadcast. Blaring forth from half a dozen radios in a closely packed apartment block, it will prove productive sound for those who *want* to listen to it. But for the other tenants who *have* to listen to it — when they might have preferred another program, or studying, or sleeping — the symphony becomes destructive sound: plain noise.

Noise will therefore be seen as a social, and not a technical, unit of measurement, developed to describe our own pollution of the natural sonic environment. This pollution corresponds closely to that of the atmospheric environment in both cause and effect. Both are an index of social waste, since both represent an incomplete or incorrect conversion of energy on the one hand, and a direct threat to health and efficiency on the other. Unlike atmospheric pollution, however, noise is almost exclusively man-made. Incredible as it may appear, we used to boast of this. All through the literature of the nineteenth century, noise was considered a symbol of creative human activity ('the hum of the city,' 'the busy roar of the shops') instead of a sure sign of waste of both human and mechanical energy. Today silence has become the symbol for efficiency in machines, though unfortunately the importance of silence to working men and women is not as generally recognized.

The connection between silence and efficiency can scarcely be overemphasized. If in your home you exchange a noisy electric fan for a silent new one, you have by definition acquired a better one. Its blades are scientifically designed to move the maximum amount of air with the minimum of power. A quiet refrigerator means closer tolerances, better manufacture and design — hence longer life and less maintenance — than a noisy one. The huge steam turbines in the power house make only a gentle hum while rotating at thirty-six hundred revolutions per minute. Here vibration must be held to an absolute minimum if the turbine is not to fly apart under its tremendous loads. Everywhere in industry the same thing holds; in motors, machine tools, locomotives, silent performance means efficient performance. In general then, it may be said that with machines noise is a result of inefficiency while with man it is a cause.

What We Hear and How

THE EAR is only the instrument of perception of this sonic environment. It is not merely the ear, but the entire body which, through its central nervous system, profits from a good sonic environment. And, except in the extreme instance of blast or concussion, it is not the ear but the entire body which suffers from a bad sonic environment. The ear is a specialized filter which stands between our internal and external environments, as much a 'window of the soul' as the eye, and functioning in much the same capacity.

Like the eye, the ear perceives only a portion of its total environment. Just as we cannot see the whole of the luminous spectrum with the naked eye, so we can hear only a portion of the total sonic environment. This environment has two dimensions. The vertical is one of intensity — that is, loudness — and extends from the threshold of audibility up to the threshold of feeling. Expressed in other terms, this runs from quiet to noisy, from silence to blast, from 'hearing nothing' to 'hearing 'til it hurts.' The unit of measurement is called a *decibel*. The horizontal dimension is one of frequency and runs from sounds of such low pitch that we cannot hear them to sounds of very high pitch such as those with which bats communicate. This dimension of the sonic environment is measured in *cycles per second*.

The perfect ear thus has a field of hearing which covers only a portion of the sonic environment; and a less-than-perfect ear covers even less of this area. But within its range, the ear, like the eye, is an extraordinarily flexible instrument. 'The range of

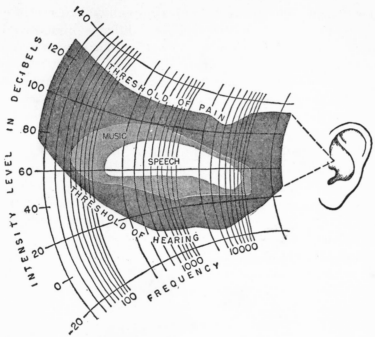

Submerged in a pulsing sea of energy, the ear perceives
only a small portion of that form called sound.

physical intensities to which the ear responds is enormous,' says
Doctor Paul E. Sabine. '. . . A sound so intense as to be painful
is of the order of *ten trillion* times the minimum audible intensity.
The intensity of speech is of the order of one to *ten million* times
the minimum audible intensity, so that conversational speech
level falls about the middle range which the human ear will
accommodate.' [1]

Nature has provided the eye with an adjustable aperture, the
iris, which permits a wide accommodation to light; in addition,
there is the eyelid which can shut out light altogether and protect the eye against the strongest natural light source — the
tropic sun.   Unlike the eye, however, the ear has no such flexible
control mechanism — probably because Nature never anticipated sounds greater than those of thunder or hurricane, both
of which are well within the ear's limit of accommodation.   But

[1] *Architectural Record* (January, 1940), p. 69.

today the average American ear is constantly exposed to a synthetic sonic environment which is very different from anything Nature had in mind. How does this affect our hearing and our health?

The hearing mechanism of the inner ear is a complex keyboard behind the eardrum, consisting of hundreds of microscopic hair clusters, each with its separate nerve connection to the brain. Here sound waves received from the outside are converted into sense impulses and telegraphed to the brain. Extended exposure to loud or excessive sound may damage this keyboard, resulting in temporary or permanent loss of hearing. This delicate mechanism is, like most parts of the human body, able to stand a lot of punishment; but, also like the rest of the body, it has fixed limits beyond which it cannot go. Hence it can be destroyed by an 'all-out' blow or worn down by the accumulation of smaller but constant blows.

As a matter of fact, most types of serious impairments to the ear are probably not due to the sonic environment at all but to pathologic conditions — catarrh, mastoids, infections. And the task of deciding what percentage are definitely traceable to noises as a primary factor is beyond the scope of this study. For persons ten to nineteen years of age a hearing loss sufficient to be a handicap under church or theater conditions affects only 1.5 per cent; but in the age group fifty to fifty-nine this proportion rises to 14.3 per cent.

There can, however, no longer be any doubt that there are whole areas of industry where the sonic environment has ceased being a mere nuisance and has become an active menace to the worker's health. Isolated noises such as whistles and blasts, pneumatic drills and riveters, damage the ear directly — that is, impair it as a hearing mechanism. But continued exposure to such sonic environments as obtain in boiler plants, shipyards, and steel fabricating shops can result in permanent deafness. So characteristic was the derangement of hearing in the Tank Corps and Air Forces during the war that it was given a special name — *tinnitus* — and its treatment considered a part of military medicine.

Sound levels can fall well below those which damage the

hearing mechanism and still be detrimental to health and efficiency. Strangely enough, due to the mechanization of office work, sound levels obtain here which are higher than in many factories. And medical authorities seem pretty generally agreed that they result in lowering both the quality and quantity of work performed. Noise has a distracting effect, making concentration on any task more difficult; hence the part played by such noise is to contribute to and accelerate fatigue.

The urban ear is not only attacked in the office or shop. Everywhere, including the home, it works under a much greater environmental load than Nature intended. The situation is all the more dangerous because it is insidious. We have already observed that the ear is powerless to exclude any noise which comes its way. Consequently, the brain makes a sort of automatic correction for many of the messages which the ear sends along — recognizes them as being of no significance and, so to speak, discards them. But this involves quite as much effort as if all the sounds had use value; in fact, it probably involves more work, since their disturbing effect has to be overcome. Thus it is that noise tires us even when we may be quite unconscious of it.

Control of the sonic environment must thus not be viewed as a problem in 'ear health' so much as general well-being. Not as a problem involving only certain types of workers exposed to very acute conditions but as one involving everybody all the time. In order to see how this rising sea of noise can be curbed, it is necessary first to understand something about sound itself.

How Sound Behaves

THE BEHAVIOR OF SOUND in the open air is strikingly like that sort of motion which occurs when a stone is dropped into a quiet pool. In both cases the energy moves away from its point of origin in successive waves. The difference between water and sound waves is that the former move outward in an expanding circle, while sound waves move out in an expanding sphere. In other words, water waves move in a horizontal plane only while sound waves move in three dimensions. In the open air, this process continues until the energy is finally dissipated in friction with the air.

Although a sound wave displaces each air particle, setting up a characteristic vibration, the particle does not move forward with the wave but rotates vertically. The time required for a given particle to complete this vibration is known as the sound's 'period'; the number of completed vibrations per second as its 'frequency'; the distance between two wave crests is called its 'wave length'; [1] and the maximum distance between the crest and the valley of the wave is its 'amplitude.' The speed of sound is much slower than that of light, and varies somewhat with the temperature of the air — for example, at 40° F. sound travels at 1,100 feet per second; at 60° F., 1120 feet per second. Like light, sound may be focused, reflected, and absorbed.

The behavior of sound in the open air is one thing. Its behavior inside buildings is quite another — constituting a whole branch of physics known as acoustics. The acoustical performance of a given room depends upon a bewildering array of factors. The type of sound, location of its source, the size, shape, and surfaces of the room, the people present, even the clothes they are wearing — all of these are important factors in whether or not the room has 'good' acoustics. But in the reaction of any room to any sound, four phenomena are to be observed: reflection, refraction, absorption, and resonance. These serve as criteria by which to measure acoustical performance.

Reflection of sound is just what the term implies — when it meets a solid obstacle, sound bounces back. In its most exaggerated form, this is the echo of our childhood. Refraction occurs when a sound wave breaks around a free standing obstacle such as a column. Here the action is identical with what happens when an ocean wave breaks around piling. No surface, however, can reflect all of a sound which strikes it. A portion is absorbed by the wall itself. The amount reflected and the amount absorbed depends upon the character of the wall: smooth-surfaced, dense materials reflect most of the sound, while rough-surfaced porous materials absorb it. The fourth phe-

[1] In the average male speaking voice this wave length is about five feet six inches.

nomenon associated with sound in buildings is resonance. This describes the special response of a room, or any part of a room, to sounds of a certain pitch or frequency. The reaction here is identical with that which takes place when one tuning-fork is set into strong vibration by striking another of the same pitch. Although seldom consciously employed in buildings hitherto, the principle has important implications for certain types such as radio studios, concert halls, and opera houses.

Today sound may be produced, stored, sold, plowed under, or distributed very much like any other commodity. The fact that we need a pot and a fire to consume coffee, while a radio or victrola is necessary to the consumption of sound, does not in any sense alter the relationship between consumer and producer. Society should produce sound, just as it should produce food or autos, for consumption. But the fact of the matter is that under our present economic system sound is produced for profit, just as are food and autos. Today's synthetic sonic environment is at once the basis and the product of a huge modern industry. Hence it can scarcely be surprising to find that our synthetic environment is characterized by chaos in production, distribution, and consumption — scarcity in the midst of plenty, deliberate restriction to maintain the price, adulteration of the product, monopolization of the means of production. At the heart of all this spectacular conquest of sound lie two relatively simple instruments — the mechanical speaker and the mechanical ear. Between them, the loudspeaker and the microphone have proved to be instruments of fantastic economic, social, and political importance. Their revolutionary effect on building design is thus but a reflection of their impact on society as a whole.

Radio and motion pictures are full-fledged industrial enterprises, manufacturing sound on a mass scale essentially as autos are produced in Detroit factories. It will not be surprising, then, to find that recent technological advance in sound control has originated in the studio — assembly room of the sound industry. This is not to forget that the telegraph and telephone created the preconditions for radio and movie technology, and also had important effects on building design.   But their impact was general, not specific.   The telephone (along with the automobile) might have made possible today's suburban home; but it did not directly modify the sonic requirements of the house itself.   It remained for the radio and movie to revolutionize our concepts of the sonic environment, to raise demands which, in being solved, have profoundly altered building technology.

In the first place, the industry gave us acoustics — science of the behavior of sound in enclosed areas.   The acoustical performance of a given studio is not determined by the broadcasting equipment alone, but by the reaction of the room as a whole to the source of sound.   To control accurately this factor it was not enough that the engineers perfect microphone and transmitter.   They had also to study the room itself — its shape and size, the textures and acoustical quality of floor and wall surfaces, even the audience and performers.   Nor could they stop with that.   Extraneous noise constitutes the same sort of hazard for radio that air pollution does for pharmaceuticals — it will ruin the product if not eliminated.   Since, as we have seen, sound is transmitted by both the air and the structures, radio engineers had to analyze the studio walls from two separate angles: insulation and isolation.

The transmission of sound through a wall is in some respects similar to that of heat.   When air-borne sound hits a wall a portion of it is reflected, a portion of it absorbed, and the remainder is transmitted through the wall to the air on the other side and to all floors or walls which join it.   These three factors vary greatly, depending upon the materials and construction of the wall in question.   Dense, hard-surfaced materials like wood, smooth plaster, or steel will reflect a large portion of the sound. Loose, porous materials such as plush, gypsum plaster, and mineral wool will absorb a large portion.   But transmission of sound depends more upon the system of construction than upon the materials.   Generally, sheer mass is the most effective barrier to sound: a solid continuous element such as a concrete floor slab or solid brick wall will transmit less sound than a thin wall. But since massive walls and floors contradict present trends toward lightness in structural design, the use of lightweight absorptive insulating materials is usually substituted, with the isolation of the various wall membranes a secondary device.

To make a wall literally impermeable to sound is a very difficult task; to make a room literally soundproof is even more so. Hence, for purposes of analysis, it is necessary to separate the sound originating within the studio from the noise originating outside. Progress in the control of sound originating inside the studio has been little short of amazing. The studios of today are no longer mere soundproofed rooms — they are precision instruments as fine as the microphone itself. Indeed, their performance today is judged not merely in such quantitative terms as 'volume' and 'intensity' but also in qualitative terms as 'brilliance' and 'resonance.' Experience has shown that each musical and dramatic form has its own acoustical requirements, and that studios should be designed to meet them. Since it would be impractical to have separate studios for all possible forms, however, the problem of flexibility arises. Several of the new studios of the Columbia Broadcasting System in New York have brilliantly solved this problem of multiple use with movable walls (Fig. 98). Here the walls consist of huge vertical or horizontal louvers which are electrically operated. The fins are surfaced in a variety of reflective and absorbent materials and, at the press of a button, can be adjusted to any desired degree. This arrangement yields great flexibility in the acoustical performance of a given room, permitting its rapid and easy adjustment to the requirements of a variety of programs.

Then there is the acoustical problem of the audience itself. Handel was well aware of this when, playing one night in London's Covent Garden, he was told by a worried management that his house was very poor. 'My music will sound the better,' he said. What he obviously meant was that, with a full house, the reverberation period of the Garden was too short for his musical technique. With fewer people — that is, less absorptive surface — he would get a longer reverberation, hence a fuller choral tone. Today, Handel's problem has been solved. Empty or full, an auditorium can be given the same reverberation period because the seating can be specially designed to absorb the same amount of sound when empty as when full.

Buildings as Sonic Instruments

THERE ARE MANY BUILDING TYPES whose major social function is the production of sound: theaters, concert and lecture halls; opera houses; radio and movie studios; classrooms; churches. Here the building must be regarded as much more than a device for keeping the rain off the parson's head. The building actually becomes an instrument of communication. The more precisely designed it is for its specific task, the better it performs. Although the first scientific formulations of the behavior of sound in enclosed spaces did not appear until the beginning of the present century (the American physicist, Wallace Sabine, was one of the early leaders in this field), there is ample evidence that an understanding of acoustical phenomena is centuries old. Indeed, from an historical point of view, it is obvious that musical and dramatic forms (both religious and secular) have been largely determined by the buildings in which they were produced. Naturally, these evolving musical and dramatic forms in turn profoundly affected the development of the building, so that their history is one of constant interaction.

Whether the production occurs indoors or out, the relationship remains essentially the same: the sonic form is modified by the environment. But the greater the control desired — that is, the more complex the form — the more it becomes essential to move the performance indoors. And the more totally enclosed the space, the more inseparable the connection between sonic form and building design. Most concert goers are apt to think of Beethoven's Fifth as an independent entity: at most they connect it only with the name of some conductor or orchestra whose rendition of it impressed them. Yet Beethoven's masterpiece has never been performed except in an auditorium of some sort and its character has always been modified by this fact. Here the building must be considered as integral a part of the symphony as the score, the conductor, or the bass viol.

Broadcast studios, theaters, and auditoria have, after all, a highly specialized function: unlike other building types, they produce sound for consumption. Their end-product is like that

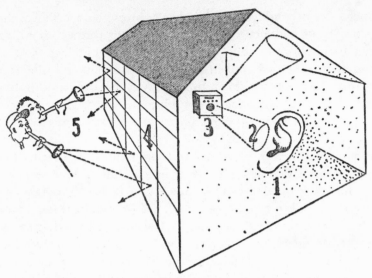

In order for the ear (1) to accomplish its task (2) with
maximum ease and efficiency, the building — through
its equipment (3) and structure (4) — must create and
maintain a wide range of sonic conditions, some of which
have no precedents in the natural environment (5).

of a restaurant — it can either be consumed on the spot or
delivered to the home.   And the product is judged, much as is
that of the restaurant, by how well it is prepared, how much
there is of it, how free it is of pollution and dilution.   The
parallel cannot be extended too far, of course.   Dramatic and
orchestral sound is produced for human beings by human beings
in an extraordinarily direct and immediate relationship.   This
involves qualitative intangibles which the consumers measure
with complex and highly subjective criteria — criteria which lie
outside the realm of acoustics and, for that matter, of this book.
Nevertheless, it is clear that the building is an essential part of
the artist-audience relationship, without which it would be
greatly impeded if not rendered impossible altogether.

These new equipments and techniques for the control of sound
do more than merely provide the optimum conditions for hearing it.   Thus, in broadcasting a symphony, the conductor —
instead of wielding the baton from a podium in the studio

proper — may conduct from inside a control booth. The orchestra can see its conductor, and the conductor can see, hear, and direct his orchestra. But, in addition, he could intervene between the orchestra's finished musical product and the radio audience. At the flip of a dial or two, he can modulate or emphasize all or any part — building up the strings, playing down the horns, intensifying a piano or a human voice.

From developments such as the foregoing — where a really precise control of the sonic environment has been essential — there has developed a new appreciation of the importance of acoustics in all types of building. Upper-class houses used always to boast a 'music room' — that is, a room where music could be produced, if not heard. Nowadays, in those few houses which can afford the space, the music room appears as a sonic instrument — its plan, surfacing, and construction designed both to provide the correct acoustical conditions for music and to isolate it from the rest of the house. The living room of the Fairchild house, by William Hamby and George Nelson, is an example of the application of these basic principles of acoustics to a multi-use room: non-parallel walls, a balance of absorptive and reflective surfaces, isolation of the entire room from the main body of the house. These same principles could easily be applied to the design of the living rooms of much more modest houses and apartments.

Sheer noise is, however, a much more pressing problem in all types of buildings than control of productive sound. And this problem, from its very nature, is as much one of good planning as of acoustics *per se*. In industry, commerce, and transportation, some noise is perhaps inevitable, though certainly not at the levels which commonly obtain. As a rule, working conditions can be vastly improved merely by the use of sound-absorbent surfacing materials and sound-deadening insulation in floors, walls, and ceilings. In housing, on the other hand, noise is usually the result of congestion and is not — in any technical sense — necessary at all. Street noises can be easily abated by reducing through streets to a minimum, placing the housing back from the street, and using heavy planting screens of trees and shrubbery as sound absorbers. Babies will always cry: but if houses and apartments were rationally planned and sited, the neighbors would rarely be disturbed by it. Even in single houses, a plan which intelligently zones the family's various activities will greatly increase the privacy and freedom from distracting noises of its members. Only in multi-family dwellings does the control of noise imply soundproof construction of at least party walls, floors, and ceilings. But even here, a good floor plan will often accomplish more than tons of sound absorbent material.

Even today, the average rural area has a sonic environment which — with minor exceptions — has remained practically unchanged since the white man came. Near the highway there may be the roar of a diesel truck; a freight train may whistle on the siding down the valley; a transport plane may drone across the sky. But these sounds are merely superimposed on a natural environment which remains substantially undisturbed, and which — for long intervals and over large areas — may sink below the threshold of hearing; that is, into silence. Such a sonic environment is physically easy on the human body. Indeed, to the sound-shocked city dweller, it usually seems idyllic. And there is little doubt that, in a purely physical sense, the farmer and the farmer's wife work in a more satisfactory sonic environment than the machinist at his lathe or the machinist's wife in her tenement flat.

The transition from country to city is gradual, the balance between natural and synthetic environments shifting so subtly as to be seldom consciously remarked. The natural retreats, the synthetic advances, until in the center of town the natural has completely disappeared. Here, sound levels run the full gamut from the absolute (and synthetic) silence of the broadcasting studio, through the hubbub of street and tenement life, to the concentrated clatter of comptometer and typewriter in the office or of automatic machinery in the factory. The city dweller has, for all practical purposes, lost the peace and quiet of the countryside. His sonic environment is infinitely more varied than that of the farmer. He has access, at least in theory, to a far wider range of productive sound — theaters, movies, bandstands, concert halls. He has greater access to telephone, radio, and television set. The trouble is, all too often, that his neighbors also own or have access to the same instruments.

Whether the city dweller works in an office, a store, or a factory, he works in a synthetic sonic environment which is hostile to his health. And whether he lives in a downtown hotel, a close-in slum or apartment, or a suburban house, he moves in much the same environment. He may have ready access to a thousand kinds of productive sound. He has no refuge from noise. To enjoy the natural sonic environment he usually has to run a gauntlet via train or car from which a week-end is too brief a time in which to recuperate.

The problem, however, is not that there are either too many or too few such instruments for the propagation of sound (though in statistical fact, there are probably far too few) but rather that they are not under social control. It is thus not a question of natural versus synthetic environments, as the agrarians and the decentralists would have us believe, but rather one of integrating the best of both for increased social productivity.

The rôle which building could play in this reintegration is of a very special character. Obviously, in the rural areas, the problem is a relatively simple one because the synthetic is very 'thinly spread' over the natural sonic environment. Not one farmer in a thousand needs a soundproofed bedroom. No street cars whiz by his window, no neighbor's radio blares near enough to keep him awake. If he is lucky enough to own a tractor or a power-driven saw, the chances are that whatever noise they make is psychologically pleasant to him. Certainly, no farm machinery reaches sonic levels which are dangerous to health. Nor does the farmer's wife object to the subjectively pleasant swish of the electric washing machine or the erratic thump of the electric pump. If she is lucky enough to have either, the sound they make will always connote work well done by hands other than her own.

No, the farmer has no need for buildings which protect him against noise; what he is short of is buildings which provide him with socially productive sound. And these are precisely the types of buildings which the farmer must have if he is to enjoy a civilized sonic environment. Band shells which carry the brasses to the farthest row on a hot July night. Theaters that direct the undistorted lines to the balcony. Opera and concert houses whose acoustical rôle is a part of the performance itself. Lecture halls that lose not a syllable of the expert's speech. Halls where a thousand can square-dance and still hear fiddle and 'caller.' This is the sort of synthetic sonic environment which would enrich the life of the American farmer.

The task of controlling the sonic environment in urban areas is infinitely more complex. The chances are that a socially and physiologically acceptable environment will not be achieved without a radical redesign of our cities. For here the problem is the reverse of that of the rural scene. Here the natural environment has been completely destroyed. It can be recreated only when our cities are laced through and surrounded by parks, playgrounds, and green belts. (There is no economically feasible way of producing bird song or absolute silence synthetically; it is only as the result of extraordinary technical

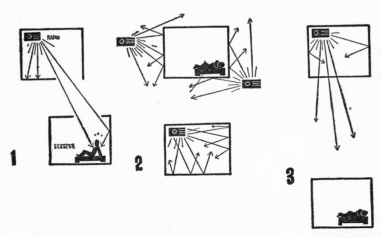

Noise is an index of waste, an enemy of health (1). Sound-proof barriers can be thrown around either the source of noise or the victim or both (2); noise can be minimized by distance (3). Social control might imply all these means and many others, including elimination of the source wherever possible.

ingenuity and at great expense that it can be achieved in the fifteen hundred-odd radio stations in the land.) We might, theoretically, isolate each city dweller in a soundproofed cell. Here he could cut out his neighbor's radio and play his own to his heart's content. Or it might be possible to outlaw the radio and automobile completely, placing each building so far from the next and all buildings so far from the street, that sound would not carry between them. It is even possible to eliminate the fire truck by making every building literally non-burnable. It is equally possible to put sound-absorbent material in every office and factory in the land or, conversely, to perfect literally noiseless typewriters and machine tools.

All of these measures and many more have their advocates. The layman is bound to wonder which one is right. The answer is clearly that no one of them by itself is sufficient. The control of sound is a social operation and the presence of noise a sign of social waste. Local measures may bring local relief; but real control of the sonic environment is part and parcel of real control of all environments. The criteria for a socially desirable sonic environment coincide at all main points with the criteria for the others.

CHAPTER FOURTEEN

The Conquest of Space and Gravity

THERE WAS A TIME, and that not long ago, when a building was considered complete when walls, floors, ceilings, and roof were finished. No equipment was built into the structure. If it were a dwelling, the family brought its furniture; if a factory, the owners moved in their machinery. But always there was a clear — indeed, a visible — distinction between the two. We have already seen how this distinction began to break down under the impact of accelerating technological advance. Today systems for the control of atmosphere, light, heat, and sound interpenetrate each other and structure itself to such an extent that they can be isolated only for the purpose of analysis. But these systems only create the optimum physical conditions under which work of all sorts can be carried on. Thanks to them, the building becomes an efficient tool onto which we can shift the load of an imperfect natural environment. Yet these systems do not (except indirectly) promote that rapid and orderly movement of flow of people, things and ideas which is the essence of modern industrial society. For this, another type of equipment, another family of tools, had to be devised.

A forty-story hotel with no elevators, a hospital without telephones or paging system, an auto factory without conveyor belts or traveling cranes — any layman would recognize such buildings as anomalies. They would be actually useless. Where would the hotel operator be without elevators to move people (incoming and departing guests, waiters and bellhops) and things (luggage for the man in 1008, supper for the Kiwanis on the roof)? How could he operate without telephones, buzzers, and bells to move messages, orders, instructions? Every factory owner knows that serial production in its simplest terms is merely that equipment necessary to move the proper things and messages to the proper workman in the proper time and place. His large and increasing investment in conveyors, cranes, hoists, and trucks is charged off to increased labor productivity. And the 'drive in' laundry in Nashville — whose curb-service men wear roller skates, deliver orders via microphones, and snatch the requested parcel off the conveyor belt from the shipping room — is merely a dramatic application of mechanization to a new building type.

In dwelling houses mechanization is at a far lower level than in any other building type. Here such equipment as automatic stokers, housephones, electric floor polishers and dishwashers are still known as 'conveniences,' though everywhere else they have long since become essentials, as much a part of the building as its roof. It is, of course, still possible to live in houses without them. Our ancestors did: and, according to the 1940 Census, most of us still do. (Twenty-two per cent of our dwellings had no electric power, sixty-six per cent had no mechanical refrigeration, fifty-eight per cent had no central heating.) Yet it is a strange case of split thinking to glorify the adding machine or the conveyor and belittle the vacuum cleaner or the electric sewing machine. Both are tools, with the identical function of freeing men for increased social productivity, not for idle ease.

It is easy to ridicule American gadgets because there is so often no adequate control of their use. Hence, juke boxes in every cross-roads joint serve to fog the absence of refrigerators in two out of every three American homes. Millions of glossy gasoline pumps and 'streamlined' soft-drink vendors obscure the absence of running water from eighty-eight per cent of our farm homes. Much of this distrust of mechanization, however, springs from a deeper source: the bitter experience of the working people themselves. As they have seen it work out in the factories and mills, mechanization has too often meant physical exhaustion and technological unemployment. In popular usage 'labor-saving device' becomes a term of derision, 'modern plant' a threat of the dole.

This aspect of mechanization is clearly a social problem. The factory has not yet been designed which can of itself prevent unemployment. But within this larger reference frame, the design of the factory is of critical importance to the workers' health. It can become an instrument which, while increasing productivity, at the same time protects and extends their health; or it can, with the same sort of mechanization, merely bleed them of their resources in health and stamina. Depending upon the character of the forces which control its design and operation, the factory can become either the source or the eliminator of fatigue.

Some Non-Architectural Aspects of Fatigue

MOST OF WHAT WE KNOW about fatigue comes from the factory. Yet research in the field has been complicated, in a sense, by the one-sided investigations of its external or objective aspects. This was perhaps the natural result of research largely subsidized by the manufacturers themselves as a means of increasing productivity. However important this approach may be, it is far from complete. For one of the most puzzling aspects of fatigue is its duality: it is at once objective and subjective, physiological and psychological. Thus, if we observe and measure it from the outside only, from the standpoint of management alone, we are ignoring the fact that the relationship between the two halves is not merely complex: it is dialectic.

Even the mechanism of fatigue is not as yet fully understood. It is obviously an entirely 'natural' phenomenon, part of the basic physiological cycle of fatigue and recovery in the living organism. But that, after all, is not saying much. More specific questions remain. Precisely how does fatigue affect production? How much fatigue can you endure this week without suffering later? How is it that modern building with all its labor-saving mechanization often seems to accelerate fatigue? What is the relation between fatigue and health? Although an analysis of the various types of fatigue may reveal a wide divergence in details, there is one fundamentally common factor: disturbance of the balance between wear and repair. We all get tired when we work. The longer we work, the more tired we grow; and the heavier the work, the less we can do of it. If overwork continues beyond a certain point, it begins to affect our health. The temporary *disturbance* between wear and repair becomes *permanent damage*. Where regular intervals of rest and recreation might have cured the first, long periods of medical or hospital treatment may be necessary to undo the latter. Nor do we all tire at the same rate. Joe seems to thrive on work which would kill Jim. Fatigue in one industry will differ sharply from that in another; while two offices doing exactly the same type of work will also vary widely as regards fatigue rates. Obviously many factors are involved in this problem and it would be an error to assume that the building and its equipment is any more important than half a dozen others. In the triangular relationship between the task, the organism and the environment, the building affords the 'working conditions' under which work is done. A well-designed building will, unit for unit of work, cause less fatigue than a badly designed one. But the length of the work week, the rate at which work is performed, the character of the work itself are also of decisive importance, as are the health, morale, and adaptability of the worker himself.

Common sense should tell anybody — especially anybody who works for a living — that a 60-hour work week is detrimental to both the individual and society as a whole. Wartime experience amply confirms this: beyond given limits, increasing the length of the work week did not bring corresponding increases in production. Indeed, over a period of time, it resulted in a net drop. A wartime report of the British Ministry of Labour cites an instance in which a group of men at heavy labor had their hours reduced from 66.7 to 56.5 hours: their total output increased by 22 per cent. The same report cites a machine which turned out 250 units per day when operated on three eight-hour shifts but only 192 units per day when operated on two twelve-hour shifts.

Fatigue affects production in another important way: the quality of the product tends to deteriorate along with decreasing quantity. An excessively long week results in a sharp increase in 'rejects,' on the one hand, and in accidents on the other. Here an interesting psychological phenomenon is observed. Toward the end of the day, after a period of declining productivity, the worker gets a 'second wind.' From a mood of depression he will spiral into a sudden excess of exhilaration and confidence. He works rapidly again and, as it seems to him, accurately. Objectively, however, he is careless. His judgment of dimension and timing — essential in industrial operations — becomes noticeably impaired. Workmanship deteriorates rapidly. In one English factory, cited in the above report, accidents were two and a half times as frequent in a twelve-hour shift as in one of only ten hours.

The character of a specific job has a lot to do with fatigue. Modern serial or mass production involves careful analysis of the process, breaking it down into its component parts, organizing them in efficient sequence, and assigning specially trained men to each phase. The manufacturing process is thereby atomized. This often leads to a similar atomization of the worker's movements and mental processes, as Ruskin so shrewdly remarked a century ago. His job may require only a portion of a man's muscular and mental capacities: but it requires that portion all the time, and with sometimes horrifying monotony. Such routines skyrocket fatigue: they can actually cause psychological trauma, as Chaplin showed with such bitter wit in his movie 'Modern Times.'

We are constantly reading in the newspapers of some new production method which 'cuts in half the time formerly required' to make something — a house, a tank, or a bomber. Such advances do not necessarily imply a speed-up in the *rate* of work. For example, a big riveted bomber will have as many as 450,000 rivets, each of which takes twenty seconds to drive or a total of 2500 man-hours. However, by changing the fabrication technique to automatic multiple welding, this time can be reduced by approximately thirty per cent. Or again, by changing the entire process from riveted metal to molded plywood, the man-hours per plane could be halved. Assuming that environmental conditions remain the same, none of these savings in time necessarily means that the men are more fatigued at day's end, even though production per man has been increased.

It is intense rationalization *within* a given process which raises the danger of the 'speed-up' or 'stretch-out.' Here the process itself is not altered. Instead, corners are cut, waste motions eliminated, men shifted, materials and tools rerouted. The time-and-motion expert studies each worker at his task, often by slow-motion photography. On the basis of such analysis, the expert can often show the worker a quicker and simpler sequence of motions which enables him to go through the same operation with a smaller expenditure of energy. Thus, if a given operation is redesigned so as to take ten per cent less time and ten per cent less energy, the worker can increase his output per hour by ten per cent with no increase in fatigue. But if the savings in time outstrip the savings in effort, net fatigue will increase unless the work day is proportionately shortened.

The simple and unadorned speed-up is the most obvious and most common technique of increasing the rate of work. This can occur in any type building, old or new, good or bad. Here time-and-motion experts and labor-saving devices are not employed. The work is simply piled on the men and forced through. A high 'norm' is established; and 'best' workers hit the pace; and the rest have to keep up or else. Unfortunately, this type of speed-up is very common, especially among small and backward manufacturers attempting to meet the competition of the great streamlined monopolies, and has done much to prejudice the public against all mechanization.

None of this is, of course, a valid argument against the historic necessity for industrial mass production, with its specialized, atomized and repetitive operations. Scientific studies of industrial efficiency have evolved the techniques and equipment which have made America what she is, enabling us to triumph over Fascist barbarism and offering us the only promise of a peaceful future. The public in general, and the working people in particular, must not repeat the error of the early weavers of Lanarkshire, who destroyed the machines in protest against their social abuse. Rather they must understand the full significance of these equipments and techniques, and demand that they be democratically applied to the subjective needs of the workers as well as to the objective requirements of the process itself.

It is apparent that the best-designed building, complete with air-conditioning and all manner of robots, does not increase the net amount of the worker's energy. Rather it protects what he has. It focuses his expenditure of energy, guarantees that a minimum be expended in unproductive work — resisting excessive cold or noise, lifting heavy weights which a crane could better handle, walking to the object rather than having it move to him. But under rational and progressive management, a well-designed building will extend and preserve the worker's health over a longer period of time.

There is probably a law of diminishing returns in the mechanization of any process, whether it be frying an egg or building a car. A point beyond which the cost and complexity of the mechanization outstrips the human labor or the time saved. This is the point which so unnecessarily exercised Aldous Huxley in *Brave New World*. Where that point lies and when we will reach it is, however, largely a metaphysical question. As long as three-fourths of the human race is underfed, underclothed, and ill housed, we have little cause to fear the 'dehumanizing' effect of techniques which increase human productivity. It is a fact that American building on the whole was sadly under-mechanized in 1940. Four years of wartime suspension of civilian production have enormously increased this deficit. If to this is added the fact that technology itself has made great strides during the course of the war, it is apparent that the saturation point has been pushed much farther into the future — beyond, in fact, any predictable point in the future. The war demonstrated conclusively that any operation can be mechanized, thereby raising to the nth power the productive capacity of the men involved. No pun is intended: the miracles of road and bridge building, airport construction, harbor repair — all under the most adverse conditions conceivable — are an index to the reproductive powers of mechanization. On the home front, the miracles of production of such complex items as synthetic rubber or penicillin showed the same forces at work.

Redesign of the Tools

THERE IS PRECIOUS LITTLE EVIDENCE of overmechanization in that building type which is most important of all to the consumer — the dwelling. Here the concept of labor-saving, of fatigue and accident prevention, has scarcely appeared. Of all our buildings, the home is the least successful as a tool precisely because it has been the least studied. We have already seen how far behind all others it lags in the control of the environments; a similar inadequacy marks the equipment, furnishings and utensils which go into it. Naturally, any mechanical comparison between a factory and a house is fallacious. Managing a jute mill and running a house have only this in common: they are both social processes. But if scientific analysis has proved clearly fruitful in the one, it is reasonable to suppose it might be helpful in the other. And it is precisely to industry, with all its shortcomings, that we must turn for precedent and guidance.

In defense of traditional design, it is often said that a chair is, after all, a chair: that sitting has not changed. But this depends upon what kind of sitting is involved. From a purely structural point of view, a more skillful design than that of the American Windsor chair has scarcely ever been produced. And for a certain kind of sitting — say letter-writing — the Windsor is still a tolerably satisfactory piece of equipment. The hooded footman's chair of Versailles and the wing chair of the English gentry were eminently suitable for the drafty halls for which they were designed. But it would be a brave antiquarian indeed who would argue that the rough benches of the little red schoolhouse were as desirable as the average school seating of today; or that today's comptometer operator could work as efficiently on a Victorian bookkeeper's stool as on a contemporary posture chair. Modern life has developed many kinds of sitting and each requires a special type of chair. For a chair is just another type of tool, the primary function of which is to take the load off the human user.

If there is one type of consumer goods which is wretchedly

designed, shoddily constructed, and consistently overpriced, it is household furniture. Exploiting the archaic and confused esthetic standards of the public, the furniture industry is apparently dedicated to Barnum's proposition. In any event, it has used modern mass-production techniques and materials to produce what is, from any standpoint, a sub-standard product. The exceptions are small and lie only in the upper price brackets: the so-called 'period' pieces (which have at least the merit of archeological precision) and a small volume of modern design (which is usually comfortable and pleasant to look at). Before the war cut them short, there were many evidences of change, however. Perhaps the most significant was the competition, held in 1940 by the Museum of Modern Art, for low-priced, mass-produced household furniture. Confined to North and South American designers, this competition produced a wealth of interesting design. The prize winners were executed in full-scale pilot models, but the contemplated commercial production was cut short by the war. Whatever their individual merits, the designs as a whole showed how keenly the younger designers were aware that they must turn to science and technology for both their materials and techniques if they were to produce truly satisfactory furniture.

How these concepts illuminate the whole field of furniture design was brilliantly demonstrated in some of the experimental work of the Design Correlation Unit of Columbia University's School of Architecture under the leadership of Professor Frederick J. Kiesler. Proceeding on the assumption that the design of even the simplest and most prosaic item of furniture was subject to radical revision and improvement, Kiesler's class chose the bookcase as a subject of analysis. It did not require much research to discover that historically the bookcase had reached its present form a long time ago and had seen little if any improvement since. How well did it meet the requirements of the user? and how well those of the books? History offered little in the way of intelligent answer. There had been more and more books published, and bigger and bigger libraries built to hold them. But if it were the task of a book storage unit to take the load off the user, then it had clearly fallen far short of its objective.   On the other hand, if it were the task of the unit to provide the books themselves with an optimal environment, here too its success had not been spectacular.

Beginning with the human body, where all building research

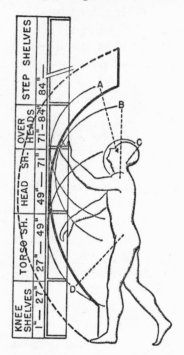

must begin,
Kiesler's group came upon a major discrepancy.   The first criterion of a bookcase would obviously be easy recognition of and access to the books themselves.   Since the sweep of both the eye and the arm is circular, the limits of both recognition and access are also circular in the vertical as well as the horizontal plane.   All existing bookcases were rectilinear in both planes, so that between the user and the tool there was only one point of actual tangency — immediately in front of him at a point between shoulder and eye level.   To read or reach any other point, the user had to stretch, squat or move sidewise.

Redesign of the bookcase involves study of the human body, whose limits of recognition and access are always circular in all planes.   Thus the ideal profile of a bookcase (heavy curve) is the sum of the orbits of eye (A), arm (B), head (C), and torso (D).

The ideal solution would be a hollow spherical bookcase, with the user at the center and the interior radius approximately that of his arm.   Other considerations would immediately modify this initial concept.   The user would not want his books directly overhead nor immediately under foot: so the sphere would be truncated top and bottom.   The center of the sphere should be somewhere near eye level: so the truncated bottom would be well off the floor.   To enter or leave the unit, the user would not want to climb over or crawl under: so the unit would be built in spheroid sections, like the outer surface of the cells of an orange, one of which would be omitted. But only the inner surface of the sphere would be accessible to the user when he was inside it: hence each of the sections would pivot upon its vertical axis, so that both surfaces would be equally accessible. And since capacity would vary with the needs of the individual user, each section should be complete in itself: as his library grew, he could add sections to complete the sphere.

What of the books themselves? Had they any properties which importantly affected this schematic solution? They were, first of all, rectilinear in form and there was little prospect of that property being modified: hence the unit could only *approach* the spherical by means of small chords. Books were comparatively heavy: so construction of the case would have to be strong and the center of gravity low. They varied in size, so the shelving would be adjustable. The whole unit should be easy to move: hence the individual sections should be mounted on noiseless casters. Easy recognition implied good lighting. Hence each unit would have its own fixture — a fluorescent tube with adjustable reflector — mounted on a universal joint.

Had books any special environmental requirements? Information was scanty here, but it was agreed that excessively dry air was as bad for paper as excessive moisture. Moving air of moderate temperature and humidity would be a satisfactory norm: so glass fronts were omitted and the shelves would be slotted. Dust was bad for books, however: so transparent plastic flaps would hang from the outer edge of each shelf, mounted on friction hinges which would stay put at any angle.

Only now was it possible for Kiesler's students to produce actual working drawings. And this involved a realistic survey of industrial resources. What materials were best suited to the design? What modifications would be imposed upon it by available fabrication methods? How could cost be held to a minimum without sacrifice of quality? These and many other questions were answered in the construction of a pilot model. The result bears little resemblance to the standard bookcase because, as a tool, it has been redesigned from the ground up. It is not the only (and may not even be the best) possible solution to the problem of book storage.[1] Its significance here lies in the *methodology* of its design. The user, the task, the tool: each has been analyzed, free of historic precedent and prejudice, to discover the best solution in terms of modern scientific knowledge. A much more productive tool is the result.

Every item of furniture and equipment in the dwelling could be fruitfully subjected to the same sort of scrutiny and redesign. Time-and-motion engineers could well turn their attention to the simplest household operations and processes. Beds, desks, chairs, wardrobes — all of them assumed their present form long ago. And today they wear an accumulation of whimsy, convention, and sheer ignorance which all but obscures their original function and greatly reduces even their original usefulness. The bed, to take an instance at random, is not so perfect a tool as might at first appear. In the light of our current knowledge, it is not at all certain that the super-soft inner-spring mattress is a guarantee of either perfect rest or satisfactory sexual intercourse. Nor are contemporary bedding and bedclothes necessarily the best solution to the problem of maintaining even body temperature during sleep. They are based on the premise that the body itself produces enough heat to maintain comfort conditions; and that all bedding need do is to slow down the rate of loss. At normal room temperatures this is true. But in a cold room, heat loss from even a well-covered body can equal the energy output of a night-long walk at two to three miles per hour. And bedding heavy enough to hold heat under these conditions will weigh enough to further increase fatigue. It is easy to conceive of lightweight, electrically heated, and thermostatically controlled bedding or bedclothes, based upon the Air Forces flying suits. There is, likewise, no reason why mattresses could not be heated in winter and cooled in summer. In fact, researchers at the John A. Pierce Foundation laboratories have gone even further and proposed the elimination of bedding and bedclothes and the substitution of a 'sleeping cabinet' which

[1] Kiesler did not overlook the fact that knowledge has not always been stored in books. At one time we used clay tablets, at another papyrus rolls; and it may not be long before the microfilm reel replaces the book. This was duly noted by the class.

would provide optimal conditions for sleep: quiet, privacy, complete darkness, exact and automatic control of both radiant and free air temperatures.

The Machine in the Kitchen

THE KITCHEN has been the object of more intelligent study than any other area of the house. This was logical, since it was the scene of some of the housewife's most important and least pleasant labors. Also it was easier, since the tools and equipment were used here and only here, and much of it was by its very nature fixed. The kitchen was easy to isolate. And much study has been given to the various operations which take place there, to organizing the equipment into those patterns which will expedite them. As a result, the kitchen is already the best-designed and best-equipped unit in the house. However, this process is by no means complete nor is its future direction fully established. For today's kitchen is not the self-contained unit of grandmother's day, dependent upon the outside world only for such items as salt and coffee. Instead, it has become merely one stage in a huge industrialized food-production belt. This belt brings us such miracles as fresh, frozen, canned, and dehydrated foods from all over the globe at all seasons. It also brings us such travesties as cereals to which the original minerals and vitamins have been partially restored. But whatever its merits or weaknesses, it is this system to which the American kitchen is geared and without which it would not be intelligible.

Some recent writers are driven near to madness at the prospect of millions of women, in millions of kitchens all over the land, simultaneously preparing millions of little parcels of food, simultaneously using millions of stoves and washing millions of pots. This, these critics say, involves a criminal duplication of effort and equipment, not to mention a huge wastage of food. In a purely quantitative sense, they are perhaps correct; and in urban areas there was, even before the war, marked evidence of revolt against this condition. Mass feeding had seen an unprecedented expansion in American cities before 1941: since then, this trend

has been tremendously (even if temporarily) expanded. Whatever its shortcomings, this service is probably the best in the
world in terms of the availability, nutritional value, and sanitary
preparation of its product.

But to say that mass feeding is a reasonably satisfactory method
for certain sections of the population under certain specific conditions is a far different thing from calling for the abolition of
the individual kitchen. Such loose and mechanistic generalizations have already done enough harm to the cause of modern
architecture. Nor need rejection of this approach throw us into
the arms of the other extreme — the food faddists to whom only
a raw carrot is a good carrot, who insist that every family should
raise its own wheat and grind its own flour. Under their influence, the kitchen would become not only the most important
but also the largest room in the house. Here the housewife
would spend a twelve-hour day (all with the most modern
equipment) buying only salt from the nearest co-operative and
generally turning the clock back to the days of candle-dipping
and soap-making.

The actual problem is not that of a choice between these two
extremes; it is rather that American building should cover the
whole spectrum of choice between them. From a cultural
standpoint, our cooking and eating habits are a rich and varied
asset. Reflecting as they do not only our diverse national origins
but also the range of our various climates and vegetations, they
constitute much the same sort of national resource as our literature or our music. Insofar as these inherited culinary standards
violate modern knowledge in the fields of diet, nutrition, or food
preparation, they should and will be modified. But they should,
at the same time, be protected from wanton destruction at the
hands of selfish commercial interests. Assuming that the whole
nation will be able to afford an adequate diet (a reasonable
assumption, surely, in view of the war we have just won), the
architectural problem becomes one of guaranteeing freedom of
choice in the means of preparing and consuming food.

The magazines, during the war, kept an avid public fairly
well informed on what to expect of the post-war kitchen. Some

of these prophecies are now beginning to appear in the flesh. One interesting tendency is reversing pre-war practice in stove and refrigerator design. Instead of being concentrated into units which looked more and more like juke boxes, there is now a tendency to break them down into their component parts. These components — ovens, griddles, plates, and broilers — are then built directly into cabinets at waist height: instead of a single stove there is a row of specialized cooking units. With the spread of quick-freezing, the same process will probably take place in the refrigerator, providing different types of cold units for cooling, freezing, and quick-freezing. This decentralization is important to both the safety and comfort of the housewife, since it concentrates all cooking operations at counter height. It also implies increased cost and complexity in the kitchen unless the whole thing is to be mass-produced as a unit.

We are promised much. But some of the knottiest problems await practical solutions — for example, dishwashing and garbage disposal. These are not only unpleasant and tedious operations, they also affect the health of the family and ultimately that of the community. Facetious remarks about paper or plastic dishes which could be used once and then discarded does not alter the fact that, from a sanitary standpoint, they are a move in the right direction. More satisfactory might be a simple low-cost dishwasher with infra-red lamps for quick drying and bacteriocidal lamps for disinfecting. Similarly, for all but farm kitchens, there is need of a simple method of garbage disposal. The electric grinder which pulverizes the waste and then flushes it into the sewer is perhaps the most effective proposal to date.

Many other fascinating conveniences for the kitchen await us in the laboratories: lighted transparent ovens and cooking utensils; high-frequency induction cooking. Kitchens whose shelves revolve, whose mechanized egg-beaters and glass-washers plug into flexible shafts like a dentist's drill; kitchens with automatic machines of all kinds. But, as Heiner and McCullough have trenchantly put it,[1] none of these devices nor all of them

---

[1] In a valuable study on kitchen planning in *Architectural Forum*, February and March, 1946.

together is any guarantee of a kitchen which, as tool, takes the maximum load off the housewife. As they put it 'a safe, labor-saving kitchen involves more than mechanizing the egg-beater ... it is at least as important that the egg-beater be located for easy accessibility as that it be motor-driven when you find it.'

The glitter of these valuable advances should not blind us to the fact that even the 1940 model kitchen, with only a gas or electric range and refrigerator and a sink, was beyond the range of over half of the American people. In 35,000,000 families, only 15,000,000 had mechanical refrigerators while 9,000,000 used ice and an equal number had no refrigeration of any sort. Only 54.2 per cent had gas or electric ranges. Two-thirds of the rural families had no electric power and eighty-two per cent had no running water: from this it is apparent that their kitchens left much to be desired in both safety and convenience. Our task here is not to produce one pluperfect kitchen so much as to make the present standard available to all. This is a technical as well as an ethical imperative: for genuine technical progress can come only from a broad base of mass production.

When the Bathroom Comes of Age

IF THERE IS ONE THING for which America is famous and of which all Americans are proud, it is that standard of living which allegedly provides a bathroom for all of us. The bathroom is the only portion of the sanitary apparatus with which the building consumer comes into first-hand contact, but it displays all the characteristics of the system as a whole. What is a bathroom? It is primarily an instrument whereby the individual can safely dispose of waste matter which accumulates on both the inside and outside of his body. It is a mechanism for controlling the flow of waste. To move or carry this waste material some sort of fluid vehicle is required. This vehicle must be of itself harmless to the body — chemically inert and pathogenically sterile. It must be a solvent of body wastes, either by itself or in conjunction with other equally harmless agents. It happens that soap and water are the mediums which best meet these criteria, although they are not the only conceivable ones.

In order to effect the transfer of wastes from the body to this fluid vehicle, we have devised three basic tools: basin, tub, and toilet. Here again it must be observed that these tools are not by any means the ultimate solution to the problem. However they do constitute a very acceptable minimum, especially since a large portion of the American people do not yet enjoy even this standard of protection, according to the 1940 Housing Census:

	U.S.A. (per cent)	North (per cent)	South (per cent)	West (per cent)
All dwellings				
with running water	69.9	79.1	46.0	82.7
with indoor private toilet	59.7	69.6	35.3	70.7
with private bathing facilities	56.2	64.7	33.3	69.8
Urban dwellings				
with running water	93.5	96.4	82.4	95.6
with indoor private toilet	83.0	87.2	66.3	87.1
with private bathing facilities	77.5	81.0	60.8	85.1
Rural farm dwellings				
with running water	17.8	23.0	8.5	46.6
with indoor private toilet	11.2	15.2	4.7	29.8
with private bathing facilities	11.8	15.2	5.4	32.6

The bathroom is much more than a mere convenience: it is a vital factor in the maintenance of health. A study by the United States Public Health Service disclosed that among persons living in households without private inside flush toilets, typhoid fever was over one hundred per cent more prevalent than among those persons who had such facilities. 'The frequency of indigestion and other stomach ailments was seventy-five per cent higher, and of diarrhea, enteritis, and colitis, forty per cent higher in the group without toilets,' the report continued. It is of course obvious that other than structural factors enter into the equation. Stomach ailments may be caused by economic insecurity or bad food as well as by bad plumbing. The point to be made is that even with no economic worries and with the best of food, the danger of gastro-intestinal infection remains. Only modern sanitary theory and equipment can prevent it.

I have said that the bathroom, in spite of being society's first successful instrument for the disposal of body wastes, was still far from being the ideal instrument for the purpose. For, though it is far from being the most dangerous area in the house, the bathroom still presents enough hazards to frighten the informed consumer.

The toilet. It is possible that for each case of typhoid, dysentery, or colitis which the flush toilet has eradicated, it has substituted a case of constipation, piles, vermin, or bacterial infection. At any rate, the conventional toilet does nothing to minimize these latter hazards. Consider the bowl itself. It has neither the correct shape nor height nor angle for the natural position of defecation: the lip is too high by several inches, horizontal instead of sloping sharply backward, poorly shaped for use by the male. This makes evacuation more difficult. Take the seat itself. Who used it previously and with what was he infected? Parasites such as lice and infections such as gonorrhea may be spread via the toilet seat. Last and most vulnerable, consider the ubiquitous toilet paper. Infection of the female reproductive system by organisms from the anal tract may be traced directly to the use of tissue as a cleansing medium. And though it can scarcely be said to cause hemorrhoids, the use of tissue certainly does not help them.

Redesign of the toilet to meet such deficiencies has been halting and sporadic, emphasis being placed instead upon the fact that it is 'available in a wide range of colors including DuBarry Pink and Nile Green' or that in flushing it is noiseless. Yet enough isolated examples of advance already exist to enable us to forecast the main outlines of the w.c. of tomorrow. From physiology itself we can guess that the bowl will be much lower than at present, sloping sharply down and back so that instead of sitting uncomfortably the user squats naturally. The seat, conforming to this contour, will disinfect itself automatically after each use. Already hopefully patented are several such designs in which the seat swings up into a sterilizing chamber at the back: here a bath of either live steam or ultra-violet rays guarantees a quick death for parasites. (An even simpler solution might be to fix an ultra-violet lamp above the bowl so as to flood the seat with its rays at all times.) Instead of tissue for cleansing, this toilet will borrow from the French *bidet*. From the bottom of the bowl there will be jets of water, at skin temperature and with suitable disinfectants added; these will be followed by jets of warm air, like the dryers sometimes found in public washrooms. Instead of flushing after use, the entire inner surface of the bowl will be washed by a smooth and silent sheet of water. The bowl will have forced ventilation.

What this utopian w.c. will look like need not concern us here, except to observe that it will bear little resemblance to contemporary 'neo-Classic' models. Instead of the cumbersome present-day procelain models, some of which weigh as much as three hundred and fifty pounds, it will probably be fabricated out of some light metal or suitable plastic. It will of necessity be an integral part of a prefabricated bathroom.

The tub. Gold faucets and verd antique marble have never successfully masked the tub's basic deficiency — that of trying to get the body cleaner in water which grows progressively dirtier. The basic advantage of the shower is that one bathes in a current rather than in a stagnant pool. Body wastes are immediately carried off by the falling water, whereas in a tub they accumulate. A combination of the two would seem desirable — a tub through whose slotted ends flowed a slow current of constantly changing water. Such tubs are in wide use in medical institutions; and their use elsewhere merely implies more accurate valves for control of temperature and volume than the present faucet.

Statistically, the number of persons who annually break their necks from falls in the tub is not enormous. But further research will unquestionably yield tubs whose contours and surfaces are less slippery, easier to clean and more comfortable to the touch than the five hundred-odd pounds of cast iron which today caress our shivering bodies.

The lavatory. Like the toilet and the tub, the physiognomy of today's lavatory is much more a result of tradition than of research. It is only a dim approximation of the shape desirable for washing the face and hands, shaving, etc. The faucets are not only unhandy and unsafe (source of contamination by back siphonage); they are absurd in an operation which exclusively involves the hands. From the hospitals tomorrow's lavatory will borrow knee- or foot-pedal controls. As in the tub the lavatory should provide a current, not a stagnant pool; and there is no technical reason why it should weigh more than ten or fifteen pounds.

It is ironical that the most onerous aspect of the bathroom is the task of keeping it clean. This is more the fault of the vehicle it employs than the instrument itself. As long as the water is hard — that is, contains enough calcium to precipitate soap — there is little that the designer can do. The obvious solution is a supply of soft water. Most of our urban water is hard. But there is no technical reason why it cannot be softened at the central plant along with the other treatments it receives in being processed. The added costs of such treatment would be more than offset in terms of soaps saved, drains unclogged, housework reduced. This does not absolve the bathroom from the responsibility of providing better surfaces than it now does. Materials which are resilient and warm to the touch, easily cleaned and waterproof, are already available; there is even the possibility of materials whose surfaces are themselves bacteriocidal. These the future bath can scarcely ignore.

In 1939, impatient with the technical backwardness of the plumbing manufacturers and undismayed by the industry's apparent determination to keep domestic sanitation at the Victorian level, Buckminster Fuller produced his famous prefab bathroom. This remarkable unit was not so much an effort to reach the optimum possibilities outlined above as to produce a complete, lightweight, self-contained unit. It was a design directed at short-circuiting the bewildering convolutions of the plumbing trade — manufacturers, jobbers, dealers, plumbers, etc. Small size, light weight, simplicity of installation are the controlling factors in the Fuller design. The finished product is a cabinet six feet square and eight feet tall, weighing some 535 pounds. It contains a full-size tub with shower, toilet, lavatory, and linen and medicine cabinets. It is fabricated in two lobes which lock together but may be used separately; one contains the tub, the other toilet and lavatory.

The entire unit was designed for die-stamping in copper, the back of the metal being sprayed with a sound-deadening mastic. It could be equally well fabricated from aluminum, plastics, even plywood. Carrying its own heating and ventilating system and integral lighting, the unit required only four connections: hot and cold water, electricity, and sewerage. Its installation would require little more skill or time than that of an electric refrigerator. Despite its many advantages, only one unit of the Fuller bathroom was produced — the hand-made pilot model; whether it ever sees full production is a matter of speculation. But the fact remains that if the American people are to get good bathrooms and plenty of them at low cost, they will have to follow the general lines established by Mr. Fuller's pioneer.

When Edward Bellamy, in his utopian Boston, eliminated all the chimneys and finished all the interiors in waterproof, washable surfaces, he was answering the housewife's prayer. For of all the tasks which face her, none is so remorseless, so physically exhausting and emotionally unrewarding, as the constant process of cleaning, polishing, and washing required to keep the dwelling in reasonable condition; and of all the operations which should be eliminated, none merit it so much as these. Yet in actual practice, the average American dwelling is not much closer to this goal than it was in 1887. Our buildings are not much more washable nor our cities much cleaner than those of the Boston of Bellamy's day. It is in this context that the mechanization of cleaning, polishing, and washing achieves an almost abnormal significance. The electrical vacuum cleaners and floor polishers, the washing machines and ironers, are tools which will not be opposed by anyone familiar with housework. The chief obstacle to their widespread use has been and is likely to remain their high cost. Only in multiple family housing does it become possible to employ these labor-saving devices on a genuinely economical basis.

Since the end of World War II there has been an accelerated tendency towards the prefabrication of all these units — kitchen, bath, laundry — not only as individual units but even towards grouping them into one package to produce the so-called mechanical core. The logic of such a trend is inescapable. It promises both reductions in cost and increases in mechanical efficiency. It makes for easier distribution, simpler installation, and easier amortization by the average family. It is, in theory at least, the only way in which these facilities can be brought within the reach of the great mass of American families. Perhaps the most ambitious package of this type is the Ingersoll Utility Unit, which includes a house heating plant as well as kitchen, bath, and laundry. Here all the basic mechanization for the average six-room house is compressed into a single lightweight package $9\frac{1}{2}$ feet square by $6\frac{1}{2}$ feet high. Although by no means as cheap as it might be, this unit offers much in contrast to the conventional handicraft assembly of disparate parts. From an engineering standpoint, the unit may seem somewhat primitive; and it may be somewhat restrictive in planning. Its significance lies in the fact that such a unit will undoubtedly be a prototype for the further mechanization of the average American home.

CHAPTER FIFTEEN

The Integration of the Environments

A$_N$ OPTIMAL CONTROL of all environmental factors in any given building is a theoretical possibility, and many a modern building shows a large measure of success in this respect. But the requirements which the various control systems impose upon buildings are often mutually irreconcilable. Thus, some special problem in illumination may make an ideal solution in acoustics impossible. In addition, structure and plan have requirements of their own to which all other systems must adapt themselves. These contradictions are internal to the building and implicit in any design problem. His success in resolving them is a measure of the designer's skill.

The designer's responsibility does not end here, however. We have already seen that optimal control of the various environments cannot, except with extraordinary effort, be achieved by individual buildings alone, no matter how advanced their design or elaborate their equipment. For buildings, like people or nations, simply cannot exist alone. It is not until each building stands in a proper and just relation to its external environment that optimal control of its internal environment becomes possible. Every aspect of the immediate physical surroundings — topography, adjacent trees and buildings, path of sun, prevailing breeze — affects and is affected by the building.

Since the individual designer seldom has any control over the general anarchy of his surroundings, he is forced in his own building to adopt defensive measures. The buildings which surround his own obstruct the prevailing breeze. Unable to exploit this natural feature, he has to install fans. Neighboring

structures not only make no intelligent use of their own share
of the sun's heat and light, they also prevent a normal distribution of sunlight on his plot. Thus, for him, insolation and daylighting remain academic questions: he has to install space
heaters and fluorescent tubes instead. Surrounded by paved
courts, masonry walls, and traffic-crowded streets, his plot is
flooded with noise: he must rely upon sound insulation to make
his building tolerably quiet. Having access only to polluted air,
he must rely upon filters to cleanse it. His building is thus
doubly on the defensive — against nature and against man.
It has to overcome the natural deficiencies of its external environment without being able to exploit those features which
are favorable. And, as though this were not bad enough, it has
also to overcome the cumulative damage which its neighbors
have already wrought upon the natural environment.

The ingenuity which American buildings display in over-
coming such peripheral obstacles is little short of miraculous.
By mechanical means, we can now create any set of environmental conditions we desire. Important as they are, the wide
use of these techniques and equipments has inherent dangers.
The contemporary designer runs the risk of accepting electrical
air filters as a satisfactory *substitute* for clean fresh air; of feeling
that electrically operated louvers are preferable to natural
foliage; of preferring sound insulation to plain ordinary silence.
There are, as we have seen, many specific situations in which
our synthetic environments are superior to nature's. But this
is no adequate basis for the mechanistic conclusion that we
don't need nature any more. On the contrary, with the complexity of modern building we need nature more than ever
before. It is not a question of air-conditioning versus sea
breezes, of neon tubes against the sun. It is rather the necessity
for integrating the two at the highest possible level.

Building Design and the Micro-Climate

SO MANY HAVE OBSERVED IT, so few have measured it: yet it is principally in this micro-climate that man must move.   The perspiring man in the street who doubts the Weather Bureau's 88° F. when his own private thermometer shows 103° F. in the shade; the irate citizen who chases his hat down a roaring street-wide gale while the instruments at the airport blandly register an eight-mile breeze; the gardener whose seedlings on the north side of the house were frozen despite an official low of 39° F.; the puzzled housewife whose radio proclaims a visibility of nine miles or better when outside her window the smog is so thick that she cannot see across the street.   All these people are the victims of a climatic contradiction.   There is nothing wrong either with their powers of observation or the instruments at the weather station.   It is merely that the same climate is being measured at two entirely different levels.   The Weather Bureau is reporting on the macro-climate while the citizen is feeling on his own back the effects of his micro-climate.

Meteorology has reached a high stage in this country, especially during the recent war.   But so far it has worked largely on a macroscopic scale, dealing in terms of continents and regions inside which important variations go largely unobserved. Historically this emphasis is not difficult to understand.   Meteorology got its earliest impetus from such activities as agriculture and maritime shipping.   In the last decade, aviation has enormously extended both its coverage and its accuracy.   This is essential knowledge, but of scant use to the designer or consumer of buildings.   For the rude and pressing needs of the individual deal with his immediate environment — conditions within his apartment, block, or place of work.   Detailed knowledge at this scale is almost totally lacking in this country.

When homely observation christens a certain intersection as 'the coldest corner in town,' the chances are that a check with instruments would confirm the fact.   Moreover, intensive research along accepted meteorological lines would reveal *why* it is the coldest corner and *how* it might be redesigned to correct the situation.   It is the character and juxtaposition of air masses which determines the weather in a given locality at a given time. But the local behavior of these air masses is in turn affected by the particular configuration of the land: the height and depth

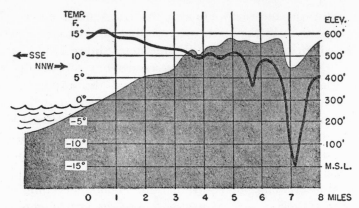

Measurement of the microclimatology of Toronto clearly shows the effect of the lake on the city's environs. On a cold winter's night it was thirty degrees colder in a suburban valley seven miles inland than it was along the lake shore.   *Architectural Forum*

of its hills and valleys; the shapes, sizes, and densities of the buildings upon it; its bodies of water, groves of trees, parks, and paved streets; finally, by the way the sun falls upon the whole ensemble.

It thus follows that every change we make upon the landscape — every house we raise or tree we cut down, each field we plow or street we pave — affects the micro-climate. This change may be small: it will certainly be definite. It may be for the better: but the chances are that, with our appalling ignorance, it will be for the worse. We cannot say, with Mark Twain, that everyone talks about the weather but no one does anything about it. As a matter of fact, we talk about the weather all the time and are never conscious of how importantly we are changing it.

Landscape design, as a specialized methodology for manipulating the natural environment, has achieved an independent professional status only since Olmsted — that is, in the past fifty years or so. This tardy recognition was but the reflection of the fact that city dwellers saw no use-value to the landscape. It has been only by degrees and haltingly that any recognition of its importance to man's health and happiness has developed. Even this recognition has been of a peculiarly limited kind, for the discovery of the landscape has been primarily in esthetic terms. Streets planted with trees are now quite generally recognized as being more attractive than streets without them. Buildings are no longer considered completed until their surroundings are landscaped. Open areas add to the beauty of a neighborhood. Parks and playgrounds are important to the health of growing children. All of this is true. Yet it does not convey an adequate picture of the complex relationship between man, building, and landscape. It does not comprehend the real physical impact of the landscape upon us and upon the microclimate, nor of our every action upon it.

Certain aspects of the landscape are susceptible to wide and flexible manipulation, the health and comfort potentials of which have been scarcely tapped by contemporary designers. Two illustrations will suffice: the use of trees and use of lawns in urban areas. Above and beyond their beauty, the scientific use of deciduous trees will accomplish any or all of the following:

> *Deflect, absorb, and reduce the heat radiation* of sun-heated roofs, walls, and paved areas in summer, while in the winter permitting fullest access of solar heat to these surfaces.
>
> *Reduce the free air temperatures* of contiguous areas (the shade effect) both by reduction of radiant temperatures and by the transpiration of the leaves, whose evaporating moisture cools air temperatures. (An oak tree with 700,000 leaves will transpire one hundred and eighty gallons of water per day.)
>
> *Filter the atmosphere.* Trees are themselves excellent air filters, catching and holding dust on the viscous surface of their leaves. Many trees, of course, pollute the atmosphere with their own pollens but since these pollens can travel great distances anyway, near-by trees do not greatly increase the hazard.
>
> *Reduce intensities and glare* both indoors and out from sun, street lights, near-by windows. (A birch and beech forest will reduce light intensities by fifty to seventy-five per cent of normal.)

Increase visual privacy in summer when more people spend much time out of doors, or with doors and windows open.

Reduce the transmission of air-borne sound. A dense planting of full-leaved trees and shrubs is an excellent insulator against noise.

In general, trees have a stabilizing effect upon their immediate surroundings, reducing all environmental extremes. Rudolph Geiger, in his excellent study on the micro-climate,[1] found that a mixed forest growth of spruce, oak, and poplar cuts off sixty-nine per cent of the sun's heat from the ground. He found that forests are cooler in summer, warmer in winter than clear land; and that a belt of trees would reduce wind velocities by as much as sixty-three per cent. In this country, measurements have shown that a shelter belt of trees will reduce wind velocities by fifty per cent and reduce fuel consumption in farmhouses thus protected by as much as thirty per cent.[2]

Much the same result will flow from the intelligent use of lawns and dense ground covers:

Temperatures will be reduced. Because of its rough texture and low color value, a grass surface will absorb more sunlight and re-radiate less heat than any paved or masonry surface. Because of transpiration, a lawn destroys a large portion of the heat it absorbs. In general, both air and radiant temperatures will be much lower above a grass plot than over a paved area of similar exposure. Observations in Texas, at 2 P.M. of an August day, revealed a temperature immediately above an unshaded asphalt pavement of 124.7° F.: above a shaded grass plot thirty feet away the temperature was 98° F. — a differential of almost 27° F![3]

Glare will be eliminated. Grass presents a glare-proof texture. Despite immensely higher illumination levels out-of-doors, glare on a natural landscape will occur only over water, snow, or sheets of rock.

[1] *Climate of the Layer of Air Near the Ground.* Munich, 1927.
[2] United States Department of Agriculture, *Climate and Man*, p. 485.
[3] C. F. Brooks, 'Parade Ground Temperatures at College Station, Texas,' *Monthly Weather Review*, United States Department of Commerce, 1919.

Dust will be reduced. Obviously a healthy lawn can be the source of very little dust; in addition, its grass blades will catch and hold a large amount of air-borne dust.

Noise will be reduced. A grass surface offers an ideal surface for the absorption of air-borne sound.

From facts such as these it is apparent that the landscape is an immensely important factor in building design — a factor which no architect can intelligently ignore. Trees, shrubs, sod, and ground cover must be viewed not as luxuries, not as ornaments, but as actual items of equipment, as essential to the efficient operation of the building as its stoker or lighting system. Their selection, disposition, feeding, and watering need not be charged off to overhead or justified as pleasant hobbies: they become serious matters of maintenance. Such an evaluation of the landscape implies new concepts for the landscape designer as well: his designs must recognize new disciplines. Purely visual considerations of composition, proportion, vista and balance will be subjected to the acid test of environmental control. Landscaped areas will then be judged by their actual performance as well as by their beauty. No more than in architecture are the two contradictory; on the contrary, such an integration will yield new and higher esthetic standards.

The most important features of the natural landscape, however, are subject to no such easy manipulation: the path of the sun, the distribution of heat and frost, topography, the location of water bodies, the paths of prevailing winds. In order to exploit these, it is the buildings themselves which must be maneuvered into the most favorable positions. This again involves a whole body of knowledge which is only beginning to take shape in this country. In one of the few investigations of its kind, the American Public Health Association measured air movement and temperatures in Harlem Houses, a public housing project in New York City. The investigation revealed wide discrepancies with the climate of this four-block area:

The northern portion is rather well exposed, and the southeast corner is completely exposed to the local [southwest] winds; but

the southwest corner is hemmed in by other structures. . . .
During the midday, temperatures at all three stations were
approximately equal at about 95° F. but wind velocities at the
open southeast corner were *two to four times as great* as those at the
southwest.   Thus, even when air temperatures were the same,
conditions on the roof at the southeast corner were quite pleasant,
while those at the southwest were virtually intolerable . . . at
10 P.M. the temperature had dropped to 76° F. at the southeast
corner but the southwest readings had dropped only to 89° F.,
a differential of 13° F., apparently dependent upon wind exposure.[1]

The same study found that in an Oklahoma City housing project,
those apartments which were placed at right angles to the prevailing wind had an inside air movement of fifty feet per minute
(the minimum deemed necessary for any feeling of relief in high
temperatures), while identical units placed parallel to the wind
had an air movement of only thirty feet per minute.   One can
assume that exposure to prevailing winds was at least one of the
factors determining the site plan of these two projects.   And
one can readily see that other factors may have prevented *all*
the units having ideal exposure to the wind.   But the fact
remains that a difference of 13° F. or twenty feet per minute
could easily prove the difference between a good and a bad
night's rest for the tenants.   Even if, for comfort, each apartment
were air-conditioned, the difference would be reflected in the
load carried by the units cooling the southwest corner.

There is, of course, a reverse side to the coin: the protection
of buildings from cold winter winds.   Since these originate at
different points of the compass from those of summer, it is
usually possible to orient the building so that a minimum surface
is exposed to them.   Heavier insulation and a minimum of
window area on such surfaces will further reduce heat losses.
In any event, average wind velocities will be lower in a city, as
in a forest, though in certain areas they may be freakishly much
higher.   For the movement of air between and through a group
of buildings is not wholly determined by the general direction
of the breeze.   It is greatly modified by local air currents set

---

[1] Allan A. Twichell, *Conditions in Occupied Housing* (New York: American Public
Health Association, 1940), p. 8.

up by walls of varying temperature, exposure, and juxtaposition. With adequate knowledge of these phenomena, it is apparent that we could organize any group of buildings so that they would not only manipulate existing breezes but deliberately create 'artificial' ones. This is in no sense utopian, for our cities create such air currents anyway. The only difference is that we would be harnessing for our comfort those whimsical gusts which today do little but scatter the papers on the street.

Harnessing the Sun

IT IS A TRUISM that cities are much hotter than the surrounding countryside in summer. Here we must rely largely upon rude observation, since most weather stations are themselves located in urban areas. In addition, their readings are usually taken atop the tallest building in town and ignore *radiant* temperatures (which, from the standpoint of comfort, are of equal or greater importance than air temperatures). This summertime differential between city and country is largely due to the preponderance of such surfaces as walls, roofs, paved streets, and courts. These absorb, hold and re-radiate heat to a far greater degree than any natural landscape. As a consequence, daytime temperatures are abnormally high and the city cannot cool off at night as rapidly as the countryside.

Contrariwise, cities would be colder in winter than their surroundings were it not for the fact that we heat them. Outside temperatures are raised by heat loss through millions of square feet of building surface. Perhaps as much as two-thirds of these same surfaces will not be even touched by the sun's rays throughout the winter. Thus, we have the paradox of a mechanism which traps far too much solar heat when it is definitely not wanted and makes no effort to trap it when it is definitely needed. It makes no effort to exploit prevailing winds when they would help and only accidentally protects us from them when they are not desired. Huge quantities of natural energy are available: all of it is ignored, while boilers and generators and cooling units work furiously to make up for the oversight.

Research in insolation, the scientific exploitation of sunlight in buildings, has seen a spotty and uneven development in this country to date. In recent years there has been a steady increase in glass areas in all types of buildings; and this is an index of our increasing awareness of the importance of sunlight. Here and there, independent investigators have done enough work to indicate the great potentials as well as the complexity of insolation. A few architects have built 'solar houses' which show great promise. Tens of thousands of houses in Southern California and Florida get their hot water from solar heaters. The owners of a group of new solar houses on the shores of Lake Michigan report fuel savings of $250 per heating season over conventional methods. It is estimated that a square foot of glass facing south in New York City will transmit 170,000 B.T.U. more solar heat during a heating season than an equal area of brick wall. Despite the fact that it has been so largely ignored, there can be no doubt of the importance of insolation to building design and city planning.

But so far, the architect has had to rely for his information upon research sponsored by various manufacturers. Much of this has been valuable, but all of it is fragmentary and disparate. There are still large areas of fact which have scarcely been surveyed. A vast amount of theoretical data requires digestion and there is need for much experimental work to confirm it. In short, there is need for a centralized research program which encompasses the principal factors in architectural insolation: solar heating, daylighting, and solar therapy.

Solar heating, daylighting, and solar therapy are merely architectural exploitations of three of the properties of sunlight — the heat of the infra-red wave band, the luminosity of the visible, and the germicidal, tanning and anti-rickets factors of the ultra-violet. A well-insolated building would thus admit a maximum of direct sunlight in the winter, a minimum in the summer; the optimal amount of sky light the year round; and a maximum of the ultra-violet band throughout the year. In theory, at least, it is not difficult to insolate a single building. It requires only that the designer know for his building site the

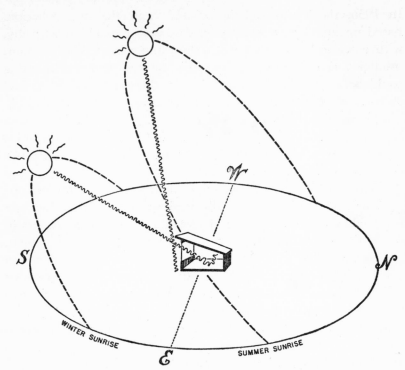

A house properly oriented to the shifting path of the sun
will gain much heat from winter sunshine while excluding
the rays of the higher summer sun. Proper use of deciduous
vines and trees can make this control still more effective.

points of the compass, the latitude, and the angles of incidence
of the sun for all seasons of the year. Given this information,
he can orient his building, arrange the rooms, compute and distribute the glass areas, determine the angle and projection of
the eaves. Thus he allows the sunlight to enter where and when
he wants it.

Actually, the problem is not so simple as it sounds. Not only
is it three-dimensional but — because of the shifting trajectory
of the sun — also curvilinear. A simple three-dimensional technique of analysis is obviously desirable; and it was supplied by
the late town planner, Henry Wright, and his son, Henry N.
Wright, in their work at Columbia's School of Architecture.

In 1936, the Wrights designed and built the first heliodon. Based on an English prototype, this was a machine whereby, with a scaled model of the building and a movable pin-point spotlight, the relationship between the sun and the building could be accurately simulated for any latitude, season or time of day. The heliodon has subsequently been considerably improved. Professor George M. Beal, of the University of Kansas Department of Architecture, has constructed one with a motor-driven light and built-in camera which greatly extends the usefulness of the instrument.

The heliodon offers an effective method for determining the *distribution* of sunlight, especially where groups of buildings are involved or where the terrain is irregular. But it is of no use in computing the *quantity* of solar energy, its value in terms of heat, light, or therapy. The question remains: How much solar heat will a scientifically insolated building absorb in winter — heat which the conventional building would lose? Conversely, how much solar heat would such a building exclude in summer — heat which the conventional designs admit? Obviously, a large number of variables are involved in the equation: climate, latitude, topography, orientation, amount of glass area, type of construction. But to demonstrate that the dividends of proper insolation would in any case be large, Henry N. Wright made what was almost certainly the first study of its kind in this country.[1]

Based on the climate of New York City, the Wright study established a reference frame of facts such as these:

> The maximum heat value of sunlight is equal to 350 B.T.U. per square foot per hour on a surface at right angles to the sun's rays.
>
> The highest average heat value of sunlight occurs precisely when it is most needed — at 4 P.M. on the winter solstice.
>
> A south wall receives almost *five times* more heat from the sun in winter than it does in summer.
>
> Whereas a west-northwest wall will get *six times* as much heat in summer as it does in winter.

[1] *Solar Radiation as Related to Summer Air-Conditioning and Winter Heating in Residences.* New York: John B. Pierce Foundation, 1936.

A south wall receives a maximum of 2300 B.T.U. per square foot per day at the winter solstice; at the same time, a north wall gets no solar heat at all.

It is apparent, then, that it makes a great deal of difference to the tenant's comfort which way a building faces.   As Wright puts it: 'houses placed broadside to the south-southwest, with most of the important rooms and large windows located on that side (and with a minimum of window area on the west-northwest end) will be a great deal easier to cool in the summer, and more pleasant to live in and easier to heat in winter.' Using a five-room cottage of conventional design, he estimated that, placed in the worst possible orientation, it would admit *nine times* as much sun heat in summer as the same house (with only minor changes in size and location of windows) in the best possible orientation.   Conversely, the properly oriented house would receive *four times* as much heat in winter as the improperly oriented one.   Expressed in other terms, this gain would average thirty-seven kilowatt hours on a bright December day.

The moment one building is close enough to cast its shadow on a neighbor, however, the problem is complicated.   For maladjustments between the buildings themselves — no matter how well designed each may be — will nullify the larger relationship between them and the sun.   Here, too, the Wright study pioneered.   Assuming a level plot and using the same five-room house, he demonstrated that an infinite number of buildings could be deployed on the landscape, each enjoying ideal year-round insolation.   No house shades its neighbor at any time of day or year; each unit gets greater visual privacy, better exposure to breeze and to view, than in the conventional gridiron layout. In terms of land coverage, paving, and utilities the solar pattern competes easily with traditional layouts.

Daylighting, as was seen in the chapter dealing with the luminous environment, must be regarded as an integral part of the illumination system.   In general, it might be said that a building which is well insolated is also well lit.   This is a necessary oversimplification, for there are many situations in which a flood of direct sunshine provides the worst possible luminous

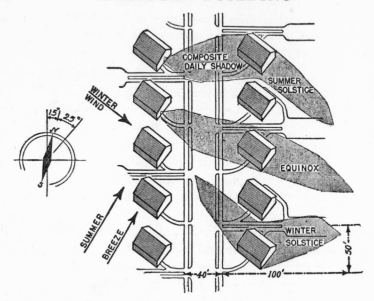

Even on fifty-foot gridiron lots, it is entirely possible to place each house so that none shades its neighbors, each has full access to prevailing summer breezes, and each has maximum outlook and privacy.   *John B. Pierce Foundation*

environment for the task in hand. In such cases, the building would probably be windowless anyway. Ordinarily, good daylighting would go hand in hand with good insolation. For situations where 'cool' sunlight is desirable, a window glass which admits only the visible and excludes the infra-red waves would be desirable: no such glass is presently available. Nor will it be since the greater portion of solar energy — when measured as heat — is visible. Heat-absorbing glass is available which comes as close as possible to this ideal. For any special manipulation of the visible wave band after it has entered the building, a wide variety of means are available — light-diffusing glasses, venetian blinds, translucent screens, etc. Finally, in the photoelectric cell we have an ideal control instrument for the integration of day- and artificial light at any given level.

The therapeutic value of the ultra-violet in sunlight is generally acknowledged but not very definitely defined. All sorts of diseases are associated with the lack of it (rickets, tuberculosis, respiratory ailments). It kills a number of air-borne bacteria. It is necessary to the production of vitamin D in the human body. The precise importance to the sick of the ultra-violet in sunlight is a question for the medical profession to answer. Meanwhile, it is safe to assume that our buildings would be healthier if they absorbed it. That they do not is due to the fact that ordinary glass is opaque to most of the band: it admits enough to permit photosynthesis in plants but not enough to tan the human skin. Ultra-violet glasses were available before the war, although they were expensive and apparently not stable — that is, their transmission of the band decreased with time. Presumably both cheap and stable glasses will be available to post-war building.

The problem of using solar energy intelligently is closely related to that of efficiently storing it. For as far as building design is concerned, the chief drawback to solar heat is not the total amount available but its uneven distribution in time — its wide daily and seasonal fluctuations. The solar water heaters of California and Florida receive enough solar heat throughout the year to yield impressive results, even though the heater itself is relatively primitive. Essentially nothing more than a copper coil in an airtight, black-painted, glass-topped case, these heaters are oriented for maximum exposure to sun — on the roof, along the wall, sometimes over windows where they also act as awnings. A heater whose area is sixty-four square feet will supply a family of six with 130° F. water the year round. In midsummer, the yield is, of course, much higher.

But heat is one of the most difficult forms of energy to store, and the solar heater is actually only a converter. What is obviously implied is an efficient method of converting energy into an easily stored form. Here again Nature offers a technique: photosynthesis. When we succeed in duplicating the physio-chemical process by which the simplest weed can convert and store energy in usable form, a Gordian knot in building design will have been cut. This is a task for physicist and chemist; and the solution is not one for which society can long wait. Once solved, there is the dazzling possibility that any building in a temperate climate could be heated, and possibly even cooled, by the sunlight which falls upon its surfaces. We can thus conceive of building skins incomparably more flexible and sentient than those of today. Membranes which transmit solar energy directly to the interior when the interior calls for it: which exclude the energy when it is not needed, converting and storing it in the form of carbons, alcohol, or electricity for use at another time. Then buildings would begin to approach the animate world in the efficient maintenance of an equilibrium between internal and external environments.

CHAPTER SIXTEEN

Plan, the Instrument of Policy

A PLAN IS MANY THINGS, depending upon how you look at it. From the point of view of society as a whole, a plan is an instrument of policy, a means of facilitating a certain line of action. Thus the plan of an American city may be regarded as an instrument of socio-economic policy for the production and exchange of goods and ideas. And the plans of individual buildings of which the city is composed are likewise expressions of smaller, individual policies. From the standpoint of the architect or physical planner, however, a plan is a representation of a horizontal plane passed through a building or a city. In such a sense, a plan is a *solution* for a given line of action. It inevitably reflects the designer's concept of how — within the limits given — a certain amount of space may be best organized for the specific operation to be housed. For the people who live or work in the completed building or city, a plan is something else again. It is a control mechanism which will, to a large extent, determine how happily they live or how well they work together.

Planning may therefore be analyzed at many different levels and from many points of view. Our concern here is with physical planning — the system of spatial relationships created by real buildings in actual cities. Here again, the most illuminating approach is from the point of view of the health of both the individual and society as a whole. The primary function of all building plans is to direct the flow of human and

mechanical energies into certain productive patterns. A successful plan is one which increases the physical and mental well-
being of the people whose energies it channelizes.

In a limited technical sense, to plan is to manipulate space.
A set of blueprints has only, so to speak, a potential energy;
but once the building is up and people are using it, its plan
ceases to be an abstraction and becomes instead a very real and
dynamic force. It modifies importantly the social relationships
of the people who use it. Thus it may be said that planning is
the manipulation of physical relationships for the purpose of
facilitating social relationships. There is, of course, no metaphysical significance to what a plan can accomplish. You can
force a family to live in a school or a church or a factory instead
of in a house. Its relationships will be adversely affected, its
well-being and productivity diminished, by forcing it to operate
in a plan not designed for it. But as a social unit it will remain
recognizably a family. It will not become either a history class,
a church congregation, or a trade union. From this it is apparent
that each social unit (class, congregation, work crew) and each
social operation (study, worship, industry) has its own private
set of spatial requirements. These can be discovered only by a
study of the internal structure of the unit and operation to be
housed. But the more precise the designer's knowledge of these
requirements, the more satisfactory his plan will be.

As an independent field, consciously and deliberately separated
from other aspects of building, planning is scarcely more than
fifty years old. Prior to that, the lack of full-time professional
planners had been a measure of the simplicity of American
society. Public and private policy had been small enough in
scale and simple enough in structure to warrant amateur solutions. Technical knowledge had been at too low a level to
detect whatever inadequacies such plans might have had, much
less to measure precisely their ill effects.

This absence of planners did not, of course, preclude the
existence of highly successful plans. As a matter of fact, this
country had a well-defined tradition of planning long before the
planner appeared as a trained specialist. This tradition had

certain characteristics which are inseparable from our building as a whole. It was rational, mechanistic, expansive. It attached great importance to order and balance and its method of achieving these qualities was in symmetry. For a long time, satisfactory plans could be produced within this tradition. Indeed, it was so satisfactory for so long that it was to form an almost obsessive basis for the professional planners when they did appear. In 1893 the Classic plan arose like a phoenix from the fifty-year interregnum of the Romanticists and the Victorians. Even today, American planning has not been liberated from the grip of this tradition.

The weaknesses of Classic plan are today all too apparent. We may still know very little about the detailed physical and psychological requirements of a family or a group of workmen in a factory. But this at least we do know — their needs are no more than approximately symmetrical, and can seldom be organized satisfactorily around a system of intersecting axes. A symmetrical plan is seldom an accurate reflection of the social processes it is supposed to facilitate; an axis is a concept from plane geometry, not biology. Yet Classic planning was progressive in its concept of ordered growth, of controlled development along predetermined lines toward socially desirable ends. Its limitations lay in a schematic approach which was two dimensional, with a pre-scientific concept of change.

But if the Classic tradition proved unsuitable to the rising industrial society of the nineteenth century, it did not follow that the planning of the Romanticists was an advance in the right direction. It is true that they discarded the axial line and the exact symmetry, and to this extent they exercised a liberating influence from the rigid and restrictive Classic. It is true also that they rediscovered the natural landscape. Yet, under the leadership of Ruskin, they turned the course of American planning backward, not forward. Like Ruskin, they began by being naïvely ignorant of the new science and technology rising around them; and like him, they ended up by being bitterly antiscientific. Their ecstasy over the natural landscape masked a profound ignorance of its inner content — Washington and Jefferson were far better botanists than the Transcendentalists

of Walden Pond. When all was said and done, the Classicists
had had perspective — both physiographic and social.

A Modern System of Plan Classification

IT IS CHARACTERISTIC of the emergence of any field of human
endeavor into an independent status that it attempt two things
— to define its area and to classify its content. It is ironic that
John Ruskin should have been one of the first to do this in the
field of planning. He was the first to recognize the growing
specialization of Victorian building and to attempt to set up a
system of categories for its planning.

> Architecture proper [said he] naturally arranges itself under
> five heads:
> Devotional — including all buildings raised for God's service
> or honor.
> Memorial — including both monuments and tombs.
> Civil — including every edifice raised by nations or societies for
> purposes of common business or pleasure.
> Military — including all private and public architecture of
> defense.
> Domestic — including every rank and kind of dwelling place.[1]

Yet even a system of categories became an instrument of reactionary propaganda in his hands. It was an ethical critique
of English building — a sermon on what he thought it should
be rather than a description of what it actually was. He established a separate category for monuments and tombs while
blandly ignoring all the new plan types which were so important
a part of contemporary life. He saw no distinction between the
plan of the Crystal Palace and that of the Houses of Parliament,
and nothing which distinguished both of them from the great
railway stations designed by Phillip Hardwick at Euston Square
(1837) or that by Francis Thompson at Derby (1839). The
factories which had already made England the leading manufacturing nation in the world cannot anywhere be crowded into

[1] John Ruskin, *Seven Lamps of Architecture* (New York: John W. Lovell, 1885), p. 17.

Ruskin's list. Clearly, when he provided for 'private military architecture of defense,' he had in mind the England of Walter Scott's novels and not that of Darwin.

Ruskin's system of classification was accepted uncritically by the American architects. It was never seriously analyzed, nor was any theoretical structure of comparable impressiveness counterposed to it. It appeared at a time when architectural theory in this country was hopelessly confused and anemic, and at its lowest ebb. It won the day by default. The Ruskinian concept was absorbed into the main stream of American theory, where many vestiges of it remain to this day.

In the last analysis, the plan of any building is determined by the peculiarities of the social process which it is evolved to house. If the process is the manufacture of stockings, then the plan 'automatically' takes on the characteristics of a hosiery mill. If the process is the education of very small children, then the enclosed space is organized in a manner characteristic of nurseries; while if the care and treatment of the sick is the process in question, the plan 'becomes' that of a hospital. Under Ruskin's classification, it is apparent that a hosiery mill needs only to produce socks for soldiers in order to be classified as military; while a hospital — endowed by and named for some dead philanthropist — can properly be called memorial.

The truth is that an accurate classification of the buildings of a given era is determined, not by abstract systems of logic, but by the character of the society itself. And no juggling of plan types according to some preconceived scale of ethical values can conceal the fact that *social process is the determinant of plan*. Moreover, it must also be observed that there is an internal relationship between each process and the others. These relationships mesh and interlock to form a cyclical system. In theory, this cycle may be entered at any point, but since industrial production is the most decisive of all contemporary processes, it seems logical to classify plan types in relation to it. The factory is the crucial building of our society. It is the factory which at once makes possible and necessary all the rich variety of modern American building. If old types such as the livery stable disappear, it is because of the factory; and if new ones like the airport appear, this is also due to the factory. It is the factory again which is responsible for the astonishing specialization in the dwelling house — the self-contained suburban cottage, the towering apartment houses and hotels, the tourist cabins and the resort hotels. There is not a single building type which does not — in its structure, equipment, and plan — reveal the impact of the factory and its products. Indeed, our very history would be unintelligible without an understanding of this relationship. Industrial production is the nodal point of our society. To be illuminating, any classification of plan types should pivot around that fact. Thus, it seems to me that any classification of modern American plan types must be of this order: [1]

Social Process or Operation	*Corresponding Plan Types to Facilitate It*
1. Production	Smelters, mills, mines, factories, etc.; farms, dairies, greenhouses, canneries, abattoirs, etc.
2. Power	Dams, hydroelectric and steam generation plants, electrical distribution systems, etc.
3. Transportation and communication	Airports, railroad and highways systems, marine terminals, etc.; telephone, telegraph, radio, television, and postal systems; newspaper and publishing plants, etc.
4. Storage	Warehouses, refrigeration plants, grain elevators, oil tanks, vaults, etc.
5. Exchange	Shops, stores, markets, warehouses; banks, stock exchanges, etc.
6. Administration	Capitols, courthouses, city halls, etc.; offices, headquarters, etc.
7. Protection	Jails, fire halls, etc.
8. Dwelling	Houses, apartments, hotels, resorts, tourist and trailer camps, dormitories, etc.

[1] This corresponds in most respects to the system set forth by K. Lönberg-Holm and C. Theodore Larson in their notable study, *Planning for Productivity* (New York: International Industrial Relations Institute, 1940).

9. Education and research	Nurseries, schools, universities; laboratories, libraries, museums; zoos, botanical gardens, experimental stations, etc.
10. Recreation	Stadia, natatoria, gymnasiums; theaters, cinemas; race tracks, ball grounds, parks, playgrounds, beaches, etc.
11. Repair and reconstruction	Clinics, health centers, hospitals, sanatoria; rest and old-age homes; orphanages, reformatories and asylums, penitentiaries, etc.
12. Religious worship	Churches, synagogues, chapels, etc.
13. Elimination and conservation of waste	Cemeteries, crematoria, etc.; water systems, sewerage systems, incinerators, etc.
14. War	Military installations of all sorts (as the recent war has demonstrated, there are few buildings which do not automatically become military under modern conditions of total war).

There is, naturally, some deviation from such a schematic classification as this in real life. Some of the simpler building types may be used for more than one process or operation without adversely affecting it. A movie theater built for entertainment may be used for certain types of visual education, an auditorium may serve for both a church service and a bingo game. Again, a given plan type may in one situation form a complete building while in another and more complex project it may be only a small unit. From biological necessity, some types are more or less constant in all buildings. Washrooms and toilets which require only a small corner of a plane will grow to large and complex buildings at the pithead of a mine.

It is generally true that American building today is organized along the lines indicated here. But whatever the advantages of this classification over that of Mr. Ruskin, it remains little more than a check list until it is amplified in two directions. Functionally, these specialized buildings must be viewed as cells in larger networks. These networks extend *vertically* to accommodate a

BLOCK	NEIGHBOR-HOOD	COMMUNITY	CITY	STATE OR REGION	NATION	
					▓	OTHER ADVANCED OR SPECIALIZED TRAINING
				▓		TEACHER'S COLLEGE
				▓		UNIVERSITY. RESEARCH AND SCIENTIFIC INSTITUTE
				▓		MENTALLY DEFECTIVE
				▓		BLIND, MUTE, DEAF
			▓			ADULT EDUCATION
			▓			TECHNICAL AND VOCATIONAL
		▓				HIGH SCHOOL
		▓				JUNIOR HIGH
	▓					GRAMMAR SCHOOL
	▓					KINDERGARTEN
▓						NURSERY

A complete educational system will provide adequate facilities for every type and level of education, for all ages and for every degree of mental and physical ability. And good planning will distribute these facilities in every block, neighborhood, town, or region which requires them.

given social process from its smallest local manifestation to a comprehensive system, national in scope. This is readily apparent in a process such as education. The larger the social unit, the more complex are its educational requirements. The more specialized the program, the more the differentiation in the buildings required to house it. For the day is long past when a 'standard' classroom will adequately meet the needs of all types of classes. Certain factors like good lighting may remain constant; but many others are undergoing continual refinement and specialization.

In the physical plant which houses each social operation listed above this characteristic development is to be observed — rooms are combined into buildings, buildings grouped to form centers, centers are organized into networks. These systems mesh, interlock, and sustain each other so that a horizontal section at any given level also reveals a characteristic pattern. For the smallest residential unit (which in modern town-planning parlance is the large, traffic-free block) the structure will be comparatively simple — housing units, a nursery and playground, perhaps a communal laundry. Several of these combine to form a *neighborhood,* with shopping center, movie, etc. These, in turn, are grouped into a *community* large enough to support a grammar school. This is generally regarded as the smallest socially self-contained unit, though they are seldom self-supporting from an economic standpoint. These communities are, in turn, the cells of the *city or metropolitan district* which, together with its surrounding agricultural area, is the basic social, economic and political unit of industrial America. Varying in size with the geography of the area, any number of these metropolitan districts combine to form a fairly homogeneous unit known as the *region.*

The foregoing constitutes a reasonably accurate description of the broad lines along which the physical plant of our country is actually organized. It facilitates an understanding of planning problems because it relates each plan type to social reality. Such a system of categories is, however, only a quantitative description. It is not meant to convey the impression that American building today offers complete or even adequate accommodations for American life. This, as any planner would be prompt to point out, is anything but the case. For our physical plant is full of inequalities, lags, and aching voids when measured by accepted standards. The reader needs only to superimpose a check-list like that given above on the actual educational facilities of his own home town to discover this himself. Are there playgrounds for each fifty families? Does each neighborhood have kindergartens to which children can easily and safely walk? Is there a school for crippled children in the city? for adult education? How far from home must blind or deaf children go for an education?

As a matter of fact, it is only in the past fifteen or twenty years that the physical planners have reached the stage where they could formulate such questions, much less answer them. They had appeared late in the day, at a time when American society was already comparatively mature. The nation was a running machine, whatever the friction or waste. Its physical apparatus was huge and complex; the contradictions between private profit and public good made diagnoses risky and remedies extremely hard to apply. The development of the field of physical planning was thus anything but easy. It involved many false starts, superficial concepts, confusions between cause and effect. Yet it has steadily advanced, broadening its concepts to the point where it can deal in terms of whole regions; deepening its perception so that the interplay of basic social and economic forces can be intelligibly plotted. It is a measure of this growing maturity that it can ask revealing questions and with reasonable accuracy answer them.

A formal classification which groups buildings according to type and relates them to social process is necessary to an understanding of the planning field: but it is not all that is necessary. Building is in constant flux, subject to the impact of general social and scientific advance in much the same way as astronomy or physics. Our society is extraordinarily fertile in invention and building is quick to reflect each advance. The auto made obsolete the buggy: coincidentally, the garage replaced the feed store and the blacksmith, the giant clover-leaf intersection replaced the dusty crossroads. Radio and movies supplanted the legitimate theater; and vaudeville houses gave way to broadcasting studios. Under such an interplay of forces, the individual plan type emerges as anything but static. It was not always what it is today, nor is it likely to remain for long what it is now. There is a subtle but steady obsolescence in all types, so that no plan of thirty years ago — theater, drug store, factory, or apartment — will be satisfactory today. Sometimes the life-cycle of a plan is very brief. Thus, a scant forty years encompasses the rise, dominance, and decline of the tuberculosis sanatorium. It appeared in response to a certain theory of combating the disease by sunshine, fresh air, and quiet. It flourished in the desert and the mountains. Now that surgery and straight hospitalization are becoming the accepted treatment, the sanatorium is slipping back and seems destined for abandonment.

These movements are not so aimless or unpredictable as they might seem at first. They appear as surface disturbances, so to speak, and long periods may elapse between the first wave and a deep-going tide of change. Such lags are especially characteristic of the building field, for buildings are hard things to liquidate, either physically or financially. Some types respond to changes much more readily than others: thus the backwardness of housing is notorious while the rate of change in commercial types is quite rapid. This unevenness of development is even more noticeable in city planning than in individual building, for here the lag is cumulative in both time and space. Nevertheless, standards in planning do change and along fairly definite lines. At the present time, several criteria are notable in planning — those looking toward:

1. Multiple use of space
2. Flexibility
3. Mechanization
4. Mobility
5. Concentration and dispersion

The Multiple Use of Space

THE MULTIPLE USE OF SPACE is a notable characteristic of modern plan. One has only to compare contemporary plan types to those of a century ago to realize the extent to which we have intensified the use of enclosed space. Though by no means the most spectacular example of this trend, the steady compression of the American home is the most familiar example. A century ago the parlor was used only for company, weddings, and funerals: if the home had any pretensions, it boasted two parlors, the front one being opened only for the most formal occasions. Today, at the same socio-economic level, there is likely to be only a living-room and this space is used all the time, by all the family, every day in the week. One corner is often used for eating, another as often as not for sleeping. The dining-room of a century ago has all but disappeared; and despite the fact that the kitchen has absorbed this function also, it is apt to be only a fraction as large as its early Victorian progenitor. This compression of a given range of activities into smaller and smaller spaces has occurred in most building types. While it is a form of overcrowding, it differs from the procrustean congestion of the slums in this important respect: it is a designed compression, with all sorts of structural and mechanical devices aimed at compensating for the lost space.

A multiple use of space may flow from physical or mechanical necessity, as in the case of a trailer or an airliner. Here weight and bulk must be held within fixed limits, yet the resulting space must provide facilities for a fixed number of operations (lounging, sleeping, cooking, eating, defecation). Since these cannot occupy the same space at the same time, the areas allotted to each must be compressed to the minimum and the space — wherever possible — organized so as to permit different uses at different times. The compartments on some of the newer streamline trains offer almost perfect examples of this trend: everything is on hinges and when not in use folds out of sight, out of the way.

The same tendency appears in buildings, but usually as the result of economic forces. Rising land values, construction costs and taxes, and a demand for high return on capital investment also tend inexorably toward compression of plan. In commercial buildings, where street frontage is at a premium, shops which thirty years ago would have been cramped with fifty feet are today able to manage with ten. In office buildings, the unit floor space per clerical worker has been reduced by perhaps two-thirds since the days of H. H. Richardson. In theaters and auditoriums of all sorts another expression of the same tendency is apparent. A movie may occupy a relatively large amount of expensive space but this space is used twelve hours a day, seven days a week. A legitimate theater will occupy the same amount of space and yet be used only twenty-four hours a week, seldom as much as twenty-six weeks per year. This uneconomic use of space has already forced most legitimate theaters to turn movie. But there is another possibility, one which is increasingly apparent in auditoriums, and that is the tendency to extend the working day of the building by providing for a greater range of activities. This leads to large auditoriums which can be subdivided into smaller ones, to seating which can be shifted or removed altogether; to floors which can tilt to create proper sight lines; rise to form platforms or sink to form pools. Here, the intense use of time is made to compensate for the comparatively lavish use of space.

It is, of course, in the 'efficiency apartment' that most Americans have become acquainted with the multiple use of space. Here, because of economic (not physical or mechanical) limitations, the processes of living have been compressed into steadily dwindling areas. A multiplicity of devices and equipment make it possible and simultaneously make it tolerable. Tables fold out of the walls, sofas pull out to become beds, kitchens fit into ventilated closets, and beds drop out of them. Soundproofing, lighting, and elevators are added to compensate for increased densities. Because there is less space for the housewife to dust, clean, and mop, because there is a place provided for everything, these apartments are often economically organized in terms of space: but it does not necessarily follow, as is so often assumed, that they are also *efficiently* organized from the standpoint of the human user.

An economical organization of space may result in a plan which, objectively, makes work easier — in other words, channelizes the energies of its tenants effectively. But an *economical* plan will only be truly *efficient* if the internal requirements of both the process and the worker involved in the process are carefully considered and substantially met. Modern kitchens are marvels of compression. Old equipment has been radically improved, new labor-saving equipment has been added (dishwashers, deep freezers, powered egg-beaters) and all of it has

been organized into a space only a fraction as large as its prototype of fifty years ago.   Insofar as the new model cuts down
waste motion on the part of the housewife, economy may coincide with efficiency.   But there is a point beyond which a
multiple use of the same space makes work harder and not
easier.   If the family eats in a small kitchen with limited counter
space, the chances are that more energy is required to prepare
the meal, serve it, and clean up afterward than would be required in an old-time layout of large kitchen, pantry, and
eighteen-foot dining-room.

The same paradox holds true for much more complex social
operations and much larger buildings.   It holds true for the
city as a whole.   For example, the compression of a range of
cultural and entertainment activities into a single building might
give a community a more satisfactory solution than a whole
series of single-purpose buildings.   There is no merit to wasting
space.   But generally speaking the tendency to scrimp on urban
space, inspired as it is by economic pressure, should not be
raised to the level of a principle.   The criterion of physical
planning must be: what space does the process require for its
fullest development, not merely how much of such-and-such
process can be crammed into a given area?

The Flexible Organization of Space

FLEXIBILITY IN MODERN PLANNING is the natural result of the
rapid rate of change which obtains in industry, commerce, and
all urban institutions in general.   In some production fields, the
rate of change in technique is very rapid.   Industrial processes
and operations are being constantly revised in the light of rapidly
broadening knowledge.   New ones appear and old ones drop
out; and the ones which persist undergo steady modification.
This flux exerts great pressure upon both structure and plan.
The total amount of enclosed space necessary to house a given
operation is changing; and the fashion in which this space is
subdivided and organized by the plan changes likewise.   Buildings designed along conventional lines, built of conventional

VI

Confluent Streams of Contemporary Design

DESIGNERS of the buildings in this section: 133, 134, Albert Kahn, Inc.; 135, 136, Raymond Hood; 137, Reinhard and Hoffmeister; Corbett, Harrison and McMurray; Hood and Fouilhoux; 138, George Howe and William Lescaze; 139, Walter Dorwin Teague; 140, Raymond Loewy Associates; 141, John Russell Pope; 142, Addison Mizner; 143, Dwight James Baum; 144–147, Frank Lloyd Wright; 148, Alden Dow; 149, Pietro Belluschi; 150, 151, Hugh Stubbins; 152, Marcel Breuer; 153, Carl Koch; 154, Harwell Hamilton Harris; 155, George Nelson and William Hamby; 156, Walter Gropius and Marcel Breuer; 157, George Fred Keck; 158, Gardner Dailey; 159, Resettlement Administration; 160, Richard Neutra; 161, Buckminster Fuller; 163, Blass and Beckman; 164, Donald Deskey Associates; 165, Kenneth Lind; 166, Walter Gropius and Konrad Wachsmann; 167, Oscar Stonorov; 168, Oren Thomas; 169, Carson and Lunlin; 170, Ketchum, Gina and Sharp; 171, Ernest J. Kump; 172, Bruce Goff; 173, William A. Ganster and William L. Pereira; 174, Wurster and Bernardi; 175, Ernest J. Kump; 176, Tennessee Valley Authority; 177, Burnham Hoyt.

ILLUSTRATIONS in this section are from the following sources: 133, 134, Hedrich-Blessing photo; 135, Ezra Stoller photo; 136, McGraw-Hill Building Corporation; 137, Phillip Gendreau photo; 138, Ben Schnall photo; 139, Eisenstadt-Pix; 140, F. S. Lincoln photo; 141, *Architectural Forum*; 142, Igor Polevitzky, Robideaux photo; 143, Samuel Gottsche photo; 144, 145, 147, Stoller photos, reprinted from *Fortune Magazine* by special permission of the Editors; 146, Schnall photo; 148, *Architectural Forum*; 149, Boychuk Studio photo; 150, 151, National Housing Agency; 152, 153, Stoller photos; 154, Maynard Parker photo; 155, *Architectural Forum*, Robert Damora photo; 156, Paul Davis photo; 157, Hedrich-Blessing photo; 158, Roger Sturtevant photo; 159, Farm Security Administration photo; 160, Julius Shulman photo; 161, *Architectural Forum*; 162, Adirondack Log Cabin Company; 163, Lustron Corporation; 164, Shelter Industry, Inc.; 165, Prefabricated Structures, Inc.; 166, General Panel Corporation; 167, W. H. Harmon Company; 168, Wickes, Inc.; 169, 170, *Architectural Forum*, Gottscho-Schleisner photos; 171, Sturtevant photo; 172, George Kidder Smith photo; 173, Hedrich-Blessing photo; 174, 175, Sturtevant photo; 176, T.V.A. photo; 177, Hedrich-Blessing photo.

Material basis of the modern esthetic is, of necessity, industrial production. In the hands of such masters as Albert Kahn, the factory itself is the best expression of this esthetic. Its directness, simplicity, and clarity mark it as lineal descendant of the earlier handicraft.

In the skyscraper — actual seat of industrial power — simplicity, economy, and efficiency become stylistic criteria. In Hood's famous buildings (135-7), these become severe, autocratic; in Howe and Lescaze's Philadelphia building (138) elegance and structural honesty yield the best multi-story structure in America.

138

Stripped of its masonry connotations, the curve reappeared in the thirties as the symbol of smooth, mechanical motion. At the New York Fair, Teague's (139) and Bel Geddes's (140) exhibits echoed the curves of flow line, highway, and motor car itself.

141

The twenties produced a whole school of eclectic designers — skillful, precise, and sterile. Famous were Pope (141), Mizner (142), Baum (143).

142

These upper-class ideologues, with their explicit dependence upon a discredited tradition, were eclipsed by the convulsive realities of the Depression.

143

FRANK LLOYD WRIGHT, in contrast, developed a brilliant romanticism of his own. In his bold and masterful compositions, any allusion to clapboard cottage, oriental garden, or Navajo village is oblique, abstracted . . .

... Big or little, Wright is always master of scale — whether in his spiral-ramped skyscraper design for the Guggenheim Museum (146) or the charming little dining nook at Taliesin (147).

148

A Michigan house by Alden Dow (1935) shows Wright's impact upon younger men.

To our domestic tradition in wood Pietro Belluschi has brought a sparse Italian elegance. His Portland houses (149) are akin to Wright's, yet not derivative.

149

Hugh Stubbins's excellent wartime houses (151) are an extension of New England wood tradition. Always America's favorite material, wood has a new-found popularity with younger designers who find that its familiar warmth and texture reduces resistance to forms not always orthodox.

Careful adaptation of building to site, characteristic of modern work, has led Marcel Breuer to build a large country house as a series of separate, loosely connected units (152), while Carl Koch has used a natural ledge to create a rock garden in his living room (153).

154

Intimate relation between indoors and out, technically possible now for any climate, is exemplified by this suburban house in California by Harwell Hamilton Harris . . .

. . . and in this town house in New York by William Hamby and George Nelson. The courtyard's deceptive simplicity inevitably suggests Japanese use of plants, gravel, and wooden screens.

155

156

The unadorned statement of function in a house by two of its leading international spokesmen, Walter Gropius and Marcel Breuer (156). Similar insistence on the supremacy of rationalism is evident in the Chicago houses of George Fred Keck (157).

157

The San Francisco climate permits Gardner Dailey a more genial design in the same idiom (158).

158

159

One of the earliest and best of America's new towns, Greenbelt, Md., was prototype . . .

. . . to such successful wartime communities as Channel Heights, designed by Richard Neutra.

160

161

163

164

165

PREFABRICATED HOUSES ran the gamut from Fuller's 1946 model dymaxion of aluminum and plastic (161) to those timidly disguised to look like handmade Cape Cod Colonials (162).

162

166

At any rate, by 1947, it looked as though the industrialized production of houses was at last an accomplished fact. Six contenders are shown at right.

167

168

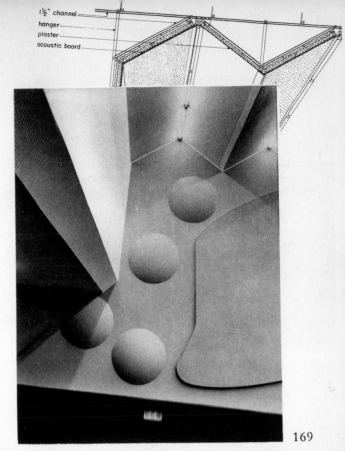

1½" channel

hanger

plaster

acoustic board

169

COMMERCIAL buildings have made adroit use of recent technical advance: essential acoustical surfacing in abstract forms decorates a studio by Carson & Lundin (169), while luminous ceilings are chief feature of a shop by Ketchum, Gina & Sharp (170).

170

Demand for resistance to earthquake, hurricane, and fire has led to single-story schools like this handsome and humane group in Carmel, Calif., by Ernest J. Kump.

Bruce Goff designed, and enlisted men built, this chapel out of the Navy's Quonset huts.

173

Advances in medicine are brilliantly paced by the glass walls and southern balconies of Ganster and Pereira's hospital at Waukegan, Ill.

174

A warmer, less imperious monumentality is apparent in both Wurster & Bernardi's office building for a factory (174) and Kump's design for the city hall of Fresno, Calif. (175).

175

The great complex of dams, powerhouses, and recreational areas of the TVA boasts some of America's most significant and most beautiful social architecture (176). In the same genre is Burnham Hoyt's magnificent open-air theater, fitted between two huge, wind-eroded buttes in a Denver park (177).

176

177

materials, are thus apt to be technologically obsolete before they are completed. Unpredictable changes in production techniques can occur, rendering all but the most flexible and farsighted plans prematurely archaic. There is thus real point to the apocryphal automobile manufacturer who said, when asked to describe the best type of building for his purpose, 'no building at all.' He meant by this that changes in his manufacturing process were so continuous and so profound that any satisfactory layout was soon out of date. He meant that most buildings were so planned and built as to make radical reorganization time-consuming and expensive. And he meant that most structural systems are so unsalvageable as to often make it more economical to build a completely new structure than to try to rebuild the old one.

Such inadequacies in individual building plans are, of course, reflected in the plans of our towns and cities. Here again, space that was organized and subdivided for one purpose is forced to serve as the container for another quite different one.

A small county seat which once served as an administrative and commercial center for a farming area becomes a manufacturing city. However inadequate the plan might have been for its original purpose, it is doubly unsuited for the new one. A single-line railroad once bisected the town with a daily wood-burning locomotive and two cars. By degrees it is converted into a sprawling complex system of spur lines, freight yards, and shops. A gridiron pattern formed by a courthouse square and two post roads is extended indefinitely to handle commercial and industrial, residential and recreational areas. The whole pattern is laced with an expensive and hard-to-change network of utilities — paving, sewers, streetlights, schools, and fire stations. Within this inflexible and rigid pattern, the pulsing life of the community is imprisoned. In this sense, at least, it would be possible to paraphrase the auto magnate and say that the best city would be no city at all.

Planners have at least learned this from the recent and tumultuous past: they might not always be certain which direction changes might take, but they could always be certain that there would be change. Not to provide for this would be disastrous. It is in such a context as this that the modern planning concept of flexibility has developed. A flexible plan, whether for the largest city or smallest house, is one which permits the organism whose energies it controls to expand and contract, or to re-arrange its internal processes without doing either. It might involve green belts as buffer areas between all the principal parts of the city. It might mean only folding, sliding, or movable partitions between the rooms of a small house. But in either case, it implies that the change should be possible with minimum effort and confusion. To achieve this quality of flexibility in our plans, many structural and mechanical devices are available. More specialized knowledge than ever before is at hand. But we have had little opportunity to date to apply these resources to large-scale physical planning.

Whether in a small house or a large city, a flexible plan im-plies control of the extent as well as of the direction of growth. This is generally recognized in the planning of individual build-ings: thus, an effective house plan will strike a balance between the requirements of the individual members and the maximum well-being of the family as a whole. Just so the community or regional plan, to be ultimately effective, will be directed at satisfying the needs of the individual to the point commensurate with the public good. But a family usually controls its size within fairly definite limits and can plan accordingly. And this is precisely what no American community, up to date, has been able to contemplate — much less to accomplish. Three cen-turies of land speculation and continuous urban expansion have created an intellectual climate in which it is heretical to suggest that there are limits beyond which no community should be permitted to grow. What these limits will be, of course, varies from one community to the next but that there is a point of diminishing returns to urban growth is no longer open to serious question. We can turn to Nature and — without drawing mechanical parallels — notice that here growth proceeds at two distinct levels: first, along the lines of cellular multiplication and, second, in the creation of entirely new individuals. Something of this sort is undoubtedly true of human settlements. The optimum size of a given community is a function of its type, age, physical environment, and relationship to other urban centers. But that there *is* an optimum size in each case cannot be doubted. Thanks to modern technology, it is probably much larger than it was in the eighteenth century; however, the limits exist and contemporary planners are increasingly aware that to ignore them is to court disaster.

Mechanization Implements Flexibility

THE MULTIPLE USE and flexible organization of space are, at the contemporary scale, inconceivable without a high degree of building mechanization. If space is at such a premium that it must be intensively used, then it must be flexibly organized, readily convertible from one use to another. To make conversion easy or at least tolerable, the process must be mechanized. The municipal auditorium of the average town offers a typical illustration of this problem. To be of maximum effectiveness, it must be adaptable to a wide range of uses. To be economically operated, it must be intensively used. Thus, an auditorium seating five thousand will be desirable for large political rallies, whereas a room seating only seven hundred and fifty might be needed for chamber music. A level floor is essential to basketball, while a sloping one is desirable for stage performances. For a boxing match, a raised platform is required; a swimming meet would imply a pool at the same spot. For dancing, a waxed hardwood floor must be furnished; for hockey, a sheet of smooth ice. And each of these activities will have its own requirements in terms of illumination, acoustics, ventilation, temperature, etc.

Fifty years ago, separate structures would have been required for most of these activities. And since it takes a comparatively large group of people to support most of them, adequate provisions were seldom found anywhere but in the largest cities. Thanks to our technical development, all such facilities can now be housed in a single building. The changes they imply can no longer be made manually, however. The scale of the elements is too large, the time available too small, the controls involved too complex. Hence the structure is mechanized. Motor-operated walls, floors, seating, and partitions rise, drop, tilt, or fold at the touch of a button. Lighting systems can be made to pin-point a soprano or flood a hockey game. Air-conditioning systems automatically adjust themselves to a cheering crowd of thousands or a sedate group at a lecture.

The complete mechanization of buildings is today quite practical. There is scarcely a situation conceivable which is not technically soluble. Nor is there any question but that the general effect of such mechanization serves to greatly increase the productivity of enclosed space. The social desirability of such measures must, however, be measured against a larger reference frame. Under short-sighted or selfish controls, such intensively used spaces may lead to needless congestion, wasteful travel, concentration of facilities in a location that is detrimental to the over-all community pattern. Generally, it would seem that such concentrations are desirable only when they cannot otherwise be effectively and economically provided.

Mobility and Plan

THE MOVEMENT OF PEOPLE AND THINGS within and between buildings, or inside and between cities and regions, has always been a controlling factor in their plans. But never has the volume and speed of such movement equaled that of the present. This has naturally led to a condition in which the provision for rapid, free-flowing movement has become a cardinal principle of modern planning. This result is everywhere evident, but nowhere so dramatically as in highway design. In this field, the pressure of vehicular traffic is so great that a very rapid evolution in forms to handle it has taken place. And if these forms are strangely reminiscent of hydraulic engineering, the resemblance is more than accidental. For it is to the highway and traffic engineers that we owe the discovery that traffic must be regarded as a liquid, obeying much the same laws and demanding much the same handling. One cannot, of course, extend the parallel too far. Vehicular traffic, unlike water, runs uphill and negotiates a clover-leaf intersection: but in general it responds to changes in pressure, direction, or grade in a manner startlingly like water. Pedestrian traffic is not substantially different. It tends to follow the line of least resistance, flows around a smooth turn better than a sharp corner and — as any storekeeper can tell you — balks at even one or two steps.

Traffic, because of these fluid properties, forces important modifications in planning as it grows heavier. The first result has been the collapse of right angle, axis, and symmetry. Traffic has an uncanny instinct for the line of least resistance. Any open space — park, campus, square — bears mute evidence of this. Formal path and walkway systems are quickly supplemented by a network of short-cuts which seldom bear any relation to the permanent system and often serve to expose its inadequacy. In any group of buildings (such as a campus) there is a complex pattern of movement between various buildings at different times. It is surprisingly difficult for a designer to anticipate the pattern of this movement in advance. And it is for this reason that there are today many planners and landscapists who — in new projects — will wait until the crowds have already traced out their own paths before laying a system of permanent walks. Under the given set of conditions — the relationship of the various buildings, the topography of the land — such a system will often prove the most efficient possible.

This is, of course, no substitute for a physical plan which takes into account all the factors involved in designing a campus. It merely indicates the strength of the internal relationships so established. Such a technique is patently impossible in the design of a building. Here the designer must anticipate the flow — in other words, understand the internal character of the operation or process to be housed. Even a small and apparently simple operation discloses a surprising intricacy when studied in this light. Thus, even the small house will have its rush hours, heavy traffic intersections, busy and quiet areas, interlocking or separate phases of activity. All of these involve the movement of people or things, and to guarantee that this movement be quiet, smooth, frictionless implies a most thorough grasp of the unit to be housed.

Increased mobility has affected American architecture in another direction as well, for many buildings have themselves become mobile. There is scarcely a type which has not already appeared on wheels. Clinics, laboratories, libraries, groceries, radio and weather stations, dwellings, and churches have all been 'trailerized.' Indeed, their widespread appearance in the past decade has already led to a whole literature of socio-technical speculation on the possibility of putting all buildings on wheels. Trailer enthusiasts paint a glowing picture of the city itself dissolving, to flow along super-highways with the seasons. This is, of course, merely decentralist escapism in modern dress. It blandly ignores the historic function of the city and is at best a vulgarization of the real significance of mobile building types — that they can be used to supplement and enrich existing fixed facilities.

These mobile types could be of enormous significance to rural areas, where the population is not dense enough either to support or to warrant many highly specialized services. Already mobile cancer, tuberculosis, and dental clinics — moving on regular routes at periodic intervals — are an important aspect of regional health and hospitalization systems. Here, the use of mobility is not merely a stopgap substitute for or adjunct to conventional hospital facilities. It becomes at the same time an independently important instrument in preventive medicine. Traveling libraries, including those for the blind, are already fairly common and suggest that the trailer could be used to distribute even more complex cultural forms to rural areas — art exhibitions, movies, plays, and concerts. Although the chief effect of the trailer, architecturally, has been compression of plan and consequent multiple use of space, many of them are as well equipped as their fixed prototypes. Properly designed, they can be 'plugged-in' to existing buildings and to a large extent duplicate the performance of more complex and specialized buildings.

Experience with mobility has had an interesting effect upon

contemporary architects and planners. They have been forced to abandon those fixed reference frames and single-point perspectives which the Renaissance developed and the Classic Revivals carried to such high points. Since the designer increasingly approaches the building from the standpoint of the tenant rather than the passer-by, he is forced to study its spatial organization in motion, as it were. He must visualize the building from many points of view, not just from the front door.

This new attitude is of great intellectual significance (though it certainly is not without important esthetic implications also). Fundamentally, it brings the building designer much closer to a scientific attitude toward his own field than ever before. For the first time, he recognizes the dynamic effect of building upon human activities.

At the level of city and regional planning, mobility has had an even broader effect. The hard and irresistible pressure of traffic, more than anything else, has served to liquidate the Classic plan, the Haussman boulevard, the City Beautiful façade. For one could not long deal with traffic without understanding that it was as blood to the body, that the streets and railroads were like the circulatory system and that the organism which they fed — the city — had a pulsing life of its own. Here again was a concept which introduced scientific breadth and precision to a field which had hitherto been eclectic and shallow.

The Dialectic of Urbanism

IN THE YEARS immediately prior to World War II, there was a tendency among many professional planners to speak of concentration and decentralization as though they were mutually exclusive criteria in physical planning. Whole schools of thought arose out of this misconception. There were those who claimed that decentralization was the remedy of all modern ills. There were those who argued to the contrary that entire cities should be compressed into a few gigantic buildings, air-conditioned, connected with aerial sidewalks, and topped by landing fields for helicopters. This controversy may have often reached almost comic proportions, but there was nothing comic in the issues involved. These proposals were efforts to analyze urban life, which was obviously unsatisfactory for most people and becoming more so all the time. They were protests against the waste and confusion and poverty of life in American cities. Some of them — like Frank Lloyd Wright's *Usonia* — were very persuasive; some of them — like the semi-serious fantasies of Hugh Ferriss — were absurd. Both schools represented a superficial analysis of the real structure of American life.

Actually, though it is still possible to find sharp contrasts between metropolis and backwoods, our country has long been preponderantly urban in character. The distinctions between city and country have been steadily disappearing — the natural result of the steady industrialization of every field of production, including agriculture and forestry. This industrialized urban society is marked by extreme fluidity. As we have seen in Chapter Seven, its urban centers show both centripetal and centrifugal forces at work — tendencies toward the centralization of certain operations and decentralization of others. This apparent contradiction is actually a basic characteristic of the American community. Structurally, it resembles the atom. Its component parts are attracted by one set of forces, repulsed by another and the resultant is a dynamic equilibrium.

This ebb and flow is compressed within an archaic plan, restricted by property rights and vested interests which tend to oppose its modification or redesign. What could — with proper planning — be an orderly and satisfactory movement becomes instead a vortex of conflicting currents which are difficult to plot and analyze. The results are anything but pretty. But effects should not be confused with causes: specifically, concentration cannot accurately be described as the cause of urban failure nor dispersion as the answer to it. The fact is that concentration is essential to the success of many phases of American life. This is true not only of an automobile center like Detroit or a merchandising center like Chicago. It is equally true on a cultural plane: a concentration of talents, skills, and facilities is essential to the movies in Hollywood or book and magazine publishing in New York. The civilizing effect of the city has been a constant throughout history; and it is still true that urban centers — that is, points of physical concentration — are essential to the production of both ideas and things.

Most 'decentralist' schemes are essentially escapist. They argue the undoubted pleasures of living near Nature and the out-of-doors; the individual's need for privacy, quiet, and leisure; the beneficent effects of sunshine and open air. But such programs neglect to point out they are totally dependent upon modern industrial society for the modern houses, the cars and electric power without which they could not operate. Even conceptually such plans reveal their urban origin — their sophisticated desires, their intellectualized approach to Nature stem from and are dependent on urban culture.

The working adult, whether he uses his hands to build autos or his head to write books, has two sets of requirements. For his work he requires easy access to the talent, skills, facilities, and materials of his field. These are always concentrated in urban centers. Even more importantly he needs the social, intellectual, and technological climates which such centers tend to generate. At the same time, however, the working adult needs privacy, seclusion, leisure for his personal life — all the more so because of the very intensity of the working day. This implies dispersion in space. For the rural population, the reverse is largely true. Here the very nature of agricultural production affords ample solitude, privacy, contact with the out-of-doors. For recreation and leisure, the rural population instinctively and correctly turns to whatever urban concentrations are accessible to it.

There is no theoretical conflict between concentration and dispersal in the field of physical planning. They are merely different aspects of the same phenomenon. Modern planners increasingly recognize this fact and their plans show it at all levels — regional, city, and individual building. The concept involved here is that of a network of concentration points or centers which are linked to each other by transport and communication facilities but separated by greenbelts, parks, and low-density residential areas. Such a pattern increases the range of choice of the individual, permitting equally easy access to centers of work, shopping, education, health, and culture. Such a pattern tends to eliminate the artificial and anachronistic barriers between urban and rural life, between man-made and natural landscapes. For the first time in history, such an inter-penetration of the two environments is entirely possible for the physical and spiritual enrichment of both. And in plans such as those for the Tennessee Valley or for some of the wartime communities, we have graphic, if fragmentary, proof of how much richer and more productive a life such concepts promise.

All physical planning, no matter what its scale, must ulti-mately rest on the earth. And the particular piece of earth upon which it rests and the way in which each is adapted to the other have a decisive effect upon the plan's effectiveness. The existing physical and economic organization of the land is the reference frame within which any planner must work. Under the best circumstances, this organization will tax his ingenuity and imagination; under the worst, it can literally paralyze him. Of the two, it is often much easier to revise the physical organiza-tion of a given area than to revise it economically. In the pre-ceding chapter, I have described the principal factors involved in adapting buildings physically to the land. Awareness of them gives contemporary plans a quite unprecedented attention to the path of the sun, the slope of the hill, the direction of the prevailing breeze. This is a qualitative gain of the highest order. One has only to compare the street patterns of some of the recent government-sponsored towns to those of the typical community to realize how great is the gain.

The economic organization of the land is by far the most severe and repressive of all limitations upon today's planners. At every turn they are confronted with a pattern of land owner-ship which seldom bears any relation to its physical configura-tion and even less to social necessity. As a matter of fact, the economic organization of American land is one of the most remarkable spectacles in history. Except for a narrow margin along the eastern seaboard, the entire country was subdivided in less than a century. This meant that 2,393,571,800 acres of land had to be parceled out in record time. And parceled it was.

The process was carried on at such an hysterical pitch that the land-planners of the time (George Washington was among them) laid down state, county, and private boundary lines which often extended off the map of the known world. In this method of plotting, natural configurations were not only ignored, they were often unknown. In the absence of any fixed points, boundaries were run from north to south and east to west. By this sort of bookkeeping, the Rocky Mountains were chopped up into the same rectangles as the flat Indiana farmlands.

As the exploration, conquest, and division of the continent continued, this pattern was naturally somewhat modified. But the basic rectilinear skeleton was reinforced by canals, highways, and railroads. The cities which developed within this reference frame adopted the same general approach to the problem. Big rectangles were cut up into smaller ones. The gridiron street pattern became the norm. This pattern perhaps did less violence to the land in the plains than it did in the mountains. It mattered less in the farmlands than in city lots. But it was a ghastly heritage for today's planners, who understand that a straight line is not necessarily the shortest distance between two points.

The irreducible requisite of any successful plan is that it direct the flow of energy consigned to it into the most productive pattern of movement. This is clearly the criterion in the design of the airplane or the hydroelectric plant. It should clearly be the criterion in building design and city planning, where the energy flow to be directed is that of human beings. Unfortunately, this criterion is seldom met in our country today. The vast productive tide of America's energy is thwarted, abused, frustrated and by-passed in the granite-hard channels of our buildings and cities. It is in this context that the statement is increasingly heard: 'What this country needs is planning!'

Superficial appearances to the contrary, this country is probably the most intensively planned area on earth. Visible and invisible, local and national, public and private, mesh after mesh of plan is thrown across the nation. Interlocking, overlapping, contradictory or mutually irreconcilable, their effect is everywhere apparent — in the desolate cut-over lands as well as in the terraced slopes of the Tennessee Valley, in the grimy coal fields as well as the sleek skyscrapers they heat, in the slums of the big cities as well as in their smartest avenues. In this complex pattern we are able to distinguish certain aspects which we call 'good' from others which we recognize as 'bad.' Where these plans impinge upon our personal lives, no expert opinion is needed. Thus the housewife in a poorly planned house complains that running it 'wears her out,' while her husband is a 'nervous wreck' from traffic jams morning and night. The same couple can see with their own eyes that a supervised playground in the neighborhood is 'grand for the children' or that the TVA's flood- and erosion-control is a 'good thing for the country.' In other words, the layman's reaction to plan is conditioned by its impact upon him — that is, how successfully it directs his energies, how much return it yields him per unit of effort expended. As a matter of fact, this is an eminently sensible method of evaluation — the same one the professional planner uses when he evaluates a plan in terms of social desirability or undesirability.

Planners and laymen alike, however, are apt to forget that the plan itself is merely the instrument of policy. Good or bad planning is the expression of good or bad policy: and their co-existence in America today is merely the expression of basic conflicts and contradictions in our national life. These issues will be resolved not by plans but by politics: democratic policy must precede democratic planning.

In the political field, the baiting of planners has become a favorite pastime. Reactionary congressmen and commentators have made almost a specialty of it. Their attacks are always organized in such a way as to make it appear that the alternative to broad-scale social planning is freedom from *all* planning. This, to put it mildly, is misleading. The alternative to a broad comprehensive plan for any field of activity is a multitude of private, local, disparate, and selfish plans. All organizations, whether public or private, must plan and must have planners. And the administration of any plan, whether private or public, involves the risk of producing a certain percentage of bureaucrats.

Much of the current opposition to local, regional, and national planning is cynical, some of it merely ignorant or uninformed. It is interesting to observe that this opposition always speaks in abstractions. The issues are described as 'rugged individualism versus planned bureaucracy,' 'moral and spiritual values are threatened by regimentation,' etc. Behind this smoke-screen of metaphor is usually to be found a hard nucleus of vested interests with private plans. Since often the motives of the opposition cannot stand the light of day, it resorts to straw men: regimentation, bureaucracy, statism become the battle-cry, when in reality the issues are cheaper electricity, better housing, more schools, improved soils.

The need for democratic long-range planning scarcely needs demonstration any longer. But the average citizen, confused by a whole literature of anti-planning propaganda, fails to understand that such planning, far from being repressive, is actually a liberating force. It tends to increase not only our material well-being but our intellectual and cultural resources as well. During the early days of the TVA much was made of the restrictive and repressive aspects of the project — graves would be moved, bottom lands flooded, farms condemned, private enterprise ruined. The positive aspects of the plan were drowned in the clamor. Yet little is heard of these charges today for the simple reason that they have been proved without foundation. The entire fabric of the region's life has been enriched by the plan: every section of the community has benefited by it, including those who were most certain it would ruin them. The people of the Valley have learned that one over-all plan, democratically conceived and administered, has proved a far better channel for their energies than the hundreds of small and inefficient ones which it replaced.

CHAPTER SEVENTEEN

The Production of Buildings

THE PRODUCTION OF BUILDINGS is one of the most complex and difficult of all operations in present-day America. To assemble the money, land, labor, materials, and equipment necessary to the production of even a small five-room house is a process which is proportionately more involved than that of building a 45,000-ton battleship. Hundreds of separate items, made by different manufacturers and distributed through various channels, must be individually assembled from a host of entrepreneurs. The talents of a whole hierarchy of skilled trades and professions must be dovetailed together and — at the present rate of technological development — this hierarchy necessarily grows larger. A network of building and zoning ordinances — often contradictory and almost always obsolete — has to be negotiated, as do all the legal processes involving transfer of land titles, financing, etc. As a result of this archaic system of production, building prices are high, quality generally low, and output inadequate.

These peculiarities flow from a central fact of historic importance: the building field has never been industrialized. It is not in any proper sense an industry at all, but an agglomeration of related interests held together in an awkard and uneasy truce. For, in addition to the horizontal conflicts which characterize all fields today — labor versus management, big versus little business, producer versus consumer — the building field has a deep vertical flaw in its structure. To one side of this fissure lie the manufacturing, fabrication, and construction interests, whose profits and wages depend upon production of new buildings. This fact naturally gives them a vested interest in a high rate of production — like the automobile industry, they would like to see yearly models. But on the other side lie the *rentier*-realty-mortgage interests, dependent for *their* profits upon ownership of existing buildings. Since many a fifty-year-old building is still yielding good returns, this portion of the building field shows an understandable tendency to restrict the production of new units to a minimum. And since these interests control the land upon which any building must ultimately rest, they wield a veto power of no small dimensions.

It is this split between profit-through-production and profit-through-ownership which has largely prevented that consolidation of capital and that centralization and mechanization of production facilities which characterizes modern industrialism. The split has been perpetuated by two facts: buildings are, by all odds, our most durable consumer goods, and land values, although socially created, are individually owned. As long as these two conditions coexist, the building field is apt to retain its peculiar characteristics. Hence, the anachronistic picture of the country's second largest field — only agriculture normally employs more people — still largely dominated by small entrepreneurs. Whatever the social advantages of small ownership, they are here obscured by the inefficiency of the production method and the technical backwardness of the product.

Nevertheless, certain sectors of the building field have been able to produce structures of extraordinary value and — as the recent war so graphically indicated — produce them quickly and in quantity. By and large, these sectors are the ones which directly service manufacturing, commerce, and business. There are intermediate zones serving public and quasi-public functions, such as law enforcement, mails, hospitalization, and education, which have produced fairly satisfactory buildings even if in inadequate numbers. But it is that sector euphemistically known as the housing industry which has failed totally to meet its responsibilities. This failure is not a recent phenomenon; on the contrary, its roots go far back in American history. Evidence of its cumulative deficit begins to appear almost exactly with the urbanization of the latter half of the nineteenth century. At its highest peak of production in 1929, the housing sector produced only some 900,000 new units; it has never approached that point since; in 1946, with a need of perhaps as many as 5,750,000 dwelling units, it produced a scant 500,000 units. And these left much to be desired in both quality and price.

There is an enormous disparity between the performance of the residential and the non-residential sectors of the building field. This disparity is reflected even in the organizational structure of the two sectors. In non-residential building, research, design, and fabrication are consolidated and centralized to a far greater extent than in housing. A couple of dozen firms will control the preponderance of industrial construction, whereas in housing, the same volume of work will be divided among literally thousands of small builders and contractors. Inevitably, this leads to a wide disparity in the end-product. Building design which meets the criteria of environmental control set forth in the preceding chapters of this book implies, among other things, continual research: but under contemporary conditions, research is an expensive process which can be amortized only by large-scale operations. The same thing is true at every level of building production: projects must either be very large or smaller ones must be continually produced in order to exploit even partially the advantages of industrialization. Because it can do this, the technical and esthetic level of non-residential building generally is fairly high. And because performance is a critical factor in the use of such types, the non-residential sector has a fairly steady demand for its services. A factory owner will have to act on the inroads of technological obsolescence years before the owner of rental housing has learned the meaning of the word.

The industrial and commercial plant of the nation, therefore, conforms closely to the effective demands of our society. Where it is inadequate, a pattern of social control is already fairly well established: fire, safety, and sanitary regulations governing the internal conditions of plants, shops, and offices; and zoning and city-plan regulations governing the disposition of non-residential buildings in the landscape. Here, it is true, existing minima are often appallingly low and/or poorly enforced. The mere presence of a factory, with its attendant traffic, noise, smoke, and gases, may often destroy a neighborhood, even though the plant itself may be designed to tolerably high standards. Again, the shops and offices of an average town may be individually acceptable, yet by their relation to each other, to the streets, and to the town itself, be wholly undesirable. Here the community must, in its own defense, often impose controls which the individual owners will regard as little short of confiscatory. Yet whatever their offense to the eye, ear, and nose, the end-products of the non-residential sector of the building field are usually more satisfactory than that of housing.

The production of housing has been largely controlled by the profit-through-ownership interests — *rentier*, mortgage banker, speculative realtor, and (increasingly) the insurance companies. Because of their basic economic orientation, these interests have severely restricted the annual production of new housing units. By the end of 1946, the resultant shortage had reached the proportions of a national scandal. Estimates of the need might vary widely — depending upon the point of view of the estimator — but few denied it and few denied that it was very large. To meet the sheer physical shortage in habitable units, National Housing Administrator Wilson Wyatt estimated that 2,700,000 units were required in the two-year period ending in 1947. To meet the long-range need, the Wagner-Ellender-Taft Housing Bill envisages a production of 12,600,000 units in ten years by a comprehensive program of public and private financing.

Estimates of the need varied with a number of factors, not least of which was the problem of the proper criteria for measuring obsolescence in housing. Should a house be considered in urgent need of replacement only if it were in danger of collapsing over the tenant's head? This was, in a general way, the criterion employed in both the Real Property Inventory of 1936 and the first National Housing Census of 1940. On this basis, somewhere between sixteen and nineteen per cent of the nation's dwellings were found (by unskilled investigators after only superficial investigation) to be in need of replacement. Or should residential replacement needs be measured against the much broader and more radical scale of industry — that is, *technological* obsolescence? This would involve, not only the actual physical condition of the house and its equipment, but an estimate of its modernity relative to current standards of comfort, convenience, and amenity. Moreover, it would include an estimate of the building's external environment — its access to parks, schools, shops, transportation, etc.; its freedom from noise, smoke, traffic.[1] If this scale were employed to assess our housing, perhaps as much as fifty per cent could be shown in need of replacement.

There was another set of figures which statisticians could juggle — those of population. The population was still increasing, though the *rate* of increase was falling. The number of families continued to rise, though the *size* of the family unit was decreasing. To these trends, both of which increased the need for housing units, were added two others: the steadily lengthening life-span of the population (which meant that more people occupied their units longer) and the millions of new marriages created by the emotional tension of World War II. Juggle these figures as one might, it was clear that the rate of housing need was increasing at the precise moment when, because of depression and war, the rate of production of new units had dropped to an all-time low; for, one year after the official close of hostilities, the building field had managed to produce a scant 400,000 units of the 1,500,000 scheduled.

The specific obstacles to an adequate housing supply are usually grouped under two heads — economic and technical; but in a very real sense, there is no technical problem, or at least none which could not readily be solved if the economic log jams were decisively broken. The concepts, skills, and materials are already available, as is proved by the accomplishments of the non-residential sectors of the field; but to utilize them fully in the production of housing it is necessary to bridge

[1] A scale of this sort, together with a technique of collecting and analyzing the data, has been evolved in *An Appraisal Method for Measuring Quality of Housing,* American Public Health Association, Committee on Hygiene of Housing, New York, 1947.

the vertical fissure which now splits the field, the paralyzing contradiction between profits-through-production and profits-through-ownership.   Only interests with immense resources at their disposal can do this on any national scale, since it involves assuming responsibility for design, fabrication, distribution, and merchandising of house and land, or (in the case of rental properties) servicing and maintenance.   In theory, at least, the initiative could originate with either industrial or *rentier* capital, great blocks of which already lie wholly or partially in the field. In actual practice, however, efforts from either side have been limited, tentative, and wholly inadequate to the task at hand.

The only private *rentier* interests which have shown either the disposition or ability to produce housing on a mass basis with no government assistance whatever are the insurance companies. Their appearance in the field is a comparatively recent event, accelerated no doubt by the proven stability of rental housing in large-scale, well-planned units.   Possessed of immense resources and seeking maximum security for their investment over a long period of time, the insurance companies' operations lack the crassly speculative aspects of the typical real-estate manipulation.   They have shown little tendency to short-cut traditional construction methods or normal channels of manufacture and supply.   This has not, in fact, been necessary.   The projects must be designed for long life, for which conventional heavy construction is satisfactory.   The projects are fairly large, which permits a measure of rationalization in construction.   The end-product is generally better, and the cost to consumer lower, because of the economies inherent in large, integrated projects. However, the insurance companies are far from being an important factor in the housing market.   At the end of 1946 they had completed less than twenty-five thousand units — scarcely enough to change the basic character of the field as a whole.

It was in this context that the only other agency strong enough to resolve the issue — the federal government itself — was forced to act.   In the thirteen years following the first inauguration of Roosevelt, the government had been wholly or partially responsible for the production of 1,440,947 dwelling units.[1]   The most

[1] Including 851,197 publicly-financed units built during World War II.

significant aspect of the government's two-pronged program was that of public housing. Although the emphasis varied (occasionally producing such sports as Greenbelt, Maryland, Norris, Tennessee, and the itinerant agricultural camps in the Southwest), the housing produced was preponderantly low-rent, multi-family, urban (Figs. 159, 160).

Despite all the charges to the contrary, this public housing was conventionally produced in strict accordance with the precepts and practices of private enterprise. Except for occasional use of the right of eminent domain, the federal and municipal housing agencies proceeded in exactly the same fashion as would any private organization. Land was assembled from private owners at current prices, local architects and engineers were engaged to design the projects, construction contracts were awarded to private firms on the basis of competitive bidding, maintenance and servicing were organized along traditional lines. Within the limits of nationally established minimum standards, economy was everywhere the rule. The capital cost per room has always compared favorably with equivalent facilities built by private industry. The only innovation was a rental subsidy covering the differential between the cost of construction, maintenance, and amortization and the ability of the tenant to pay. This subsidy has averaged 23 per cent.[1]

Physically, public housing has tended to be conservative in structure and appearance, minimal in its space standards and amenities. At the level of site- and community-planning, however, it has always followed standards incomparably higher than those of typical lower-income neighborhoods. Structural conservatism was largely dictated by the fact that most projects were financially set up for a period of sixty years: hence, long-lived, low-upkeep buildings were imperative. Advanced site-planning and landscaping, on the other hand, were a recognition of the fact that the ultimate livability of a dwelling unit is profoundly affected by its external environment. Community facilities — parks and playgrounds, recreation halls, nurseries

[1] *Public Housing*, p. 36 (Washington; Federal Public Housing Agency, 1946). This subsidy amounted to $7.19 per unit in 1944: for the period 1933–1944 the entire cost of the subsidy on 105,600 low-rental units was only $38,775,000.

and laundries — are actually compensatory for lack of such facilities in the home itself.   Whatever its deficiencies, public housing has — like TVA in power — put a floor under housing standards by which all housing production must hitherto be judged.

The second prong of the government's housing program has been the Federal Housing Authority.   Primarily an insurance operation, guaranteeing up to ninety per cent of the mortgage, the FHA was aimed at encouraging the profit-through-ownership sector of the field to produce housing.   At the end of 1945, the FHA had been instrumental in producing 1,246,915 units, of which some 75,000 units were in medium-rental, multi-family projects.   In exchange for its loan insurance service, the FHA reserved a fairly complete control over the construction, appearance, and location of all insured units.   Its control was not always beneficent.   Especially in the small-house field, the agency has been notoriously conservative; nor have its space and structural standards reached more than an acceptable minimum.   However, in its multi-family projects for middle-income groups, the FHA has set fairly high standards in site and architectural planning.   Despite its penchant for phoney chimneys and meaningless colonnades, the agency's work in apartment houses has measurably raised the level of design in a field that sorely needed it.

Thus, the federal government has intervened in the housing crisis in two efforts to bridge the contradiction.   Both have been projected from the *rentier*-landlord rather than the industrial side of the field.   In the case of public housing, the government assumed all the functions of the typical landlord.   In the case of FHA, the government merely acted to guarantee the operations of existing landlords and mortgagees.

Prefabrication — the Paradox

FROM THE INDUSTRIAL side of the housing field has come a series of small but highly significant efforts to solve the housing crisis by largely technical means. These efforts have been loosely encompassed by the term 'prefabrication.' For well over a decade, now, the imagination of the house-hungry public has been stirred by this word. The concept of factory-made houses is first and foremost a technician's answer to the housing problem. But it caught the public's fancy because it corresponded to the realities of American experience — namely, that the only way to produce enough goods for everybody is industrially. The layman might be ignorant of many of the intricate details of the building field; but his instincts were correct in telling him that the industrialization of the house-building field was long overdue, an historic necessity. It is highly doubtful if the American people will ever have *enough* housing without it. It is certain that they will never have *good* housing without it: for the criteria of environmental control established in this book can be met *only* through the fullest application of science and technology to housing. And only an industrialized field can make these applications.

'Prefabrication' is a term which — like the word 'peace' — has been stretched to cover a wide range of conditions. Actually, the term describes the process rather than the product. Prefabrication has always envisaged the volume production of completely shop-fabricated dwelling units which could be delivered ready to be plugged-in like a refrigerator or radio. This would involve a transference of labor from scattered, open-air field operations to the controlled conditions of centralized mass production. Ideally, as much as ninety-five per cent of the total labor would be moved indoors. All the force of fact is behind such a shift. It would yield more and cheaper houses and permit the adoption of radically improved standards of performance and appearance (Fig. 161).

If the problem were solely technical, the shift from field to factory would be simple enough. But it was early apparent that there was more to it than this. The concentration of design, production, distribution, and merchandising of a complete, ready-to-use house into a single operation is a task to tax the resources of all but the largest organizations. Although there are many parallels between the automobile industry and prefabricated housing, most analogies tend to ignore two immensely important differences: even the smallest house is too bulky and heavy to be readily delivered in completed form like an auto; and no house, however complete, is ready to use until it has a piece of land to rest upon.

There are many interests on the profits-through-production side of the field with adequate resources to tackle even these problems, but few of them have shown any willingness to assume the risk. Prior to the war, the big companies had shown little disposition to enter the prefabrication field. The investment required was large, the risks not small, and the resistance of the existing building field to such innovations was enormous. Thus, by default, exploratory work fell more or less to small, inadequately financed independents. Almost without exception, the background of these independents was industrial. At least in their earlier stage, most of their products reflected that fact — that is, their designs and fabrication methods sought to increase production and reduce unit costs by typically industrial techniques. These men dreamed of producing a complete, ready-to-live-in house which could be bought from a showroom floor and delivered like an automobile. However, if distribution, merchandising, and advertising were dismaying problems for the big companies, for the small independents they soon proved all but insuperable. The only way in which they could hope to get their product onto the market was by using the existing facilities of the traditional house-building field. But to utilize these facilities, they had to have a product which involved no major upset to existing interests and relationships in the field. This, in turn, led the independent producer into a maze of compromises which slowly but surely robbed his product of the inherent advantages of industrial mass production.

The bathroom, for example, could not be stamped out of one piece of stainless steel — not so much because of the cost of the dies (though that, of course, was an item) as because it threatened local fixture dealers, master plumbers, plumbers' unions, etc. The structural shell could not employ advanced engineering principles both because the factory to make it would be expensive and because local materials dealers, building codes, and building trades unions would be opposed to it. Even the appearance of the finished house was dictated, not by functional analysis but by local prejudice, strictly enforced by local banks, realty interests, and lending institutions. The attempt to meet limitations such as these established the other limit of the prefabrication spectrum — the so-called 'packaged' house. Here, both design and materials were traditional and work in a central factory was confined to those aspects which did not threaten the *status quo*.

The history of prefabrication to date is a story of shuttling back and forth between these two extremes. A technical solution was conceived; it was measured against economic realities; its design was then revised downward to prove acceptable to those realities. The halfway point between a genuine industrial product and a packaged unit lay approximately at 'panel construction' and it is not surprising that a majority of the surviving prefabs employ the panel as the basic structural unit. There are, of course, all sorts of technical and economic compromises which are theoretically open to the small independent prefabricator. And many of these hardy souls have shown great ability at circumventing one or another of their problems. But so far not one of them has successfully circumvented *all* of them in real life.

At the end of World War II, it was clear that a huge potential market existed for the prefabricated house. But it was also clear that the demand would be filled only by (1) large national organizations with industrial know-how, manufacturing facilities, skilled labor reserves, and adequate capital or (2) by a program of government aid to the small independents to enable them to achieve the same status. There was some evidence, especially among the war-swollen plane and shipbuilding companies, that industrial capital was at last preparing to move into prefabrication in a decisive way. From a technical standpoint this was entirely natural, since there was much in common between the manufacture of planes or ships and houses. But the federal government, unable to count on such a development, included a broad program of aid to existing prefabricators in its

Veterans' Emergency Housing Act of 1946. In many ways this was an unprecedented move. Previously, the government had always entered housing from an economic standpoint; it had never displayed much interest in the technical aspects of the crisis. Here, for the first time, was a recognition of the technological backwardness of the field and a concrete plan for reducing the lag.

Briefly, the government offered the prefabricators these inducements: a guarantee to purchase a stipulated number of units from manufacturers whose houses met its standards; to grant loans to those needing them, the purchase contracts serving as collateral; to give the prefabricators priorities to essential materials at fixed prices; to sell or lease them surplus war plants and manufacturing facilities; and to accelerate by all means the new materials and equipment called for by many of the new houses. Novel as it was for the building field, this subsidy was in essence no different from that granted all industry in the recent war. And, as Administrator Wyatt dryly remarked, provision of decent housing for the veteran in peace was no less a necessity than providing him with ammunition in war. Finally, the subsidy to the prefabricators was not discriminatory, since it was only part of a much larger program. It rounded out the most comprehensive and most generous program of aid yet offered by the government to every portion of the private housing field. Yet, from the start, the Veterans' Emergency Housing Program was subjected to merciless attack — most of it from within the field and specifically from the profits-through-ownership interests. As 1946 drew to a close, the entire program had been undermined by the abandonment of priorities and price controls. Wilson Wyatt had resigned because of his inability to secure RFC loans to selected prefabricators; and it did not seem likely that any portion of the program would survive.

Nevertheless, advances of both a theoretical and practical significance had been registered in prefabrication. Many new firms had been attracted to the field. Some of them had secured the necessary assistance from Wyatt before he resigned and others, having sufficient private capital, did not need it. In terms of strength, fire-resistance, and long life, many of these post-war prefabs promised to give the conventional house a run for its money.   In terms of appearance, they were at the least on a par.   And if any of them managed to get into full production, it seemed certain that they could compete in price.

There is thus little in its recent history to indicate that the building field can, unaided and uncontrolled, give the American people the kind of housing to which their technical accomplishments entitle them.   The immediate post-war period has not been auspicious — the field seems to have forgotten nothing and learned nothing.   For, while it has bitterly resisted federal and municipal intervention, even at the points of most critical need, it has been unable to present a program of its own.   Its internal contradictions remain unsolved.   Here and there, it is true, it has produced well-designed, well-built houses and apartments, even occasionally entire neighborhoods.   These have been within the reach, economically, of only the topmost layers of the population.   There is a hoary thesis — currently popular again — that the housing field need produces only new units for this strata of the population.   Their discarded housing units will in turn become available for the next lowest income group and so on down the line until, according to the theory, everyone will be housed.   While this 'escalator' has always operated in American housing, it has never filled the need and never will.   Statistically, the production of upper-class housing has always represented a portion of the national total so small as to be insignificant.   Philosophically, this theory is even less defensible.   If the American people were told that their society could offer them no better perspective than an existence in which they would wear only second-hand clothes, drive only second-hand cars, sleep only in discarded bedding, and read only hand-me-down books — in short, were to have access only to consumer goods handed down to them by the income group above — they would certainly rebel.   Yet this is precisely the perspective which the apologists for private housing advance.

Another theory which is currently resurgent holds that government needs only to retire from the picture in order to solve the housing crisis.   But this overlooks the fact that the crisis existed for decades before the government ventured to intervene in the field at all. The proponents of this latter-day *laissez-faire* also handily omit to mention that they hope to *maintain* government intervention in the form of such agencies as the FHA (to insure loans), Federal Home Loan Bank (to make loans), Home Owners' Loan Corporation (to take over distressed loans). They do not, in other words, envisage complete retirement by government from the field, but merely from those areas in which they happen to have no interest.

Actually, since the days of Roosevelt's first inaugural, a fairly comprehensive pattern of housing aid, control, and initiative had been evolved by the federal government. However haphazard or unplanned the process, this experience had developed into a minimal program of public and private housing: most of its features were included in the Wagner-Ellender-Taft Housing Bill which, at the end of 1946, had not been acted upon. Its passage seemed far from certain. Yet the fact remained: whether renovation of the housing field came from within or was imposed from without, renovation would come. For its anarchic and archaic condition was something which the American people could not indefinitely afford.

CHAPTER EIGHTEEN

Toward a Democratic Esthetic

T HE EVOLUTION OF ESTHETIC STANDARDS in American building over a period of three centuries can be understood only when seen in relation to the underlying technical, economic, and social forces which conditioned their development. In the preceding sections of this book I have traced the main lines of development of these forces, indicating how they interlocked and interacted to produce the significant architectural styles of our country's past. This has served to place esthetics in a realistic and intelligible reference frame and gives us a perspective which enables us to see them as the syntheses of an enormously complex social process. This was all the more necessary because the esthetic content of architecture has too long and too exclusively occupied the attention of architect, critic, and historian. Moreover, their discussions were carried on in terms of literature, not life, so that the meaning and usefulness of their esthetics was doubly obscure.

The senses — on whose stimuli the esthetic reaction must necessarily depend — are the least reliable means of objectively measuring a building's performance; but to say that they are unreliable is not to imply that they are unimportant. The primary function of building is the maintenance of man's health; and I have indicated how building design can provide the optimum conditions for man's requirements; but to say that control of the physical environments is basic to man's physical and mental well-being is not to say that such control is exclusively the basis of his happiness. In other words, I do not for a moment

348

imply that such materialistic factors as light, heat, sound — that is, those forces whose objective existence and impact upon men we can scientifically measure — are the only elements in architecture worthy of consideration. To do so would violate the evidence of history itself. It is obvious that a building can meet all objective criteria of physical performance and still be esthetically unsatisfactory to a given person or group of persons. It is likewise apparent that a building can be hopelessly obsolete when judged by such criteria and yet be esthetically satisfactory to many people. This is merely another way of saying that, to be genuinely effective, a building must conform to esthetic as well as physiological standards of performance.

But to formulate and analyze these esthetic standards we are forced to consider a whole range of social, cultural, and ideological phenomena. We are forced to examine not building but man. The whole tradition of architectural criticism in this country — like criticism in other fields — is permeated with metaphysical abstraction. Consistently the attempt was made to divorce esthetics from life, to emphasize only its subjective aspects. This tradition led to a paradox: while consistently overemphasizing the importance of beauty in architecture, it stubbornly insisted at the same time that beauty was not and could not be subject to an orderly, scientific investigation. On the one hand we were told that 'a thing of beauty is a joy forever'; on the other that 'beauty lies in the eye of the beholder.' According to dicta like these, beauty is thus simultaneously a property of (1) the object, and (2) the beholder. Yet the whole history of art exists to prove the fallacy of both. Most art forms once considered beautiful have outlived that prestige, to fall ultimately into disuse and obliquity: while disagreement in any mixed group as to the esthetic value of a given object is axiomatic.

The facts would seem to indicate that esthetics in architecture must be discussed at two different levels: the *reaction* of the individual and the *standard* of the group. The reaction is not a property of either the individual or the building but of the relationship between the two. As a process, it is the result of the individual's intricate psychological and physiological response to external stimuli. It will vary with objective circumstances — whether he is hot or cold, rested or tired, hungry or well fed. But the individual's evaluation of the reaction — his sense of satisfaction (beauty) or dissatisfaction (ugliness) — will be largely conditioned by his social and cultural background. Agreement between individuals as to the esthetic merit of a given building is therefore largely a matter of similar social and cultural background. From this it follows that esthetic standards are expressions of social agreement, of a common outlook or attitude towards this particular aspect of human experience. These standards will vary from one period to another. And in any given period they may vary somewhat between this class and that, although the relation between the popular taste and the dominant high style is intimate. The folk arts echo the idiom of the fine arts. The latter are, in turn, an expression of the outlook, ambitions and prejudices of the dominant class of the period.

Good Taste and the Populace

THIS ENTIRE ESTHETIC PROCESS is firmly rooted in social reality and operates in American architecture as in every other phase of American life. Yet here the problem is complicated by special factors which prevent a mechanical comparison between buildings and other art forms or artifacts. The field as a whole is lethargic in responding to changes in esthetic standards. Because buildings are very large, expensive, and permanent things, the field will at any given time show strata upon strata of conflicting styles. Their sheer, physical persistence is reflected in subsequent standards, so that both high style and popular taste are full of echoes and repercussions of the past which, in any other medium, would have long since died away.

It is this confusion of cause and effect which has troubled every critic since Ruskin. The esthetic standards of architecture, when measured against the great periods of the past, were demonstrably low. What caused this? How could the process be reversed? In its most familiar form this problem was reduced to a hen-and-egg conundrum: which came first — bad design or low popular taste? Since the discussion has been almost exclusively the property of specialists in esthetics — architects, editors, and critics — it was perhaps not surprising to find that the verdict was against the people. Low popular taste was responsible for bad building design. Yet the question is actually meaningless, for it ignores both the *constant interaction* between popular taste and high style and their *joint subordination* to the exigencies of our society as a whole.

The esthetic standards of the people are basically sound. Modern scholarship has established this beyond question, both in the folk arts of pre-industrial Western civilization and in the great primitive cultures of Africa, Asia, and the South Seas. Under handicraft methods of production for use there is no such thing as bad taste; popular standards cannot be corrupted or debased. This is not due to any moral imperatives but rather to the simple fact that, in such societies, esthetic standards are constantly disciplined by the production method itself. Here design is so intimately linked to execution as to make any divergence between the two most difficult. Designer, producer, and consumer are one and the same person. There is consequently neither incentive nor opportunity for adulteration of workmanship or design. It would, of course, be absurd to hold that even in primitive cultures every individual is able to make every item he needs, or that everyone is equally skilled or gifted in making them. Even here there is specialization. Yet each member of the community remains close to actual production, can from his own experience judge what craftsman or artist is trying to do and how well he has succeeded in doing it. This creates a situation in which the average level of esthetic judgment is extraordinarily high — a fruitful environment for both artist and consumer. It also makes possible the striking unity of primitive art wherein there is no qualitative difference between the design of a lowly wooden bowl and an important ceremonial canoe. It creates a situation in which popular taste and high style are one and the same.

Much the same forces operated to create the folk arts of pre-capitalist, pre-industrial Europe and America. Here too handi-

craft production — despite a relatively high degree of specialization — involved a large part of the people in the actual work of
design and fabrication of buildings and artifacts. Here too was
production for use with its inherent resistance to adulteration of
workmanship and corruption of design. This folk art coexisted
with the high style of the ruling classes, to which it loaned and
from which it borrowed liberally. Despite this continuous
interaction, however, folk art preserved a large measure of
independence. It was slow to respond to the abrupt changes of
upper-class taste. Indeed, until production relations were altered by the capitalists, it could not change. As a result, the
folk arts were expressions of popular taste of an uncommonly
high average level. They may have never reached the pinnacles
of achievement of the high styles but they always avoided their
disastrous collapses. It was this quality which, beginning with
Ruskin and Morris and continuing down to the present-day
interest in Latin and South American handicrafts, has held such
fascination for modern artists and architects. They might, like
Ruskin, have failed to understand the material conditions which
produced these esthetic standards. They might have romantic
ideas as to how such conditions could be recreated. But they
recognized that until the past century popular taste had always
proved itself sound.

Under modern industrial capitalism, this relationship is quite
disrupted. The design process is separated from that of fabrication. It is put into the hands of a very small group of specialists
who, by the same token, are isolated from the work and the
workmen. Since production is no longer for use, the entire
production process is subjected to the remorseless pressure of
the profit motive. This makes possible an unprecedented advance in both technical and esthetic standards. At the same
time, however, it introduces the motive and the opportunity for
deterioration — adulteration in workmanship and materials at
the level of fabrication; artificiality, irresponsibility, and vulgarity at the level of design.

The cycle is not yet complete, however, for the people generally have been converted into consumers. They too have
been removed from actual participation in the work, their critical

capacity correspondingly weakened and confused. They are confronted with a vast array of commodities about which they can actually know very little. At the same time, the vast and pervasive power of advertising is turned upon them. As consumers, they are surrounded by an environment of social pressures to conform to standards of taste which are established by the dominant groups. Unless these standards too flagrantly contradict reality, they are adopted by the people generally. If they happen to be corrupt or retrogressive standards, they can and do lower the level of popular taste. It is in this sense, and this sense only, that low standards of popular taste can be blamed on the populace.

There are, fortunately, other forces in modern society which tend to resist the corruption or debasement of popular esthetic standards. In the first place, the overwhelming majority of Americans are working people directly involved in production — even though they may produce only a small part of some article which they themselves may never use. This experience gives them a certain critical foundation, if only in judging materials, workmanship, finish, etc. Also as working people the majority of them are involved in trade unions, consumer groups, the broad democratic movement generally. These new forces, as they approach maturity, pay increasing attention to problems of popular culture. This necessarily involves the formulation of esthetic standards which more directly reflect the aspirations and outlook of the popular forces. There is, finally, the effect of education: whatever its limitations, this too serves to develop and strengthen the critical faculties of the people.

A study of the esthetic tradition in American building reveals that the hen-and-egg conundrum did not appear — indeed *could not* appear — until around the middle of the last century. It was not until industrialization had successfully infiltrated the major fields of production that design began to be removed from the hands of millions of anonymous, independent artisans and put into the control of a handful of specialized designers. Whatever else it accomplished, this process of centralization automatically isolated design from the healthy democratic base of popular participation. A new esthetic idiom began to emerge, leaving its subtle imprint upon every article of daily use — art forms, buildings, clothes, china, furniture, and trains. It was the idiom of the Victorian mill and factory: whether it was better or worse than its predecessors might have been subject to some argument, but there was no need for confusion as to the responsibility for the change. It was the Victorian manufacturer, not the consumer, who brought it about.

There were those critics who, while admitting this, still maintained that the consumer was to blame for buying such products. By so doing, they said, he objectively subsidized bad design. This frivolous position on the part of the critics ignored the blunt reality of the new consumer's position, who primarily bought what he *could*, not what he necessarily preferred. Even more disastrously, it ignored the fact that an 'ugly' industrial product was far better than no product at all. From the smug comfort of an editor's chair in New York or Boston it was all too easy to overlook the avidity with which the vast rural reaches of nineteenth-century America hungered for the labor-saving products of industry — a yard of machine-made cloth, a pair of machine-made shoes, a fine cast-iron kitchen range, or a Currier and Ives engraving. Victorian industry was not merely replacing 'beautiful' candelabra with 'ugly' kerosene lamps; it was introducing a reliable source of artificial light where not even candles had been before. Its ornate parlor heaters did not merely put an end to the neo-Grec Franklin stove; they brought comfort to tens of thousands of houses which had never known real comfort before.

The democratic esthetic of pre-industrial America had had its base in handicraft production: both folk art and high style had been nourished on it. Nor can there be any doubt that industrialism destroyed both the material base and its esthetic expression. Yet such was the extraordinary tenacity of folk art that the struggle extended well over half a century. Evidence of this conflict laces the fabric of late Victorian life, with machine-made objects preserving many traces of their handicraft predecessors. Railroad cars and trolleys wore all the hand decorations of the horse-drawn buggies, electric lights looked like candelabra, linoleum pretended to be tile, and oilcloth to be linen. On the other hand, the arts-and-crafts movements inspired by Ruskin and William Morris were frantically at work on simon-pure handicraft — hand-painting china, hand-weaving scarves, hand-tooling leather. These movements involved only a small section of middle-class intelligentsia: the rich had not the time for such homilies and the poor had not the money. Thus, as the century closed, the very existence of all handicraft was made increasingly precarious. Industry was robbing it of an economic base in all but the most backward and unimportant areas. At the same time, with its fabulous extension of the means of communication, industry was subjecting handicraft to the withering propaganda of product advertising until at last the very term 'homemade' had become one of opprobrium.

At the level of high style, the upper-class arbiters of taste had never displayed much interest in the esthetic potentialities of either the machine or machine-made products. For a short while after the Civil War, which had marked the victory of industrialism over all other methods of production, there was some evidence in the clothes they wore and the houses they built that the industrialists themselves might raise machine production to the level of esthetic principle. But the tides soon changed and they turned to the importation of a whole range of styles which, by implication, denied even the existence of the machine. This trend culminated in the Chicago Fair of 1893.

This process had its exact counterpart in building. Increasingly concentrated in the cities, it came under progressively narrower economic controls. Public buildings had always been an extremely responsive instrument of upper-class taste. Commercial and industrial structures had long expressed the standards of merchant and mill-owner. Now the same thing began to happen to residential building. Millions of people, who a century previously would have lived in structures of their own design and construction, now flocked into the row-houses, apartments, and tenements which — from the seventies on — began to flood the cities. Needless to say, the tenants had no more voice in the design of this housing than in that of the shoes they wore or the trolleys they rode in. Here again the specialists had taken over the design as a necessary corollary of centralized production and ownership. Small entrepreneurs continued to exist and thousands of individuals continued to build their own homes; but here, as in other fields, they tended to follow the dominant standards of taste established at the top.

Here again it is necessary to remember that, whatever it looked like, this housing by and large offered the consumer new levels of comfort and convenience. Running water, toilets, and tubs; gas and electric lights; central heating — these appeared to the pragmatic Victorians to more than offset the losses in light, air, and privacy; and the curlicues and gingerbread were, according to the magazines and newspapers, in the highest elegance. At any rate, the area of choice in which the individual could express a dissenting opinion was very small. The demand for housing in the bursting cities was so great that he took what was available. Adjustment to the new esthetic standards was perhaps the least of the problems with which life in modern American cities confronted him.

Confluent Tendencies

TODAY, THE BASE of the democratic esthetic is of necessity the factory. Handicraft production has all but disappeared, continuing only as a hothouse exotic for small sections of the luxury trades. Its last echoes have died away in the popular consciousness. A new idiom based upon machine production has replaced it — an idiom which at its best has those same qualities of directness, simplicity, and honesty which always characterized the old folk arts. It is as though the American people, after a century of fumbling with the machine, have at last begun to discover its esthetic implications. The plane is a case in point. Here is an industrial product whose design cannot, for purely practical reasons, tolerate nostalgic evocations of the past. There is probably no product in all history whose design has been more strictly or continuously conditioned by material considerations than that of the airplane. Yet most Americans undoubtedly consider it beautiful. It so completely satisfies our national

passion for speed that its form has become a fetish. So overwhelming is our admiration of its high technical and esthetic
standards that we now permit aerodynamics to influence the
design of objects which have nothing in common with it. The
local results of such enthusiasm may often be disastrous; but
they cannot obscure the central fact that in the plane the mortal
schism between technique and esthetic has for the first time in a
century been resolved.

If we have a standard of popular taste — an industrial equivalent of folk art, so to speak — the plane is its best expression.
In similar fashion, the nexus of today's dominant high style lies
in the field of modern architecture, sculpture, and painting.
These two levels of taste are organically related. Like the
modern plane, modern art and architecture could not for practical, and would not for theoretical, reasons tolerate dictation
by the forms and idioms of the past. History itself forced this
climactic break and, in the preceding sections of this book, I
have traced the forces that led up to it in architecture. It
remains to show how, in specific men and buildings, these
currently find expression at the esthetic level.

Of the three broad tendencies which flowed together to form
that body of theory and practice known as modern architecture,
the first and most characteristic was native common sense.
Despite its surface appearance of extravagance and eccentricity
American life had always had a basic orderliness. It demanded
simplification, efficiency, economy. It was 'willing to try anything reasonable' to achieve these qualities and, in certain very
important areas, it got them. In the present century, this
demand had been raised most sharply by the advanced sections
of business, industry, and commerce.

Once their demands were met on a purely practical plane,
it was not long before certain essential qualities began to be
expressed at a higher, more abstract level. Simplicity, economy,
and efficiency became stylistic criteria. A whole body of work
appeared in which this common denominator underlies the
vagaries of individual architect and client.

While this movement was large and its boundaries not always
distinct, its essential character can be circumscribed with a

handful of names: the long series of industrial plants designed by the office of Albert Kahn; the skyscrapers for the *Daily News* and the McGraw-Hill Publishing Company in New York designed by Raymond Hood; the group of buildings at New York's Rockefeller Center — joint work of three firms, including Hood's [1]; the General Motors Exhibit by Norman Bel Geddes and the Ford Motor Company Exhibit — both at the 1939 New York World Fair. These structures reveal one striking characteristic in common — even beyond the necessities of structure and plan, they depend chiefly upon simplification for effect.

Stylistic simplification was the expression on the esthetic plane of the underlying pressure for economy. Economy of initial cost, economy of maintenance, economy of space, man-power, and mechanical energy. In its crassest form, economy meant simply cheapness. A landlord wanted the most for his money — the largest area possible in this apartment or that factory for the least possible cost. Under such a set of pressures, something in conventional building had to give way. Rationalization of construction methods yielded some cost reductions. A certain amount of cheapening or adulteration was possible in the structure proper — although this was limited by the building codes. The rest of the paring had to come out of the fat of the building — its ornamental or decorative features. There had to be less of them, or they had to be cheaper, or both. In the early part of the century, this necessity had led to a flourishing business in 'mail-order Classic' — plaster and terra-cotta ornament stamped out by the thousands and sold by the yard. These were cheaper than carved wood or stone details, but — after the crash of 1929 — not cheap enough. Ornament as such had to go. For a brief transitional period, the old devices hung on, the pilasters, flutings, and swags reduced to nothing more than etched lines on the skin of the structure. Finally they disappeared altogether.

Building design gained from their disappearance, even though the improvement was superficial and the essential mass and articulation of such structures remained unchanged. For the architects themselves, the process was a blessing in disguise. It

---

[1] Reinhard & Hoffmeister; Corbett, Harrison & MacMurray; Hood & Fouilhoux.

was the first time that many of them had been forced to face the problem of genuinely economical structure; and, in the solution of such problems, it was inevitable that the principles thus evolved would find expression in new esthetic concepts.

Simplification could spring from more valid motives than mere penny-pinching, however; and, as expressed in the outstanding buildings of this group, it could lead to more significant results than merely stripping the façade of useless ornament. It could and did produce hundreds of buildings which were handsome in quite a new fashion — buildings whose appearance of orderly precise articulation was clearly the result of a radically different approach to the design process. Thus, in many of the Kahn factories there is a very high esthetic standard which appears as an almost incidental by-product of the main work at hand — a pragmatic solution to a set of very practical problems. Appearance and purpose, function and form, are so intimately related that it is difficult to separate the two. One might almost imagine that any formulation of their esthetic principles must have *followed* the actual invention and development of the idiom (Figs. 133–34).

Yet in the *Daily News* or Rockefeller Center Buildings, the same esthetics are at work as a conscious principle, deliberately applied. Here in visual terms is a statement of the power of simplification. The reference to industrial production is inescapable. In the factory it leads to impersonal, continual, and precise multiplication. In the skyscrapers it produces the cold and polished surface, the endless soaring line, the meticulous geometry of intersecting column and girder. At the two Fair exhibits, the same principles are at work in even more explicit terms. The curve — so studiously avoided in the early thirties because of its connotations of the masonry arch — has reappeared as a symbol of smooth, mechanical motion. The curving lines of the Teague and Bel Geddes designs make the rectangularity of the skyscrapers seem naïve (Figs. 139–40). By implication, they register the immense advance of a short decade in our understanding of flow lines, whether of stresses in a steel member or traffic on a factory floor. Teague's use of the spiral ramps with their moving, multi-colored cars thus evokes both the smooth highways on which they glide and the assembly lines on which they are born. In Bel Geddes' design for General Motors the right angle has disappeared altogether. The very forms are reminiscent of the streamlined vehicle. Though the stucco skin belies it, the structure is externally modeled into shapes which recall those of a Diesel locomotive or a motor-car body. It is a totem to industrial production.

For all their handsomeness, the buildings of this group are often surprisingly cold and mechanistic. Almost without exception they are severe — in their more formal aspects, even autocratic. Stylistic simplification could itself become a fad: thus the continuous vertical piers of the Rockefeller skyscrapers are only a partial statement of the structural problem. The gross overemphasis given them here is itself dishonest. Clearly, simplicity and efficiency were not a broad enough base, upon which to erect the esthetic of modern architecture.

There was a second current within the modern movement whose sources can be plotted in the works of Richardson, Sullivan, and Wright. It represented another and equally persistent set of American traits: the idealist's demand for a way of life in which artistic imagination and intuition could play upon and fertilize the bare facts of material existence. There was only a small segment of the building field in which this tendency could express itself, however: upper-class residential work, an occasional church, an even rarer public building or tomb. Business, industry, and commerce were generally opposed to poetic overtones for both practical and philosophical reasons. And — disregarding the personal factors of background, temperament, and opportunity which gave them the direction they took — it is apparent that the large and stormy individualism of men like Wright and Sullivan made them ill-fitted for the life of a successful corporation architect. This was fortunate for modern architecture, for domestic design permitted more esthetic experimentation than any other segment of the field.

The ravishing perspectives of Wright's own house at Taliesen may well serve as index to the concepts of the whole group. The exotic forms and magnificent compositions; the artless yet cunning integration of indoors and out, landscape and structure; the always human scale; the warm colors and sensuous textures — these are the elements of an esthetic very different from that of Kahn (Figs. 144, 147). The qualities which first distinguished the Wright houses are now widely diffused among the work of a whole school of younger men. With these men there is apt to be less eccentricity than with Wright, even at the risk of diminished richness or audacity. Whimsy is tempered with rationality. A sharpened interest in science and technology tends to restrain intuitive solutions.

In view of their restricted area of operations, the influence of this group upon the whole body of architectural thought has been remarkable. It must be remembered that their dominance in residential design was not won without a long and bitter struggle. Expensive residence work had long been considered the preserve of a whole group of highly skilled eclectics: the famous firms of Delano and Aldrich; Mellor, Meigs and Howe; Addison Mizner; Frank Forster and Harrie Lindeberg. These men were also imaginative, skilled at composition, texture, and color. For decades they had been the unchallenged ideologues of high style, spokesmen for the wealthiest families in America. Their privileged position was destroyed by the depression of 1929–33. An abrupt end was brought to the succession of great houses which had dominated the domestic scene for so long. At the same time, the ideals and perspectives of the class which built them were suspect, discredited (Figs. 141–43).

If Wright's designs suddenly seemed incomparably fresher, more valid and authentic than those of Harrie Lindeberg, it was at least partially due to the fact that Wright's work contained no literary allusions to a past so thoroughly discredited. Both men had used traditional materials — brick, stone, tile, and wood — which were rich in association and evocation of the past. But Lindeberg had used them in an explicitly nostalgic way. Broad, blind gables; towering chimneys topped by sculptured pots; immense, steeply sloping tiled roofs — no literate person could look at these without conjuring up a whole romantic literature of English country life. Wright's houses had no such dependence on the past. Where allusion did occur it was oblique, abstracted. Here and there one might catch a fleeting color from the American Indians, a glint of burnished copper and polished wood from some Quaker kitchen, a shingled eave which evanescently recalled the frontier cabins of Audubon and Daniel Boone. These images were subtle — the layman was never quite sure whether they lay in the building or in his own head. They reflected the best aspects of American experience — its humanity, its hospitality, its lack of aristocratic pretension.

As the decade passed, it became increasingly clear that the shallow, repetitious allusions of the eclectic idiom had nothing but a surface glint. Without significant content, it could not achieve significant form. It led nowhere, had no fertilizing powers. Against this esthetic bankruptcy was the astonishing productivity of Wright and the younger idealists. They had evolved a richer and more humane idiom than the industrial mechanists, yet they were not hostile to either science or technology. They were able to absorb the technical advances of industrialism while at the same time preserving a healthy skepticism about the social and economic implications of monopoly. In this sense they reflected the temper of the American people in the decade of the New Deal.

Shortly before, and increasingly after, the first World War, a number of young European architects had come to this country, among them Frederick Kiesler, Lawrence Kocher, William Lescaze, Moholy-Nagy, Richard Neutra, Antonin Raymond. These men established our first liaison with the great centers of European modernism, Paris, Vienna, the German Bauhaus. They may thus be said to have introduced still a third element into modern architecture in this country, the rationalism of the so-called International style. The rise of Fascism in Europe brought many more architects to this country until, at the end of the second war, a large part of Europe's best-known men were here: Curt Behrendt, Marcel Breuer, Walter Gropius, Eric Mendelssohn, Mies van der Rohe, José Sert, and many others. Coming from practically every country in Europe, this group brought with them a rich and varied experience and their influence was to be very wide — the more so because many of them have become teachers in American universities.

To more than outline the principal contributions of the Europeans is beyond the scope of this book. It may be presumptuous even to class them as a group. But their work has certain qualities in common which differentiates them from the native modernists. The idiom which they brought with them from pre-Hitler Europe was highly developed, complex. It lay somewhere between the work of Wright and Kahn (both of which, incidentally, had been studied earlier and more intently in Europe than in America) but it had a rational elegance which distinguished it from both. It reflected the same revolt against the senile Beaux Arts system of esthetics which had taken place in this country. But it was a revolt which was colored by the more sophisticated cultural climate in which it had taken place. Thus, while the International style was based upon the potentials of industrial production and sought to exemplify them in sternly utilitarian designs, its best buildings often managed to avoid the heavy-handed literalness of the American mechanists. This dexterity and lightness was clear in Gropius' design for the Bauhaus at Dessau, in van der Rohe's house for the Tugenstadts, in Le Corbusier's dormitory for the Swiss at the University of Paris. The same quality found an American expression in the Philadelphia skyscraper which George Howe and William Lescaze designed for the Public Society for Savings (Fig. 138).

One of the Europeans who exercised immense influence here was Le Corbusier. Although he stayed in Paris except for occasional short visits, he played an important rôle in both North and South America. Along with Wright, he has for years been the world's leading architectural theoretician, beaming his ideas across frontiers and language barriers like a high-powered broadcasting station. Le Corbusier's philosophy is at once more formal and more intellectualized than Wright's, more coherent and explicitly social than that of Gropius. Embodying many of the best qualities of French culture — its precision, scholarship, wit and elegance — Le Corbusier's designs at the same time have a certain emotional aridity. His concepts are exquisitely worked out; but they tend to be repetitious. They sometimes boast a magnificent scale, as in his plan for rebuilding Paris along the 'heliothermic axis' into a huge, skyscraper-studded park. But he first proposed this scheme in 1925. He has never substantially altered it and presumably still considers it an ideal solution, not only for Paris but for communities as disparate as Algiers and the little provincial town of Saint-Die in Normandy. Le Corbusier can thus be dogmatic. He can also be curiously mechanistic, as in his famous dicta: 'Une maison est une machine à habiter' and 'L'histoire de l'architecture moderne, c'est une histoire de fenêtres.'

Perhaps because of their earlier interest and fairly wide experience in multi-family housing, the Germans and Swiss brought to us a maturity which we lacked in this field. One has only to compare our earliest efforts in PWA slum clearance to some of the wartime communities to understand how immensely productive their influence was. And one has only to compare these later communities with the German and Swiss *Siedlungen* to establish the directness of the heritage.

Only from the Viennese and the Scandinavians came any note of genuine gaiety or lightness. They had evolved a happy mingling of folk art and modern idiom which was especially successful in interior design. However, it was a tender plant, the product of a very special cultural climate, and it did not stand transplanting very well. To date, its influence has been chiefly felt in better-class shops and cafés, where it has certainly been a beneficent counter-agent to the banalities of the Grand Rapids store-fixture school.

Among the Europeans there was also a group of lyrical romanticists — Eliel Saarinen, Joseph Urban, and the sculptor, Carl Milles. Rebels of an older generation, these men did not belong to the modern movement in the strictest sense of the word, although their work had certain qualities in common with it. In spirit, they were much nearer to Bertram Goodhue in his later period than to Wright. Their special metier was the monumental public or quasi-public building; and this was precisely the building type on which the classicists had the firmest grip. Urban's design for the Ziegfeld Theater and the

Saarinen-Milles collaboration on the buildings for the Cranbrook School have had but a scanty progeny. Like Goodhue, their talents were inappropriate to the times.

The Problems Ahead

BY THE END of World War II these three main tributaries of modern architecture had met and substantially merged into one movement. The war had itself accelerated the process under the highly favorable conditions of national unity. There had been an unprecedented amount of essential construction. While most of it had been strictly utilitarian and much of it ugly and incompetent, there was still evidence aplenty that, in not much more than a decade, the movement had matured, become by all counts the only consistently vigorous and productive force in American architecture. The next phase was opening.

If modern architecture had proved its validity to the point where it could no longer be challenged intellectually, it did not necessarily follow that its ascendancy was absolute and secure. Actually, this was far from the case. At the close of World War II, only a small portion of the existing buildings in the country could be classed as expressions of the movement. This might perhaps have been expected since nowhere does style change more slowly than in architecture. But there was also ample evidence that wide sections of the American people were indifferent to its implications, while certain smaller groups were actively hostile to it. The hostility is easier to explain than the indifference. However indirect or circuitous the connection, modern architecture has been generally considered an expression of social advance. Hitler, with insane logic, saw Communism in its concepts of health, comfort, simple human well-being. American Tories were quick to see sedition in its internationalism, dangerous radicalism in its sharp break with the eclectic past — blandly ignoring, of course, the foreign origins and international character of all the other great styles. And the hostility among conservative architects and critics was a reflection both of their vested interest in eclecticism and of their distrust of progressive ideological implications buried deep within the movement.

Of far more importance to its future is the indifference of wide sections of the public to modern architecture. This can spring either from the public's ignorance of what contemporary design promises the building consumer in the way of health and happiness, or from some inner lack, some failure to meet a need, on the part of the buildings themselves. The chances are that both factors are involved. The specialists are prone to forget that the sharp theoretical battles of the recent past have been fought almost exclusively by professional architects, writers, critics. However important the issues or correct the ultimate decisions may have been, only a minuscule proportion of the laity has been involved. This isolation has worked to the detriment of both parties. The layman has not been fully informed as to what the architect was trying to do for him. The architect has not been fully aware of what the layman needs or wants in his buildings.

The average man is wretchedly informed as to what performance he has a right to demand of buildings; and it has been the central purpose of this book to explain what he should demand and why. But it is apparent that above and beyond physical performance, laymen ask something more of buildings, some quality which they have found in the traditional design and miss in the modern one. What is this quality?

The quality, it seems to me, is sentiment. The modern movement, firmly grounded in the physical sciences, has severely restricted the play of sentiment in building design. This was an urgent historical necessity, for sentimentality had not only corrupted the esthetic standards of American architecture, it had robbed them of technical and social usefulness as well. The whole tottering structure had to be razed and rebuilt from the ground up. This task the modern architect has substantially accomplished. Is it possible that he overlooked some element, which, rightly or wrongly, the tenants will demand? Must modern design afford a greater play of sentiment to achieve widespread popular support? If so, what specific form and direction shall it take?

Historically, sentiment in building design has been expressed through devices which, through repetitive use, tended to become symbols. While they all came to have an ideological significance, these devices were not necessarily explicit in statement or literal in message. Examined by themselves, independent of their cultural matrix, many of them would appear to be quite empty of content. Thus for one reproduction of a Greek sculpture, the Greek Revival in this country employed a hundred plain and fluted columns, a thousand gable ends, uncounted cornices and pediments — geometric abstractions, all of them. Yet together, and supported by all the other cultural media of the period (painting, music, literature, drama, etc.), they added up to a sum much greater than the individual parts. And now that the period has receded a century and more into history, this particular system of symbols has acquired all sorts of connotations and significance of which it cannot be divested. The same thing is true for each of the other periods of American architecture. They have become part of our cultural heritage, the good along with the bad, and they constitute the background against which today's layman makes his esthetic judgment.

For reasons which should by now be apparent, modern architecture cannot permit sentiment to dictate the actual configuration of a building or the shape, size, and articulation of its various elements. The pitch of its roof, the size of its windows, the presence or absence of columns — these must be determined by objective criteria. But it is precisely these elements of traditional form and proportion which have always hitherto carried the principal burden of sentiment in architecture. The dormer needs no added ornament to evoke a picture of snug colonial comfort. The column alone can give the portico its connotations of bewigged and beribboned leisure. The mere silhouette of a church steeple gives it emotional significance long before the detailed symbols of cross and saint are visible. In fact, in the typical Protestant church of eighteenth-century New England there was no art, no ornament. For emotional impact, it relied entirely upon a characteristic form. These traditional forms and proportions — however appropriate to the structural and planning concepts of previous epochs — were usually of such an arbitrary nature as to impair if not prevent a contemporary solution of problems of structure, plan, and environmental control. The modern architect had no choice but to discard them.

The use of art forms for the explicit statement of sentiment presented the modern movement with a somewhat different problem. A stylized eagle in the pediment of a door, a marbeline figure of Psyche in a stair hall niche, a bust of Franklin in the library, or an heroic figure of some local statesman on the courthouse lawn — these were well within the limits of the American tradition. By themselves, they would not have been as restrictive as the dormer or the portico. But the endless reproduction of such forms, the vulgarity of their design and idiocy of their use had, by the nineteen-twenties, made them the actual symbols of eclectic decay. Since the sculpture and painting they found around them was rotten, the modern rationalists revolted against all art forms. Since all existing systems of applied ornament were trivial and corrupt, they supplanted it with only that pattern and texture which was integral to the materials of which they built. For the realistic curves of Psyche's torso, the modernists substituted the abstract spiral of a cantilevered concrete stairway. Instead of the pallid idealism of a Puvis de Chavannes mural, they used matched sheets of richly colored marble: instead of the arabesques of chintz, the stripes of a zebra skin: instead of the pastoral landscapes of wallpaper, the pattern of plywood.

Nor was it altogether an ideological problem. In respect to sculpture, it was also technical. The modern movement, in its passion for structural efficiency, had revolted against solid masonry construction. In differentiating between skeleton and skin, it had done more than revolutionize structural theory; it had also made lightness a dominant esthetic criterion. Buildings were conceived as enclosing space — not displacing it. This served to discredit not merely stone buildings but stone itself, with its real weight and symbolic massiveness. As long as sculpture used marble or granite as a medium, it could scarcely escape a similar connotation. Such sculpture thus presented the modern architect with a really knotty problem. The art form was heavy in both fact and appearance. If it stood free of the building, as in a fountain, it might have the value of contrast. But incorporated into the structure proper, it required support, physically and visually. Once committed to using stone sculpture, the architect was apt to find himself caught in a train of logic from which it was difficult to escape. Classic instance of this is to be found in Goodhue's Nebraska State Capitol. Here an honest effort to integrate sculptural forms into the building had led to their actually dictating the building's design. In the process of offering adequate visual support for the sculptural masses, the building assumed the quite deceptive appearance of being formed of solid blocks of stone. In the Capitol, Goodhue desired to memorialize the vanished legends of the Great Plains country — the Indians, the buffalo, the shining, windswept prairies. He could accomplish this only through the explicit statement of art. But he chose stone sculptures as the medium. Esthetic consistency then led him to sheathe a light steel-framed office building with stone until it looked like a solid monolith. To 'carry' the sculptures alongside the entrance and stone-clad dome at the top of the tower, Goodhue introduced very wide stone piers. In the entrance this led to false pylons; in the tower it cost him the best office space on each floor. The building's mass and articulation was everywhere subordinated to sculptural concepts, which, however valid in the abstract, had disastrous results both as to efficient plan and esthetic honesty.

It was from experiences such as these that modern architecture undertook the Spartan exorcism of art forms from building. The measure was therapeutic, as necessary to decoration as to structure; and, in a short fifteen years, it has succeeded in producing an entire idiom which is probably unparalleled in all architectural history for its lack of sculpture, painting, and ornament. In the process, what began as a simple necessity had by degrees been raised to an esthetic principle: *all* art was rejected, not merely the bad. Thus, the richest and most productive period in American art history — the programs of the

Works Progress Administration and the Treasury Procurement Division — went largely unremarked by modern architects. It is true that, because of the character of the programs, most of this material was incorporated into public buildings which were largely under the control of architectural bureaus in which the modernists had little voice. But even in the buildings which they did design, this work played little or no rôle. The situation was doubly ironic, because much of the art was good and much of it expressed a point of view very closely related to that of modern architecture.

Whatever the merits of the case, the anti-art tendencies of the movement served to worsen the already unhappy plight of the artist. Robbed of the reference frame of architecture, he was forced to project his ideas in a partial vacuum. Unable to execute sculpture and murals at an architectural scale, he was reduced to that of easel painting. Unable to speak directly to the public, he was forced more and more to speak only to the collector and connoisseur. Fortunately, there is increasing evidence that modern architects are revising their mechanistic attitude toward art. They begin to wonder if perhaps the baby was not thrown out along with the bathwater. For however necessary it might have been to exorcise the flood of eclectic art forms inherited from the nineteenth century, it has yet to be established that all art forms can be excluded from architecture. Such a program, indefinitely extended, impoverishes both artist and building designer. Some resolution of the conflict can and will be found, though what exact configuration such a synthesis will take is a matter for speculation.

In view of the anarchy and general backwardness of the building field, it is hardly surprising that the vast majority of our building stands at an appallingly low level, technically and esthetically. This creates a cultural lag between popular taste and the regnant high style of modern architecture. The average building consumer has no esthetic standards sufficiently realistic to enable him to measure the size of this lag. Moreover, the creation of such standards awaits objective conditions which will permit him to actively participate in the use and enjoyment of modern architecture. In the last analysis, there is no other way in which the consumer can be convinced of the validity of its claims or persuaded to adopt its standards as his own.

On the other hand, the building designer's standards are themselves open to improvement and modification. Almost without exception, the buildings already cited in this chapter for their high performance will be found to have some detail which detracts from, or lack some factor which might have added to, their esthetic value. This, too, is a reflection of the conditions of the field. To erect a modern building, as to build a modern plane, there is required a large, complex, and integrated staff of specialists in research, design, and fabrication. To achieve rising standards — that is, to narrow the gap between theory and practice — such a staff would have to build many structures and build them regularly. In short, produce them on an industrial basis: and this is precisely what no staff is able to do under present-day conditions.

Here again is graphic illustration of the relation of quantity to quality in building design: you cannot have the latter without the former. (This proposition cannot be read backwards, however: for quantity is merely the *prerequisite* of quality, not its *guarantee*.) The qualitatively great works of the past are merely the visible apices of whole pyramids of intense (and probably mediocre) creative activity. The heroes of the Renaissance stand no more independently of their less gifted (and/or less fortunate) contemporaries than do Wright or Le Corbusier. Moreover, progressively advancing standards are based as much upon *continuity* of production as upon *volume*; and this is nowhere more apparent than in building, where periodic slumps tend to dissipate the cumulative momentum of periods of intense activity.

American building as it stands today, at the end of World War II, is too broad in scope, complex in function, varied in form and material, to be easily related to any private set of esthetic standards. Judged relative to those currently operative in the modern movement, most of our building seems poor. But the issue is not simply one of whose standards are best — the layman's or the specialist's. It may be true, as is often charged, that the average American has a low level of taste; but it may also be true that the standards which the architect and artist are offering him are incorrect in the light of social reality; for the mortal dichotomy between esthetic and technique, between fine art and folk art, is in the last analysis an expression of the deeper conflicts in our society itself.   To free American building from the contradictions which paralyze it today, building designer and building consumer must join with all Americans of good will in building a society of peace, freedom, and plenty. In doing so they will inevitably lay the basis for a flowering, rich and wide, of a truly democratic esthetic.

THE END

Index

Index